D1151871

# 60
# GREAT FOUNDERS

## GEOFFREY HANKS

CHRISTIAN FOCUS PUBLICATIONS

Geoffrey Hanks lives with his wife, Celia, in Worthing on the south coast of England. He is the author of the bestselling *70 Great Christians*, also published by Christian Focus Publication. Previously he was Co-Editor of the Faith in Action series of biographies for young people. Geoffrey has written many articles for the Christian Herald.

© Geoffrey Hanks
ISBN 1-85792-140-2

Published in 1995
by
Christian Focus Publications Ltd.
Geanies House, Fearn, Ross-shire,
IV20 1TW, Scotland, Great Britain.

Cover design by Donna Macleod

Maps by Holmwood Maps and Plans.

Printed in Great Britain by
J. W. Arrowsmith Ltd, Bristol

# Contents

## 5. NATIONAL MISSIONS

## 6. SERVING THE COMMUNITY

# INFORMATION BOXES

# FURTHER READING

The author wishes to acknowledge reference to the following publications for background material, and recommends them to the reader:

*By Their Blood*, James & Marti Hefley, Mott Media 1979.

*Christianity in America*, (Edited), Lion Publishing 1983.

*Evangelicalism in Modern Britain*, D W Bebbington, Unwin Hyman 1989.

*Evangelicals in Action*, Kathleen Heasman, Geoffrey Bles 1962.

*George Williams & the YMCA*, Clyde Binfield, William Heinemann 1973.

*70 Great Christians*, Geoffrey Hanks, Christian Focus Publications, 1992.

*The Guinness Legend*, Michele Guinness, Hodder & Stoughton 1990.

*A History of the Expansion of Christianity* (6 vols), Kenneth Scott Latourette, Harper & Row 1937-45 (The Paternoster Press 1971).

*History of Christianity*, (Edited), Lion Publishing 1977.

*Moody Without Sankey*, John Pollock, Christian Focus Publications, 1995.

*Operation World*, Patrick Johnstone, OM Publishing 1995 (Revised).

*Prophecy Today* magazine, PWM Trust.

*Religion in the Victorian Era* (2 vols), Leonard Elliott-Binns, Lutterworth 1936.

*Saints in Politics*, Ernest Marshall Howse, George Allen & Unwin 1953.

# PREFACE

This is the second of three volumes designed to cover aspects of Church history in a readable and easy-to-digest form. The first two books are based on the biographies of great Christians, men and women who have made a significant contribution to the growth and development of Christianity. A third volume, in preparation, recounts 50 great events in Church history in the light of their historical setting.

In this current volume, the focus of attention is on the past two centuries. These years have witnessed the founding of a large number of enterprises by which Christianity has spread to parts of the globe previously unreached by the gospel. It also tells of men and women who have been used of God to bring relief to untold millions of people, often neglected by governments and their fellow men, who would otherwise have been left to their own devices.

Much of the material in this second volume originally appeared as a series of articles in the *Christian Herald* weekly newspaper under the title 'Footprints of Faith'. For the sake of clarity, the subjects are grouped together under sectional headings, though some of them could easily have fallen into more than one category. And while all of the organisations represented here were founded by Christian men and women, a few are included that were formed for humanitarian purposes rather than in furtherance of the gospel. These societies continue to do splendid work and are commended to the public.

The author wishes to place on record his gratitude to Colin Reeves, managing editor of the *Christian Herald*, for his permission to make use of these articles, and for his personal contribution towards the chapter on the Rev Michael Baxter, founder of the *Christian Herald*. Thanks is also due to Bruce Hardy and Jackie Stead of the editorial staff who carefully prepared the series for publication.

Many organisations have readily co-operated by providing access to source materials, and each article has been checked for accuracy by a representative. It must be remembered, however, that their ministry is continually in a state of flux and details given here can quickly change.

Geoffrey Hanks,
Worthing, West Sussex, 1995.

# INTRODUCTION

With the exception of the early years of the Church, the past two centuries have been amongst the most exciting times in the history of Christianity. Although by the beginning of the 19th century Christianity had been planted in all the five continents, the way was opened up for a further expansion of the Faith. Missionary societies were founded to carry the gospel to peoples and tribes previously unreached, and more than ever before attention was given to caring for the poor and under-privileged masses of society.

These movements owed their origin to a revitalisation of the Faith that began towards the end of the 17th century. Starting in Germany, the revival spread through parts of Europe, and the following century reached Britain and America. Further revivals were experienced in the 19th century, climaxing in the 1857 Awakening which originated in North America and reached the British Isles two years later.

## The Great Century

The 18th century Evangelical Revival arose within the Church of England (though most denominations were ultimately affected), beginning in Wales (1735) before influencing England (1739) and Scotland (1742). Its emphasis was on the need for a personal encounter with God, leading to a changed life. It was from among these people that the modern Protestant foreign missionary movement had its origins.

Yet it was from America that eventually the majority of Protestant missionaries and more than half the funding came. Initially the churches in the older American states were concerned for the spread of the gospel among the settlements along its western frontiers, though some Americans were sending money to support British missions. It was not until 1810 that the American Board of Commissioners for Foreign Missions, a Congregational foundation, was set up and sent out Adoniram Judson as one of its first missionaries.

As the century progressed, a number of developments took place within the missionary movement that significantly shaped its future.

Whereas missionaries had for the most part been ordained ministers, increasingly the role was filled by lay Christians. In the second half of the century, more and more women were accepted by missionary societies, so that by 1914 they constituted half the missionary force.

At the same time, foreign missions began to assume a greater importance in the Church. It resulted in more volunteers for the mission field, and led  to an increase in prayer and financial support for missionary causes. In America, the Student Volunteer Movement, founded in 1886 under the watchword, 'The evangelisation of the world in this generation', stirred thousands of young people to offer for foreign missions.

One other movement that deserves attention is the rise of Jewish missions. Europe in the 19th century was home to hundreds of thousands of Jews; large numbers of them had settled in Russia (including Poland), Germany and Romania, and there was a sizeable Jewish population in the USA. The London Society for Promoting Christianity among the Jews (now CMJ) was formed in 1809, and was a means of influencing churches in Scotland and on the Continent to take an interest in Jewish evangelism.

## Social Concern
In Britain, the Industrial Revolution created large cities with over-crowded slums, resulting in immense misery for large numbers of the poorer classes. It was against this background that Evangelicals - amongst others - formed a wide variety of charitable institutions, often run by volunteers, who were moved to translate their new-found faith into action.

City missions, which first appeared in the 1820s, were founded to carry the gospel into the slums. Started by David Nasmith in Glasgow, they were to be found in many of the major cities of Britain and America. Voluntary workers, including many middle-class ladies, visited homes to assess the needs and endeavour to bring relief.

Over the century, other agencies were founded to minister to particular groups, and children were among the first to receive attention. Of the great orphanages, the George Müller foundations led the way (1835), and his principle of 'living by faith' was an inspiration to many Christian leaders. And although a society for the protection of animals had been started in 1824, it was not until nearly sixty years later that a society was formed (in 1881) to deal with the problem of child abuse.

Medical missions, providing care for those who could not afford to pay for treatment, began around the middle of the century. Started in Edinburgh under the influence of Dr Burns-Thompson, they spread to other major cities during the following fifty years.

The Sunday School movement and the ragged schools provided free education for poor children, until the introduction of the Education Act in 1870, when attendances began to decline. A wide variety of agencies catered for teenagers, who had for the most part been overlooked. Initially intended to minister to their spiritual condition, the vision quickly broadened to embrace physical, social and educational needs.

Societies were also started to care for the handicapped and the elderly; the temperance movement fought against the evil consequences of drink, and the Lord's Day Observance Society campaigned to keep Sunday special.

All was not well, however, and attacks made on the authority of the Bible caused alarm among Protestants. In his book, *The Origin of Species*, Charles Darwin propounded the idea of evolution which undermined the biblical teaching about Creation. Added to this, German 'liberal' theologians denied the miracles and other supernatural elements of the Gospels, claiming the books were largely mythology. Another disturbing idea to emerge was the 'social gospel', which interpreted the kingdom of God solely in terms of social reform and political action.

**Renewal**

Many of these views were accepted within the Church, tending to rob the gospel of its power. Yet both America and Britain experienced times of renewal. The Azusa Street Mission in Los Angeles (1906) led to the rise of the modern Pentecostal movement, now with a world membership of over 360 million. The evangelical movement gained in strength as in the 1940s scholars who believed the Bible to be the Word of God came to prominence. And towards the end of the 1950s the charismatic movement erupted in North America, reaching Britain shortly afterwards.

Despite the theological turbulence within the Church, two world wars and the rise of Communism, missions continued to thrive and even expand. It took some while for the Church to respond to the pleas of believers behind the Iron Curtain for help as Communism attempted to stamp out religion, especially Christianity. Thousands of believers were martyred, yet the Church continued to grow.

In the West, new missions were formed and old-established ones began to adapt to 20th century conditions. As foreign missionaries were withdrawn from Africa, India and China, native believers took over responsibility for running their own churches. The role of a number of missions changed, a matter often denoted by the adoption of a new name.

Two societies – Operation Mobilisation and Youth With A Mission – recognised that young people had much to offer and could be involved in evangelism without the usual Bible college training. Each year these missions accept hundreds of young people for short-term periods of service, and after initial preparation send them off in groups to various parts of the world.

Christian concern for the under-privileged has in no way diminished, and new agencies have been founded this century. Although many admirable charities have been set up to operate on a humanitarian basis, Christian societies such as Langley House Trust and St Christopher's Hospice have an extra dimension of caring to offer.

The past two centuries have seen a phenomenal church growth around the world as the gospel has been planted in hitherto unreached regions. This, however, is only part of a widespread revival of religion taking place, as is witnessed by the interest in the occult and spiritism, the popularity of the New Age movement, the resurgence of Islam and the revivals among Asian religions.

There is obviously a tremendous spiritual hunger waiting to be met, and Christians are convinced that this can only be satisfied in Jesus. The 2,000th celebration of his birth should serve to remind his followers that there is much yet to be done before the Lord's return if we are to 'make disciples of all nations'.

# 1

# INTERNATIONAL
# MISSIONS

# THE SUDAN (1900)

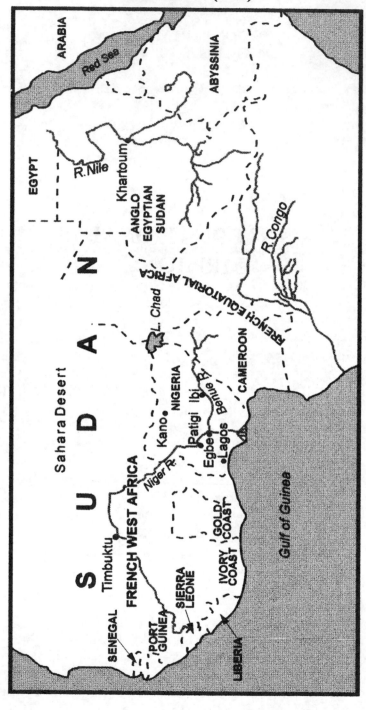

# 1. ACTION PARTNERS (1904)
## Dr Karl Kumm (1874-1930)

In recent years a number of Protestant evangelical missionary societies have undergone considerable changes. They have been forced to reconsider their role and adapt to new developments.

This was certainly the case with the Sudan United Mission, which began a gospel work in Nigeria in 1904. Renamed Action Partners, it now works to further the cause of Christ in partnership with African churches and other Christian agencies rather than operating as an independent body.

In the 19th century much of Africa was colonised chiefly by the British, Germans and French, though Portugal, Italy and Spain were also involved. Realising the vastness of the continent's natural resources and keen to take advantage of them, a group of European superpowers met in 1884 at the Conference of Berlin to divide the greater part of the continent between them.

The land was shared out on the basis of tribal areas, which meant that seeds of dissension were sown that were to continue causing strife into the 20th century. Under the Treaty, Nigeria was handed over to the British, though it did not become a Protectorate until 1902. The remaining area of Anglo-Egyptian Sudan was shared between the British and French.

At this time, the Sudan ('land of the blacks') covered a vast area of land south of the Sahara desert, stretching for almost 3,000 miles from the Atlantic coast to the Red Sea. Few explorers had ventured into the region; it was a land of darkness, where Islam was becoming more firmly entrenched. Its population numbered around 50 million, but could only muster some half dozen mission stations along its borders.

It was to this immense expanse of land that Karl and Lucy Kumm felt led by God.

## Heart To God

Karl Kumm, a native of Germany, was the fourth son of an officer in the Regiment of Guards. Following in his father's footsteps, he joined the German army, but stayed for only a year.

On a visit to friends in London in 1895, he wandered one day into a mission hall in the East End. It was there that he heard Edward Glenny speak of his work with the North Africa Mission. Kumm's immediate response was to give 'his heart to God and his life for service in Africa'.

Straightway he took steps to prepare himself for his call. He began a course of study in Arabic, and attended Harley College in the East End, where he came under the influence of the principal, Dr Henry Grattan Guinness. Dr Guinness at that time published a monthly magazine, *The Sudan and the Regions Beyond*, which may well have planted in the student the seed of his call.

Realising the need to improve his command of Arabic, Kumm went to work among Muslims in Egypt under the auspices of the North Africa Mission. It was in Egypt that Kumm met Lucy Guinness, one of Dr Grattan Guinness' talented daughters, who was touring the Middle East with her father. She was a cultured young lady, a brilliant musician with the making of a concert pianist, and reckoned to be the finest Christian editor in the British Isles. Above all, she was on fire for God.

Although several years her junior, Kumm was a mature young man with a love for music, and was studying for a doctorate in Egyptology. He acted as guide, interpreter and escort to the father and daughter, and before long the two young people had fallen in love.

They were engaged in January 1900, and married the following month in Cairo. The match was more than a romance, for they both had a fervent longing to take the gospel to the peoples of the Sudan. Both of them, however, were aware of the sacrifices that would face them, with long separations while Karl travelled in Africa.

Back in England the Kumms settled at Castleton, near Sheffield, where Kumm had set up his headquarters. Their home was not far from Cliff House (now Cliff College), the Guinnesses' country extension to Harley College.

### The Greater Sudan

Gathered with a small group of friends at the Sheffield YMCA in the autumn of 1902 to pray about the Sudan, they felt it was the time to turn their vision into a reality. A council was formed and the Sudan Pioneer Mission launched as an interdenominational society. Its object was the evangelization of the pagan peoples of the Greater Sudan (the Sahel).

Kumm approached a number of the leading missionary societies of the day for help. None of them felt able to undertake any additional responsibilities, though all of them were sympathetic to his ideas. Undismayed, Kumm determined to plough ahead. He paid a brief visit

## HARLEY COLLEGE

Karl Kumm was trained at Harley College, a missionary training institution opened in 1873 by Dr H Grattan Guinness (1835-1910), the leading British evangelist of his day. The college was originally located in Stepney and was known as Stepney Institute. It was based in the East End of London on the grounds that if trainee missionaries could not cope with the conditions of life in the East End, they would not be able to manage the work of a missionary in China.

Of the 100 applicants for the first courses, 32 were accepted. The students, who slept on the premises, were not charged any fees, as the college was run on a faith basis. Conditions were sparse but adequate. As the Stepney building – supervised by the young Tom Barnardo, who had recently opened a boys' home nearby – was quickly judged too small, he rented a larger place in Bow, called Harley House.

The gift of Cliff House in Derbyshire (in 1875) provided the Guinness family and their students with a northern extension to the college, and a place for needy holidays. It was given by a Mrs Hulme, and was intended for lay people training to be missionaries at home and abroad.

To cater for the increasing number of students seeking training, a new college was built in the grounds of Harley House. It opened in the autumn of 1878 as Harley College – the East London Institute for Home and Foreign Missions. The work was brought to an end in 1914 by the onset of World War 1.

In 1889 Harley College became the basis for missionary work in the Congo, when the Congo and Balolo Mission, later to become the Regions Beyond Missionary Union, was founded to support the work of Harley students.

to Libya to gain some knowledge of the Hausa language, one of the main languages spoken in central Sudan and northern Nigeria.

During his absence, Lucy Kumm worked hard on behalf of the infant mission. She travelled around the country and applied her literary gift to writing numerous letters seeking support. In Edinburgh, a meeting was arranged by supporters in St George's Church, where the minister was Dr Alexander Whyte.

When Kumm returned home, the work was reorganised under the new name of the Sudan United Mission, a name suggested by Dr Whyte. Preparations were begun for an expedition to the Bauchi hill country of north eastern Nigeria, an area suggested to him by a British government official in Libya.

**Volunteers**

Three young men, including a doctor, were moved by Kumm's challenge to join him on an initial visit to West Africa, in July 1904. The four of them entered the Sudan by its western gate, Nigeria, and on the advice of the High Commissioner decided to begin work among the hill tribes around the Muslim town of Wase. The tribespeople were spirit-worshippers whose lives were ruled by fear. Slave-raiding threatened them all, infant mortality was appalling and disease was rampant, especially leprosy and malaria.

The party journeyed up the River Benue to Ibi, from where the 80 mile trek to their destination took them over a month. From the beginning the venture was beset by problems. In addition to the difficulties of learning the language and culture of the natives, Kumm's three young companions were taken ill and Dr Bateman had to return to England. Despite their problems, the three remaining missionaries carried on and set up a base.

The following year the trio were joined by other volunteers, from Britain and the United States. By now, Kumm felt the work was established enough for him to leave his colleagues and return to the UK. He reasoned that it would be better to organise the work from the homeland, from where he could continue his appeal for workers, prayer partners and funds.

Kumm returned home in time to celebrate Christmas with Lucy and the children. For nearly 18 months Lucy had been alone, caring for their young family and pursuing her efforts to rally support for the Mission.

The strain on her frail frame was considerable, added to which she had often gone for weeks without a word from her husband.

But Kumm was not still for long. Although more British candidates offered themselves for service, all of them engineers with practical skills to offer, Kumm left for a tour of the United States early in 1906 to seek further openings for the work. Shortly, Lucy and the children joined him and they stayed at a cottage close to the Moody conference centre at Northfield.

## Parting

While the tour of the USA proved fruitful for the work – an American branch of the mission was founded – the call of the Sudan soon lured Kumm back to Africa. He said goodbye to Lucy on 2 July, both of them realising that their parting could be for several years.

Travelling via England, Kumm stopped off to speak at the annual Keswick Convention. Six days after he left the States, Lucy was taken ill, but refused treatment in order to complete a book she was writing about slavery in the Congo. She finally agreed to surgery in August, but too late; her condition deteriorated quickly, and she died.

Kumm arrived back at Northfield ten days after her death, where a memorial service had been conducted by Dr R. A. Torrey and Dr Campbell Morgan. Her death was a grievous loss not only to Kumm, but also to the mission, for she had been responsible for widely-publicising the work by her writings.

The task of establishing the work continued, and Kumm made further tours of English-speaking countries to promote the Mission. Over the years more branches were founded – in South Africa (1907) and Australia and New Zealand (1911). Others branches were formed in Denmark (1912), Norway (1922) and Canada (1924).

As a result, the work was able to continue in Nigeria and a start was made in the Anglo-Egyptian Sudan (now the Republic of the Sudan). In between his tours, Kumm returned to Nigeria to supervise the work and to make exploratory expeditions for the purpose of planning new stations.

## Developments

With their limited knowledge of the Hausa language, the missionaries began efforts to preach the gospel. It was not long before they made the

KARL KUMM

important discovery that they had to adopt a different approach to pagans and Muslims from the methods used in the UK. In a few instances men were converted who earlier had come under the influence of Church Missionary Society missionaries, and indeed some tribes were even sympathetic to the gospel,.

As the gospel gained a firmer foothold in Nigeria, more stations were opened and a Field Superintendent appointed with headquarters at Ibi and later at Jos. Missionaries learned to overcome their problems, enabling a number of other developments to take place. It was not long, for example, before they realised the importance of medical work as a means of expressing the gospel, even before they could speak the language.

It became the practice to set up a small dispensary at each mission station, where tribespeople could receive simple treatment. Eventually, the Mission's medical work developed to include several hospitals, the first at Vom in 1922. This later developed into a full 250-bed hospital, training nurses for other hospitals over the North.

In 1908 plans were laid for a project to care for freed slave children, an idea put forward by friends of the society. The home opened its doors in August the following year, with 115 girls and women, and 49 boys.

They were under the care of two African matrons and an African house father. It was named in honour of Lucy Kumm and was officially opened by the Acting Governor of the Protectorate, Sir William Wallace.

As tribespeople were won to Christ and asked for baptism, it became necessary to provide them with some form of education. Classes for religious instruction were started for adults and children, to teach them to read a Gospel and enable them to understand the Faith.

Starting a class often produced more permanent results, leading to the foundation of a church or primary school. Increasing attention was paid to Christian education, and in later years the Mission opened a number of secondary schools and started to train its own day school teachers.

Karl Kumm paid his last visit to Africa in 1923, when a severe attack of dysentery left him weak for the rest of his tour. Unable to recover, he resigned from the mission in 1925, and continued in a poor state of health until his death in 1930.

The work amongst leprosy sufferers was first started at Vom in 1925. Later, the mission was given government permission to open a leprosy colony at Maiduguri, a Muslim area in the north-east. It resembled a village, with its own market, school and church. Such was its reputation that many Muslim patients flocked to the colony for treatment, where for the first time they heard the gospel.

**Further developments**

The first regularly organised church had been brought into being by the mission at Donga in the Benue valley in 1917. But though the Mission had a vision of 'the evangelization of Africa by Africans', it was not until 1934 that a training school was founded at Gindiri to train Africans to reach out to their own people.

The Bible School at Gindiri has now developed into a full theological college, where pastors for the Church are trained. The biggest development at Gindiri, in terms of numbers, was the development of secondary schools and teacher training, so that today many Gindiri 'graduates' occupy high positions in government service, especially on the Plateau.

One outcome of this work was the Faith and Farm project, which involved trained lay evangelists working with farmers to teach them better farming methods. In 1938 three men who had converted from paganism were ordained and given charge of their own congregations.

The aim was eventually to establish an African Church that was self-supporting, self-propagating and self-governing.

Over the years, an interest in the Greater Sudan (i.e. the Sahel) was awakened in a number of other countries and more branches established: Switzerland (1950), France (1961) and, more recently, the Netherlands (1976) and Germany (1994). Mission stations have been set up in French Equatorial Africa (now the Republic of Chad).

## Mode of Operation

SUM's mode of operation is rather different from that of other missions. Each branch of the Mission is autonomous, and is free to develop as guided by God. Assigned to their own areas of operation, branches are responsible for raising and spending their own funds, and for appointing and supporting their own missionaries.

Though plans had frequently been discussed for an indigenous Church, they did not materialise until the mission's jubilee year. A constitution was approved in 1955 and the *Tarrayyar Ekklesiyoyin Kristi a Nigeria* (TEKAN), the Fellowship of the Churches of Christ in Nigeria, was born. In 1977 the British branch of SUM relinquished its control of its work, and COCIN (Church of Christ in Africa), one of the churches of TEKAN, and the one which had developed from the British branch of SUM, took responsibility for all missionaries.

In the late 1980s, the leadership of the British branch of the SUM re-assessed the mission's role, which led to a number of exciting new developments. Under the new name of Action Partners (prayerfully chosen to reflect the new emphasis), SUM entered into partnership with a number of indigenous churches and missionary agencies in Africa. The idea was, and is, to provide support in the fields of Bible Training, medicine, education, agriculture, engineering and other crucial areas, so that the work of the gospel can be more effective. The long-term aim is to reach the regions beyond with the national church. A developing emphasis is the unreached people groups of the Sahel – the zone of encounter with Islam.

In the UK the Mission moved into new headquarters at Bawtry (South Yorkshire). Bawtry Hall, a Georgian mansion purchased in 1988, houses Action Partners and other mission agencies which now share the building. More than that, it is being used as a Christian conference centre and to train and encourage Christian workers to develop skills that can be used on the mission field, and to prepare them for new patterns of ministry.

While Action Partners is developing links with churches and Christian agencies in Africa, it is also in close co-operation with the Australian and New Zealand Branch. Shared field work goes on in Nigeria and the Sudan, as well as Ghana, Cameroon, Chad, Egypt and Kenya. More recently the Mission has taken over the work of the Regions Beyond Missionary Union in Zaire.. Whilst the aim is still to bring the gospel to the people of the Sahel, now it is in partnership with other international groups, and with indigenous missions and churches.

The call is to work with others to build the kingdom of God, and help build up a mature Christian Church.

**ACTION PARTNERS STATEMENT OF PURPOSE**

Communicating the Good News about Jesus Christ in partnership with Churches and Christian Organisations in Africa and the world.

Combining resources to bring people to a saving knowledge of God through Christ alone.

Equipping and training for Christian service.

Ministering to spiritual, emotional and physical needs.

## CENTRAL & SOTHERN AFRICA

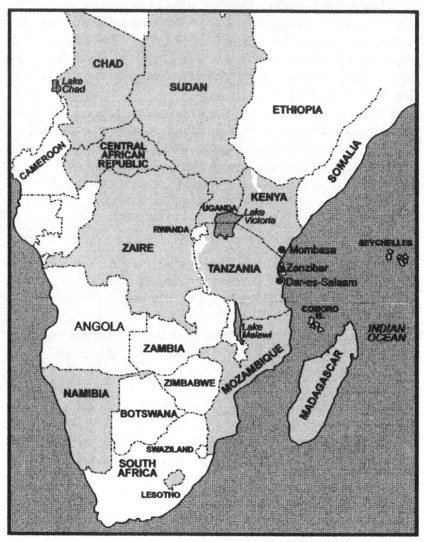

AIM's area of operation today —

## 2. AFRICA INLAND MISSION INTERNATIONAL (1891)
### Peter Cameron Scott (1867-1896)

To become a Christian is to enter the realm of faith. That is not to say that all reason is abandoned, but that the believer learns to live within the providence of God. There are many examples within the modern missionary movement of men and women who have known how to rely completely upon God, and have achieved by faith what humanly seemed impossible.

Hudson Taylor's China Inland Mission was the first of a number of 'faith missions' set up to exemplify this principle. Without the backing of a denomination or other influential body, Taylor set out to win China for Christ. He determined from the beginning (in 1865) that adopting the faith principle meant, for example, there should be no appeals for funds, but that he would rely entirely on seeking God in prayer.

In this matter, Taylor was considerably encouraged by the friendship and support of George Müller, founder of the children's homes at Bristol. At the same time, his decision to form a new mission was taken in the aftermath of the great revival of 1859. Many thousands of men and women had experienced a spiritual awakening; they understood something of what it meant to 'live by faith', and were anxious to win others for Christ.

The Africa Inland Mission was founded on the basis of such a faith. Peter Cameron Scott, the founder, was convinced that as the new mission was of God then he would supply their needs. While there were often times of shortage and missionaries faced frequent dangers, especially from fatal diseases such as malaria, God always fulfilled his promises.

### Missionary-Explorers
Scott began his work in British East Africa, now known as Kenya, and built on the work of a number of missionary-explorers who had gone before him.

One man who led the way was Johann Ludwig Krapf, a German Lutheran minister with the Basle Missionary Institution. Released to work with the Church Missionary Society, he was sent to Ethiopia in 1837, but opposition from the government and the Coptic Church forced him to move south. In 1844 Krapf founded the first Protestant mission station in East Africa, at Mombasa. Afterwards he moved inland, where his linguistic researches did much to prepare the way for future missionary achievements.

His vision was to set up a chain of mission stations across the continent to Gabon. He termed it an 'Apostle Street' of mission stations, as each one was to be named after an apostle. 'This idea I bequeath to every missionary coming to East Africa,' he proposed. 'Though many missionaries may fall in the fight, yet the survivors will pass over the slain into the trenches and take this great African fortress for the Lord.'

David Livingstone of the London Missionary Society and the New York journalist H M Stanley also paved the way for an entry into East Africa, and at Kampala, Uganda. Other societies took up the work where they left off, especially the Church

## Africa Martyrs

The foundation of Christianity in Africa has been a costly affair. Not only have a great number of missionaries died in the cause, but thousands of African believers have been killed in standing firm for their faith.

The first churches on the continent were in North Africa, and from early days they were subject to bitter persecution. Representative of those first years is the death of Perpetua, a young mother of 22 years of age. Refusing to offer incense to the heathen gods, she was killed by wild beasts in the theatre at Carthage (c 202).

The Church in North Africa was destroyed in the 7th century by the militant forces of Islam, which continually campaigned against any remnants of Christianity. Towards the end of the 13th century Raymond Lull of Majorca entered Tunis alone, to witness to the Muslims. After years of meeting in secret with a group of believers, he publicly denounced Islam and at the age of 79 was stoned to death. A 25 year old Arab Christian was arrested by the Turkish governor of Algiers in 1569. When he continued to hold fast to Christ, he was cruelly put to death; bound hand and foot, he was thrown into liquid concrete.

After the exploratory journeys of Livingstone, the pace of evangelization in Africa began to gather speed. As it did, the number of martyrs dramatically increased. During the 19th and 20th centuries more believers died in Africa for their faith than ever before, as Christianity confronted the forces of Islam, paganism and nationalism. Yet in one church after another there was revival, and the Church grew strong as a result of its sufferings.

Missionary Society, which concentrated its efforts around the freed slave ministry at Frere Town, near Mombasa, though the regions they covered were further south.

In addition, the Roman Catholics, the United Methodist Free Churches, the Universities' Mission to Central Africa, the Society of Friends and the Scottish Industrial Mission had made a tentative start, endeavouring to build on the foundation laid down by their forerunners.

By 1895 the missionary societies had gained a firm foothold on the coast of British East Africa, though the vast area of the interior was virtually untouched. The time was ready for someone to go where no-one had so far succeeded, someone with a call from God to reach the lost peoples of the East African highlands.

It was to this land that Peter Cameron Scott, an expatriate Scotsman, was called, and it was in Westminster Abbey while kneeling at the tomb of his compatriot, David Livingstone, that he received the vision.

## Glorify God

Born in Glasgow of earnest Christian parents, Peter Scott was taken to America in 1879 where the family settled in Philadelphia. After starting work in a printer's office, he had a breakdown in health and was sent back to Scotland where it was hoped he would recover.

Kneeling one day at the graveside of a little sister, he vowed that if God spared his life he would dedicate himself to the Lord's service. His health immediately began to improve, and though not completely recovered, by the following year he was able to return to America. His vow to the Lord, however, was forgotten.

Blessed with an exceptionally fine singing voice for which he had received training, Scott applied to the Opera House for a position in the chorus. For some while he

PETER CAMERON SCOTT

had been haunted by a verse of Scripture, 'Ye are not your own, ye are bought with a price, therefore glorify God in your body and your spirit, which are God's.' As he entered the theatre a voice whispered, 'Are you going to glorify God by going in there?'

For a moment he paused on the steps, then carried on; but the voice spoke again. Convinced it was the Lord speaking to him, he turned round and hurried back home where in his room he made a full surrender to God. Now at peace, he felt able to trust the Lord not only for spiritual health but for physical restoration as well. His condition improved remarkably, and his eye sight which had troubled him for four years began to improve.

From then on, events began to move at a rapid pace. In 1889 he started a three year missionary training course. By November the following year (1890) Scott had been accepted by the International Missionary Alliance and was on his way to the West Coast of Africa.

His first tour of duty, in the Congo (Zaire), was brief and marred by tragedy. A few months after his arrival he was joined by his brother John, who died following a brief illness. Scott had himself to make the coffin, dig the grave and lay his brother to rest. He also went down with fever and became so ill that he had to leave Africa, wondering whether he would ever return.

Scott travelled home by way of England, where he stayed with friends in London, a Mr and Mrs Brodie. With careful nursing he gradually recovered his health and strength, but all the time his mind was on Africa.

He studied the possibility of returning to an area where the physical conditions were more favourable. Soon, his mind became fixed on British East Africa, an upland region which straddled the equator. The fact that it was an elevated plateau appeared to offer a lesser threat to health and would, therefore, be less likely to prove fatal for missionaries. He hoped that Africans more resistant to malaria could be trained as evangelists and sent to the people on the plains.

During his stay in London, Mrs Brodie took him to Westminster Abbey to visit the tomb of David Livingstone. Captivated by the words of Scripture on the monument, 'Other sheep I have which are not of this fold; them also I must bring,' he knelt for some while in quiet, and heard again the call of God. Those moments crystallized the thoughts of the past weeks and his decision was made. He would return to Africa and establish a line of mission stations across 2,000 miles of the continent from where he could reach the tribes of the interior.

## Faith Mission

Back home in America, Scott shared his vision with Dr A T Pierson, a missionary-statesman, who was enthused by his plans. It was decided to form a new society, and a committee was formed to launch the mission. It was to be called the Africa Inland Mission (AIM), with its headquarters in their home town of Philadelphia. The President was the Rev Charles Hurlburt, who was later to succeed Scott as Director.

Although other missions were short of funds, Scott was convinced of the rightness of his new venture. As the committee prayed about the work, it was decided not to make any appeals for money or to incur debts. From its inception, it was a 'faith mission', and has continued to operate on this basis ever since. Among the first volunteers for service was Scott's own sister. Later, his parents were also called to join him on the mission field, so that his whole family was involved.

Following a farewell and dedication meeting in August 1895, a party of seven missionaries set sail. Joined by one other missionary from Scotland, the group reached the island port of Zanzibar in the October, before moving to Mombasa on the mainland. There were already several missions at work along the coast, and the Church Missionary Society very kindly provided a house for the ladies to stay.

Before long, the men decided to go off and explore the interior. A large number of porters were employed and the party was given a military escort, making a total of some 300 men in all on the safari. With considerable difficulty and hardship they were able to penetrate the uplands and reach the village of Nzawi, some 250 miles from the coast.

The chief welcomed them, but was reluctant to let them have the plot of land they wanted. It took careful negotiations by Scott before the village elders permitted them to choose their own spot, close to a water supply. Not only was their first station established here, but eventually some of the villagers were brought to faith and the first church of the Africa Inland Mission was founded.

When the ladies from Mombasa joined the men, it was judged there were too many workers for the one station. After two months, Scott set off to survey the area for another suitable site. When the villagers at Sakai refused his request for land, he employed his skill at juggling, tumbling and balancing sticks and knives to prevail upon them to change their minds. He won them over and they allowed him to settle in the village.

As a second party of missionaries was on its way, which included his parents and a younger sister, Scott moved on and established a third station, at Kilungu. On 3 October a fourth station was opened at Kangundo, where the party took over the use of a brick-built military post.

## Gratitude

Scott's first annual report, which proved also to be his last, was one of immense gratitude to God. In it, he recounted that in less than ten months four stations had been opened, with houses built of bricks. Elementary school work had begun and simple medical treatment was made available.

All this was accomplished with little knowledge of the language and despite considerable sickness among the missionaries – none of them had been free from fever. He concluded, 'We have had times of trial, also times of blessing; times of sorrow and times of joy. Patience has been put to the test, but God has answered our prayer.'

After spending 14 months in British East Africa, Scott planned to return to America as escort to one of the missionaries who was sick, and for consultations with the Home Council. He calculated that during these months he had walked over 2,600 miles, which had obviously taken a toll on his health.

One day, after a long and tiring journey, he began to vomit and suffer severe pains; blackwater fever set in. His mother stayed at his side, and his father and sister were sent for. But too late; he died on 4th December 1896. His last words were, 'I want the arm of the Lord of hosts around me.' The following day his body was laid to rest in front of the little thatched house in which he had lived.

For some years after Scott's death the Mission went through a period of 'dark waters', when it was thought the work might come to an end. The threat to health was real, despite living on the upland plateau. A number of workers fell prey to African diseases; some resigned, and one left to set up a station for the Socicty of Friends. Soon there remained only one missionary, who readily admitted to loneliness. Back in Philadelphia questions were raised: 'Was it worth it ?' and 'Should we carry on ?'

It was decided that Charles Hurlburt should go out to study the situation on the field. Hurlburt was a dynamic character with clear gifts of leadership, recognised as a spiritual giant. It was said of him as a missionary that 'he loves more, gives more and does more'. With his wife and five children, Hurlburt went to British East Africa in 1901, to carry on where Scott had left off.

Under his direction, the work revived and began to grow. In 1903 the AIM headquarters was moved to Kangundo and a start made to push inland. After three years, the Mission had 31 missionaries and had opened seven stations, all the time moving further west.

Meanwhile other societies entered the field, and the Church of Scotland (Presbyterian), the American Church of God, the Methodists and the Seventh Day Adventists all opened stations in the interior.

Scott's last entry in his diary – 'Here I am, Lord, use me in life or in death' – has been wonderfully fulfilled, and AIM's 750 missionaries now serve in 14 countries in Africa and its adjacent islands.

God used Peter Cameron Scott's brief ministry to begin a work that has been built up into a thriving Mission, and the churches that have been founded under the AIM banner are built on the foundations he laid down.

## MISSION STATEMENT OF AIM INTERNATIONAL

AIM International has two primary aims: (1) to take the gospel of the Lord Jesus Christ to people groups which do not have a viable church of their own which is able to evangelise their own members; (2) to enable churches to grow more mature by the training of national leaders.

In addition to evangelism and theological education, AIM's activities include medical care, community development, agriculture, literacy training, literature production, Bible translation and education.

AIM International is an interdenominational and international mission with an evangelical basis of faith.

# 3. ARAB WORLD MINISTRIES (1881)
## George Pearse (1814-1902), Dr Grattan Guinness (1835-1910) and Edward Glenny (1854-1926).

It was not until towards the end of the second century that Christianity was established in North Africa. Despite terrible persecutions, there emerged a thriving Church that produced a number of outstanding leaders.

Some 500 years later, after the death of Mohammed in 632, Muslim armies swept westwards from Arabia. They established control over the northern coastal regions of the continent as far as the Atlantic, destroying churches or converting them to mosques. Apart from the Coptic community in Egypt, practically all evidence of Christianity was wiped out and the population eventually assimilated the Islamic religion and culture.

For twelve centuries North Africa remained under the sway of Islam before serious attempts were made to regain the land for the Cross. While Christians could convert to Islam, under Muslim law there were severe penalties – even the threat of death – for Muslims who chose to become Christian. And although Christians were acknowledged as 'people of the Book', they were regarded by Muslims as inferior.

Following the Crusades, Christianity was distrusted by Muslims because of its association with European imperialism. Hence attempts by Europeans to spread Christianity among the non-Christians of North Africa met with little success.

From the end of the 18th century several European powers – notably France, Spain and Great Britain – began to take a commercial interest in North Africa, and eventually the region came under their control. In the 1830s and 1840s France extended its authority over Algiers and Tunisia, and later France and Spain gained a foothold in Morocco. Britain took control of Egypt in 1882 following the British army's intervention in an armed revolt. During these years a large number of Roman Catholics from France, Italy and Spain settled in North Africa, many of them merchants and traders. Though Catholic missions were founded to win over the non-Christians, including the many Jews living there, they made little progress.

There was also a small Protestant presence, and from the 1830s modest missionary incursions were made into the region. Among them were the British and Foreign Bible Society and the London Society for

Promoting Christianity amongst the Jews, now the Church's Ministry among the Jews (CMJ). The Southern Morocco Mission, with its headquarters in Scotland, sent their first two missionaries in 1888. At the same time Lilias Trotter and a number of others began a work in Algiers which became known as the Algiers Mission Band.

The largest effort to reach the Muslims, however, was made by the North Africa Mission, which viewed the whole of the coastal area as its mission field.

## Common Desire

The North Africa Mission (NAM), which traces its origins back to the influence of the 1859 Evangelical Revival, was one of several non-denominational missions operating at this time north of the Sahara. Three men were involved in establishing the mission, drawn together by their common desire to see Muslims converted to Christ. Each one made his own particular contribution to the work, though the initial impetus came from George Pearse, a stockbroker.

As a result of his business acumen, Pearse made enough money for him to be able to indulge his interest in mission. He had already founded the Chinese Evangelisation Society (in 1850) which sent out Hudson Taylor to China, and was anxious to do more. When he retired in 1870

at the age of 55, he began to spend much of his time in France in an effort to evangelise French soldiers.

Clerical opposition, however, made his task virtually impossible, and in 1876 he moved to the French colony of Algeria where he hoped to continue his work. While staying in Algiers his attention was drawn to the Kabyles, a tribe of Berber people who lived in the mountains between Tunisia and Morocco.

The thought of reaching them for Christ was re-affirmed one bright moonlight night. As Mrs Pearse looked out from their hotel window she saw what appeared to

GEORGE PEARSE

be a bundle of rags on the pavement. She quickly realised the 'bundle' was, in fact, a man, his ghastly face upturned to the moon. The following morning she discovered that the man had died, one of hundreds of victims of a terrible epidemic. The incident impressed itself upon the Pearses and they determined to do something for these people.

The Pearses consulted their friend Dr Grattan Guinness, who shared their vision for North Africa. He encouraged them in the work, and in the light of his considerable support was recognised as one of the mission's co-founders. Pearse determined to press ahead with the project, despite now having attained 65 years of age.

His booklet, *Mission to the Kabyles*, challenging Christians to consider this work, was well-received. As a result, three young men volunteered to join him: a young Swiss missionary, a Syrian converted from Islam, and Edward Glenny who had a gospel work in Barking, East London, where he supervised a number of mission halls.

Glenny, the third acknowledged co-founder of the mission, had early in life come under the influence of George Müller, and had learned the principle of living by faith. A businessman with an extensive ministry of writing and preaching, Glenny one day read of agricultural schemes in Algeria to produce exports for English markets. Interested in an opportunity for mission work among the Arabs, he saw the possibility of combining the two activities.

Introduced to George Pearse, he was able to join the first party of missionaries shortly going out to North Africa. The party arrived in Algeria on 5 November 1881. Its headquarters were set up at Djemma Sahridj, a little way outside the port of Algiers, where the Pearses had bought a plot of land.

### Evangelism

With European governments in control of North Africa, it seemed that openings for evangelism might be possible, though not without difficulty. The French authorities in Algeria, however, supported the Catholic cause and forbade Protestants to preach in the open air. As the missionaries were under constant surveillance, contact with people had consequently to be at a personal level.

Many of the government officials were Roman Catholic and they purposely opposed the Protestant missionaries, charging them with espionage and distributing arms and gunpowder. It was only the timely

# NORTH AFRICA (1900)

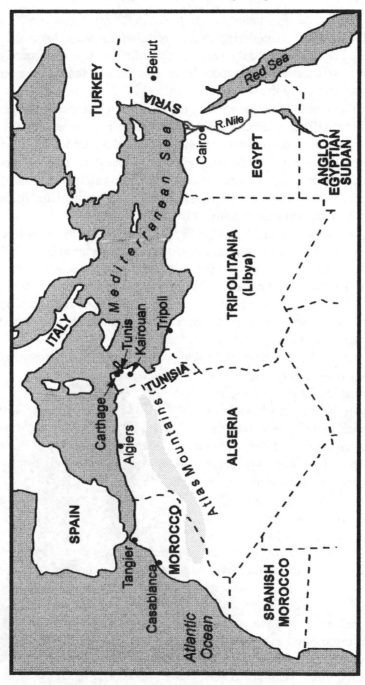

protestations of representatives of the French Reformed Church, who commended the missionaries for their unselfish service, that ended the trouble. Despite two early resignations, the new mission survived. Other missionaries soon swelled their numbers and they spread out to distant parts along the coast.

Initially called Mission to the Kabyles, the work seemed to go easier among the hill tribes, especially where women missionaries with simple medical skills were able to visit the villagers in their homes. Many of the villagers apparently listened to the message, but they had no conviction of sin and were unable to respond to the gospel. Others claimed to believe in Jesus, but often lacked the courage to break away from Islam. To make an open confession meant putting their lives in danger.

After two years on the field, Edward Glenny was appointed Honorary General Secretary, and he returned to Barking where he set up their new headquarters. Pearse handed over the control of the Mission to a Council in London, then he and his wife returned to North Africa. Their home at Djemma Sahridj became the centre of the work in Algeria, from where they continued their witness to the Kabyles and engaged in literature distribution.

From the headquarters in Barking, Glenny began deputation work around the country, encouraging support for the young mission. He kept in touch with the overseas work by paying occasional visits to the field, and in this way was able to co-ordinate their activities. In Barking, he took over five further houses for the use of missionaries coming home on furlough, where new recruits were able to spend about a year in training before going out.

EDWARD GLENNY

## Expansion

By the middle of the 1880s NAM had extended its sphere of activity westwards to Tangier, a Spanish possession in Morocco. Here, two main programmes were set up in an effort to break through the Muslims' fear of contact with Christianity. The first was a medical work, begun in Tangier in 1884 by the wife of an American missionary. When Dr T G Churcher arrived in Morocco the following year the mission was able to open the first ever hospital in that country.

The Tulloch Memorial Hospital, which was later to include a school for training nurses, soon gained a reputation for giving a loving and

### Militant Islam

Mohammed, the founder of Islam, believed himself to be 'the apostle of God' and that he had a duty to warn people of the Day of Judgment. When his message was rejected, he determined to use force to win over converts. He raised an army and marched through the Arabian peninsula on a holy war (*jihad*). Under the threat of death, pagans were forced to accept Islam; Jews and Christians were given a choice, either convert to Islam, or submit and pay tribute money. Whilst many of the Christians in Arabia submitted, many Jews refused and were put to the sword. By the time of his death, Mohammed had conquered most of the peninsula.

Under the Caliphs ('successors') the policy of aggression continued. Between 635 and 651 they overwhelmed the Middle East and turned towards Christendom. Within a hundred years many of the lands around the Mediterranean basin had fallen to Islam: Egypt, Palestine, Syria, North Africa and Spain.

Although parts of the Muslim empire were recovered by the Crusaders in the 12th century, fresh Muslim advances in 13th-16th centuries led to the capture of Constantinople and the fall of the Byzantine empire. Macedonia and the Balkans were over-run, and in 1529 Muslim armies reached the gates of Vienna, where they were finally stopped.

In recent centuries, economic and cultural factors have often been the means of expansion, rather than military might, especially in south east Asia. Emigration has further enabled Islam to gain a foothold in the West, where its influence is steadily increasing.

Militant Islamic factions are again active, and a number of Muslim countries are strongly influenced by Islamic fundamentalism. In Sudan, forces from the north are campaigning against the Christianised south to convert it to Islam, while in Algeria thousands have died in violence between Islamic fundamentalists and the government. Islamic groups in Israel are continuing their *jihad* against Israel and will not be satisfied until the Jews are driven into the sea.

caring service. Local people referred to it as 'the house of God'. Prejudices were broken down, so that when a government hospital was eventually established, many patients still preferred to be treated at the mission hospital.

There was also a successful evangelism programme, set up by a gifted Irish lady, Emma Herdman. She realised that in a Muslim country men were better fitted to reach the upper classes and command their attention to the gospel, so she gathered together a team of Christian men – all of them Muslim converts – to train as colporteurs and teachers. For 11 years they travelled through the northern part of Morocco, selling Christian literature and teaching the Bible. There were a number of conversions, but before any church could be established Emma Herdman fell ill and died.

**Few Converts**
In Tunisia, a simple medical work was begun among women and children at Kairouan, a staunch centre of Islam. A few converts were made, but such were the pressures upon them that they did not stand. Further eastwards, the mission sent a representative to Egypt in 1892, to begin a work among the Muslims, and a few years later they were able to establish a centre at Tripoli (Libya). For a brief period there were also missionaries in Beirut ministering among Bedouins.

Other missions, which also laboured among the Muslims in these lands, found the work equally demanding and faced similar obstacles. But by the end of the century, NAM had 115 missionaries operating in 17 centres, from Morocco along the coast to Egypt. As always, converts were few.

A number of tragedies occurred to missionaries in the early years which indicate the sacrificial nature of their calling. When Casablanca, in Morocco, was attacked and looted by tribesmen, the small NAM hospital in the city was destroyed. While on this occasion the workers were spared, there were other times when missionaries met with a violent death. The country was also plagued by diseases, and lack of hygiene controls or proper hospital facilities resulted in further missionary deaths.

Since 1945 the Europeans have been forced to withdraw from North Africa, leaving behind strong nationalist governments influenced by Islamic fundamentalism. Tighter restrictions have been placed on

Christian work, and NAM schools and hospitals have been closed and proselytism forbidden.

The North Africa Mission merged in the 1960s with the Algiers Mission Band and the Southern Morocco Mission to become the Arab World Ministries. Now there are nearly 300 members drawn from over 12 nations, united in a call to share God's love with Muslims throughout the whole of the Arab World, as well as reaching Arab world Muslims living in Europe.

The world of Islam is a hostile environment for Christian witness, and alternative approaches have to be made. Radio broadcasts from a new media centre in the south of France, Bible correspondence courses and an attractive literature programme are used to present the gospel.

The term 'missionary' has been replaced by 'Special Service Worker', which denotes a believer who undertakes a secular job in an Arab country in order to live as a Christian witness. Through friendship evangelism, 'tentmaker' missionaries build a foundation on which to share the Lord.

In this sort of environment, members need more than simply faith and love. It is what the apostle Paul describes as the 'patience of hope'.

## ARAB WORLD MINISTRIES MISSION STATEMENT

Our purpose is to proclaim the Good News of Jesus Christ to Muslims of the Arab world, wherever they may be found, and to help those who believe to be integrated into local churches.

VISION
Our vision is to see mature and vibrant churches among Muslims of the Arab world.

AIMS
* To recruit and train personnel for the placing of teams in strategic centres.
* To communicate effectively the gospel using all appropriate means.
* To make disciples and, wherever necessary, plant churches.
* To work together with national believers and local churches who share our vision.
* To mobilise prayer and financial resources.
* To increase the extent and effectiveness of our ministries in major urban concentrations of Arab world Muslim populations.

## 4. EUROPEAN CHRISTIAN MISSION (1904)
### G P Raud (1882-1953)

After Christianity spread throughout Europe during the early centuries of the Church, the Continent became the chief bastion of the Faith. It was from Europe, following the 16th century Reformation, that the Church began to send out missionaries to other parts of the globe. By the beginning of the 19th century Christianity had made gains in all of the world's five continents.

The 19th century witnessed a fresh outburst of Christian missionary activity emanating from Europe. The main impetus was the consequence of a series of revivals experienced in Germany, Great Britain and America, whilst the Roman Catholic Church also displayed a new determination to make further conquests. A wide variety of missionary societies were founded to reach people in places that were previously inaccessible, while other agencies were set up to evangelize different religious and racial groups.

In addition to new missionary initiatives, Protestants engaged in a wide variety of good causes, which influenced all levels of society throughout Europe. Many social reforms were inspired by men and women motivated by a new-found faith, and the teachings of Jesus formed the basis of much new legislation. The formation of the great Protestant orphanages, mission hospitals and nursing institutions, care of the physically and mentally disabled, and provision for the poor, the prisoner and the homeless, all owed much to the reforming zeal exhibited during this period.

Yet despite an impressive witness to the power of the gospel, only a minority of Europeans were to be found within the fold of the Church. There were at least two reasons for this state of affairs.

One was that, as a result of the Industrial Revolution, large numbers of the population moved from the countryside into the towns. Separated from their usual environment, thousands of them tended to drop their religious observances and the beliefs they had long held. They consequently severed their links with the Church, and either repudiated the Faith or simply ignored it.

Then, of those claiming church membership, many appeared to have only a superficial grasp of their religion. Europeans had, for the most part, settled down as third or fourth generation Christians, and were to a large extent only nominal church members. Very little attempt had been made to present the claims of the gospel afresh to each succeeding generation.

## Challenge

In 1904, Ganz Petrovitch Raud, a young man from Estonia, accepted the vision and challenge of Europe as a mission field. Some people scorned the idea of evangelizing 'Christian' Europe, but Raud was convinced that the Continent more than ever needed the gospel and that this was God's will for his life.

At the beginning of the 20th century, Estonia was part of the Russian Empire, ruled by Tsar Nicholas II (1894-1918). It did not gain its independence until 1918. At this time, Russia was a divided nation, with a huge gap between the rich aristocrats and the starving peasantry. A series of bad harvests, together with a period of industrial and political unrest, led to a short-lived revolution in 1905. The problems were never resolved, and in 1917 there was another revolution and the Bolsheviks took control of the country.

There were a large number of Protestants living in the empire, especially in the Baltic provinces, and many German communities had been created in the Ukraine. In the second half of the century there was a revival among the German immigrants, largely the work of American Baptists. Lord Radstock, an English evangelical peer, visited Russia and preached among the upper classes. There were many converts among the landowners, some of whom shared the gospel with their tenants and retainers.

From around 1875 the Russian Orthodox Church began to persecute these evangelical Christians. A number of Baptist churches had been established, and they bore the brunt of the Church's attacks. Although religious liberty was accorded the German Baptists in 1879, the Orthodox Church saw dissent as heresy and as a threat to society, hence the efforts to curb it.

Believers faced threats and intimidation from the police and the militia, meetings were broken up and preachers arrested. Many Baptists lost their jobs, others were exiled and died far away from home. As only Orthodox Church weddings were legal, Baptist marriages could not be registered. In which case, any children born of such a union were considered to be illegitimate and were denied educational opportunities. It was against this background that Ganz Raud was brought up.

## Godly Family

Raud was born into a godly family. His father, Pertel, was a preacher and a man of prayer, and made a great impression on the young Ganz. Even as a small child, his father's prayers were a blessing to him. 'In prayer my father was an example to us all. We had family prayers night and morning. They were happy times I did not want to miss, because my father made them almost irresistible through his life and devotion to the Lord.'

Sometimes, when he knew his father was privately at prayer, Ganz would slip up quietly to the bedroom door, to listen and hear what he was saying to the Lord about him. 'My father and mother were godly people, who in their daily walk showed their love for the Lord Jesus Christ. Their life was so beautiful that it was the power which drew me to God.'

His older brother, Will, was already a pioneer evangelist and church-planter in Estonia. He often travelled the country, gathering crowds to hear the gospel, and many came to the Lord through his ministry.

Ganz Raud sometimes accompanied his brother and father on their journeys, which gave him opportunities to preach, visit hospitals and distribute the Scriptures. His activities quickly became known, and he was classified by the Church and civil authorities as a dissenter. On occasions they were arrested, and once his father told the arresting officer, 'You cannot do me any harm without God's permission.'

Believing he was also called to become a preacher of the gospel, Raud began to seek God's will for his life. Some of his friends urged him to pursue an academic training, but Raud felt God had other plans and launched out on his own as an evangelist.

## Tour

Challenged by his father's daily prayers for Russia and all of Europe, Raud's attention became focused on the need of this great continent to hear again the message of the Bible. From shortly after his conversion he prayed, 'I am only 18, Lord, but I want to be sure of your will for my life.' A number of mature Christians also prayed with him and for him, but it was three years before he received an answer to his prayer. The confirmation came in quite a dramatic way during the Christmas season of 1903.

Despite the atrocious weather conditions, the three men felt bound to keep their commitment to undertake an evangelistic tour. During their ten-day mission they visited a number of towns and villages, travelling in a horse-drawn sleigh. It was New Year's Eve, and they had arrived at a border village where a meeting had been arranged in the local baronial castle.

The baron, a committed Christian, had made his castle – known as a 'Prayer House' – available, and a large gathering was ready to hear the preachers. The meeting began at eight o'clock that night. First father Pertel, then Will spoke, and finally it was Gans' turn. As he rose to his feet, the baron came in to say that plain clothes Russian policemen had come with handcuffs to arrest the preachers.

But the people were already deeply absorbed in what they had heard in the messages, and were under a strong conviction. Many of them, hearing the gospel for the first time, had begun to cry out to God for mercy, so that the Spirit of God was powerfully at work as Ganz got up to speak.

The three policemen approached the table from which Ganz was speaking, but waited for him to finish before arresting him. His message was based on Revelations 20, and he called on his listeners to repent and give themselves to the Lord, lest they find themselves under judgment.

What happened next was a miracle of grace, reported Ganz. The Holy Spirit touched the heart of the police chief, who began to feel the burden of his sins. There and then he accepted Christ as his Saviour. His two colleagues turned and fled, fearing that what had afflicted their chief might also take hold of them.

**Guidance**

That night 40 people found the Lord, and the gathering was afterwards given over to an all-night prayer meeting. At one point they prayed for guidance for Ganz, that he should know from the Lord immediately. A word was given that the Lord would thrust him out soon, that he would be used to reach great numbers for him, even far away from the place where they were praying.

To Ganz, this was the Lord's confirmation of his call to Europe. Afterwards, he always considered this all-night prayer meeting and the following day – 1 January 1904 – as the beginning of his later organized work for the mission.

A month later, shortly after his 22nd birthday, Raud was invited to Tallin (the capital of Estonia) to hear a well-known visiting German

Bible teacher. Afterwards he sought out the teacher and asked his advice concerning his future plans. The man's counsel was specific: 'Leave Estonia as soon as possible and acquire as much Bible knowledge as possible. See what God is doing in other countries, and how the work of God is being carried out. In other words, enlarge your vision and horizons.'

Raud later admitted to the wisdom of this counsel. 'If I had remained where I was living,' he later confessed, 'I would probably have lost my life in the (1905) revolution, the war that followed and the flood of Communism that swept over the land.'

### England

A Christian nobleman offered Raud enough financial help for him to be able to undertake his European trip, and to get the work started. For the next ten years Raud travelled the Continent, chiefly with the idea of gathering knowledge about Europe's religious condition.

He began his tour in England in 1905, where he spent much time in

GANZ PETROVITCH RAUD

prayer and Bible study. He also listened to some eminent Bible teachers at Keswick and other conventions, and experienced the Welsh revival. In France he learned something of the history of the Huguenots, and was impressed, and in Switzerland and Scandinavia he was able to witness a work of God.

However, his attention was particularly focused on Germany, where he spent some time in learning the language and – following the advice given him – studying in a Bible school. In Berlin, he worked with a Bible teacher, and was able to speak at meetings and Bible conferences. But the evidence of theological trends towards Higher Criticism in the German universities both shocked and saddened him.

It was during these years that Raud called out the first workers to join him in the mission, although as yet he had not given the work a name. He began by providing financial support for several gospel preachers, enabling them to return to their countries and start church-planting work. Whilst aware that the greatest need was in Eastern Europe, his first two workers were sent to France. Two others were later sent to Russia, where a thriving gospel work was started in Kiev, until anti-Christian regulations were introduced.

Three weeks before the outbreak of the First World War Raud left Germany and, in February 1915, sailed for America on the last trip of the *Lusitania*. Convinced that it was from here that God would have him continue his work, he headed for New York.

Over the next two years he gradually gathered support for his work in Europe, ready for when the end of the war would allow a resumption of his mission. Prayer groups were formed and finance started to come in. It was in 1917 that his plans took a definite shape. With the help of the Rev and Mrs MacDonald from Washington DC, he formally inaugurated the Russian and Slavonic Bible Union, with the aim of establishing a gospel work in all the countries of Europe.

## Developments

The work began to gather momentum, and over the next few years a number of developments took place. By 1922 the Union had acquired headquarters in Brooklyn, New York, which also served as a Bible school for training workers. As Raud's vision for post-war Europe became clearer, he changed the title to the European Christian Mission (ECM).

## EUROVISION

Despite ECM's commitment to Europe as a mission field, other societies also minister to the Continent. But whereas the ECM opened its work in Western Europe, Eurovision has focused on Eastern Europe and Russia, with a special concern for Siberia. Eurovision was founded by Pastor David Hathaway (author of the book Czech-mate) who has been ministering behind the former Iron Curtain for over 30 years. Called in 1964 to reach out to Eastern Europe, Hathaway formed a travel company called Crusader Tours, taking groups overland to Israel. From 1968, Bibles, secretly concealed in the coach, were delivered to believers in Communist countries en route. Arrested and imprisoned in the former Czechoslovakia in 1972, Hathaway experienced a remarkable release 18 months later.

His work on the behalf of believers behind the Iron Curtain continued, and four years later he was able to return to ministry in Eastern Europe, including (from 1984) evangelistic crusades. At a Eurovision East/West conference in Karlsruhe (Germany) in 1986 God gave Hathaway a prophecy that the Iron Curtain would fall and that revival would come to Eastern Europe. Another prophecy (1989) warned of a second curtain to fall, by economic collapse, military takeover and by spiritual force.

With the onset of glasnost (openness) and perestroika (reform) in the former USSR (in 1987), and the collapse of Communism (1991), the way was open for further evangelism, and crusades have been held in Bulgaria, Hungary, Russia (Kiev) and the Ukraine. But after a leading from God in 1992 Hathaway felt directed to approach Russia from the East. Eurovision now also operates in Siberia, where thousands have been converted, many miracles witnessed and new churches planted.

In Brooklyn he set up his own printing works, which saved the Mission thousands of dollars. What is more, it enabled him to produce a wider selection of tracts and booklets, as well as to expand the Bible ministry. The staff were employed on the same basis as the missionaries – people dedicated to serving the Lord, without a guaranteed salary.

By 1927, there were 81 missionaries, mostly nationals in their respective countries, but including British, American and Canadian men, with a further 243 national helpers. Between them, they ran 132 gospel halls, a large proportion of which were in Russia. Offices were opened in London (1927) and Canada. Soon the Mission had over 100 missionaries operating in 12 countries.

Raud was a tireless worker in the Lord's service, and most years he spent several months visiting the missionaries from his base in America. In addition to giving his support, he preached at revival meetings, arranged conferences and supervised the construction of new gospel halls. Much of the work was in Eastern Europe – Russia, Estonia, Lithuania, Poland, Bulgaria and the former Czechoslovakia, lands where a gospel witness was hardly known.

The Second World War brought inevitable disruption to the work, and British and American missionaries were forced to withdraw. Although the Mission maintained contact with some of the missionaries, the sphere of activity was switched from the Continent to Britain and America.

Throughout these difficult years the work of evangelism continued in both countries, covered by daily prayer, and funds continued to come in.

## Cold War

Changed political conditions in 1945 made it necessary to re-establish the work. But the aim was still to establish a mission in every country where there was freedom to do so. New centres were opened in Western Europe, and during the years of the so-called Cold War the Mission remained active in the former Communist bloc of Eastern Europe. Couriers took in God's Word, and they cared for the suffering Church by providing relief for those in need.

The work later expanded to include Australia, New Zealand and South Africa, and a centre was founded in Northern Ireland.

The great physical demands of supervising the work across Europe, as well as numerous other spiritual concerns, placed a great strain on Raud. Despite having a diagnosed heart condition which called for rest and care, in 1953 he insisted on making a trip to Europe. In October he arrived in Paris at the end of the tour, worn out by his exertions. One morning he was found in a coma in his hotel bedroom, his head resting on his Bible, open at Psalm 143. He had obviously been praying when the heart attack occurred.

Ganz Petrovich Raud was a man who had been faithful to the heavenly vision given to him while yet in his teens. For fifty years he had been obedient to the will of God, and had the joy of seeing the kingdom of God being built in lands where the gospel had long been neglected.

ECM is today deeply involved in a variety of exciting gospel projects, witnessing to Europe's 800 millions in the midst of turbulent political and social changes.

More than ever, the call is to 'pray to the owner of the harvest that he will send out workers to gather in his harvest.'

## MISSION STATEMENT OF EUROPEAN CHRISTIAN MISSION

### Our Origins

European Christian Mission traces its origins to an all-night prayer meeting in Estonia in 1904 when a young man by the name of Ganz Raud was called by God to serve him in Europe. The work developed under Ganz Raud's leadership and has continued since his death in 1953. Prayer has always held a central place in the life of ECM, together with the recognition that the work is God's and we are workers together with him in the evangelisation of Europe.

### Our Membership

We are an international and interdenominational fellowship committed to the evangelisation of Europe. We are evangelical in doctrine, non-political in action and international in outreach. The inspired Word of God is our only rule for faith and action. All members subscribe to the Statement of Faith.

The supporting sections of ECM around the world share in full partnership together having the corporate goal of reaching Europeans for Christ.

### Our Identity

ECM is also committed to cooperation with other organisations which have similar objectives in Europe. Our policy is to seek an identity with a national evangelical body in each country of ministry. We also work in partnership with agencies in recruitment of personnel and in the pursuit of specialist ministries.

### Our Vision

The vision of ECM is to reach Europeans with the message of the gospel of Jesus Christ through evangelism, church planting and church development, with the goal of establishing ministries in each country of Europe as the Lord opens doors of opportunity.

# 5. FULL GOSPEL BUSINESS MEN'S
## FELLOWSHIP INTERNATIONAL (1952)
### Demos Shakarian (1913-1993)

A census by MARC Europe in 1990 highlighted what was already generally known, that more women than men attend church.

This imbalance has been in evidence at least since the 18th century Evangelical Revival, when according to John Wesley more women were converted than men. Whatever the reason for this, whether it provided an emotional outlet or they were simply in need of greater reassurance, the Church often afforded them a vehicle for their talents and energies.

During the 19th century, however, a number of agencies were set up in Britain aimed specifically at boys and men, to win them for the kingdom of God.

These organisations were often founded in the context of a particular social environment, and were intended to meet physical as well as spiritual needs. There were hostels and clubs for working boys, the seamen had their missions and the soldiers their institutes.

At the same time, some societies were established simply for the purpose of evangelism. Men, however, were more difficult to reach; partly because of their long hours of employment, but also because of the influence of secular ideas. One organisation aimed solely at men was the Young Men's Christian Association (founded 1844) which flourished on both sides of the Atlantic.

In the USA a similar disparity of numbers existed between the sexes in certain sections of the Church. Between 1890 and 1917, the era of crusades, Protestants were mobilised on a wide scale for Christian missions and service. The YMCA was among the leading parachurch organisations, many of them imported from Britain, aimed at evangelizing young men working in cities and college students. In time the scope was widened to provide also for the intellectual, social and physical development of boys and young men.

It was not until 1952, when Demos Shakarian founded the Full Gospel Business Men's Fellowship International (FGBMFI) in America, that another organisation was set up with the avowed aim of winning men for Christ.

Shakarian was a highly successful dairy farmer and business man,

## THE CHURCH IN ARMENIA

Until recently, Armenia was a Soviet republic and a member of the former USSR. It is located south of the Caucasus mountains, with Turkey on the west and Iran to the south.

The origins of the Church are obscure, though it seems that the gospel penetrated the land at an early date. Gregory the Illuminator (c 240-332) is recognised as the one who established Christianity in the land at the beginning of the fourth century. Under King Tiridates (c 238-314), Gregory attained to high honour in Armenia. As a result of his witness the king was converted and baptised. Armenia was 'converted' en masse and became the first country to have a Christian ruler. Gregory was consecrated bishop at Caesarea and became leader of the young churches. He called in Greek and Syriac missionaries to help him teach the people.

Sandwiched between the Russian, Turkish and Persian empires, the Armenians have for centuries been subject to persecution. In the 19th century, evangelical Protestant missionaries entered the country and there was a revival. The Turks reacted against this movement: a number of Armenian leaders were imprisoned by the Turkish (Muslim) government, and in 1864 Muslim converts to Christianity were imprisoned.

Between 1895-96 nearly 100,000 Armenians were killed and there were mass deportations. The Turks claimed that the Armenians were planning to rise against them and embarked on a programme of genocide. They began to massacre the Armenians, using the most cruel methods. Both evangelicals and members of the Orthodox Church went to their death. It is said that in 1915 as many as 600,000 Armenians died on one day alone – 24 April, now observed as Memorial Day. Armenia was annexed by the Soviet Union in 1920.

brought up in the Armenian Pentecostal Church. He was accustomed to seeing whole families attend Sunday worship, when the numbers of men and women in the congregation were more or less equal.

But during the course of an evangelistic campaign in 1944, he noticed that the women in the meetings outnumbered the men by as many as ten to one.

It was this realisation that implanted the germ of an idea in Shakarian's mind, and when he founded the FGBMFI it was with the purpose of reaching business and professional men with the gospel.

## Prophecy

In 1905 the Shakarian family emigrated from Armenia, on the borders of north east Turkey and Russia, and settled in Los Angeles, California. Their move was the result of a prophecy given by a remarkable 'Boy Prophet' who lived in their village. The prophecy told of a terrible danger that would come upon the Armenians, and God warned them that when the time came everyone must flee.

Nearly 50 years passed before the 'boy' announced the fulfilment of the words of prophecy. 'We must flee to America. All who remain here will perish,' he warned.

Groups of Pentecostal Armenians took heed of the word and left for the New World. Those who failed to heed the message were massacred by the Turks in 1914, when one and half million Armenians died, including the inhabitants of the Shakarians' village.

In obedience to the prophecy, the Armenians settled on the west coast of America, around Los Angeles. This was the year before the famous Azusa Street Pentecostal revival, which was to spark off a charismatic renewal around the world.

Shakarian's father was only a 13-year-old boy when they emigrated, but he was soon at work supplementing the family income. When God gave him a prophecy, that he would 'bless the fruit of your ground, the increase of your cattle', Isaac Shakarian gave in his notice at the factory and began his own business buying and selling vegetables. The word from God proved true, and eventually Isaac set up as a farmer and built up a large herd of dairy cattle, the largest in California.

When Demos was 17 his father gave him his own herd to manage, and the boy was soon earning more than his day school teachers. The family business prospered, even during the depression, and the Shakarians found themselves moving among politicians, businessmen and community leaders.

At the age of 13 Demos was baptised in the Holy Spirit, and his hearing miraculously restored. (A doctor later confirmed a 90% recovery.) 'Lord,' he said, 'I know that when you heal people it's because you have work for them to do.' So from then on, he began to pray about the future work God had for him.

His marriage to Rose Gabrielian in 1933 was strictly according to Armenian tradition, but it was truly a marriage 'made in heaven'. The couple were one together in God, and both intended that they should serve him in whatever work he gave them to do. They became increasingly aware that God wanted them to do something with people. This resolve was strengthened when on two different occasions they were given a prophecy which told that one day they would speak with heads of state around the world.

At the beginning of the Second World War God gave Shakarian and his wife a vision for evangelism. The two of them organised a series of Sunday afternoon open-air meetings in Lincoln Park, Los Angeles, where as many as 4,000 people often turned out for a picnic. The summer meetings proved a great success, and although numbers were not great, there were many who were converted to Christ. As further opportunities for evangelism arose Shakarian started to plan other campaigns.

He brought pastors from all denominations to work and pray together, and invited well-known evangelists to undertake the preaching. This work confirmed to him that his true gift was rather as a helper; organising these campaigns was what God wanted him to do.

## Chicken Dinner

One of the most memorable of these occasions was a gospel rally in 1945, held in the famous Hollywood Bowl and attended by over 20,000 people. At a chicken dinner given beforehand for Christian businessmen, to seek their financial support for the rally, Shakarian invited a number of the guests to tell of what God had done for them.

The effect was electric as the hundred men and their wives heard of marriages restored, alcoholism overcome and business partners reconciled. At the end, Shakarian described what they had heard as the 'full gospel', as every aspect of the good news had been heard. This approach later became the Fellowship's own brand of evangelism, by which thousands of men and women have been won to Christ.

For the first time, Shakarian began to appreciate the part laymen could play in evangelism. But the idea did not begin to take shape, however, for another six years. It was the occasion when he and his wife set up a 16-day campaign in Los Angeles for the evangelist Oral Roberts.

By now he was beginning to feel restless, as though God was trying to show him something different to do. He told Roberts about his idea of using ordinary businessmen to reach other men with the gospel. The evangelist was thrilled with the thought but was a bit non-plussed with the proposed title: The Full Gospel Business Men's Fellowship International. Each of the words was essential, Shakarian argued, as they precisely indicated what the movement was about.

The initial meeting was held at Clifton's Cafeteria, downtown Los Angeles, on a Saturday morning in December 1951. But instead of the hundreds Shakarian expected, a mere 18 men turned up for breakfast. As he explained his ideas to the men, Shakarian was disappointed by their evident lack of enthusiasm.

It was not until Oral Roberts prayed for a thousand chapters, spread across the world, that the atmosphere changed. The men appeared to capture the vision and the meeting ended with a hearty rendering of 'Onward Christian soldiers'. A few weeks later, in January 1952, a board of directors was appointed and the Fellowship legally constituted.

Yet despite the vast amount of effort Shakarian put into promoting his new organisation, not a single new chapter was started. The following months were ones of frustration, and in December that year it finally seemed as though the venture would have to be abandoned.

**The Vision**

The night before the last Fellowship breakfast was due to be held, Demos spent some time in prayer. As he prayed, he realised that he had been so busy organising the work that he had not allowed God to have his way. When he cried out, 'Lord Jesus, forgive me', God reminded him that it was he alone who could open doors.

At that point Demos had a tremendous vision in which God told him that he was about to show him the purpose of his life. As the vision unfolded, he saw millions of men with their hands lifted towards heaven, linked together in a community of love across Asia, Africa and America. By 3.30 that morning, the Shakarians realised that God intended the work to go on.

During that same night God also spoke to two other men about the Fellowship, telling them to offer their help. One of them, who the previous week had said the outfit 'wasn't worth five cents', donated $1,000 for the work, and another, who travelled 400 miles through the night to be there, offered his press for printing a magazine. After all, if the Fellowship was to go round the world, Tom Nickel reasoned, then it would need a 'voice'.

DEMOS SHAKARIAN

This proved to be the turning point. By the summer of that year 10 chapters had been started, and in October, nearly two years after the first meeting at Clifton's, the first National Convention attracted 600 men.

## International

The Fellowship became 'international' in 1956 when a chapter was set up in Canada, but it was four years before the movement spread further afield. The next chapter to open was Haiti, where the infamous 'Papa Doc' was the dictator. Despite opposition at their first evangelistic rally, when it was infiltrated by a group of voodoo priests, thousands of people were converted.

Before long the Fellowship began to spread further afield – to Europe, Australasia, India and the Far East. Although Shakarian was a Pentecostal, he was in no way denominationally-minded. One of the results of his ministry was to encourage the spread of the charismatic experience throughout the Church, affecting Catholics, Nonconformists and Episcopalians alike.

His aim was to proclaim a 'full gospel', with the purpose of winning men to Christ. An emphasis was placed upon the baptism of the Holy Spirit, accompanied by speaking in tongues; healings and other miraculous events were also an expected part of the normal Christian experience.

In 1965 a FGBMFI World Convention was held in London, purposely to encourage the start of a similar laymen's ministry in the UK. Organised by a Fleet Street prayer group headed by such men as Michael Harper and Ernest Walton-Lewsey, some 400 North American businessmen descended on the capital for a series of evangelistic meetings. Many conversions were reported, but despite such a powerful witness the movement was slow to take hold.

Although chapters were started in London and four other major cities, there was a suspicion of anything Pentecostal, and no real growth was possible until the charismatic movement had become established in the churches in the late 1970s. Now there are 270 chapters in the UK and Ireland, with members from across the complete denominational spectrum.

### MISSION STATEMENT OF THE FULL GOSPEL BUSINESS MEN'S FELLOWSHIP INTERNATIONAL

#### THE VISION

'The Vision for the Fellowship is based upon a series of prophetic messages having occurred over a period of time and confirmed by a literal vision from God.

'In the Vision, untold masses of men from every continent and nation, once having been spiritually dead, are now alive. They are set free, filled with the power of God's Holy Spirit, faces radiant with glory, hands raised high and voices lifting their praises to heaven.

'We see a vast global movement of millions of laymen, being used mightily by God to bring this last great harvest through the outpourings of God's Holy Spirit before the return of our Lord Jesus Christ.'

This Vision, given to Demos Shakarian in 1952, is explained in detail in the book The Happiest People on Earth.

#### THE MISSION

* To reach men in all nations for Jesus Christ.
* To call men back to God.
* To help believers to be Baptised with the Holy Spirit and to grow spiritually.
* To train and equip men to fulfil the great commission.
* To provide an opportunity for Christian fellowship.
* To contribute to a greater unity among all people in the Body of Christ.

# 6. INTERNATIONAL NEPAL FELLOWSHIP (1936)
## Dr Lily O'Hanlon (1904-1982) and Hilda Steele (1907-1992)

The mountainous kingdom of Nepal is situated on the northern border of India, and extends along the southern slopes of the great Himalayan range. To the north lies the high Tibetan plateau of China; to the south a narrow strip of low-lying jungle separates the country from subtropical India. A land of outstanding beauty, it has for centuries been virtually cut off from the rest of the world, not so much by any physical barrier, but by the policy of its rulers. Owing to the jealously exclusive policy of the Gurkhas, the predominant tribe of Nepal, little was known about the country until more recent times.

Contact with Christianity was first made in the 17th century, when a band of Jesuit missionaries passed through the land en route for Tibet. But it was not until the following century that a more determined Catholic attempt was made to establish a mission in the country. Despite opposition from Hindu Brahmins, a group of Capuchins settled in Nepal in 1715. They succeeded in gaining the first Christian converts within the country, and by the middle of the century two churches, complete with cemeteries, had been built.

The 80 native believers were assured by their rulers that they would be free to practise their religion. Although continued harassment from the Brahmin priests and persecution by relatives and friends caused much suffering, most of them maintained their faith.

The religious climate changed when, in 1769, Prithvi Narayan Shah, the tough and brilliant leader of the kingdom of Gorkha, expelled the ruling house and took control of the land. He conquered the various petty Nepali kingdoms and united them under his rule. Today he is generally regarded as the 'father' of the nation.

Prithvi forced the Catholic priests to quit the country. Together with the converts, they chose to go into exile in north India, rather than face an insecure future, and even death. They resettled in a Christian colony in the town of Chuhari, in Bihar. For almost 200 years the door to the gospel in Nepal remained closed; Nepal was a Hindu kingdom, and the presence of Christians was said to defile it.

In 1846 the country was taken over by another despotic family, the Ranas. For over a hundred years the Ranas controlled both king and government, and met any opposition with violence and bloodshed. With the exception of a few diplomats, no foreigners were allowed to live or work within its borders. Thousands of ordinary Nepalis fled the country and, like the Christians before them, settled in northern India.

Around this time the British were beginning to develop the hill country of Darjeeling (Sikkim), and labourers were recruited from among the exiles. It was here, where there was freedom of religion, that the gospel began to take root : a Nepali church was founded and the Bible translated into the Nepali language.

The real beginning of the Nepali Church was due to the efforts of a Church of Scotland missionary, the Rev William Macfarlane. In 1870 he set up the Eastern Himalayan Mission at Darjeeling, then an important hill station for the British. Bible studies attracted a number of young students, and the first one to bear witness was baptised in 1874. Despite opposition and persecution, the church grew to 2,500 by the turn of the century, and to almost 14,000 by 1945.

Constant efforts were made by Protestant missionaries to enter Nepal with the gospel, but the door remained firmly shut. Sundar Singh (1889-1929/33), the famous Indian Christian sadhu, often preached in Nepal as he made his way over the Himalayas to Tibet. In one small town, he was arrested for preaching about Jesus, but was later rescued by secret believers. Obviously, the gospel was bearing fruit, though the time was not yet ready for an open declaration.

Nevertheless, efforts continued; by the distribution of gospel tracts, through personal contacts with travellers from Nepal, and by preaching, the seed of the gospel was sown. Some heard the good news and believed, but felt it necessary to remain secret disciples. The work of preparation for when Nepal opened its doors went ahead, praying for the day when the Lord would give the opportunity.

It was not until 1951 that the border of Nepal was tentatively opened to foreigners. This followed a revolution against the Rana regime, which led to its downfall and the restoration of the king to power. Within two years Christians were allowed into the country and many Nepalis returned to their homeland.

## Vision
In the early 1930s two young missionaries shared a vision for Nepal, and were called – quite separately – to serve God among the Nepali people. Following a time of prayer and fasting while on furlough in Ireland, Dr

# NEPAL

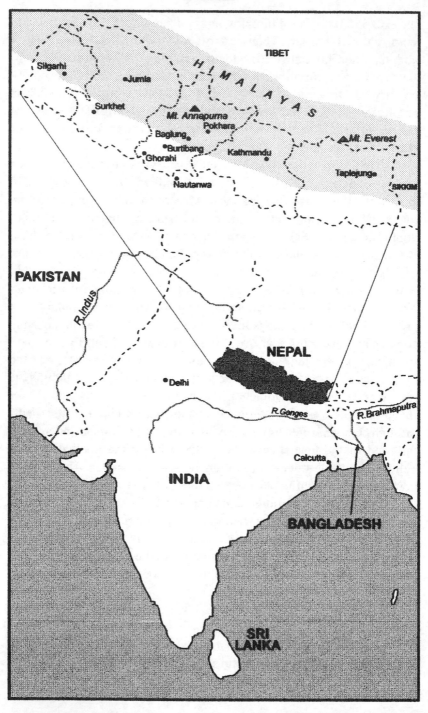

Lily (Pat) O'Hanlon of the Ludhiana Medical College in the Punjab, and Hilda Steele of the Zenana Bible Medical Mission, determined to begin a medical work together. In this way, they hoped to reach Nepalis with the gospel and train them in readiness for returning to their own land.

It was during one of these times of fellowship that the Lord gave them his pattern for the work : they were to be 'a band of men ... whose hearts God had touched.' During the succeeding years, God called a number of men and women to enter the land, to form the nucleus of a church in the town of Pokhra. The Lord also gave them the name of the mission, which was to be the Nepali Evangelistic Band.

The two missionaries opened a dispensary in 1936 among the exiled Nepali people at Nautanwa, four miles south of the border of Nepal. The small town was the home of over 1,000 Nepali exiles, while hundreds of others passed through the town each year on their way to and from India.

Their new home was a small 'end of terrace' house with mud walls and a tin roof, where they set up the front room as a clinic. As the natives distrusted foreigners, none of them would at first come to the clinic. The breakthrough came from a group of boys, who had suggested the two ladies start a school for them. Without any previous experience, the missionaries opened their home to the boys, and as a result of their Scripture lessons a number of them were won to Christ.

At the same time, pupils began to bring their relatives along to the dispensary, and the medical work gradually opened up. Villagers from around the town began to visit the clinic on market days, and after three months the missionaries even began to receive pleas for medical help from across the border.

From the beginning, the policy was not to send in western missionaries, but rather to raise up a band of Nepalis who would be evangelists and church-planters among their own people. It was not until 1939, however, that the first Nepali workers joined the two missionaries. They were Daniel and Martha Pradhan, who worked with them for a while at Nautanwa before going up to Shillong, the capital of Assam, to open a small church among the Gurkha soldiers and the 2,000 resident Nepalis.

The following year three further Nepali Christians, including a married couple, were added to the mission. David Mukhia already had ten years' experience as an evangelist when he and his wife joined the small team. Their presence enabled the mission to widen the scope of their evangelism. Evening lantern talks, and Sunday and open-air services attracted interested crowds, while hundreds of Gospels were sold to travellers at the railway station.

David Mukhia undertook preaching tours and colportage work; he started a school and helped in the dispensary. As it was felt necessary to have someone ready to officiate at baptisms, he was ordained pastor at a non-denominational ceremony in Calcutta. A natural choice, he was the first Nepali pastor outside Darjeeling dedicated to Nepal itself.

As Nepal was still not open to foreigners, their efforts were directed towards Nepalis living in the northern parts of India. But Dr O'Hanlon's prayers were still for the land itself, and for 15 years the mountain barrier seemed as impregnable as ever.

**Revolution**

It was in the winter of 1950-51 that the totally unexpected happened. The Rana regime was deposed and King Tribhuvana restored to his rightful position. With a Prime Minister chosen from among the people the king returned to rule his kingdom.

Plans were made to improve the country with foreign aid and advice. A contact with the British ambassador to Nepal paved the way for permission for 'the staff of Dr O'Hanlon's hospital' to enter the country. This was on condition that there was to be no proselytising, though on the compounds they would be allowed to 'serve and worship God according to their consciences'.

Six missionaries, including Dr O'Hanlon and Hilda Steele, five Nepali Christians and 19 carriers made up the first party to enter the land in November 1952. They established their headquarters at Pokhra, a small town surrounded by snowcapped mountains to the west of Kathmandu, the capital. It was in a strategic position, and was recommended as an excellent place for a hospital.

'If you go there,' they were told, 'many patients will visit you because it is the centre of a big district and everyone knows about it.'

David Mukhia and Premi followed some months after, bringing their newly-born child. As the senior Nepali pastor, with 22 years' service along the Nepali border, Mukhia became the first pastor of the church at Pokhra. There was already a small congregation, and others were soon added to it. Wisely, he decided to maintain a distance between the mission compound and his native church, to prevent any suggestion that it was a Western church planted on Nepali soil.

## Shining Hospital

Nepal is a subtropical land and is subject to a wide variety of diseases, aggravated by primitive living conditions and religious superstition. Tuberculosis, leprosy and midwifery cases are the most needy groups, and when Dr O'Hanlon set up a dispensary outside the town there was a heavy demand for her services.

The following year, the government made a plot of land nearer the town centre available for a hospital. Building work began immediately, though patients had at first to be accommodated in thatch and bamboo huts. In 1954 prefabricated aluminium huts were erected, which eventually provided four wards, a theatre block, a maternity unit and an outpatients' department. It became known as Shining Hospital, a name suggested by the patients.

One of the greatest needs, however, was for specialist care for the victims of leprosy. A further grant of land, received in 1959, enabled Dr O'Hanlon to build a leprosarium; they named it 'Green Pastures'. Temporary huts were erected, and treatment had to be carried out in the corner of one of the patients' wards. Minor operations were performed either on the floor or on one of the patient's beds.

It was some years later (1966) before the foundations of a permanent building were laid. When completed, it provided facilities for a wider range of operations, including plastic surgery and operations performed for drop-foot and clawed hands.

But the Nepalis were fearful of leprosy. Although timely treatment could prevent it spreading, patients had often to be sent home with a signed certificate, re-assuring sceptical relatives of their cure.

Through all these years Lily O'Hanlon never lost sight of her overriding aim, that of making the gospel known to a people living in the darkness of idol worship and evil spirits. Few Nepalis had ever heard the incredible message of a God who loves, but saw it reflected in the lives and work of the believers.

## Opposition

From the beginning, there was opposition to the gospel message. At one point students forced ward services at Shining Hospital to be stopped. Because the law forbade anyone in Nepal to change their religion, the gospel could only be shared on a personal basis, usually through opportunities given at surgeries and on home visits. It was left to the

Nepali Christians to engage in direct evangelism.

The first resident to come to faith (in 1956) was Lucius, a farmer who was searching for peace with God. He returned home and told the villagers what he had heard, and within a few months nine others openly confessed their faith in Jesus.

Despite the threat of punishment, the new converts were determined to make a stand and went ahead with their baptism. In 1960, however, the pastor and eight new Christians in the town of Tansen were imprisoned for their faith. The believers at Pokhara were struck with fear and for a period further baptisms were suspended.

As the workers established a presence at Pokhara, the medical programme was expanded to take in outlying villages and some of the more distant areas. Attention was particularly focused on towns west of Pokhara, and in April 1961 a dispensary was opened in Baglung. Whilst

## ADVANCE IN NEPAL

The kingdom of Nepal is slightly larger than England, and about the same size as Florida, USA, with a population of around 20 million people. It is claimed that 95% of the people are Hindu, while the Christian population is estimated to be about 50,000 strong.

After Dr O'Hanlon gained entry into the country in 1952, the way was opened for other ministries to follow. Two years later the United Medical Mission to Nepal , which consisted of seven founding agencies, was formed to take advantage of a government offer of a small hospital in Kathmandu. A team began work in the small town of Tansen, and work started in Kathmandu in 1954 under the leadership of Dr Bethel Fleming. The first woman doctor was an American missionary, Dr Marjory Fleming, who joined the team at Tansen in 1956.

Since then the mission presence within Nepal has enlarged to include the Leprosy Mission, the Nepal Leprosy Trust, TEAM Mission, Campus Crusade and Operation Mobilisation.

Under a new law it is now possible to change one's religion, though it still remains illegal to attempt to persuade someone else to change their faith. When the law was introduced, King Birendra granted an amnesty for all Nepalis prosecuted for their religious activities and further charges were dropped. However, Christians in remoter areas of the country continue to be subject to persecution, as evangelism is still technically illegal. The National Churches Fellowship has lodged a formal appeal, but the government is trying to discourage Christian activity.

the people there welcomed the medical care, there was resistance to the gospel. It was three years before the workers experienced a response, when a high caste Hindu lady came to the Lord.

Education has always been recognised as an essential element of the mission's work. In the church, annual Bible schools were held for both adults and young people, supplemented by the work of vacation camps for boys and girls.

Secular education has also been given high priority. In co-operation with the local government, a boarding school for boys was opened in Pokhara, and eventually girls were taken in as well. For a time it was able to maintain its Christian ethos, but the school was taken over by the government and several Hindu teachers appointed.

In fact, the work of outside agencies in the country was brought under government control. Now, the mission is working in partnership with national workers in community health and hygiene projects, though some projects are still undertaken solely by Christian organisations.

Shining Hospital finally closed its doors in September 1990, but Green Pastures continued to retain its independency and maintain its unique Christian witness.

While the name of the mission has been changed to the International Nepal Fellowship, the original aim of bringing in the kingdom of God has continued unabated. And despite the changing circumstances and recent political unrest, it is intended – to quote Dr O'Hanlon – that the mission 'will work in Nepal for as long as it is the Lord's will ... but the Church will remain.'

### INF STATEMENT OF MISSION

INF is an evangelical, international and interdenominational Christian mission whose object is, 'to uphold and strengthen the national church and serve the people of Nepal'.

INF operates a variety of medical and development projects and works alongside and in support of the national church of Nepal.

INF members are guests in Nepal, and are subject to the laws of the country. They pray for the nation and its leaders, and through their presence and work they seek to make a lasting contribution to the life and development of the nation. Expatriates working with INF (the INF members) all need visas for government and agreed posts.

# 7. INTERSERVE (1855)
## Lady Mary Jane Kinnaird (1816-1888)

One of the great contributions made by Christian missionaries in India was in the field of education. As in many other lands, for hundreds of years education in India had been of a religious nature, and was provided for boys only. From the early decades of the 19th century, the British, aroused by Evangelicals, began to awaken to their responsibility towards the empire and the need to provide an educational system for their subjects.

Missionaries such as William Carey (Baptist) and Alexander Duff (Free Church of Scotland) not only opened mission stations, but schools and colleges as well. Duff, in fact, was one of a circle of Free Church of Scotland missionaries whose aim was to plant a mission in India centred around a system of schools. It was Duff's contention that the youth of India could be reached with the gospel through education.

There was a demand for Western type education in India, and schools run by missionaries attracted boys from high caste families. When conversions happened, as they did, parents threatened to have the schools closed, though the education on offer was usually enough to restrain such action.

At the beginning of the century there was as yet no educational provision for girls, for Hindu and Muslim men would not tolerate the idea of a school for their daughters. 'If they were educated,' they argued, 'then we should not be able to manage them at all.' Others insisted, 'A female child can never learn to read.' Consequently, out of the 40 million women in British India in the 1820s, it was estimated that less than 400 had acquired the ability to read.

## Prejudices

Girls were considered to be of no value, and their lives, like those of their mothers, were governed by deep-rooted prejudices of caste and religion. Female babies were often left to die of exposure or were thrown to the crocodiles as an offering to the sacred River Ganges.

High caste Hindu girls were married as young as five years of age, and were kept in life-long captivity by their husband's family in the filth and semi-darkness of the zenana. (The zenana was that part of a house in which the women lived, which was designed to prevent them from looking out or anyone else from seeing in.)

### The East India Company

The company was a British trading corporation authorised under a charter granted by Queen Elizabeth (1600) to trade in the East Indies. Trading stations were also sanctioned on the Indian subcontinent. By 1765 the company had become the official administrators of the Indian province of Bengal, of which Calcutta was the capital. The India Act of 1784 introduced a dual control between the company and a committee responsible to parliament. Its authority included matters relating to religion.

Anxious not to offend the Hindu and Muslim sections of the population, the company remained religiously neutral; it was more concerned about profits. Although it employed chaplains for its officials and employees (such as Henry Martyn, later of Persia), it would not permit Christian missionaries to preach in its territories. William Carey, for example, was forced to move to Serampore, where there was a Danish governor, to begin missionary work.

In 1793 when the company's charter was up for renewal in parliament, the Clapham Sect – under the leadership of Wilberforce and Charles Grant, formerly a director of the company – endeavoured to have a clause inserted which would require the company to send out school masters and missionaries. The bill failed at its third reading.

Thanks to the persistent efforts of Wilberforce, however, when the charter was renewed by parliament in 1813 a great victory was won. Missionaries were allowed to enter India and provision was made for an Anglican bishopric.

Following the mutiny in 1857, which attempted to restore the Mogul empire, the Company's rule in India came to an end. Control of India was formally transferred to the crown.

A number of attempts were made by missionaries to introduce education for girls, which horrified even the more enlightened Indians. In 1821 a Miss Cooke of the British and Foreign School Society landed in Calcutta, aiming to begin the organisation of schools for girls. The following year she was able to start a class for low caste girls, but under the roof of a boys' school. Several years later a separate building was erected, the gift of a Hindu rajah, which became the Female Central School.

By 1823 there were 22 schools opened, and a Ladies' Society for Native Female Education in Calcutta was organised to care for these schools. After some years the Society for Promoting Female Education in the East was set up in London by Mary Jane Kinnaird, in 1834, to provide teachers and funds for the work.

Little progress was made beyond Calcutta

until the 1840s, however, when two high caste girls who had been taught to read, obtained access to a Bible and without human aid had come to Christ. One of the girls fell ill and died; the other was banished to the sacred city of Benares, but in 1851 was publicly baptised. The episode served to demonstrate what could be achieved if India's zenanas were opened to the gospel. If more girls could be taught, and provided with Bibles, the effect could be incalculable.

### Trained Women

Mrs Mackenzie, wife of an English merchant and a member of the Central School Committee, recognised the need for a group of trained women, who would be ready to enter the zenanas when they were opened. She set about promoting the idea of a teacher-training school, the Normal School for Christian Female Teachers, English and Native.

An appeal for funds was launched, and her letter home captured the interest of Mary Jane Kinnaird, wife of the Hon Arthur Kinnaird (later the 10th baron), a Scottish Liberal MP. Mrs Kinnaird was a dynamic young woman with a lively faith, and was a leading figure among British evangelical upper class families in London. With an interest in a variety of missionary and philanthropic causes, she had already set up the Society for Promoting Female Education in the East, and was later to become co-founder of the YWCA.

Mary Kinnaird gathered together a number of her friends from different denominations and formed a London Auxiliary Committee. Although a staunch member of the Church of Scotland, she insisted that all true Christians should be able to work together. She told the committee, 'If we can give them the power to read, and the Book to read, God will bless his Word.'

The Committee engaged two sisters, the Misses Suter, to begin the work. One was appointed to the Central School, the other to take charge of the new venture, the Calcutta Normal School. It was at this latter establishment where the most intelligent girls, including 'respectable native women', would be trained as teachers.

### Breakthrough

On 1 March 1852, the date which was regarded as the birthday of the Zenana Bible Mission, the Calcutta Normal School was opened. The time was approaching when a breakthrough into girls' education was imminent. In 1854, as the first pupils at the Normal School were completing their training, the British government published a despatch which accepted that the Bible could be taught in state-controlled schools, and that girls ought to receive some education.

A Eurasian (i.e. Anglo-Indian) governess from the Normal School had recently been accepted into a Hindu home, but it was not until the following January that a second teacher was able to gain access to a zenana. Now it was on the express understanding that she was free to teach the Bible and the Christian faith.

The Indian Mutiny of 1857 threatened to extinguish the School's work, as the fighting took place largely in the province of Bengal, where Calcutta was the chief city. By the following year the rebellion had been put down. The London Auxiliary increased its support, and the two schools were amalgamated to form one institution.

With the British government now in control of India, more religious freedom gave further impetus to evangelism throughout the subcontinent. In 1860 it was decided to extend the work of the Zenana Mission. Mrs Kinnaird was able to send out missionaries under the aegis of the Calcutta School's Society, to train teachers as paid governesses for the zenanas, and to organise systematic visiting of zenanas in Calcutta by past students.

After two years, in 1862, only eight zenanas were open among more than half a million people. But the principle had been established, and two missionaries were soon to start work, one in southern India and the other in Delhi.

**New Title**
As the Society's work grew, it adopted a new title – The Indian Female Normal School and Instruction Society, or Zenana Mission. Although closely linked to the Church Missionary Society, whose missionaries acted as their field secretaries, Mary Kinnaird insisted that the work should remain on an interdenominational basis.

Writing of her mother, Mary Kinnaird's daughter remarked, 'She had a great hope that women would answer the missionary call to carry the gospel to India unfettered by ecclesiastical or imperial connections, that they would work not as a sect but as handmaids to all the churches.'

Before long, the Zenana Mission had caught the imagination of the Christian public in England. India was of personal interest to so many

# INDIA

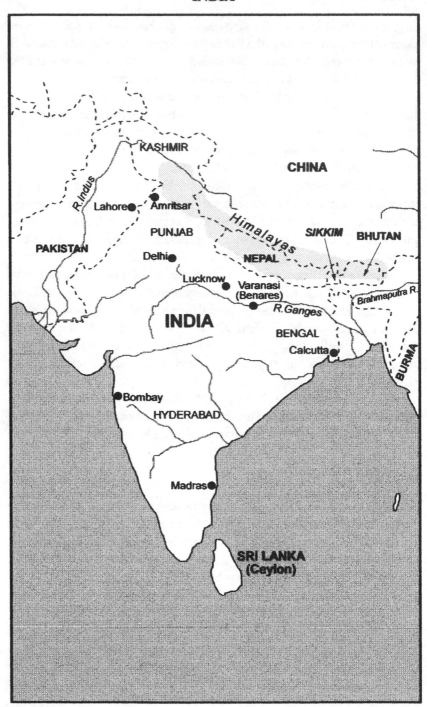

of the upper classes, doubtless through family links with the army or the East India Trading Company. The Mission was able to rely upon the support of many distinguished men, and local associations were springing up around the country. The Marchioness of Cholmondeley became President, and Lord Kinnaird was Treasurer.

In 1867, Calcutta, which so far had been the headquarters of the Society, recognised the London Committee as the parent body. There were now ten English women and a number of Eurasians and Indians at work in nine mission stations. More zenanas were opening their doors, with 72 in Calcutta alone. One woman, despite intense opposition from her husband and family, had been baptised.

### Medical Missions

In 1871, Dr William Elmslie, a Scottish medical missionary home on furlough from the Kashmir, startled the Zenana Committee by suggesting that they should launch 'female medical missions'. Dr Elmslie pointed out that the death rate among Indian women and children was enormous and quite out of proportion to the men. At least an attempt should be made to lessen pain and save human life, he argued.

'Native nurses and midwives were ignorant, and even government-trained doctors could not gain access to the zenanas. A female medical missionary,' he went on, 'would find an entrance where the educational missionary had failed, and would be able to reach Muslim zenanas as well. She would soften bigotry, remove prejudice and dispel ignorance, and would be able to unobtrusively deposit the all-pervading leaven of the gospel in numberless hearts and homes.'

Although the Committee was impressed by the arguments, medical training for women at that time had barely begun. Mrs Garrett Anderson had lately obtained her MD at Paris, and Florence Nightingale had made nursing begin to look respectable. But finding qualified workers was a problem.

Mrs Anderson suggested to the Committee that women willing to be trained should be sent abroad. But it was decided to place them as private pupils with medical professors at British hospitals, until a women's college could be established. Three candidates offered themselves for India; but one shortly withdrew, and of the other two, first one and then the other died.

Nevertheless, in December 1875, a Miss Elizabeth Bielby, with four years' nursing experience, sailed for India and began work in Lucknow. The city was largely populated by Muslims, but it was a more strategic centre for a medical mission than a predominantly Hindu place such as Benares.

## Visiting

Joining a team of Zenana missionaries, Eurasians and native Biblewomen already labouring in the city at the request of CMS, Miss Bielby began medical visiting. She was seldom called on until after the native *hakims* (doctors) and *dais* (midwives) had admitted defeat. They left her the most dreadful cases, which she had to treat in generally filthy conditions. On entering the zenana, she was always careful to make it plain that she came as a missionary, not merely a doctor, and insisted that the Bible should be read, the Christian life taught and any medicine she prescribed be taken.

By the end of 1876 Elizabeth Bielby was a physical wreck, and felt quite dispirited, for her hopes of founding a hospital had so far come to nothing. Forced to return to England, she was able to undertake further study and completed a full-length course not open to her back in 1875.

October 1878 found her again at Lucknow, and in the November she opened the Mission's first hospital in a rickety, hired house in the city. She started with one patient, then two and in a week's time there were five. She even gained entrance into a zenana, through being invited to treat one of the servants.

The work proved to be a success. The Deputy Commissioner in Lucknow wrote that the Mission was 'doing immense good. It is much appreciated by the natives of the city.' One of the Zenana missionaries commented, 'The women value the hospital very greatly and say that Miss Bielby is a messenger direct from heaven.'

Two years later, the Mission adopted a new title – Zenana Bible and Medical Mission. Four other hospitals were opened, at Amritsar, Varanasi, Patna and Nasik.

## Catholic Basis

In 1867 the seeds of a division within the Zenana Committee were sown, which led eventually to the formation of a second Zenana Mission. This was the year in which the London Committee accepted responsibility as parent body of the Mission. At their request, the aged Henry Venn drew up a statement of Fundamental Principles, which was designed to establish the catholic basis of the work.

The fact was, however, that the Mission had originated by the zeal of members of the Church of England, much of the work remained linked to the CMS and it was largely supported by the giving of Anglican people. It was the Committee's intention not to have any ecclesiastical links, but to be free to be the handmaid of all missions.

In taking this stance, the Mission's interdenominational constitution was a new development in missionary organisation. Several previous societies had been founded on a co-operative basis, such as the British and Foreign Bible Society, but they were not missions. The China Inland Mission, founded two years before Venn's statement of 1867, did not work alongside different Churches. Rather it was a body of individual believers who had shed their denominational loyalties to undertake work no 'official' Church society would tackle.

Ten years later, a dispute flared up when the question of the Mission's catholicity was again raised. Several Anglican Committee members suggested that the Mission should remain under Church Missionary Society control. Mrs Kinnaird was convinced that it should continue on a non-sectarian basis and there should be no change to the constitution. But there were strong feelings on the part of a group of 13 Anglican Committee members, and the debate persisted for several months.

The Anglican rebels eventually resigned and in 1880 founded the Church of England Zenana Missionary Society. Nearly half the missionaries decided to join the Anglican mission, so that the older mission lost nearly half its work and three quarters of its income.

### Secession

Shaken by the secession, ZBMM survived and even recovered; its income steadily increased and it maintained a close relationship with its sister organisation. For both missions, in the goodness of God it led to an expansion of the sphere of activity and to the furtherance of the gospel.

Towards the end of the century, India was hit by severe famine and plague, and thousands died, emptying entire cities and districts. The devastation opened up new spheres of service for ZBMM work, which was pioneered by Rosalie Harvey, who already had two decades of missionary experience behind her.

Among the evacuees were leprosy sufferers and orphans, homeless and with no one to care for them. As Miss Harvey adopted an increasing number of orphans, her quarters became an official babies' home; as a result, two large orphanages were opened near Bombay. In 1900, a permanent home for the healthy children of leprosy patients was built, followed by wards for men and women, a dispensary and a school room.

Other developments included a Converts' Training Home and a Widows' Home at Allahbad, and (in 1913) the Kinnaird College for Women at Lahore.

The Mission's name was changed in 1957 to the Bible and Medical Mission Fellowship; more recently it became Interserve. This avoids the term 'Bible' and 'missionary', which in Hindu and Muslim countries conveys the idea of proselytising.

There are now about 400 workers from all over the world, serving in South Asia, the Middle East and North Africa. It is the aim of Interserve to work alongside national churches in building the worldwide Church of Jesus Christ.

### MISSION STATEMENT OF INTERSERVE

The Aim of Interserve is to proclaim in word and deed that Jesus Christ is Lord and Saviour. As an international fellowship committed to serving the Christian Church, we wish to contribute directly or indirectly to the making of disciples of Jesus Christ, particularly in countries of south and central Asia, the Gulf, Middle East and North Africa, and in other countries where there are significant groups of migrants from these countries. We invite men and women of all races who sense God's call to join us in showing God's love and in communicating the gospel.

IN SEEKING TO FULFIL THIS PRIMARY AIM,

1. We affirm the crucial significance of the Church, whether expressed denominationally or congregationally, and we wish to share in the planting, nurturing and renewing of believing communities.

2. We believe that all congregations are to be involved in God's mission in the world. As God's fellow-workers, we seek to encourage local churches, parachurch agencies and individuals in the worldwide mission of the Church, and wish to share in cross-cultural ministry for the mutual benefit of churches worldwide.

3. We believe that the training of leadership is crucial for the growth of the Church and the development of communities and therefore emphasise this ministry.

4. We affirm the special place that ministry to the poor has in the mission of the Lord Jesus Christ, and emphasise service to the needy and oppressed.

5. We are a fellowship of Partners whose aim as disciples of the Lord Jesus Christ is to glorify God in everything we do. We aim to provide support for each other in finding and fulfilling our individual roles.

IN EXERCISING OUR VARIOUS MINISTRIES,

6. We seek to demonstrate God's love and the unity of all believers in the body of Christ. We commit ourselves to cooperate with the existing churches and Christian agencies in our areas of service, who share in similar goals and Biblical emphasis. Holding firmly to Biblical truth in love, we wish to promote genuine unity and in the interests of good stewardship, we seek to avoid unnecessary duplication in Christian work.

7. We emphasise the need for quality and high standards in all our varied ministries. Humanitarian services are not a propaganda tool for the message of spiritual salvation but part of ministry to the whole person. We respect the unique ministry to which each Partner is called, recognising that although our roles are different, our primary objective is to make disciples.

8. We respect the laws of the countries in which we serve.

9. We recognize that we are engaged in a spiritual conflict, not with human enemies, but against spiritual forces, and we commit ourselves to work for the coming of God's Kingdom in the power of his Spirit, using the resources he has given us, especially the Word of God and prayer.

## 8. THE JAPAN EVANGELISTIC BAND (1903)
### Paget Wilkes (1871-1934) and Rev Barclay F Buxton (1860-1946)

Christianity was first introduced into Japan, 'the Land of the Rising Sun', by the Jesuits in the 16th century. Missionaries faced a series of severe persecutions, when thousands of converts and their priests were massacred. The Jesuits were driven out of the land, and by 1638 Christianity in Japan appeared to be extinct. Yet the new religion lingered on in a number of outlying areas for nearly 200 years, as the descendents of the early converts maintained their identity in secret.

That Christians were unable to re-establish their religion was largely due to the government's hostile attitude to things foreign. Japan was virtually a sealed nation against Westerners, who were not allowed to gain an entrance into the land. Only the Dutch were given trading rights, and then only through one port.

Christianity was declared an illegal religion in the 19th century. Edict boards denouncing the Faith were widely posted and numerous anti-Christian measures were vigorously enforced. It was not until the middle of the century that Japan began to dismantle the barriers in order to adopt Western culture. Opportunities for missionary activity consequently revived.

There was also an increasing interest among the educated classes for learning English, which opened the door to the publication of literature in English, especially Bibles. Many of the first converts were youths from the samurai, the military class which enjoyed special privileges under the Japanese feudal regime.

A number of tentative attempts to introduce the gospel had been made by private individuals from as early as 1818, but to no avail. When later in the century several Western nations made commercial treaties with the Japanese, however, they insisted on a clause allowing missionaries into the country.

The Catholics were first to re-enter the land, in 1855, followed by the Russian Orthodox Church in the 1860s. Despite the renewed persecution of Japanese Christians between 1867 and 1873, when several thousand new believers were arrested, imprisoned and even tortured, Protestant missionaries were despatched to Japan. The largest contingent was from the USA. The Church Missionary Society sent representatives in 1869, followed by the Society for the Propagation of the

Gospel. After the cessation of attacks in 1873 the United Presbyterian Church of Scotland, the Dutch Reform Church and a host of other missionary bodies also entered the country.

Ultimately, it was the Protestant missions which proved to be the more effective. By 1914 they could claim to have twice as many church members as the Roman Catholics and Russian Orthodox put together, and a far greater number of missionaries. Even so, the percentage of Christians was small.

### Jesuits in Japan

The Christian religion was first introduced into Japan by the Jesuit priest and missionary, Francis Xavier. Although he only stayed two years, he made a number of converts and was able to leave behind colleagues who continued the work. By 1582 the number of Catholics had reached 150,000 and there were 200 churches.

The rise to power of rulers unsympathetic to the Catholic cause resulted in two periods of persecution. From 1587 attacks on converts increased, and 26 of them were crucified and churches destroyed.

The opening years of the 17th century marked the zenith of Catholicism in Japan. As the Church grew (there were possibly over 200,000 Catholics in the land), a new ruling family came to power. Believing the Catholics to be a threat to Japanese sovereignty, a fresh round of persecutions was begun which lasted about 30 years.

Missionaries were expelled, the import of Christian books was forbidden and churches destroyed. Adherence to the Christian religion was made a capital offence: converts were either crucified, beheaded or burnt to death. Although several thousand of them rose in rebellion against the persecution in 1637-38, it was overwhelmingly put down.

A number of converts escaped into the hills of Kyushu, the most southerly of the four main islands. When missionaries returned two centuries later they found a number of villages where there was a knowledge of the names of God, Jesus and the Virgin Mary, and of Joseph, Christmas and Lent, and where they had continued the practice of baptism.

Catholics now comprise around one third of the country's Christian population (which is about 2%). Among other religious groups in Japan are Mormons, Jehovah's Witnesses, Unitarians and the Unification Church (Moonies).

**God's Copybook**

It was this Protestant presence which nevertheless provided an opening for Barclay Buxton to begin a work on the west coast of Honshu Island, the largest of the Japanese group of islands. The Japan Evangelistic Band (JEB) was not set up until 1903, when a mission was opened at Kobe, on the eastern side of the island, under the leadership of Paget Wilkes.

A tall, athletic young man, Buxton had been converted under D L Moody at the historic Cambridge mission of November 1882, when over 200 undergraduates stood to accept Christ. Soon afterwards he received a 'strong conviction for holiness' and was baptised in the Holy Spirit. Throughout his life he was recognised as a Christian who evidenced the power of Christ and was described as 'God's copybook of a holy life'.

Ordained into the Church of England in 1885, Buxton felt called to the mission field and, after the manner of Paul, gathered around him a number of like-minded people to accompany him. The group sailed for Japan in October 1890, Buxton as a CMS missionary, while the others remained independent though under his direction.

BARCLAY F BUXTON

During a period of language study at Kobe, he began to preach 'the great truths of holiness'. His booklet on the baptism of the Holy Spirit was sent to all his missionaries and Japanese workers, to encourage them in a closer walk with God.

The missionaries made their centre at Matsuye on the west coast of Honshu Island, where there was already a small church. By the end of 1892 seven new churches had been founded, the smallest one starting with only four people worshipping in a home. Aiming to build an indigenous church, Buxton encouraged the

# CHINA & JAPAN

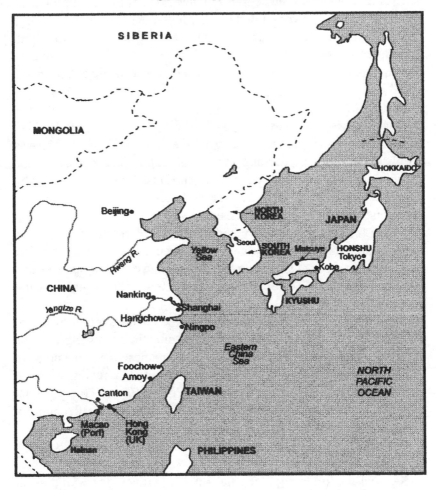

Japanese believers to lead the worship and take responsibility for the preaching.

In 1897 the Buxtons were joined by Paget and Gertrude Wilkes who had a similar desire to see people won to Christ. Wilkes, a graduate of Oxford who was converted under F B Meyer, had accepted Buxton's invitation to join him in Japan. Despite having to work through an interpreter, he soon had the joy of leading a 20-year-old young man to Christ, a man for whom he realised he had prayed while at Oxford!

## Pentecost

During his first five years in Japan, Wilkes came under Barclay Buxton's ministry and, like many of the Japanese Christians, was deeply stirred by his preaching. It was not long before Wilkes experienced his own 'Pentecost', which happened at a service conducted by a Japanese pastor. From that day Paget Wilkes was a changed man and his ministry took on a new dimension.

When the Buxtons felt they had to return to England to look after their children's education, Wilkes began to reconsider his position. The idea began to grow of gathering together a band of men, Japanese and 'foreign', filled with the Spirit, who would undertake evangelism and preach scriptural holiness.

On furlough in 1902, this thought received further support from two quite different sources. The Wilkes spent some time assisting Thomas Hogben in distributing New Testaments to Japanese seamen who were at Portsmouth for King Edward VII's coronation naval review. Hogben was the founder of the 'One by One Working Band' for personal evangelism, and discussed with Wilkes the possibility of sending a similar team of missionaries to Japan.

## Keswick

At Keswick the following year, a half-night of prayer to seek God's will concerning the proposal gave Wilkes the final confirmation that he needed. A council was formed to oversee the mission, which included Thomas Hogben and Barclay Buxton as chairman. The new mission was initially known as the One by One Band of Japan and, as Wilkes envisioned, was to be a fellowship of Japanese workers and missionaries free of denominational ties.

Paget and Gertrude, accompanied by one other missionary, returned to Japan and established their headquarters at Kobe. They acquired a shop which they turned into a mission hall, and were joined by a number of Japanese believers from Matsuye. Despite occasional differences, the Band enjoyed a real unity of the Spirit and the work 'went forward with a rush, for the power of God was behind it'.

Japan's principal religion is Shintoism, 'the way of the gods' (or rather 'demons'), which has exerted a powerful influence in national life. Thousands of shrines and temples are dedicated to these gods and, in Wilkes' days, homes had a 'god-shelf' where the spirits of family ancestors were worshipped. Shinto has no written moral code, and hardly any concept of God except something they call *kami*, which is anything that possesses spiritual power. So despite being a gifted people and skilled in craftsmanship, Wilkes discovered a widespread spiritual hunger that gave him a greater longing to reach them with the gospel.

## Heart Holiness

The Japan Evangelistic Band was founded primarily for the purpose of evangelism. From Kobe, evangelistic sorties were made into the surrounding areas and to the further ends of the country. Conversions followed, and as new church groups were formed it became necessary to provide for their care and shepherding. Many of these groups were linked up with the autonomous, indigenous Japan Jesus Christ Church, the *Nippon Iesu Kirisuto Kyodan* (NIKK).

At the same time, Wilkes was equally concerned to deepen the spiritual lives of the converts by teaching them biblical truths. Following Buxton's practice of holding an annual convention, Wilkes continued to reaffirm the message of 'heart holiness' – first a cleansing from indwelling sin, followed by the infilling

PAGET WILKES

## KOBE EARTHQUAKE

The severe earthquake that devastated much of Kobe city early in the morning of 17 January 1995 left nearly 5,500 people dead and 300,000 homeless. Many Christians lost their lives, while others have been forced to move out of the city to safer areas. All JEB missionaries and Japanese evangelists came through without harm. Many of the city's 345 Protestant and 34 Catholic church buildings survived, and JEB buildings, including the headquarters, Bible College and main Mission Hall, sustained only slight damage. Many church buildings were opened to offer accommodation for the homeless, and to act as food distribution centres.

Throughout this time, surviving churches have taken the opportunity to witness to the gospel. As the result of a vision given to a JEB evangelist, the Barnabas Volunteer Group was formed to reach out to people with acts and words of comfort. Helpers from several churches travelled each day into Kobe to minister to one of the many 'tent villages' that had sprung up, serving about 200 meals a day and distributing clothing and gospel tracts. Others visited refugee centres to prepare hot soup for the evening meal; the children were given Bible talks, and again scripture material was given out. Already a small number of men and women have believed and been baptised.

There is considerable idolatry and ancestor worship in Japan, and national Shintoism is undergoing a resurgence. Various sects such as Moonies and Jehovah's Witnesses are in evidence, and the Aum Supreme Truth religion (said to be responsible for the Tokyo subway gas attack) is leading many astray. Despite there being some 3,000 missionaries in the country, Christians consist of only 2.5 percent of the population, though they exert a moral and social influence out of proportion to their numbers .

of the Holy Spirit. Only in this way, he taught, could the believer become like Christ.

As many new Christians applied to work with the Band, it soon became necessary to start a Bible School. Suitable premises were found in Kobe and students were admitted without academic qualifications; the idea was to produce evangelists, not theologians. They were given a firm grounding in the Scriptures and engaged in outreach from the mission hall. Although the work continued to grow, there were never more than 30 JEB missionaries on the field.

## Swanwick

The Wilkes made occasional visits home, not only for the purpose of 'rest' but also to further the work. Furloughs were crowded with meetings, where the message of scriptural holiness was emphasised. The annual JEB convention at Swanwick was always a highlight, and many received their call to the mission field at these meetings.

In 1923 Wilkes returned from furlough to face a number of problems in the mission. There were difficulties with the administration of the mission, and a number of workers had resigned because of his firm theological stance. Perhaps, he wondered, the time had come for him to resign? For some while he continued to serve in Japan, but ill-health forced him to return to England. Prevented from returning to Japan, he spent time in Canada, America and South Africa, promoting the mission's work. In 1930 he returned to Kobe for the 25th anniversary of the opening of the mission hall.

Wilkes' final years were spent mostly in prayer for Japan, and in writing the story of the Japan Evangelistic Band. He died from a heart attack, following years of considerable activity and hardship. His uncompromising stand for the gospel had earned him the epithet, 'the best loved or the most hated man in Japan'.

While in many other areas of the world, missionary work has diversified to include doctors, teachers and agriculturalists, Japan's need is for specialists in pioneer evangelism and church-planting. Most of the Band's workers today are Japanese, trained in the Bible College. But as ninety-nine percent of Japan's population are not yet Christian, the prayer is that the Lord will call more workers to the mission field.

### MISSION STATEMENT OF JAPAN EVANGELISTIC BAND

*Objective*
To preach the gospel of Christ in Japan and in any other place where Japanese people may be found.

*Personnel*
The missionaries are men and women from various denominations who have banded together with the common desire to win Japanese for Christ. Japanese workers are immediately associated with the missionaries in the work and include pastors, evangelists and Bible women.

## 9. THE MESSIANIC TESTIMONY (1876)
### Rev John Wilkinson (1824-1907), David Baron (1855-1926) and C A Schönberger (1841-1924)

In the days of the early Church many thousands of Jewish people, including priests, came to faith in Jesus as their promised Messiah. But as an increasing number of Gentiles became believers, the idea arose that God had rejected Israel. This appeared to be confirmed, first when Jerusalem was destroyed by the Romans in AD 70, and then in 135 when a second revolt failed and Jews were banished from Jerusalem.

The apostle Paul's practice of preaching 'to the Jew first' fell into disuse, and Christians claimed for the Church the biblical promises concerning Israel. It was not until the 16th century Reformation, when there was a return to Scripture as the only basis for faith, that God's purposes for Israel were once again recognised.

Foremost in rediscovering these long-neglected biblical truths were the Puritans, a group of Protestant Christians. It was they who reminded the Church of its Jewish roots; it was incumbent upon believers – they argued – to honour God's ancient people, to be concerned for their welfare and to pray for their conversion.

The first to offer himself as a missionary to the Jews was a learned Puritan called Hugh Broughton (1549-1612), but the bishops turned down his proposal. And though the bishops also rejected his suggestion of a Hebrew translation of the New Testament for the Jews, his writings served to remind the Christian public of God's Chosen People.

It was not until the end of the 18th century that the Church in England began to display a zeal for mission, a direct result of the Wesleyan revival. At one period, between 1793 and 1834, thirteen missionary societies were founded in England, including the first society formed specifically for the conversion of Jews.

The Rev Lewis Way, together with Samuel Frey, a Jewish believer from Berlin, founded the London Society for Promoting Christianity among the Jews (often known as the London Jews Society, now CMJ) in 1809. But as the number of Jews entering Britain increased, other societies were formed, including the British Society for the Propagation of the Gospel among the Jews (1842), now renamed as Christian Witness to Israel.

In Scotland as early as 1818 two societies were established for the purpose of Jewish mission, respectively the Glasgow and Edinburgh Society for Promoting Christianity among the Jews. A second surge of missionary activity dates from around 1840 when other Scottish societies were set up, to make known the gospel to the Jews on the Continent, in parts of Africa and in the Middle East.

By around the middle of the 19th century there were some 20,000 Jews living in the East End of London. When the economic, social and religious conditions in Europe during the third quarter of the century forced many Jews to seek asylum elsewhere, an increasing number of Jewish immigrants entered Britain. Before the end of the century the number of Jews settled in the East End had risen to 110,000.

Among the younger British missions set up in London to minister to the new arrivals was the Mildmay Mission to the Jews (MMJ), formed in 1876, and the Hebrew Christian Testimony to Israel (HCTI) in 1893.

### Scottish Missions to Jews

Scotland has played a prominent part in world missions. From the end of the 18th century a new wave of missionary endeavour arose, including a surge in interest in Jewish mission. From 1818, both Glasgow and Edinburgh had societies for promoting Christianity among the Jews.

In 1837 a plea for setting up a Jewish mission was laid before the General Assembly of the Church of Scotland. It resulted, two years later, in sending four ministers (including Robert M'Cheyne and Andrew Bonar) on a Mission of Inquiry to Palestine, Egypt, Asia Minor and Europe. Their report stirred the dissenting Churches of the British Isles, and several societies for Jewish mission were formed.

John ('Rabbi') Duncan was the first Church of Scotland missionary to the Jews, and in 1841 he set out with two other missionaries for Budapest. His work there was fruitful, and his two years in Hungary resulted in the conversion of Jews such as the Saphir family, who became wonderful witnesses for the gospel.

After the Disruption (1843), when the Free Church of Scotland was formed by the secession of 474 ministers from the parent Church, both Churches maintained their interest in Jewish mission. Missionaries were sent to the Continent, to North Africa and to Palestine.

Nor were the communities of Jews living in Scotland neglected. The Scottish Home Mission to the Jews and other societies were formed in the 1880s. And around the same time, David Baron, then with the Mildmay Mission, spent over two years successfully ministering to Jewish families in Glasgow.

## Israel

John Wilkinson, founder of MMJ, was a Methodist local preacher in Lincolnshire when at the age of 27 he was called to minister to Jews. He applied to the British Society for the Propagation of the Gospel among the Jews for admittance to their training college in Stamford Street, Blackfriars. In 1854 he left college to begin life as a missionary, and spent 25 years working for the British Society.

With no rooms from which to operate, his day consisted of seeking out Jews in the city of London. Every day he walked to the city from Barnsbury to visit Jews in their shops and homes, distribute tracts and speak to individuals in the street. Jews at that time were not accustomed to being approached by a Christian missionary, and they were largely free from the sort of prejudice noticeable today.

An intelligent man with an easy flow of conversation, Wilkinson worked alone for six to eight hours a day. Many of the Jews to whom he spoke were amazed by his facility for quoting the Scriptures in Hebrew, and he frequently used Isaiah 53 in presenting the Messiah. Although sometimes scorned and abused, within a few months he could claim friendly access to some 60 Jewish families.

A tireless worker on the behalf of the Jews, he visited a number of provincial towns – Brighton, Bath, Bristol and others – in search of Jews with whom he might share the gospel. But the British Society was anxious to awaken the interest of Christians concerning Israel. He was asked by the society to visit churches as well, and this proved to be the pattern of his ministry for the next 20 years.

To make his entrance into these churches easier, in 1855 Wilkinson was ordained, and a few days later was speeding north on this errand. With his flair for overcoming difficulties, he was often instrumental in persuading Christians to change their attitude towards God's covenant people and support Jewish evangelism.

Eventually he began to regret that most of his energy was being spent in preaching *about* the Jews rather than *to* them. Believing that the time of Israel's restoration to Palestine was near, he felt he should concentrate on witnessing to Jews about their Messiah. He resigned from the British Society, and the very next day – 1 June 1876 – founded the Mildmay Mission to the Jews.

## Mildmay

The new mission was named 'Mildmay' to indicate its link with the Mildmay Institution, set up by the Rev William Pennefather of St Jude's Church, Mildmay. (Pennefather and his wife were the inspiration behind several remarkable social and gospel activities designed to cater for the needs of London's East Enders.) Although the attachment only lasted for a few years, the familiar name was retained. He teamed up with a Jewish Christian, James Adler, a scholarly young man with missionary zeal. Others were gradually added to their number.

With no money behind him, Wilkinson had to look to the Lord for the future. His guiding principle was always, 'Ask the Lord, and tell his people'. Under his leadership, the Mildmay Mission to the Jews experienced a noteworthy success, and Mission centres were established both in England and on the Continent.

In addition to personal evangelism and open-air meetings, Wilkinson conducted weekly gospel services at the mission room in Wellclose Square, Whitechapel. His workers made house-to-house visits in other areas of the East End.

His concern for Jewish people was not confined to their 'spiritual' needs; he was also aware of people's physical well-being. This led him to set up a wide variety of social agencies: a Night School for Children, a Medical Mission, a Workshop and Home for Inquirers, a Convalescent Home, and a Training Home and School for Destitute Jewish Children.

## Developments

As the work developed, a mission station was opened in Liverpool under Solomon Davidson, and one in Birmingham with Elijah Samuel in charge. Two missionaries were sent to Morocco and one was stationed in Cape Town, South Africa. On the Continent, book depots were opened in five Russian cities, where practical support was given to Jews being persecuted. All the while the emphasis was on reaching individual Jews, to read the Scriptures to them and present the claims of Jesus.

One of the most notable achievements was the publication and free distribution of the Hebrew New Testament: one quarter of a million copies of the New Testament and 100,000 portions of another translation into Judeo-German. The total number of copies of the Scriptures distributed by their agency between 1887 and 1901 amounted to over one million.

New headquarters, the Central Hall in Philpot Street, were opened in 1892, and were described by one writer as 'the most complete Jewish mission building in the world'. The staff employed there was larger than that of any other existing mission station.

Although the major part of the work was in London, Wilkinson made frequent tours of the larger provincial towns where Jews were to be found. It was on such a tour that he was first introduced to David Baron, an Orthodox Jew from Russian Poland, later to become founder of the Hebrew Christian Testimony to Israel.

**Feared God**

Fluent in Hebrew from his early years, Baron entered a rabbinical college at the age of ten, where he became one of its most distinguished scholars. And though he 'feared God', he was often troubled by a need to be right with God. He longed for a temple, a priest and a lamb, that he might confess his sins and roll away the burden of his heart.

An accident whilst a boy left him seriously injured, and he was not expected to live long. Distressed because he was aware that, if he were to die, he would be unfit to enter the presence of a holy God, he shared

JOHN WILKINSON AND DAVID BARON

this anxiety with his mother. She tried to reassure him that he would go straight to heaven. 'Oh, no,' he cried, 'I have not been good, and if my getting to heaven depends on my own goodness I shall never get there.'

The boy recovered, but his anxiety remained. It was a matter that troubled him for many years. He wandered about from place to place, seeking to find rest of mind but could find none, to bind up his broken heart and apply the 'balm of Gilead' to his soul.

At the age of 22 he set off with one of his brothers-in-law who had decided to emigrate to America. Stranded in Hull without money or friends, it was here that he met a Jewish Christian, a Mr Koenig, from the Mildmay Mission. Though bitterly prejudiced against Christians, whom he had been brought up to detest, Baron was impressed by the kindness and courtesy of the missionary. Certainly he could not help but notice that this *meshummad* (apostate Jew), though not rich, was far happier than he was.

Invited to attend a gospel meeting, he accepted in deference to the kindness shown him, but went rather to attempt to disprove the missionary's arguments for the Messiahship of Jesus. He argued with him, and displayed all his knowledge of the Hebrew Scriptures and Talmud in an attempt to disprove his every assertion, but he could not break down the man's testimony; he seemed to know God as Father, as the loving God.

Given a New Testament, however, he was amazed to read the story of Jesus. How, he wondered, could such holy words and sublime teaching proceed from the heart of one said by the Talmudists to be 'the greatest sinner in Israel'? His prejudice towards Christians and the name of Jesus gradually crumbled.

When he visited London to renew his acquaintance with Wilkinson, whom he had also met in Hull, he was told that his only hope was to put his faith in Christ. It took over 12 months of anguish before he was able to put his trust in Jesus. Overwhelmed by the heart of Jesus, he one evening knelt down and exclaimed, 'Oh, my God, if thou canst not save me on any other condition but faith in Jesus, be pleased to give me that faith, and help me to love the most precious name which I have so long hated and despised.'

## Harley College

Baron spent the next two years (1879-1881) at Harley College under Dr Grattan Guinness, preparing for missionary work, in the meanwhile helping MMJ with its work of evangelism.

From 1881 to 1893 he worked full-time with Mildmay, in Scotland and then on tour through England and parts of Europe, speaking to Jews of the dispersion. He was delighted to find in Scotland that there was a real love for the Jews among many Christian people. He stayed for two years in Glasgow, ministering to Jewish families and immigrants passing through the city.

Whilst touring in Europe in 1887, he met Charles Schönberger, an Orthodox Jew from Hungary, at that time associated with the British Society. They found in one another kindred spirits, especially with regard to the principle of Jewish believers witnessing to their own people. It was to be several years before their thoughts bore fruit.

For nearly two years Baron was the mission's agent in Jaffa, Palestine, where he ministered to Jewish immigrants entering the Holy Land. It was during this period that he became convinced that it was more appropriate for Jewish Christians to undertake the work of evangelizing their own people. Only Jews who had received Christ, he concluded, could fully sympathise with 'their brethren after the flesh'.

He resigned from Mildmay, and together with C A Schönberger began a new work in 1893 that they believed would appeal more to Jewish people. The two men had natural gifts that complemented each other: Baron was a great expositor of Scripture, and Schönberger an accomplished preacher. Both were, by then, experienced in mission work, and were well-fitted for the task by their background, education and training.

The name for the new mission was prayerfully chosen, and was based on Scripture. Psalm 122 : 4 (RV) speaks of 'a testimony to Israel', which was descriptive of their intent and purpose. Hence the full name became the Hebrew Christian Testimony to Israel.

## Special Feature

Without a mission centre, the two men began as itinerant missionaries and evangelists in the East End, at a time when Jews were still fleeing Russia and Poland for the security of Britain. But the following year they commenced what was to be the special feature of their ministry – regular, systematic preaching and teaching of the Scriptures.

Initially, meetings were held in the school room of Brunswick Chapel, Mile End Road. But there was a need for a more permanent centre, and for six years a dilapidated shop was hired in Whitechapel Road. Every day at 4 pm (except Saturdays and Sundays, when special services were held), meetings were held attended by between 60 and 100 men. There were also meetings for women, and for children who had permission from their parents.

It was one of HCTI's principles not to make appeals for money, and the only advertisements made were for the Annual Meeting and gatherings for prayer. Nor did Baron take any money for himself, but relied solely on the Lord.

In 1901 the Testimony was able to open its own premises in Whitechapel Road, without making any appeal. It remained the headquarters until 1985, when the building was sold and the office moved to its present site in Barking. As the Jewish population of Whitechapel had almost disappeared, having moved out to the more affluent suburbs of the capital, the a timely move.

## Zionist Congress

From the earliest days of the HCTI, Baron took a patriotic interest in Zionism. He attended the first Zionist Congress at Basle (Switzerland) in August 1897, and thereafter for several years. Although a Christian missionary, he gained admittance on the ground of being a 'reporter' (i.e. for the HCTI magazine, *The Scattered Nation*).

On one occasion, a delegate spoke disparagingly about Hebrew Christian missionaries. At which point, the congress chairman, Dr Herzl, left the rostrum and sat with David Baron and the other missionaries, showing his appreciation of their support.

The congress came to a unanimous decision concerning its aim, which was 'to create a legally assured home in Palestine'.

This was to be achieved by (1) promoting the settlement in Palestine of Jewish agriculturists, craftsmen, industrialists, and those following a profession; (2) the centralisation of the Jewish people by means of general institutions acceptable to the laws of the land; (3) by strengthening Jewish sentiment and national conscience; and (4) by obtaining the sanction of governments to the carrying out of the objects of Zionism.

Herzl's enthusiasm for a Jewish homeland was infectious, and he prophesied that the Jews would return to Palestine, if not within five years, then certainly within fifty. His prophecy was fulfilled.

The second emphasis of the Testimony's ministry was the publication of literature specially produced for Jewish readers. In its first 25 years, 38 books and pamphlets in Hebrew, Yiddish and several European languages were published. HCTI was in the vanguard of this work, and other missions were consequently awakened to the need for more suitable Christian literature for use in Jewish evangelism.

**Abroad**

David Baron made a number of tours abroad, across Europe and to North America, preaching to Jewish people and distributing New Testaments. Often as many as 500 men would gather to listen to the gospel, and some were even ready to pay for admission. After the First World War, the HCTI opened mission centres in Paris and Berlin, and resident workers were stationed in Russia, Syria, Palestine and Morocco.

Following the death of their founders, both missions maintained their witness under the leadership of highly respected men. Evangelism continued as the main focus of their activities in both Eastern and Western Europe until the Second World War, when the work was disrupted.

The two missions merged in 1973 and adopted a new title. The term 'Hebrew Christian' was dropped in favour of 'Messianic', a term currently used to denote Jews who believe in Jesus as Messiah.

The Jewish world has changed dramatically since the days of Wilkinson and Baron, though the same message is given to Jewish people by Messianic Testimony workers: that Jesus is the Jewish Messiah and the one way of salvation. As in the days of David Baron, evangelism is not limited to the UK, and missionaries once again operate throughout Europe, the former Soviet Union and in Israel.

A bi-monthly evangelistic paper for Jewish people is produced in France, and two workers are involved in reaching out effectively to the large Jewish community in the Marseille area.

The changes in Eastern Europe have opened doors for several UK workers to visit the scattered Jewish communities there. This has seen a great deal of fruit, especially in St Petersburg (Russia) and Minsk (Belarus).

Assistance is given to Jewish believers in Israel, and the Testimony co-operates in the production and distribution of Bibles in Hebrew and Russian, as well as Hebrew editions of relevant Christian books.

Although there are more Jewish believers in Jesus today than at any other time in the history of the Church, the apostle Paul's emphasis on the priority of Jewish evangelism continues to be relevant. For the gospel is still 'the power of God for the salvation of everyone who believes: 'first for the Jew ...'.

## THE PURPOSE OF THE MESSIANIC TESTIMONY

We reach out to Jewish people with the message of God's love revealed in Jesus – through visiting homes, distributing Bibles and evangelistic literature, putting on relevant meetings and giving practical help where needed. We also encourage Christians to reach out to Jewish people in a sensitive and compassionate way, mindful of the hurt that has been done to them by the false Christian teaching that has accused the Jews of being 'Christ-killers' and persecuted them in the name of Jesus. We help Jewish people who have come to the Lord to grow in their faith and relate to others in the Body of Messiah.

We wish to be a resource to the Church providing relevant material on such subjects as:

* How to reach Jewish people with the gospel
* God's Covenant with Israel and its outworking in history
* The significance of Jewish festivals and Passover demonstrations
* Background information on events in Israel and the situation for the Jewish people worldwide
* Anti-semitism past and present
* Exhibits of Biblical material and items of Jewish interest
* Testimonies of Jewish believers

We have books and tapes available on these subjects and can arrange meetings on request.

## 10. OAC INTERNATIONAL (1892)
## E P Field (1855-1928)

Preaching is the public proclamation of the Word of God. From Bible times it has been a means used by God to speak to people, so that the Old Testament patriarchs and prophets were preachers in the literal sense of the word. They traversed the land of Israel, speaking to all who would listen to their message. John the Baptist and Jesus maintained this tradition, and they drew large crowds after them as they wandered the countryside.

The practice of preaching in the open-air continued during the years of the Apostles and beyond. However, when Constantine the Great (312-337), the first Christian emperor, had many fine new churches built, Christianity became respectable and preaching was mostly confined to the pulpit.

There were exceptions to this rule – such as the Franciscan and Dominican friars of the 13th century, and the Lollards at the end of the following century – but they were few. With the establishment of the Church of Rome, the authority of God's Word tended to be replaced by that of the Pope.

In the 16th century, the Lutheran Reformation restored the authority of the Scriptures, which became the basis of Protestant preaching and doctrine. Even so, clergymen for the most part confined their preaching to inside churches. It was not until the 18th century that open-air preaching was undertaken on a grand scale, when it was popularised by the English evangelists George Whitefield and John Wesley.

### Field Preaching

At the beginning of his ministry, Whitefield followed the convention of his day and preached from the pulpit. His simple, biblically based sermons were hugely popular and the churches where he preached were crowded. But he was anxious to reach the untouched masses outside church. In the course of his correspondence with the dynamic Howell Harris, he learned of the Welshman's preaching to immense crowds out of doors, which God had used in saving hundreds of his countrymen.

The thought of 'field preaching' appealed to Whitefield, for it offered him the freedom to speak the Word of God, outside church buildings, and independent of Church authority. In those days open-air preaching was not so commonplace; it was felt that such a display of 'enthusiasm' could lead to trouble and public disorder, and was therefore frowned upon.

Aware that he would earn the contempt of many of his fellow clergymen, Whitefield nevertheless took the step. In February 1739 he addressed a crowd of some 200 coal miners at Kingswood, Bristol; at a later date he preached there to a crowd of 10,000. Thrilled to be able to teach in the open fields, he continued the practice throughout his ministry. In America, which he visited seven times, he drew similar-sized crowds, and with Jonathan Edwards experienced the Great Awakening when hundreds were brought into the kingdom.

The practice of open-air work was carried over into the following century, as Wesley's local preachers followed in the evangelists' footsteps. Door to door visitation also became part of the strategy as the need to meet outsiders where they were impressed itself more and more upon a number of Evangelicals.

Just over a hundred years ago, in 1892, Open Air Campaigners (OAC) was founded in Sydney, Australia, to do just this – to reach the vast majority of people who never entered a church. It owes its early inspiration to the work of a barrister, Edward Field, the son of General Sir John Field, aide-de-camp to Queen Victoria and a fearless witness for Christ.

### Prospect of Death
Field was born in India and educated at public schools in England. He afterwards went up to Cambridge University, but left before taking his degree. Anxious to tear himself away from his parents' influence, he emigrated to Australia in 1876 and settled in Sydney. After having numerous jobs, he studied law and was called to the bar in 1884. As a lawyer totally absorbed in his profession, Field became well-known in the city and was fully involved in the round of social life. His practice blossomed and he grew prosperous.

This success, however, came to an abrupt end when in 1890 a specialist diagnosed cancer of the throat. The sudden prospect of death led Field to review his life and consider his ways. As a result he was brought to his knees and turned his life over to Christ as Lord and Saviour. He vowed that if he were spared, then he would dedicate himself to God's service.

Advised to return to England, he consulted a London surgeon who gave him a thorough examination, and exclaimed, 'But you have been operated on already!' Unbeknown to the patient, a quiet healing process had been taking place.

True to his promise, Field returned to Sydney in 1892 where he followed his father's example, of hospital visiting and open-air preaching. An enthusiastic preacher, many converts came to faith through his witness at his meetings both in the centre of Sydney and in the suburbs. The success of his work greatly encouraged him, and he gathered together a band of 28 helpers and formed the Cogee Open Air Mission (three years later renamed the New South Wales Prayer Band).

Field's energy appeared to know no bounds. He not only organised church evangelistic campaigns, but continued with his daily open-air preaching engagements. Among his regular preaching meetings was a Sunday service at Cogee Beach, a suburb of the city, which attracted large numbers of people. Such was the impact of the Mission's work that the city experienced a revival, with hundreds coming to faith.

But the pace of work was too much for Field and in 1897 he was finally forced to give up the Mission. With his wife and family he returned to live permanently in England where he continued to witness to his faith. Although he never started a similar work in Britain, he was involved in various evangelical causes. He joined the Evangelical Alliance where, again following in his father's footsteps, he served as General Secretary from 1899-1904.

**Outback**
Though the work in Sydney was maintained, without its leader the Evangelistic Band lost some of its momentum. However, it revived in 1913 under the name of the New South Wales Evangelistic Prayer Band. Though still based in Sydney, the state capital, its vision was to visit the outback where there was often no church.

The Band was now led by William Bradley, formerly with the Egypt General Mission, who had the ability to attract the right kind of men. Some of those Bradley brought onto the staff were gifted Bible teachers or open-air speakers, and once more the Band began to make a more effective impact around New South Wales. By 1922, when the name was again changed – to Open Air Campaigners – there were already several full-time staff evangelists, supported by a number of gospel vans.

The evangelists gathered around them groups of voluntary helpers, and in teams they spread out to cover the city. There was a weekly programme of lunch-time open-airs, with meetings in parks and at factory gates, plus a Sunday evening meeting near the Town Hall. Crowds were so big that on occasions the authorities were forced to move the evangelists to another spot. Cogee Beach was once again a special centre for preaching. It became noted for its children's meetings,

## EFFECTIVE EVANGELISM

An increasingly large percentage of the world's population live in large towns and cities. Many of those who live in suburbs work and shop in city centres. Open-air evangelism can be used to reach people in parks, shopping precincts, high streets, beaches or almost anywhere else that people gather. In many parts of the world it is not unusual for crowds of several hundred to gather to hear the gospel preached in the open-air. Most of those listening will probably have had little contact with the Church. A series of open-air meetings, even of quite modest size, can reach thousands of people over the course of a year.

Effective evangelism should always result in a Christian talking to a non-Christian, and in open-air meetings this is relatively easy to arrange. Christians in the crowd can simply turn to the next person to them at the end of the meeting (those not interested will have left by then) and share Christ with them.

Open Air Campaigners is able to help Christians communicate more effectively, and offers a variety of training seminars with practical sessions to follow. Seminars include Communicating to Adults ... to Young People ... to Children. Weekend seminars on 'Gospel Magic' are designed to assist those who speak to all-age groups in schools, youth clubs, prisons, even night clubs! Methods include drama, sketchboard, visual aids and testimony.

held on Sunday afternoons, when hundreds of young people listened with rapt attention to illustrated Bible talks.

But the outback of New South Wales, six times the size of England, also needed the gospel, and plans were made to move out of the city. From Sydney, country branches were formed throughout the state and evangelistic tours made, with short stops at county towns and villages, and longer ones at farming communities. One of the biggest campaigns held was at Hunter Valley, the state's principal coalfield. Despite local opposition to the gospel, hundreds of miners were converted.

In the early 1920s, the OAC worked among Australian soldiers engaged in compulsory military training. When the Second World War started, OAC was again invited to open recreation centres for army personnel. Known as Welfare Officers, the evangelists provided leisure time facilities for the troops, held services and had opportunities for counselling or praying with men. Because of the war-time situation, OAC staff had to wear a uniform, a practice which persisted for many years after the war.

## Ladder Lettering

Evangelists use different methods to get the message across, but the most novel form of presenting the gospel was first used by OAC evangelist Jim Duffecy in 1952. Known as 'ladder or lightning lettering', it is a technique Duffecy had seen used at the Royal Sydney Show. A poster artist was working on an oversized board with paint and chalk. He made a couple of 'ladders' on the sheet of white paper with a big paintbrush, then added large circles and slabs of colour with chalk.

A crowd gathered, watching with intrigue as the puzzle was unravelled. With a few strokes each square of the ladder became a letter, and the letters became words. Suddenly, it revealed an advertising slogan – and the crowd was delighted !

Fascinated by this act, Duffecy realised that the best product in the world – the gospel – could also be advertised in this way. Already in the habit of using a sketchboard when speaking to children, he adopted this new evangelistic method. The sketchboard has now become OAC's trademark, and the ladder technique is still widely used.

When years later Duffecy revisited the Royal Sydney Show, he met the artist, who was gratified to learn that his technique had been used to make the gospel more easy to understand.

Up to this point, OAC's impact had been confined to Australia, but Duffecy's links with Youth For Christ led to an overseas extension of the work. YFC invited him to the Empire Games campaign in New Zealand, and so the first overseas branch was opened there in 1954. Open-air meetings were held in Auckland, which quickly attracted the support of well-known Christians such as Robert Laidlaw, who helped finance the first gospel van.

An invitation to North America led to other branches being formed in the USA in 1956, and in Canada the following year. Jim Duffecy led a team from Australia and New Zealand to hold evangelistic meetings in the People's Church, Toronto, where the pastor was the famous missionary, Oswald Smith. Although the work has become established in Canada, the severe winter conditions make the usual OAC style of ministry impossible.

Since then, OAC has set up branches in eight European countries (with the prospect of expansion into Eastern Europe), the Philippines, South America and the Caribbean. And in many Third World countries OAC runs a programme under the name of Sowers International.

The increasingly widespread ministry of OAC led in 1965 to a conference at which delegates set up OAC International. The aim of this was to plan and co-ordinate international development, as well as to strengthen fellowship.

## Britain

The British branch was established by David Fanstone, the present Director, and the first open-air meeting took place at Brighton on Easter Day 1968. There are now over 20 staff evangelists working in 14 branches throughout the UK.

In addition to open-air evangelism, OAC staff also serve alongside churches and other agencies. They have worked in co-operation with such societies as Operation Mobilisation, Home Evangelism and the South American Missionary Society.

Its schools ministry is probably the largest of any organisation in Britain, taking assemblies and reaching thousands of children each year. The Bristol branch takes on average between 35-40 school assemblies and classes each week, reaching some 21,000 children a month with the gospel.

To help individuals develop their preaching skills, it provides specialist training in effective open-air evangelism, geared to both adults and children, and organises outreach campaigns in co-operation with churches and missionary societies. Seminars and workshops on pastoral care are an essential element in the programme, and a wide range of equipment and training manuals in several languages is available.

The British branch is involved in developing a ministry on the Continent and there are resident workers in ten European countries.

Evangelistic trips have ben made to former Communist bloc countries that are now open to the gospel.

With the wider development of OAC's ministry, it has been decided to change the name in Britain to OAC Ministries, expressing the variety of evangelism in which staff members are involved. But priority continues to be given to the open-air preaching of the Word, for which OAC was originally raised up.

C H Spurgeon used to tell his students, 'No sort of defence is needed for preaching out of doors, but it would need very potent arguments to prove a man had done his duty who has never preached beyond the walls of his meeting house.'

OAC evangelists say it is a privilege and not simply a duty, as they see old and young people won to Christ.

### MISSION STATEMENT OF OAC MINISTRIES

To preach the gospel of Christ by all means with the church with particular emphasis on open air and going out evangelism.

Their motto is 'Presenting Christ by all means everywhere'.

## 13. OMF INTERNATIONAL (1865)
## J Hudson Taylor (1832-1905)

When Protestant missionaries first attempted to gain a foothold for the gospel in the Chinese empire, they faced – humanly speaking – an almost impossible task. Like Japan, Chinese rulers had long maintained a position of isolation, and few foreigners had been allowed to enter the land.

The world's largest nation, its population of nearly 400 million people, scattered over largely mountainous terrain, was deeply steeped in ancient idolatrous religions. Any suggestion of change was vigorously opposed, and there was an imperial edict in force that denounced Christianity.

Attempts in earlier centuries to introduce Christianity into the land had been unsuccessful. In the seventh century a Nestorian Christian from Syria – a member of an heretical sect – was welcomed by the emperor. Although churches were built, the religion was suppressed in the ninth century. Franciscan friars entered China in the 13th century, but their influence gradually declined.

Three centuries later Jesuit missionaries established a work in the Portuguese colony of Macao. Their attempts to move inland met with varying degrees of success, and though converts were won the missionaries faced persecution and imprisonment. By the beginning of the 19th century the numbers of converts had dwindled.

By this time, however, Protestant missions were being established along the Chinese coast. The way was paved for the beginning of a quite remarkable work of God, the China Inland Mission (CIM), which was unique among those working on behalf of the gospel in China. Arising out of the devotion and courage of J Hudson Taylor, and without the backing of a denominational or any other ecclesiastical body, CIM became the largest 'faith mission' founded during the century.

Focusing on the one land, the Mission captured the imagination of a wide spectrum of the Christian public, coming, as it did, on the wave of the 1859 Evangelical Revival. The revival gave an impetus to missionary work, and CIM channelled the zeal of hundreds of young believers into offering for China.

## Protestant Presence in China

The first Protestant missionary to enter China was Robert Morrison of the London Missionary Society, who landed at the trading port of Canton in 1807. Within 18 months Morrison managed to acquire a knowledge of the Mandarin dialect. Appointed interpreter to the East India Company, he still found time to fulfil his calling. He translated the entire Bible into Mandarin, and compiled a Chinese-English dictionary and grammar. It was this work that provided a foundation for future missionary activity in China.

A second factor that helped pave the way for a Protestant presence was the Treaty of Nanking, signed between Britain and China following the Opium War of 1840-42. By the treaty, five ports – Canton, Amoy, Foochow, Ningpo and Shanghai – were opened to Westerners for residence and trade. They were also allowed to learn the Chinese language, build houses, schools, hospitals and places of worship.

A number of denominational societies were soon to be found represented in these ports: the American Baptists and Presbyterians, the Church Missionary Society, the English Presbyterians, Baptists and Wesleyans, and several other smaller societies. Among these was the Chinese Evangelisation Society, founded by Mr George Pearse (also a co-founder of the North Africa Mission), a member of the London stock exchange.

## Set Apart

Taylor was born in Barnsley, a small Yorkshire town nestling in the foothills of the Pennines. At his birth the child was 'set apart unto the Lord' by his parents, for did not the Lord have a right to claim the best of his own giving?

His father, James Taylor, had a chemist's shop in the market place, at 21 Cheapside, and was active as a Methodist local preacher. Nurtured on local preachers' talk about overseas missions, from the age of five or six the boy was determined to be a missionary to China. But it was not until after his conversion, at the age of seventeen, when he put himself completely at God's disposal, that the Lord said to him, 'Then go for me to China.'

Ready to prepare himself for his call, Taylor began to pray for guidance and to learn all he could about his future mission field. He borrowed a copy of St Luke in Mandarin Chinese, and with a copy of the English version made a beginning on finding out the meaning of the Chinese characters. He studied missionary magazines and read Dr Medhurst's book, *China*, which challenged him about the value of medical work on the mission field.

Having spent some time working with his father in the pharmacy, in 1851 Taylor took a position as assistant to a Dr Hardey, a distant relative in Hull, to further his medical knowledge. Following his father's maxim of 'See what you can do without', he lived a very frugal existence to save all he could for China. But the experience of living and working among the poor people of Hull proved challenging in more ways than one. It was here that he learned one of the greatest lessons of his life: how to move man through God by prayer alone.

One Sunday Taylor was down to his last half crown as his quarter's salary fell due, with the need to pay his rent and buy food. He had determined never to remind the doctor about his salary, as requested, but to leave the matter of payment with God.

That night a man asked him to go and pray with his dying wife, as the priest had refused. Taylor was led into a wretched room where four or five starving children stood by their exhausted mother.

Having prayed with the woman, he was in conflict over the half crown piece he had in his pocket. Unable to divide the sum into two, he finally felt persuaded to give him the coin, believing that he should trust God to meet his needs; he immediately felt at peace about the matter.

The following morning he received in the post a pair of kid gloves from a stranger, from which fell half a sovereign. 'Praise the Lord,' he exclaimed. '400 per cent for twelve hours' investment – that is good interest!' It was the memory of this incident that frequently helped him through many difficulties later on.

**To China**
Now aged 20, Taylor spent the next two years in London, undergoing further medical studies prior to going out to China under the auspices of the Chinese Evangelisation Society (CES). He landed at Shanghai in March 1854, where he found his first home in the London Missionary Society compound with Dr Medhurst, whose book had first led him to undertake medical studies.

The early years spent in China were formative ones; they were years of hardship and testing, during which time God was laying a foundation for a much greater work. Priority was given to learning the language, and he commenced a study of the Mandarin dialect, devoting five hours

### Living by Faith

In 1824, Edward Irving (1792-1834) preached a sermon before the London Missionary Society that was to have far-reaching effects. He challenged missionaries to imitate the first apostles, and to go out relying on God alone. Faith, he argued, was the basis of all missionary work, and entailed relying on God for things spiritual and material.

Around this time, others were beginning to live by this same principle. George Müller (1805-1898), a member of the new Brethren movement, was an early example of living by faith. When appointed minister of Ebenezer Chapel in Teignmouth, he and his wife felt it not right to receive a fixed salary, but rather they should depend upon God alone for their needs. A box was placed in the chapel for contributions, and from then on they made their requests known only to God. When he founded the orphanage in Bristol, he had five homes and 2,050 children to care for every day, and money came in direct answer to prayer.

The policy of relying entirely on God became an established feature of an increasing number of missionary societies, and CIM was one of several to operate in this way. Other missions included the Regions Beyond Missionary Union (1872), the Hebrew Christian Testimony to Israel (1893, now the Messianic Testimony) and the Sudan United Mission (1903, now Action Partners). Non-denominational missionary colleges, such as Harley College (1873), Ridgelands (1919) and All Nations (1923) were founded to further this aim.

every day to this task until fluent enough to preach in the language. He also kept up his medical studies, intending to use this work as a means of gaining an entry for the gospel.

From the first Sunday after landing, Taylor went out with another CES worker, Dr Parker, to evangelise in the city and surrounding villages. They gave away tracts and attended to simple ailments. But his vision was that of reaching the interior, and by the end of the year he was able to make the first of a number of journeys further inland in company with one or another of the missionaries. On one journey, they preached in 58 towns and villages, 51 of which had never heard the gospel before.

These excursions showed him the truth of Dr Medhurst's contention concerning medical help, and when he saw what could be accomplished he was greatly encouraged. In one period of three months, with Dr Parker he distributed 3,000 New Testaments and Scripture portions, and more than 7,000 other books and tracts. His medical cures, however, occasionally attracted the wrath of local doctors and druggists, who were losing patients to the foreigner.

**Decisions**
During these years Taylor took three important decisions that were to significantly alter the direction of his life and ministry.

The first related to the CES, with whom his relationship had become increasingly difficult. The fact was that the Committee was not punctual

JAMES HUDSON TAYLOR

in paying his allowance, and at times he was left extremely short of funds. He was even more saddened to discover that the Society had acquired a reputation for mismanagement.

After three years in China, Taylor felt he must resign from the Society because of its willingness to fall into debt. To borrow money, he argued, implied a contradiction of Scripture. It also meant that he was living on borrowed money, and he did not think that God was unable or unwilling to supply the needs of his children. Despite the break, he continued afterwards to enjoy a good relationship with the Committee, especially with George Pearse.

Now living in the treaty port of Ningpo, it was about this time that he hung a pair of scrolls on the wall of his home. They carried the inscriptions: Ebenezer, 'Hitherto hath the Lord helped us', and Jehovah Jireh, 'The Lord will provide'. Completely alone, it meant throwing himself more than ever upon the Lord for his needs.

During these days, the thought of wearing Chinese dress increasingly impressed itself upon his mind. On one of his inland journeys he was at one point left on his own and in need of new quarters. He described finding a new home as a 'wearisome work', and went on, 'if I do not succeed soon I shall adopt Chinese dress and seek a place in the country.'

The idea of wearing native clothing was quite novel, but in order to identify himself more closely with the people he finally took this step – plus chopsticks, Chinese cooking, and even the queue (pigtail) – even though it met with objections from Europeans. Afterwards, he was usually assumed to be Chinese; it was not until he began to distribute books and see patients that his identity became known.

His marriage to Maria Dyer in January 1858 was the union of two like souls, as they both had a desire to be useful to God and a longing for holiness. Maria, the orphan daughter of missionary parents, was fluent in the Ningpo dialect and had been a helper in the first school to be opened for Chinese girls.

Neither of them, however, enjoyed good health, and the possibility of Taylor having a breakdown persuaded them of the need to take a break. Towards the end of 1860 they set sail for England with their young daughter, Gracie.

## Growing Vision

Taylor saw this enforced rest as a time for serving the Chinese people, even at such a distance. A more correct translation of the Ningpo New Testament was needed, as well as a hymn book; and he had decided to complete his medical studies. The obvious place to settle was in the East End of London, close to the London Hospital and to some of the influential societies whose help would be invaluable to him.

In addition to his studies and translation work, his days were filled with meetings, visitors, correspondence and various other engagements. But he never lost sight of a growing vision for an inland work in China, with a thousand stations manned by hundreds of missionaries, and he was able to send out a number of workers to China.

His medical studies successfully completed in 1862, he felt freer to look ahead. With returning strength, the longing grew upon him to be back in China, but he recognised it was not yet the Lord's time.

Meanwhile, the knowledge that a million people a month in China were dying without God stirred Taylor's heart afresh. He had already prayed for and sent out missionaries to the Ningpo Mission, but believed that God would send more. What should he do?

The crisis point came while recovering from an illness in George Pearse's Brighton home. One quiet Sunday morning in June 1865 he had gone for a stroll on the beach, pondering the need for missionaries for inland China. Aware of the burden upon him of sending workers into such a threatening environment, he suddenly realised, 'Why, if we are obeying the Lord, the responsibility rests with him, not with us!'

He then prayed that the Lord would raise up 24 missionaries for China – two for each of the eleven unoccupied provinces, and two for Chinese Tartary. With the waves breaking around his feet, he wrote in his Bible, 'Prayed for 24 willing, skilful labourers at Brighton, June 25th 1865.'

Two days later he went with Pearse to the London & County Bank, and with £10 opened an account for the China Inland Mission.

## Claims of China

His next task was to lay before the Christian public the claims of China. In the following September he was given an opportunity to address the Perth Conference for Deepening the Spiritual Life (the Scottish equivalent of the Mildmay Conference founded by the Rev. Pennefather). His moving appeal made an impression on the 2,000 strong assembly and placed CIM on the missionary map.

In October he published a booklet, *China's Spiritual Need and Claims*, in which he wrote of the task that lay before the new Mission and set out some of his thinking. Taylor was happy to accept believers from any denomination, provided they held fully to the inspiration of God's Word, and with no other guarantee than that given in the Scriptures. Thus from the beginning, the Mission was a non-denominational work.

Contrary to the usual practice, workers did not need a formal education or training. They would not have a fixed salary, but would have to trust God to supply their needs. There would be no appeal for funds or collections taken at meetings, but all wants would be brought before God in prayer. And they would be required to wear Chinese dress and be prepared to go inland.

In May 1866 a party of 16 adults, plus Taylor and his family, set sail from London to join the nine who had already left for China. Many were anxious about the well-being of the new Mission and warned them of the dangers. But Taylor trusted the promises of God, which he took at face value, and was not afraid of the future.

The Mission's affairs in Britain were left in the hands of W T Berger, a wealthy businessman and a friend from CES days. He was to be responsible for sending out new recruits, collecting and forwarding funds, and keeping in contact by correspondence. The direction of the Mission was in China, in the hands of Hudson Taylor. It was not until some time later that a council of senior missionaries was set up to advise him and superintend specific districts.

Soon after their arrival, the party adopted Chinese dress before settling in the coastal town of Hangchow. A dispensary was opened, a printing press set up and a church formed. After some months of language study, the time was ready to move into the countryside.

## Purpose

The main purpose of the Mission was not to win converts or to build a Chinese church, but rather to spread a knowledge of the gospel throughout the empire as quickly as possible. The practice was to make preliminary journeys of exploration prior to entering a province. Stations were opened in prefectural cities, concentrating on areas untouched by other Protestant agencies. Once the gospel had been proclaimed, it was likely that the fruits of conversion would be gathered by others.

By 1870 the number of missionaries had risen to 33, serving in 13 stations and eight out-stations in four provinces. From time to time Taylor prayed for specific numbers of additional workers, and invariably received more than he had asked for. He prayed for 18 in 1875, for 70 in 1881 and 100 in 1886. His appeal in 1890 for 1,000 missionaries resulted in 1,153 responding to the call.

By 1895 the Mission provided nearly half the foreign missionaries then in China, many of them drawn from Scandinavia, North America and Australasia. There were, in addition, 462 Chinese helpers working on 260 stations and out-stations in 14 provinces.

One discovery that Taylor made was the immense value to the Mission of women workers. The new practice of wearing Chinese dress had made it possible for women missionaries to gain an entrance into homes where men had failed. But as with many innovations, the use of single – and married – women in the interior had its critics.

Needless to say, the work was never without its problems. Soon after he had first begun in Hangchow, a small group of missionaries in an out-station became discontented. Some refused to continue wearing Chinese dress, while another made serious charges against Taylor's leadership; they even disassociated themselves from the Mission. Although the storm was weathered – the offenders were later removed – it did not help the Mission's cause.

For Taylor, health was a continual battle and he was often laid aside because of illness or a recurrence of a spinal injury. His wife, Maria, and two of his children died, and he had to send his other three youngsters back to England for their welfare.

### Attacks

Although legislation in China had been enacted that directed officials to give protection to foreigners, missionaries were at times subject to attacks or caught up in riots. Nevertheless, the Mission escaped serious injury until 1898, when W S Fleming was murdered in a previously unexplored region of the empire. This was but a prelude to a yet more terrible disaster about to fall the Mission and all believers in China, which happened while Taylor was away in England.

Political unrest fuelled by hostility to missionary activity led to widespread attacks on foreigners by a secret society known as *I Ho Ch'uan* ('Righteous and Harmonious Fists', or the Boxers). In addition to the deaths of hundreds of Chinese Christians, Protestant missionary societies lost 127 adults and 44 children killed, of which 58 missionaries and 21 children had belonged to CIM.

In the years that followed the rebellion, however, China experienced a mass movement towards Christianity, from which all missions benefited. More stations were opened, and many Chinese gave money for building gospel halls.

By now Taylor's health was fast failing him, and in 1902 he relinquished direct control of the Mission. When his second wife died in 1904, he returned to China for the last time. Happily, he was able to know something of the revival before going to be with the Lord in June of the following year.

Near the close of his life, Hudson Taylor at a CIM annual meeting gave the following testimony: 'I have sometimes met people who said, "Trusting God is a beautiful theory, but it won't work." Well, thank God it has worked, and it does work. I remember a dear friend, an aged minister in London, who said to me in the year 1866, "You are making a great mistake in going to China with no organisation behind you. We live in a busy world, and you will all be forgotten, and the Mission won't live for seven years." That was the prophecy of this good man – and a wise one too.'

But he was mistaken.

In October 1949 the Communist People's Liberation Army overthrew the Nationalist government of China and set up the People's Government. Soon there began a carefully planned government scheme to immobilise the Church and render it ineffective. The government brought pressure to bear on the Church, to get rid of all Western imperialist influences. Doors closed to missionary activities and CIM was forced to redeploy its workers in other countries of East Asia.

In June 1966, the centenary of its birth, the name was changed to Overseas Missionary Fellowship, adopted to reflect the new responsibility being undertaken.

## MISSION STATEMENT OMF INTERNATIONAL

Our goal: To glorify God by the Urgent Evangelization of East Asia's millions.

### We are an International Team

of men and women committed to sharing and showing the love of Jesus Christ to East Asian people in Asia, and in other countries too. We believe the Bible is God's Word. We believe that sin is a universal problem. We pray and work, in the power of the Holy Spirit, to spread the only answer to this problem: Jesus Christ, crucified and risen.

### We work with Local Christians

in places where churches already exist, to share the good news of Jesus our Lord. We preach, teach, encourage and train workers. We respect national Christians highly and aim for more effective teamwork in local and world evangelization.

### We reach the Unreached

in strategic places and among strategic people-groups where there are no Christians. We start churches where none existed before. We pioneer in huge cities, towns, villages and in remote areas. We tell people about Jesus Christ. We write, translate and publish literature that will communicate the good news.

### We care for the Uncared-for

sick people; alcoholics; the exploited, abused, poor; prosperous but lonely people; young and old; religious and non-religious. Most of them do not know Jesus. We want to bring them healing and wholeness in him.

### We Persevere

in bringing the good news of Jesus to people. We learn their language and their culture. We try to identify with them and be their friends. We take risks, face hardships and make mistakes but we hold on to the faithfulness of God. We trust him for guidance, for success, for money. We may fail but he never will; as a mission we have proved this again and again since 1865. We are full of hope, because God has promised to build his church.

## THE CHURCH IN CHINA

When the Communists assumed power in 1949, the new government began to put subtle pressure on church leaders and pastors to rid themselves of Western missionaries (though ultimately the aim was to root out all religious groups). Missionary societies, recognising the reality of the situation, began to withdraw their staffs, and without even issuing an edict China was able to drive out all foreign missionaries by 1952.

The Church was in future to belong to the Three Self Patriotic Movement (TSPM), based on an idea adopted from the missionaries. The principle of self-extension, self-government and self-support was revived to make the Chinese Church independent of 'imperialistic' contact and support. The Catholic Church was similarly brought under the control of the Catholic Patriotic Association. Some churches refused to belong to the TSPM and hundreds of leaders were arraigned before 'accusation meetings', or were imprisoned and tortured.

Church delegations visiting China were led to believe that the Church was flourishing, and that those in prison had brought the trouble upon themselves. But the so-called Cultural Revolution (1966-1976), set up to purge China of any remaining elements of anti-Marxist dogmas, led to further persecution. More churches were closed, religious symbols removed and homes ransacked for Bibles and Christian literature.

In 1979, with the accession to power of Deng Xiaoping, Christians were able to enjoy some freedom. But from 1983-1985, then again since the Tiananmen Square massacre in 1989, the Church has been subject to severe persecution. The main targets are the unregistered house churches, which in some instances have been closed down by security police and the homes of believers ransacked and their goods stolen.

Instead of stamping out Christianity, millions of people have believed and been baptised. In 1949 there was an estimated one million Protestant and three millions Catholics in China. A recent survey shows there are at least 30 million Protestants (an official government source has indicated 63 million) and 12 million Catholics. In fact there are more Christians in China than Communist Party members.

# CHINA & JAPAN

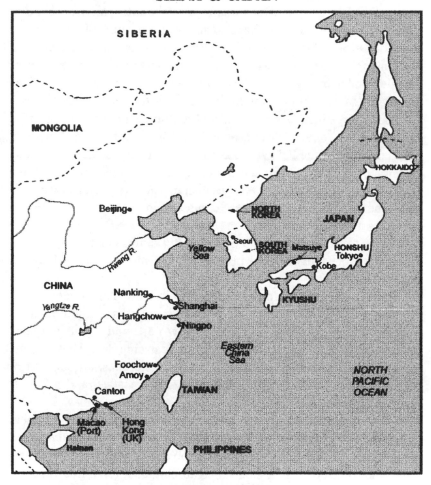

## 12. OMS INTERNATIONAL (1901)
### Charles E Cowman (1868-1924)

American Protestants were active in foreign missions from the early years of the 19th century. But it was not until the latter part of the century that renewed efforts were made to advance the cause of Christianity abroad. During this period the United States had been engaged in pushing its frontiers westwards, and much of its missionary enterprise was devoted to evangelising the newly-founded settlements, as well as immigrants from Europe, the Indians and the former African slaves.

The upsurge in missionary zeal and activity in the second half of the century was in some part a consequence of British influence. American magazines published news of British missionary societies, British missionaries often visited the States to seek recruits and encourage support, and branches of several British missionary societies were set up in the United States. All these contacts generated much interest in foreign missions.

Added to this was a series of spiritual awakenings that brought fresh life to the Protestant churches in America. The most telling revival was that of 1857.

Weekly prayer meetings were started in New York under a City Missionary, Jeremiah Lanphier. Within six months, 10,000 business men were daily gathering for prayer in New York, and within two years a million converts had been added to American churches. The outcome was a deepening of the spiritual life of the churches, an outburst of enthusiasm for voluntary organisations and crusades, and a keener interest in mission.

Prominent among the new movements was the Student Volunteer Movement, inspired by the evangelist D L Moody, and started in 1886. With the watchword, 'The evangelisation of the world in this generation', thousands of young men sailed abroad for foreign missions.

American churches followed the lead set by Britain, and a growing number of North American missionary enterprises were founded: among them, the Sudan Interior Mission (1893), the Africa Inland Mission (1895) and, under the leadership of Charles Cowman, the Oriental Missionary Society (1901).

## Godly Parents

When only two weeks old, Charles Cowman was dedicated to the Lord's service by his godly parents. Although as a boy he committed his life to God, he drifted away from the faith of his youth and neglected church attendance. At the age of 15 he trained as a telegraph operator and made rapid promotion, above many of his older colleagues.

Married at the age of 21 to his teenage sweetheart, Lettie Burd, he was soon faced with a crisis. Lettie developed heart trouble, and weakness gave way to severe illness. As his young wife lay dying, he flung himself down onto his knees at her bedside and prayed, 'Oh God, spare her life! Remember the boy who used to pray.'

Lettie's health was restored; in fact she would outlive her husband by 36 years, living until after her ninetieth birthday in 1960. Her devotional writings, *Streams in the Desert*, have outlived her and are bringing blessing to millions of people, especially in China.

Charles Cowman quickly forgot the vow he had made to the Lord, and for four years the couple enjoyed the delights of social life in Chicago. Invited to a special service just before Christmas 1893, Lettie gave her heart to Christ.

When she informed her husband of her decision, he simply scoffed at her. A month later, however, Cowman was forced to face the same challenge at a Sunday evening service. He surrendered his life to the Lord and peace came flooding into his heart. The change in him was marked because it was so radical, and being a Christian became the most important thing in his life.

## Witnessing

Immediately he began witnessing to the men in the Western Union telegraph office where he worked, even though he knew little of the Bible or what he ought to say. There were 500 men in the Chicago office, and within six months he had led 75 of them to the Lord.

His first attempt to speak to a colleague of the Lord was quite memorable. One man was sitting in the corner of a long room, apparently with a few moments to spare. After trying to summon up courage, Cowman finally approached him and engaged him in a one-sided conversation about his soul. There was no apparent response, and Cowman went home feeling downhearted.

The following morning the young man came to him as soon as he entered the office, and told him, 'I went home last night and did just what you told me. It is all settled; I gave myself to Christ.' The two men became life-long friends, and Ernest Kilbourne and his wife later followed the Cowmans to serve in Japan.

Because of their awkward working hours, it was difficult for many of the men to get to church. So Cowman rented a room in a nearby hotel for Sunday afternoon fellowship. Known as The Telegraphers' Mission Band, it became the foundation of a great missionary society. The men wrote to telegraph operators all over the United States, Great Britain and Australia, and other operators were won to Christ.

Concerned for the welfare of down-and-out men who frequented local mission halls, he became involved in an area of Chicago known as 'Little Hell'. He opened a room for them, offering overnight accommodation, free, if they first attended the preaching service. Hundreds of them were converted and many of them later became his first supporters in Japan.

### Blessing

After a year as a believer Cowman became troubled by a lack in his spiritual life. A friend shared with him a blessing he had received, referred to as 'entire sanctification'. At first Cowman saw no need of

CHARLES AND LETTIE COWMAN

this blessing, but was forced to change his mind. Afterwards he wrote in his notebook, 'I have committed myself and my all into God's hands, and he has accepted the offering. Life henceforth can never be the same.' From that day on, his service was marked by a new power and his ministry began to touch more lives.

## STUDENT VOLUNTEER MOVEMENT

The SVM arose in 1886 under the inspiration of the American evangelist, D L Moody, and made a considerable contribution towards the growing number of Americans serving as missionaries abroad. From 1880 Moody began an annual conference in the grounds of Mount Hermon School, a school he had founded close to his Northfield (Massachusetts) home. In 1886 the first conference for students was held, when 250 delegates from a hundred colleges gathered for a month of recreation, music and Bible study. Already stirred by the story of the Cambridge Seven – a group of British graduates of upper class standing and athletic prowess who two years earlier had volunteered for China – one hundred young men declared their willingness to serve overseas.

Under the watchword, 'The evangelisation of the world in this generation', the movement spread rapidly across America. In less than two years over 2,000 undergraduates had signed the declaration: 'I am willing and desirous, God permitting, to become a foreign missionary.' The movement was influential in Britain, though it was not formally organised until 1891; a start was made in Edinburgh the following year.

Moody invited many eminent lecturers to the summer camps – Hudson Taylor, Professor Henry Drummond of Edinburgh and J E K Studd amongst others, all of whom made a great impact upon the students. Although Taylor had only visited Northfield 'to give a few addresses on his way to China', it actually led to missionaries from North America joining CIM.

Not all who signed the declaration, however, went on to serve as a missionary. By 1920 around 8,140 former American college students who had joined the SVM had actually sailed abroad, including some 2,500 to China, 1,500 to India and 900 to Africa.

God's call to overseas mission came to both Charles and Lettie Cowman in 1894, at a missionary convention. They had been sent as delegates by their church, Grace Methodist Episcopal Church, Chicago. Challenged by the call to overseas mission, when the speaker asked for volunteers to go out as missionaries, Cowman turned to his wife and whispered, 'That means you and me. Let's stand and show our colours.'

At first they thought of going to India, but Cowman met Dr A T Pierson who advised, 'Young man, wait God's hour.' It was advice he never regretted. Feeling his lack of Bible knowledge, he followed a course of study at the Garrett Biblical Institute in Evanston (Illinois), and for six years both he and Lettie attended morning classes at the Moody Bible Institute.

At a Sunday morning service in 1897 the Cowmans met the Rev Juji Nakada, a young Japanese pastor and evangelist who was studying at the Moody Bible Institute. Invited to a holiness meeting, the pastor was filled with the Holy Spirit, and afterwards felt he should return to his people to preach 'full salvation' to them. The Telegraph Mission Band assumed support for him, and he travelled Japan holding evangelistic services.

## Japan

It was not until three years later that the Cowmans were both, separately, called to Japan as missionaries. They applied to a mission board and were accepted as teachers in a mission school. But before long God challenged them to launch out apart from a missionary society. Without the backing of a missionary society, or a home office, or a deputation secretary to raise funds, the Cowmans sailed for Japan in February 1901.

They were met at the docks by Juji Nakada, to join him in his work of evangelism. The challenge of presenting the gospel to a heathen nation did not daunt Cowman, who wrote in his diary, 'We expect great and mighty things to come to pass.'

In Japan, Cowman felt the power of 'the spiritual forces and the fiends of darkness' that seemed to be over the land. He was conscious of the battle about to take place, one that could exhaust the resources even of the best.

In Tokyo, the Cowmans rented a two-storey building in a street called Jimbo-cho, 'Street of God's Support', near the heart of the city. It was owned by a landlord who, on hearing their need, smiled and said, 'I have wished to rent my buildings to Christians as I have found them so reliable and prompt in paying their bills.'

There was enough space upstairs for the two missionaries, as well as rooms for students. Below was a good-sized room for a gospel hall for

Brother Nakada. Outside the hall they hung a sign in large characters:

Jesus Doctrine Mission Hall
Services Every Night
Everybody Welcome

Night after night, people crowded into the hall to hear Nakada preach, and many responded to his appeal. Within the first month almost 100 people came to the Lord, among them idol worshippers, drunkards and gamblers. The first was an educated man, searching for something new, who called in to enquire about the hall. He was given a New Testament; every evening he attended the services and was soon won to Christ.

## Telegraph Operator
Unable to speak the language, Cowman found it very frustrating. After one evening service there were not enough personal workers to deal with enquirers. Cowman was asked to speak with one young man who knew a little English. On learning of a God who loved him, the man believed. To Cowman's delight, he discovered the young man worked at the Central Telegraph Office – so the first one Cowman led to the Lord in Japan was a telegraph operator! The next evening the young man returned with two other operators, and before the end of the week seven of them had been converted. They formed a Telegraphers' Mission Band and began reaching out to their colleagues.

The converts were invited to attend a Bible School opened by the two evangelists, and a number of young men and women responded. They studied during the mornings, in the afternoon they held street meetings, and in the evenings attended the mission hall services. The aim of the school was not to produce scholars, but young men and women, steeped in the Bible, who could proclaim the gospel to all classes of people.

As Cowman watched Nakada at work, he began to realise the impossibility of evangelising the Orient by Western agencies alone. 'The task of the missionaries,' he wrote, 'is to train the national to pastor and evangelise his own people.'

It would have to be done by devoted Japanese, as only they could move the hearts of their own people. Further, he determined not to be seen as a leader, but rather to allow the Japanese Christians to come to the fore, so that the missionary could make himself unnecessary as quickly as possible. He also insisted that local churches should be entirely national – self-supporting, self-governing and self-propagating.

Every night, without exception, people came to the Lord, sometimes as many as 20 or more. The work grew, and the hall became so crowded that they began to pray for larger premises. A gift of $1,000 enabled them to purchase a splendid mission hall with enough space for the Bible school. Services continued every night for the next ten years, during which time 15,000 people found Christ.

With the work expanding, Cowman felt the need in 1902 for a fellow worker, and Ernest Kilbourne, the first man he led to the Lord, responded to the call. The two men were eminently suited to each other, and worked together in close harmony for 25 years.

It was that same year that a small missionary news periodical was started, called *Electric Messages* (later changed to the *OMS Standard*). From such a small beginning, a publishing department developed which sends out large quantities of missionary literature.

**Countryside**
With the mission hall and Bible school established in Tokyo, Cowman turned his thoughts to the millions of people beyond still untouched by the gospel. Before the end of his second year in Japan he began a series of countryside tours, which were to continue for most of the rest of his life.

Three Japanese evangelists and seven students accompanied him on the first tour. Again he found a great spiritual hunger among the people, many of them dissatisfied with the idol temples that dotted the hillsides, and the stone images and shrines that lined the road.

Services were held every day and evening, and about 1,000 people came to Christ in less than six weeks. 'I always knew there ought to be a God like that,' one woman remarked after hearing of Jesus for the first time. During the next 20 years no less than 160 interior stations were established, each one under the care of a national leader.

Cowman and Kilbourne determined that Bible school training was the quickest method of evangelising the country, and they should focus their attention on teaching Japanese nationals.

In 1903 they began to pray for the finances needed to build a large Bible Training Institute. A three acre plot of land was found on the outskirts of Tokyo. As the money came in, it was possible to build a large hall seating 2,000 (in native fashion), dormitories, lecture rooms and

## OMS Worldwide

OMS ministers on five continents: in Japan (1901), Korea (1907), India (1941), Colombia (1943), Brazil (1950), Taiwan (1950), Ecuador (1952), Hong Kong (1954), Haiti (1958), Indonesia (1971), Spain (1972), Philippines (1982), Mexico (1990), Hungary (1992), Russia (1993), Mozambique (1994). This worldwide outreach necessitated a name change, and in 1973 the former Oriental Missionary Society became known as OMS International.

OMS International works in partnership with more than 9,000 national pastors and lay-workers, and there are 550 missionaries on the field and in homeland ministries. There are around 3,000 established national churches, with a membership approaching 1,000,000 believers.

The Society operates Bible colleges and seminaries to train nationals for the ministry and for leadership. There are secondary and primary vocational schools on several fields, and radio stations in Haiti and Ecuador. In co-operation with national churches, compassionate ministries to the disadvantaged provide care for orphans, widows and delinquents. Men for Missions International (MFM) is the unique laymen's voice of OMS, and since its inception in 1954 has involved lay people in the cause of world missions. Over 12,000 men and women have participated in work and witness crusades to OMS fields around the world.

missionary bungalows. It became a centre for great conventions, which Cowman felt should be duplicated in every city in the Orient. From Japan, the society's work spread to other eastern lands.

In 1904 three Korean Christians presented themselves for training at the Bible school. The students stayed three years, and after they returned home it became possible for OMS to expand its work into Korea. Two English Christians, John and Emily Thomas, were sent to Seoul to take charge of the work. Despite opposition, a Bible Training Institute was founded, and young people who were called to preach opened up a work in the countryside, as in Japan.

## China

For some years Cowman had prayed for a number of oriental nations, one of which was China. Kilbourne also shared the same conviction, which was confirmed to them in 1907 when they paid a visit to Shanghai in order to study the working methods of other societies. One day, while in their separate rooms, both men experienced a distinct call to open a work in China. It was not until 1925, however, that an opportunity arose for the work to begin – one year after Cowman's death.

God had told him to 'Go into all the world', and yet despite his efforts 80% of Japan's population had still not received the gospel. Startled by the thought, in 1911 Cowman drew up a plan to distribute a Gospel to every home in Japan. The Great Village Campaign started with only five dollars in the mission treasury, but funds came in from the homelands. He bought millions of Scripture portions and teams of workers began the daunting task. It took four months to cover the first province, finally finishing the whole country in 1918.

During these years he continued with his evangelistic tours and kept up a voluminous correspondence with friends and fellow missionaries. In addition, he had the responsibility, with Kilbourne, for the churches and running the Bible schools.

The pace was now beginning to tell on Cowman, and though reluctant to admit defeat he was finally forced to return to the United States for a prolonged rest. He had a number of heart attacks and suffered six long years of painful illness before going to be with the Lord in September, 1924.

One national Christian wrote of him, 'We have lost our kind, loving shepherd, and the flock is bleating.' But though their leader was gone, the flock was not without shepherds, for he had left behind well-trained and Spirit-led men to carry on the work.

### MISSION STATEMENT OF OMS INTERNATIONAL

*Mission*
OMS International exists to promote missionary interest and outreach worldwide by deploying manpower and financial resources using a Biblical based and historically proven missiological strategy of emphasizing evangelism, church-planting, leadership training and partnership, resulting in transformed individuals, communities and nations.

*Vision*
OMS International envisions participating together with OMS-related national churches to marshall the combined worldwide resources to facilitate global inter-agency cooperation, communication and collaboration, to expand and accelerate world outreach for the cause of Christ in fulfilment of the Great Commission.

## 11. OPERATION MOBILISATION (1957)
### George Verwer (born 1938)

It was while a student at the Presbyterian College, Maryville, Tennessee, that George Verwer had a vision for world evangelism. Beginning with a gospel literature distribution in Mexico during his summer vacation in 1957, he next turned his sights towards Europe and the Middle East. Under the title Operation Mobilisation (OM), the work gradually developed to cover all five continents of the world. As a result, over 400 million pieces of literature have been given out and thousands of people brought into touch with the living God.

OM's aim is 'to go into all the world and preach the good news', a calling which has been increasingly characterised by the principle of 'globalization'. This term denotes something more than a mission operating internationally or in a multinational partnership. Rather, it involves operating trans-nationally, not tied to a single national base, but carrying out ministry across a variety of regions and cultures.

It also embraces the resourcing, governing, planning and organising of missions by involving the local church. Whereas international agencies cross national barriers, global organizations transcend them.

In practice, this means that OM teams are composed of members from different nationalities and backgrounds, supporting and ministering with national workers as equals. As these workers have crossed cultures to minister in other nations and in the OM ships, so the OM fellowship has become increasingly richer and more complex. Today, OM can claim to be one of the most thoroughly globalized evangelical missions.

### Roots

OM traces its roots back to the faith of a housewife from Ramsey, New Jersey. Dorothea Clapp prayed for 17 years for students at her local High School, that the Lord would save some of them and send them overseas as missionaries. She one day sent 14-year-old George Verwer a copy of John's Gospel, which George read regularly for three years until, in 1955 (at a Billy Graham rally in New York), he was 'born again'.

The day following his conversion, Verwer began a task that ever since has been the main thrust of his work. He invested a large portion of his money in Gospels to give to other students and to send to Africa. With a group of students he began to witness at the High School and around 200 young people came to the Lord.

Like Dorothea Clapp, Verwer appreciated the power of the written word, especially the Word of God. He also became increasingly aware there were millions of people in unevangelised parts of the world who had no access to the Scriptures. Despite the great advances made in translation and publication, he concluded that the biggest drawback was the problem of distribution. The most effective means of getting the Scriptures to the unsaved, he decided, was to give it into their hands.

When he left High School and entered Maryville College, he gathered a few students together for nights of prayer for world evangelism. He was disturbed by the fact that many people around the world did not have any portion of Scripture, which included Mexico, just south of the border.

One evening whilst praying in his room, Verwer suddenly got up from his knees and exclaimed, 'I've got it !' He had the idea that they should go down to Mexico, some 500 miles to the south, to distribute tracts during their summer vacation. Although aware that Mexico was a Catholic country where the government was hostile to the gospel, he felt sure this idea was from the Lord.

Still only 19 years old, he was commended to God by his home church. He set off for Mexico in an old truck filled with tracts and 10,000 Gospels of John in Spanish, accompanied by two college friends, Dale Rhoton and Walter Borchard. Their aim was to distribute the literature, and to learn to work together with missionaries and local pastors.

The following Christmas he returned to Mexico, and with an increasing number of other helpers made regular visits over the next two years. During that time, the young missionaries had the thrill of seeing many people won to Christ, national workers raised up, six Christian bookstores opened and weekly Christian radio broadcasts started (even though they had been forbidden by the government).

### Send The Light

In the autumn of 1958, now sure that God wanted him on the mission field, Verwer transferred to Moody Bible Institute, Chicago. As donations for the work started to come, it was felt necessary to put it on an official footing. Initially known as Send The Light, a committee was formed and his room became a temporary base.

The students who joined him in his expeditions sold their posses-

GEORGE VERWER

sions to buy literature and to support Mexican workers. Between campaigns, they held weekly nights of prayer for the Muslim and Communist worlds, at the same time as preparing for the next Mexico visit.

Their radical commitment inspired the President of the Emmaus Bible College, William MacDonald, to comment upon it in his book, *True Discipleship*. He stated that Christians have somehow concluded that the principles of discipleship in the New Testament were too extreme and impracticable for the age in which we live. But he had met a group of young believers 'who set out to demonstrate that the Saviour's terms of discipleship ... are the only terms which will ever result in the evangelization of the world.'

When Verwer graduated from Moody in 1960, he left the work in Mexico in the hands of others. With his wife, Drena – whom he met at Moody – he moved to Spain with two other believers, all of them in their early twenties. Amongst other countries, they had been praying for Spain, a land at that time virtually closed to missionary activity.

They gathered together a group of Spanish Christians to assist them in the task of evangelism. As well as distributing tracts, which offered either a Gospel or a Bible correspondence course, they mailed addresses taken from a telephone directory. The result was more than 20,000 requests for the free Gospel and correspondence course during the first two years.

## Communist World

Having prayed for the Communist world, in 1961 Verwer decided to take a break from the work in Spain in order to investigate the situation in the Soviet Union. Accompanied by a friend, he made the trip by car, concealing Gospels, simple printing equipment and paper in the door panels. The two men printed tracts and mailed them to addresses they took from a telephone directory.

But a margarine grease-mark on a Gospel brought about their downfall.

'Better flush that Gospel down the toilet,' Verwer's companion advised. 'No, no !' he objected. 'We don't want to waste the Word of God! Let's put it where someone will find it and read it.'

So it was discreetly – they thought – dropped out of the car. Ten miles further on they ran into a road block. The two men were arrested by the Secret Police and subjected to two days' interrogation. Their equipment and literature was confiscated, they were escorted to the Austrian border and expelled.

Haunted by his failure, after a few days Verwer went off alone into the mountains to spend a day in fasting and prayer, perched up a tree (one of his favourite places for contemplation). Recalling his experience in mobilising students to work in Mexico, he began to think in a new direction.

'We foreigners can make only a tiny dent in the great need. But what if the churches in Europe could be mobilised to reach their own lands? We could call it Operation Mobilisation.'

## Short-term

When he returned to Spain, he shared his vision with the Spanish believers, and, later, with some of the American veterans from Mexico. The idea of short-term missions was at that time virtually unknown. So it was, from 1962, hundreds of European and American young people began travelling the Continent and the Middle East on outreaches that lasted from two weeks to two years.

The next step was to move out from Spain to the larger towns of Western Europe. They prayed for 100 young workers who would be prepared to join them in literature distribution on a short-term basis over the summer months. Almost 200 from 25 different countries came to share in the work.

'Once these people become personally involved and see how God can use them,' Verwer maintained, 'they will want to continue on even after we have left them to go somewhere else.'

After a time of preparation in the mountains, the young people set out in small teams from Madrid for the different countries of the Continent. As more help was needed, the teams mobilised local churches to take part in the outreach. During the day, they distributed tracts and shared the gospel. In the evenings, they visited local churches to explain the plans God had given them for evangelism.

The following summer (1963), the aim was to involve 1,000 young people in visiting towns and villages in the Catholic lands of south-west Europe. Nearly 2,000 young people from 30 countries took part in the campaign. They worked in co-operation with 25 missionary societies and 400 local fellowships.

Around 80,000 towns and villages were visited and hundreds of people were converted to Christ. In France several new churches were planted. Clearly God was at work, and many churches and missions asked for a return visit.

The summer of 1964 was devoted to follow-up work, planned under the guidance of local pastors and missionaries. Meanwhile, thousands of young people have continued to be recruited over the summer months to engage in evangelistic campaigns. The strategy of using large numbers of short-term workers was established, though Verwer and his team have a life-long commitment to world evangelism.

### Islam

Since its conception, OM has been characterised by extended times of prayer, and the Islamic world was their main target. Their first incursion into a Muslim land was in 1961, when two young people visited Turkey; others followed a year later. Although the constitution of the country guarantees religious freedom, some of the workers involved in evangelism were arrested.

The main outreach in Turkey has been longer-term work, carried out by those who learn the language and adapt to local customs and culture. Like other missionary societies, OM has discovered that in Muslim countries the best approach is that of the 'tent-maker', by which missionaries combine a secular job with that of sharing the gospel. In this kind of environment, an emphasis is placed on Bible correspondence courses, to which thousands of people have responded.

In 1962 a team travelled through the whole of North Africa, and the following year a couple started work in Iran. All this was in preparation for regular OM operations in the Middle East. Today the Muslim world is OM's number one priority, and leaders are looking to the Lord to send out more workers into this difficult area.

For several reasons, however, it was decided that Lebanon would be the best starting place for outreach in the Arab world and the Middle East, and the first teams set out in 1963. Since then, OM has sent many travelling teams into various parts of the Arab world with a message of hope.

Israel is also an OM field of operation. In addition to distributing tracts (a dangerous undertaking, especially in Jerusalem) OMers have also engaged in street theatre, and it is the intention to reach every home with a portion of Christian literature setting out the claims of Jesus as the promised Messiah. Though concentrating heavily on Tel Aviv and other central suburban areas, where 30% of the population lives, teams have also visited towns and villages on the so-called West Bank.

## India

From the early days, transporting team members and their supplies over what were sometimes large distances remained a constant problem. This was most evident when the first OM team set out for India (1963). Because of limited funds, the team travelled by battered trucks on a gruelling two month overland trip, over mountains and through barren wastelands.

As often the case, Verwer travelled with the initial outreach team, and made the uncomfortable journey to India on the back of a truck. As he jolted up and down he reflected on the problem of transport, and thought there must be a better way to combine travelling with the ministry of distributing literature. It was on this journey that the idea of using a ship started to form in his mind, a thought later confirmed by other OMers who had made the same suggestion.

On New Year's Day, 1964, the OM team from Europe entered India and headed for Delhi. After a time of cvangelising, they moved east to Uttar Pradesh, and by the end of the year were joined by another team. They opened an office in Bombay, from where a number of local Christians were recruited to join in an outreach to some of the northern

## THE 10/40 WINDOW

This is the name given to a region of the world extending from West Africa to East Asia, from ten degrees north to forty degrees north of the equator. The 'Window' encompasses the majority of the world's Muslims, Hindus and Buddhists, and where some 82% of the world's poorest people live. It is sometimes called 'The Resistant Belt', for it is here that the greatest resistance comes to the gospel.

While it constitutes only one-third of the earth's land area, nearly four billion people – two-thirds of the world's population – reside within the Window. These people, whose knowledge of the gospel is either minimal or even non-existent, have no valid opportunity to respond to it. There are 61 countries within this region, which includes 37 of the world's least evangelised countries and contains three of the world's dominant religious blocs.

Writing in The 10/40 Window : Getting to the Core of the Core, Luis Bush, International Director of the AD 2000 & Beyond Movement, comments: 'If we take seriously the mandate to preach the gospel to every person, to make disciples of all peoples, and to be Christ's witnesses to the uttermost part of the earth, we must recognise the priority of concentrating our efforts on The 10/40 Window. No other area is so blatantly in need of the truth that salvation is only in Jesus.'

The aim of the AD 2000 & Beyond Movement is 'a church for every people and the gospel for every person by the year 2,000'.

states. As it was important for women to evangelise women, a women's team had to be formed and special training provided.

Beginning in Madras, south India, the second team co-operated with Bakht Singh in an extensive church-planting programme. Then they worked their way north through Bangalore, Hyderabad and Pune to Bombay. These campaigns entailed the use of a great number of pieces of literature in at least ten languages, and educational books were for the first time used to promote the distribution.

As more states were evangelised and local Christians joined the outreach, it became necessary to set up a locally-based training course. The courses are both biblical and practical. Ten weeks are spent evangelising in towns and villages, followed by ten weeks classroom teaching, which covers topics such as Islam and Hinduism.

### Logos

The idea of a ship at first seemed crazy, and one respected Christian leader counselled Verwer, 'Forget the idea ! ...Stick to the ministry God has given you. What do you know about running a ship? Nothing!'

As the OM leaders began to

pray about the idea, it seemed as though it was of God. Yet it was five years before a suitable vessel was found and the dream became a reality. In 1970 God provided both the money and the qualified seamen, and a ship was bought. Renamed *Logos* (Greek for 'word'), after visiting several European ports she set sail the following year for India.

Having a ship, of course, offered tremendous advantages. Apart from the saving on costs in transporting workers, the ship allowed space for training and conference facilities, for storing materials and for carrying vehicles to be used on shore. Equally exciting was the book exhibition on board which attracted thousands of visitors, and often provided a legitimate reason for the ship's acceptance by non-Christian governments.

In the next 17 years the ship visited 258 ports in 103 countries around the world, distributing Christian books and literature, and using every possible opportunity for evangelism.

The success of the venture led to the purchase of a second vessel in 1977. Much bigger and older than *Logos*, *Doulos* (meaning 'slave' or 'servant') set off the following year on a tour of Latin American countries, carrying a massive book exhibition with 4,000 titles. Like its sister ship, it has facilities for holding training programmes and conferences, and serves as a base for evangelistic campaigns.

**God is So Good**

Tragedy occurred just before midnight on 4 January 1988, when the *MV Logos* ran aground off the coast of South America, driven onto rocks by fierce currents. The crew and staff reacted magnificently, and the ship was abandoned without loss of life or injury. As the lifeboats pulled away, some began to pray, and then spontaneously everyone started to sing, 'God is so good'. For as one of the survivors wrote, 'God had been so faithful, he made sure that every life was saved against impossible odds.'

The response from OM supporters around the world was incredible, and by the autumn of that same year enough money had come in to buy a passenger ferry, renamed *Logos II*. In 1990 the new vessel set off on its maiden voyage for Spain, and North and West Africa.

Since the OM ship ministry started in 1970, around 25 million visitors have been welcomed on board the ships in over 365 different ports and 125 countries around the world.

Today, OM's role in the body of Christ is to motivate, develop and equip people for world evangelism, and to strengthen and help plant churches, especially among the unreached in the Middle East, South and Central Asia, and Europe.

George Verwer sees Christianity as a 'revolution of love', a message expressed by OM not only through evangelism, but also in its extensive relief programme.

Driven by the urgency to make known the love of God, OM ministers in all five continents under the conviction that the only revolution that can change the world is that brought about by the Lord Jesus Christ.

## MISSION STATEMENT OF OPERATION MOBILISATION

Bringing hope to the peoples of the world

Operation Mobilisation's role in the body of Christ is to motivate, develop and equip people for world evangelisation, and to strengthen and help plant churches, especially among the unreached in the Middle East, South and Central Asia and Europe.

OUR VISION
    *Focusing on the unreached
    *Partnering with churches
    *Caring for our members
    *Training and equipping world Christians
    *Mobilising the next generation
    *Globalising our ministry
    *Strengthening our organisation

OUR CORE VALUES
    *Knowing and glorifying God
    *Living in submission to God's Word
    *Being people of grace and integrity
    *Serving sacrificially
    *Loving and valuing people
    *Evangelising the world
    *Reflecting the diversity of the body of Christ
    *Global intercession
    *Esteeming the church

## 14. QUA IBOE FELLOWSHIP (1887)
### Samuel Bill (1863-1942)

The Qua Iboe Church is a thriving, indigenous African Church in south-east Nigeria. It owes its origin to the faith and vision of Ulsterman Samuel Bill who, as the result of an unusual letter, responded to God's call to Africa.

Humanly speaking, Bill was ill-equipped for the task. Without money or the backing of a mission, he was alone and facing life among an unknown tribe in a vast area of dense forests, swamps and treacherous rivers. He relied entirely on the prayers of a small group of friends at the Island Street Mission Hall, Belfast. But he was quietly confident that this was where the Lord wanted him, and from the beginning God's seal was upon his decision.

In preparation for missionary service in Africa, Bill spent two years in training at Harley College, in the East End of London. The principal, Dr Grattan Guinness, was Britain's leading evangelist of the day, a Bible expositor and missionary statesman. Guinness' chief missionary concern was Africa, a vision caught both by his family and his students.

After nearly two years at Harley and the end of his training in sight, Bill still had no indication where God wanted him to be. It would have been a simple matter to join the students going out from Harley with the Congo and Balolo Mission, but he did not feel in himself that this was right.

It was meal-time one day in June 1887, and the principal rose to speak to his students seated around the dining room table. Guinness was accustomed to receiving correspondence from around the world, but he had never before received a letter like the one he held in his hand.

'Gentlemen,' he began, 'I have here a remarkable letter. It has been written by a trader at the request of some West African chiefs. They want a white man to live among their people and teach them about God. The Scottish Mission at Calabar has lost so many workers, through illness and death, that it is unable to answer this call, and it has been sent to me.'

Throwing the envelope down onto the table, he looked around at the young men gathered with him. 'It's a fever-ridden climate,' he went on, 'and cannibalism is not unknown in the area. You would have no mission behind you, but will one of you young men offer to go?'

As the students dispersed, Bill quietly considered whether this was the call he had been looking for. Since hearing the missionary John

McKitterick speak about the Congo at his home church, his imagination had been fired; he realised that God wanted him to be a missionary.

## Guidance

Now, here was the guidance for which he had been praying, and he presented himself to Dr Guinness ready to be that volunteer. A cheque for £100 from a lady he never knew, to cover his passage to West Africa, was the final confirmation. Dr and Mrs Guinness helped Bill prepare for his mission; they were unable to accept any long-term commitment, but watched over his affairs for the first year.

Bill set sail from Liverpool in September, while his fiancée, Grace Kerr, enrolled as a student at Doric Lodge, the women's section of Harley College. It was to be nearly three years before they were to see each other again.

Three weeks later Bill landed at Calabar, south-east Nigeria. It was to this part of Nigeria that the intrepid Mary Slessor had come, some ten years earlier, working among the Efiks some miles to the north. The name of Mary Slessor was already known to him, as her exploits were becoming known in missionary circles in Britain.

Early in the New Year Bill made the short journey up the Qua Iboe River to the village of Ibuno, where the people were expecting him. The villagers provided him with a house, and an African trader's wife ensured he had enough to eat and his clothes were washed.

Although he soon began to make friends with the people, he spent the first year as the only white man in the area. Often, he desired the fellowship of another believer, someone to come alongside and help him.

Bill had not been long in the village before he discovered that the Ibunos' request for a missionary was not motivated by a desire to hear the gospel. Rather it was a matter of protection from other tribes. 'If a white man lived among us, our enemies might fear to attack,' one chief had argued. Another, with more insight, added, 'Our children might learn book and become better traders.'

The Ibunos were a gentle, peaceable people and expert fishermen; they traded as middlemen between the Europeans at Calabar and the tribes of the interior. Sadly, they were introduced to the evils of rum and gin, and drink became their greatest curse. By religion they were animists, and though they had a vague idea of a Supreme Being, their lives were governed by a belief in spirits which needed to be propitiated by frequent offerings.

Even though Bill was not a trader the people received him warmly and were ready to listen to what he had to say. One of the boys acted as his interpreter, and armed with a small manual of Bible texts in English and the local Efik language, Bill tried to explain the gospel to the tribespeople as best he could. Gradually, his command of the native language improved and his scope for evangelism widened.

From the beginning he held a day school for a few boys on the verandah of his house. Lessons were very irregular, however, partly because the boys were often absent, needed to help on the farms; but also because Bill suffered from weekly bouts of fever, which left him weak.

It was not long before Bill felt the need for a separate building to serve as a church and school, and he was gladly assisted by the villagers. When he started Sunday services, around 100 people were attracted to the meetings each week. He taught them some hymns – the young people always loved to sing – and he told them Bible stories. Soon there was a core of regular attenders who were anxious to learn more.

### HARLEY COLLEGE & AFRICA

The Grattan Guinness family and Harley College made an important contribution to missionary causes, especially in Africa. Under the aegis of the college, the Livingstone Inland Mission was set up in 1878. A party of Harley students went out to explore the Congo River, with a view to establishing mission stations. The students were aware of the dangers they faced, and despite one death, other students pledged themselves to continue the work.

Dr Grattan Guinness was involved in the foundation of the North Africa Mission (1881 – now called Arab World Ministries). In 1889 the Congo and Balolo Mission (later to become the Regions Beyond Missionary Union) was set up by Harry Guinness, son of the principal, to evangelise the savage Balolo people of the upper Congo. John McKitterick and a team of six Harley students left for the Congo. It took three years to establish the first four stations.

Lucy Guinness married a former Harley student, Karl Kumm, who founded the Sudan United Mission (now Action Partners). Geraldine Guinness, however, sailed for China, where she met – and married – her childhood friend, Dr Howard Taylor, son of the CIM founder Hudson Taylor.

During the first year Bill wrote many letters to his boyhood friend, Archie Bailie, who was spending a year in missionary training at Harley. To his delight, Bailie came out to Ibuno in 1888, to help in the work. At last, there was someone to pray with and to share the burden of the gospel.

Day after day the two men poured out their prayer to God on behalf of the people: 'O Lord, call out from among this people a church of 200 believers, for the glory of thy name. Break the powers of darkness that bind them, and open their eyes to see Jesus as their Saviour.'

Before long people began to respond to the gospel. One of the first Ibunos to come to faith and be baptised was David Ekong, son of a principal chief and grandson of the High Priest at Ekong. Then there was Etia, formerly the wife of a chief; accused of witchcraft, she had survived the ordeal of trial by poison.

Chief Egbo-Egbo, a regular attender at the church services, was the third convert. He informed Bill quite simply, 'I want to follow God.' After four days' instruction from the young David Ekong, the chief came to faith. This event was later to have significance, for David matured to become a devoted follower of Christ and the church's first evangelist and pastor.

There were other signs of encouragement, too. In November 1889 the two men set out to explore the possibilities of reaching other members of the tribe. As at Ibuno, they met with 'dark superstition, polygamy and slavery'. The effects of rum and gin, supplied by English traders, was even worse than at Ibuno. 'It is killing many of our people,' bemoaned one man. Yet in village after village the missionaries were well-received, and often the chiefs confessed they would like to hear more of the gospel.

In the following month, December, five new believers were baptised in the river, publicly witnessing to their faith in Christ. Six weeks later, they celebrated the Lord's Supper for the first time. There were around 100 people in the congregation, and they were 'most orderly and attentive'. Eleven believers sat down at table to partake of the symbols of the Lord's death, and Archie Bailie spoke from Isaiah 53. 'It was a blessed time,' observed Bill.

### A Wife

It was usually considered wise not to spend more than two years on the mission field before returning home on furlough. In June 1890, accompanied by David Ekong, Bill returned to Belfast to marry Grace. But there was more to do than taking a wife.

Much time was spent in Belfast, Dublin, Scotland and London, meeting with interested friends and raising further support. Already a few loyal friends from the Island Street Mission Hall, Belfast, had banded together to form a Qua Iboe Missionary Association, to encour-

# CALABAR REGION

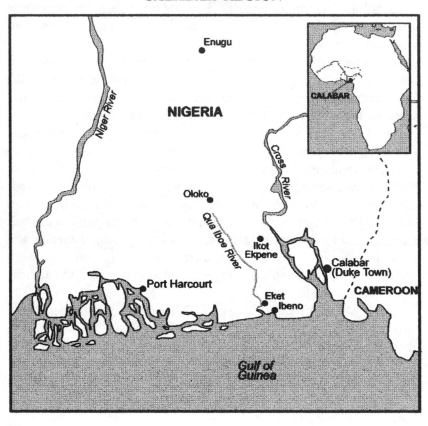

age prayer and giving for the two missionaries. Now, a Missionary Council was set up to place the work on an official basis and to provide a point of reference, with the official title of the Qua Iboe Mission.

When time came to return to Ibuno, he took with him a wife, David Ekong, an artesian pump, a second-hand organ, some surgical instruments and medical books, plus a bell with which to summon the people to worship.

From the beginning, Bill followed the principle of 'committing the truth to faithful men, who would be able to teach others'. David Ekong was the first Ibuno to put this into practice, when along with a group of other young men he began to preach in public and hold meetings in the courtyards of some of the chiefs. Many of these men were converted, and they joined Bill's class for inquirers where they were given a firm grounding in the Scriptures.

Despite persecution from their own people, the lives of the Ibuno Christians were marked by prayer and love. Strong links were forged between the missionaries and the believers. The women of the church were very practical in their witness. They visited the sick, and administered a poor fund for the relief of widows and others suffering hardship.

**Growth**
As the first church building at Ibuno was crumbling under the attacks of ants, the Christians wanted to provide a more permanent structure. Money and materials were expensive, but the gift of a sawmill from the Mission Council made the project possible. A plot of land was given them a mile up river, formerly the site of the principle idol house. It was here that the members erected a new church, capable of seating 500 people.

The early years of the mission were marked by steady growth, as the faith of the first Ibuno believers matured. They learned to meet for prayer, particularly at times of crisis, and to witness. However, as Bill's aim was to build an indigenous church which would take responsibility for its own affairs, it soon became necessary to appoint elders.

Eight men were chosen to oversee the Ibuno church, including Chief Egbo and three other men already in full-time service. They were inducted before a congregation of 300 members, around half of whom had been admitted that year. Before long, David Ekong began to assume his role as pastor, and preached virtually every Sunday. Both Bill and his wife always found his ministry inspiring.

In time, more workers – Bill rarely used the term missionary – were called, and joined with the Ibuno Christians in planting new churches in the interior. Abasi Mfon, for example, founded a church at Okorotip in 1899, which by 1920 numbered over 200 baptised members.

The provision of a power-driven boat by the Mission Council made travelling easier and safer, and both workers and heavy loads could be transported to outlying areas. When they were given a printing press, they were able to produce primers, Bibles and other reading materials.

By the turn of the century, the whole region seemed to be opening up to the gospel, and there was an obvious need for more missionaries. But Bill was reluctant to make widespread appeals, dreading the recruitment of 'misfits'. 'I leave the matter in God's hands,' he wrote. Within a short space of time, the right man – a teacher from Londonderry – came forward to join the team.

### Cost
The advancing years were never without their hardships and sufferings. Although the work continued to grow, it took its toll. Missionaries went down with the fever and in some cases were forced to return home, while a number of church leaders died (life expectancy for men in those days was only 45 years).

Alongside the work of evangelism, there were many practical

SAMUEL AND GRACE BILL WITH JACK AND EMMA

expressions of the gospel. In addition to the day school, an Industrial Branch was set up to train young men to earn a living. Medical care formed an essential element of the ministry, and to supplement the work of the local dispensaries already providing for the villagers, a hospital was opened at Etinan in 1928. Five years later, the work was expanded to include a leprosy settlement. No doubt the pressures of the work, bringing up a family and frequent illnesses took their toll on both Sam and Grace Bill. But they were great survivors, and both of them reached a good age.

In 1984 the name of the Qua Iboe Mission was changed to Fellowship in order to express its partnership with the Church in missionary activity.

With around 1,100 congregations and nearly 150,000 members, the Qua Iboe Church now has its own theological colleges and numerous schools. Its missionary programme has expanded, and the Fellowship works alongside Action Partners in Ghana and Ichad and with WEC International in Burkino Faso.

But whereas in 1887 the battle was against idol worship and secret societies, the threat today comes from a militant Islam, which is seeking to gain full control of Nigeria.

## AIMS OF QUA IBOE FELLOWSHIP

The aim of the Mission from the onset has been to preach the gospel of Christ, to disciple new believers and to establish self-governing, self-propagating churches dependant on God according to the biblical pattern. It is now in reality a large indigenous Nigerian church, totally responsible for its own affairs, with approximately one thousand congregations.

In pursuing its objective The QIF works in partnership with the Qua Iboe Church in Nigeria and with the local church to which missionaries are seconded. Expatriate workers sent out by the Fellowship become members of the indigenous Church in the country where they work and are expected to integrate fully into its life and witness and serve under its leaders. In recent years the Home Council, following the aims of the founders and under the guidance of God's Spirit, has kept the vision of Mission very much to the fore in its thinking and future planning. It hopes within the near future to send out new workers with a clear call from God, to Burkina Faso and to Ghana in partnership with like-minded evangelical organisations.

## 15. SIM INTERNATIONAL (1893)
### Dr Rowland V Bingham (1872-1943)

The American movement for foreign missions was slower to build up than that in Britain, and for most of the 19th century followed the British lead. Although the Roman Catholics still considered North America as a mission field until after the Civil War, the major Protestant denominations in the USA had already begun to send out missionaries from the early part of the century. Even so, by the 1870s there were but a few hundred Americans on the mission field.

The scene changed dramatically within a short space of time, however, the result of several contributory factors. Though religious life in America was at a low ebb in the middle of the century, the 1858 awakening radically transformed the Church. There was a quickening of interest in mission work, further influenced by the preaching of D L Moody. He drew attention to the world's millions of 'Christless souls' and the comparative few Western Christians who were prepared to serve overseas.

An added stimulus was the formation of the Student Volunteer Movement (SVM), which followed an appeal by Moody in 1886. Through SVM hundreds of college students pledged to become a foreign missionary, 'if God permit'. By 1920 nearly 7,000 students had left for the mission field. The total number of American missionaries serving abroad had risen to around 900 by 1890, reaching more than 13,000 by 1925. This figure represented half the global total of Protestant missionaries.

It was in the 1890s that two North American interdenominational missions were founded: the Sudan Interior Mission headed by Rowland V Bingham (1893), and the Africa Inland Mission under Peter Scott (1895). Both were based on the 'faith principle', following the pattern of the British missionary J Hudson Taylor of CIM.

### Graveyard

Africa, the second largest continent, was for many years known as 'the whiteman's graveyard'. The average life expectancy for a missionary was only eight years. It prompted one missionary to write, 'God bids us first build a cemetery before we build a church or a dwelling house.' The first SIM missionaries fared even worse, for within 12 months two of the party of three men who landed in Nigeria had died, and those who followed later were continually threatened by fatal diseases.

The realisation that there were some 60 to 90 million people in Central Sudan without Christ – or even a missionary – was a startling discovery to British-born Rowland Bingham, and he determined to make every effort to reach them with the gospel. In the spring of 1893 he teamed up with two other young men, Walter Gowans and Tom Kent, who had a similar vision.

Bingham had received a call to overseas mission after listening to that great man of God, Adoniram Judson of Burma. His focus on the Sudan, however, was the result of a meeting with the mother of Walter Gowans of Toronto, who aroused his concern for that vast expanse of territory. Mrs Gowans told him that her son was at that moment in England endeavouring to find a society that would support his hope of reaching the Sudan.

En route to join Gowans, Bingham met Tom Kent in New York and he became the third man of the team. They discovered that recent efforts to reach Central Sudan had failed: the Christian and Mission Alliance (founded 1881) had abandoned an attempt, while two CMS missionaries had died close to the border. Unable to find a society to support their cause, the three men decided to press on. Without the backing of any church or society, and with only $150 to cover their needs in Nigeria, they set sail from Liverpool in November 1893.

**Darkness**

For several years the picture was one of 'darkness, barrenness and death', when it seemed as though the work of the new mission would collapse. But Gowans, the leader of the three, contended that no field could remain closed before a praying Church, obedient missionaries and the Lord's command to 'Go into all the world'. There were difficulties, he conceded, but the door was not closed.

Sudan at that time was a vast area of land south of the Sahara desert, stretching across Africa for nearly 3,000 miles. The northern half of the territory was inhabited by Muslims who were known for their cruel treatment of Christians, while pagan tribes, who practised cannibalism, were established in the south.

The three men chose to approach the Sudan through the western gateway of Nigeria, a British possession, and landed at the capital,

Lagos. They made contact with missionaries from three societies already established along the coast, and attempts were made to dissuade them from venturing into the interior. Only ten days previously, of a party of six missionaries who had set out from Lagos four had died from fever or other diseases.

The Superintendent of the Methodist Mission in Lagos warned them, 'Young men, you will never see the Sudan; your children will never see the Sudan; your grandchildren may.' But the three young men went ahead with their plans.

It was decided that Bingham, who was suffering from malaria, should stay on the coast to organise supplies, while the other two attempted to reach the town of Kano. But Bingham's condition worsened; his case was pronounced 'hopeless' and his two companions informed that he would not survive the night. However, Bishop Hill of CMS gathered all the missionaries together and had a special time of prayer for the dying man. As they got up from their knees the bishop remarked, 'I believe that young man is going to be raised up !' And he was.

With native bearers to carry a range of items such as cotton goods, cloth, knives and trinkets with which to barter, Gowans and Kent left Bingham to recover and began their fatal journey. Following the course of the Niger River, it took them through the dense coastal forest and out into the long grass of the interior.

Although the two men managed to sail a considerable way up the river, their mission ended in disaster. While Kent returned to the coast for more supplies, Gowans was captured by a tribal king on a slave-trading expedition. Later released, he was seized with an illness and died in the village of Girku. When Kent returned he contracted malaria from which he too died.

The news of his two companions eventually filtered through to him, and Bingham decided to return home. With no mission board behind him to send out help, it was essential to arouse further interest in the work. All there was to show for their efforts was two graves.

## Missionary Council

Back home, Bingham undertook a period of medical training, followed by further Bible study. Rather than form a new society, he accepted a call to a Baptist church at Newburgh in the state of New York, with the understanding that his emphasis would be upon missionary work.

# THE SUDAN (1900)

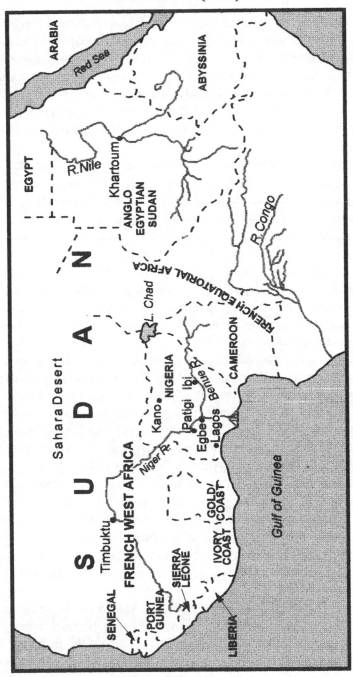

With a young bride at his side, Bingham toured churches in America and Canada, pleading the cause of the Sudanese people. As he started to arouse interest in the mission, the question of church affiliation was raised. His intention had been to begin a Baptist work in the Sudan, but a donation from a Presbyterian lady caused him to re-examine the basis of his mission. He concluded that denominational differences could cause division, and decided that the new mission should be interdenominational.

The greatest interest and response came in the city of Toronto where he was able to form a missionary council. As it happened, the moment was opportune, for a revival in his church proved the right time for him to make a break. With his wife he moved to Toronto and began preparations for his next expedition to the Sudan.

In 1900 Bingham set off again with two other young men, to try once more to establish a work in the Sudan. His reception from the missionaries in Lagos was unsympathetic, and the picture they painted of the situation discouraged his companions. Within three weeks of landing in Nigeria he went down with malaria again and at the government hospital was advised to return to Canada.

Discouraged by missionaries, the two men followed Bingham home on the next boat. In despair, the council in Toronto appeared ready to abandon the work; they were utterly disheartened. Only one member urged him to continue; he could 'see stars in the heavens when all others only saw clouds'. And, of course, there was Mrs Gowans, one of the greatest prayer-helpers, whose fervent prayer was that God would raise up a witness in the village where her son had died.

Despite everything, within six months four more young men had offered to accompany Bingham back to the Sudan. After some training in the Hausa language and missionary methods, the group left at the beginning of 1901 for a third attempt to enter the Sudan. The timing was providential, in that a British military expedition had recently been sent to crush the slave-raiding Muslim kings of Central Sudan, making the region much safer.

Under British protection, the party was able to sail 500 miles up the Niger River and open a station at the town of Patigi. Because river valleys were markedly unhealthy locations for a station, the buildings they erected were away from the river banks. Illness, however, forced two of the party to return home, though they were replaced by other volunteers.

During the next seven years there were only two deaths, including their first lady missionary; both were replaced by other workers. Despite setbacks, the young mission managed to gain a firm foothold at Patigi, teaching the gospel and ministering to the natives' needs.

## Beginning of Fruit

Of two new missionaries taken on, one was a mechanic who quickly proved his worth in a totally unexpected way. He set himself the task of learning the native language, Nupe, and surprisingly completed a dictionary and translated the four Gospels. When he went home on furlough the British and Foreign Bible Society printed these Scriptures which he was able to bring back with him. Realising the importance of the printed word, Bingham decided the mission should have its own printing press, which proved an immense asset to the whole mission field.

The other addition was a medical man, Dr Stirrett, a dedicated and resourceful worker. With a great burden for both Hausa people and Muslims, he served the mission staff and the tribespeople for over 40 years.

It was some while before a second station was opened, this time in response to an appeal for help from a lone Christian in the village of Egbe. A new missionary, Tommy Titcombe, was placed with the tribe. Without any other missionary to work with him, he learned the language and was soon able to start sharing the gospel with the people. A gifted evangelist, the gospel gripped the hearts of these people and men and women began to take a stand for Christ.

There were many converts, the first fruits of the harvest, and when Bingham visited the village in 1914 for Egbe's first Bible conference, he was able to participate in the baptism of over a hundred believers. It had taken over 20 years of prayer and dedication before the gospel produced tangible results.

The new Christians were keen to evangelise their neighbours, and from this village the gospel spread among the nearby Yagba people. It was at Egbe that the mission's first Bible college was founded, and it became the centre of a thriving church and outreach work, with more than 100 mission centres in the surrounding area.

## New Areas

The appointment of a Field Director gave Bingham, now officially the General Director, the freedom to visit missionaries and explore new areas. As the work expanded, every year was marked by the opening of

## RADIO ELWA

SIM's Radio ELWA (Eternal Love Winning Africa), established in 1954, was Africa's first missionary radio station. It penetrated regions hitherto unreached by missionaries, enabling the gospel to go ahead of them and prepare the hearts of millions of Africans to receive the Word of God.

Based in Liberia's capital, Monrovia, the two 50-kw transmitters broadcast the gospel in 40 languages across parts of North, West and Central Africa, an area that embraces millions of Muslims. Civil war in 1990, however, led to the destruction of the transmitters, studio, programme complex and power generating plant. Staff members returned 18 months later to clean and repair the few facilities left. A 250-watt transmitter was built and began broadcasting over a 100-mile radius.

God has used the tragedy to transform SIM radio into a more dynamic force for the gospel. The Mission has renewed its vision of decentralisation – broadcasting from many small sites rather than one central location, working closely with local churches to set up small stations and take advantage of national airwaves. SIM is also one of four missionary broadcasters, including Radio HCJB and FEBA Radio, who have joined together in project World by 2000. The aim is to make the gospel available by radio to the world's unreached 2.5 billion people by the end of the century.

Stan Bruning, SIM Radio Coordinator, has observed, 'When God closes one door – even temporarily – it is often his way of getting his people to look around at all of the other doors. Now that we see those new doors, we must make the commitment to go through them. That takes prayer and willing hearts.'

new stations and the translation of some portion of the Scripture. In some instances even the whole New Testament was translated into a previously unknown language.

One tribe Bingham wanted to reach, the Tangale people, were cannibals, yet with two companions he managed to enter their villages and return safely. Within two years, two young men went into the tribe, translated the Gospel of Matthew and planted a church. Many of the villagers, including two witches, were converted to Christ and their lives completely transformed.

## Ethiopia

Work in eastern Sudan was made possible by linking up in 1927 with the newly-formed Abyssinian Frontiers Mission. This enabled a group of nine missionaries to start work in Ethiopia where they received considerable support from Haile Selassie, later to become Emperor. When he came to the throne, his help made it possible to open more stations, including a leprosarium. Bingham was in frequent touch with the Emperor who, despite being in exile during the Italian occupation, remained a firm friend of the mission.

One of the mission's greatest

victories came in the early 1930s when, for the first time, SIM was able to begin work among the Muslims of northern Nigeria. Following the conquest of the Muslim emirs (or rulers) in that region, British government officials had for many years refused them permission to begin a missionary work in that area. Some of the British Residents (the local governors) even actively worked against the Mission's attempts to establish a work. After persistent representations to the government and to the International Council of Missions, however, permission was finally granted.

With the approval of the Muslim emirs, a work was started among leprosy sufferers, though no secret was made of the aim to present the Christian message. Later, Bingham was able to tour other provinces of northern Nigeria and the French territories, where he opened further stations.

Since Rowland Bingham's death in 1943 the mission has continued to expand its boundaries and has established stations in several other West African countries. Later, as a result of two mergers – with the Andes Evangelical Mission (1982) and the International Christian Fellowship (1989) – SIM now also operates in South America, India and Asia. Over 6,700 congregations have come into being through SIM ministry, all of them self-sustaining and self-governing.

SIM's aim is to evangelise the unsaved and to minister to man's needs. This involves planting churches and discipling believers, so that they may reach people in their own and neighbouring countries. Its ministries include hospitals and health care, agriculture, literacy work, linguistics and Scripture translations, and publishing. In 1954 SIM set up the first missionary radio station in Africa when Radio ELWA was opened in Liberia.

SIM seeks to extend its outreach even more and needs over 700 missionaries to help fulfil its call. 'Making disciples of all nations,' writes the General Director, Dr Ian Hay, 'is not an impossible task. Our part is to obey. God's Holy Spirit will do the rest.'

### MISSION STATEMENT OF SIM

The purpose of SIM is to glorify God by evangelising the unreached and ministering to human need, discipling believers into churches equipped to fulfil Christ's Commission.

## 16. SOUTH AMERICAN MISSION SOCIETY (1844)
### Captain Allen Gardiner (1794-1851)

Following Luther's revolt against the Roman Catholic Church in the 16th century, a movement began which set out to regain ground lost to the Protestants. Under Pope Paul III, the Council of Trent (1545-1563) met to draw up a response to the challenge of Protestantism. Known as the Counter-Reformation, it was spearheaded by the newly-formed Society of Jesus, and led to a revival of Catholic missionary zeal that enabled Rome to make new conquests.

As the Council met, Catholic missionaries were already making fresh gains in India, Asia and the New World, though with mixed results. The mission to the Far East ultimately failed and the missionaries had to withdraw. But in the Americas attempts met with a more lasting success.

### Latin America
Latin America was colonised by Spanish and Portuguese armies, who claimed sovereignty over vast areas of territory from Mexico to the Straits of Magellan. It began with the discoveries of Columbus, the Italian explorer, in 1492. He was sent by the Spanish monarch to find a route to India in order to open up the way for trade with the Indians. At the same time, he was directed 'to learn their disposition and the proper method of conveying the holy faith'.

The Spanish sent a military expedition to Mexico, where in a matter of two years it had easily subjected the Aztecs. Between 1524 and 1535 Spain conquered the Incas of Peru and Bolivia, and entered Argentina. Spanish sovereignty was gradually extended throughout many of the remaining territories of the continent, with the exception of Brazil and several areas on the north-east coast which were acquired by the British, French and Dutch.

As the Pope had delegated control for propagating the Faith to the Spanish and Portuguese crowns, their authority was absolute. As their armies conquered large tracts of the Americas, monks either accompanied their armies or followed after the soldiers, giving them a firm hold over the Indians. Large numbers of Indians were baptised into the Catholic Church, and before the end of the century Rome had gained an extensive foothold throughout South America.

## SOUTH AMERICA (SOUTHERN PART)

## Problems

Brazil was colonized by the Portuguese during the 1500s, when various contingents of Catholic missionaries worked among the aborigines. The Catholics were faced by two special problems in their new colony. One was the vastness of the country, the climate and the difficulties of the terrain, all of which made the missionaries' task immensely difficult.

The other was that whereas the Spanish had found advanced Indian civilizations in several centres, the Portuguese missions by contrast were largely among uncivilized tribes. In both cases, however, Catholic missionaries made rapid progress, and large numbers of Indians exchanged their primitive beliefs for the religion of their new masters.

Yet, despite the hundreds of missionaries dedicated to spreading the new religion, in some respects they achieved only a superficial success. Whilst Roman rituals and practices were observed, they were often mixed with elements of superstition.

Furthermore, Catholic Christianity was passive; it was not self-propagating, and growth was rather the result of missionary activity. Nor did it succeed in placing 'the imprint of Jesus' upon the life of the land, as in the days of the early Church.

It was not until the 1830s, after some of the countries had won their independence, that Protestant missionaries were able to gain an entrance into Catholic territories, first in Brazil and then in Chile. To safeguard their position, the Catholics took steps to prevent any heretical doctrines entering the conquered lands. Laws were enacted to exclude anyone newly-converted from Judaism or Islam from entering the colonies, nor were Protestants or others associated with unorthodox ideas allowed in.

## Adventurer for Christ

Although the Church of Rome remains a major force on the continent, there has been a rapid spread of evangelical and Pentecostal Christianity. One of the early Protestant missions to enter the continent was the South American Mission Society (SAMS), founded by Captain Allen Gardiner of Wallingford (Oxfordshire), a sailor and adventurer for Christ. Originally called the Patagonian Missionary Society, it was founded in 1844 to bring the gospel to the aboriginal Indians of southern Argentina.

Gardiner entered Naval College at Portsmouth at the age of 14, and two years later was posted to a man-of-war, *HMS Fortune*, under Captain Vansittart. He quickly adjusted to the strict discipline of life at sea, and acquitted himself well.

Although brought up in a Christian home where family prayers were a daily practice, it had not made any difference to his way of life. He joined in all the usual activities to which young naval officers were accustomed, and gave no evidence of spiritual life. But back in Portsmouth he had bought a Bible, which he kept hidden from his fellow officers. His thoughts about death and what lay beyond it had begun to disturb him, and he wanted to know some answers.

While in the Far East he was unexpectedly faced with a crisis, when he received a letter telling of his mother's death. Her letters had always been evidence of her love for him, and he was aware of her prayers for his well-being. Now she was gone, and his mind turned back to the conversations they had had concerning the need for a faith in Jesus Christ. The challenge came to him afresh, and it was while strolling through a temple in a Chinese port that life in Christ became a reality to him.

From this time on he began to live a transformed life. He became known as an officer who read his Bible, and took every opportunity to speak to others about things relating to the Christian life. The change was also noticeable in relation to his attitude towards other people, and he became increasingly aware of their need of the gospel.

Across the Pacific, while on shore leave in Peru and Chile, he saw the plight of nomadic Indians, who were being ruthlessly exploited by white men. Though the Jesuits had endeavoured to show a genuine concern for the Indians, his overwhelming impression was of the widespread influence of Rome, achieved by threat and oppression.

In contrast, when his ship called in at the Pacific island of Tahiti, he was impressed by the bearing of the natives there who had been converted to Christianity. It was the result of the work of a band of missionaries sent out by the London Missionary Society (now Council for World Mission) in 1796, who had faithfully preached the gospel. Here, the people were smiling and the atmosphere was quiet and calm. Their Christian faith had not only changed their lives, but it had brought about a great improvement in daily living.

The contrast between this Christian community on Tahiti and the effects of idolatry and superstition on the South American Indians was

ALLEN GARDINER

something he could not get out of his mind. Surely, he asked himself, something similar could be achieved among them as had been accomplished in Tahiti?

By the time his ship had reached home he had determined that if God opened the way, he would go as a missionary to the tribes in the South American interior. As far as he knew, no one else appeared to be making an effort to reach them and he felt compelled to take the gospel to them.

## Disappointment

Full of expectation, he made his way to the headquarters of the London Missionary Society and set his proposals before them, adding that he was willing to go at his own expense. To his surprise and disappointment, his offer was not accepted; the mission had enough on its hands already.

With this door closed, he wondered whether he should enter the Anglican ministry. But even this possible avenue of service led nowhere. In which case, he had to continue at sea until the way forward was made known.

He was given command of *HMS Clinker*, but his active naval career ended in 1826 when his tour of duty ended and there was no other post available. Now a happily married man with a young family, it seems he spent some years active on behalf of the Church Missionary Society, which he undertook with his brother-in-law, a canon of Winchester Cathedral.

But the death of his wife in 1834 was a great blow to him. As she lay dying, in her presence he re-dedicated himself to extending the kingdom of God in regions where Christ was not yet known.

Four months after her death, he reluctantly parted from his three children and set off on the first of his adventures in search of an opportunity to open up a new mission field. As the door to South America seemed closed, he chose to go to the most notorious tribe of South Africa – the Zulus.

His search for the feared Zulu chief, Dingarn, met with success, and he returned to England a national hero for having reached a peaceful agreement with the chieftain on behalf of the British government. A plan to send a missionary to the Zulus had to be abandoned, however, when fighting broke out among the tribes.

**Patagonia**
With this door closed, Gardiner turned his attention to his original scheme. Having married again, he set off for South America in 1837 with his new wife and children, travelling via South Africa. His intention was to search for a suitable opening to begin a gospel work among the tribes people. Landing at Rio de Janeiro (Brazil), he spent four months taking stock of the situation and making enquiries about possible openings.

From Rio he sailed to Buenos Aires (Argentina), where enquiries about the possibility of starting a work among the tribes drew a blank. The natives both feared and hated the white man, while the authorities would not encourage any attempt to improve the lot of their charges. From Argentina, Gardiner travelled across the Andes to Chile on the west coast. From there he made several exploratory expeditions into the interior of the continent's southern regions, again without success.

These failures at least taught him two lessons: that wherever he went, he needed to be able to speak the language, and that the Roman Catholic hierarchy continued to exert a hold over the people. The only way to gain a footing, he realised, was to go where neither government officials nor RC priests had extended their influence.

In 1840 he visited the Falkland Islands and then travelled to Patagonia, where at last there appeared to be some hope. Here he met Wissale, chief of the Hawanchis, who agreed to allow a missionary to settle in the tribe. After spending a year with them, Gardiner and his family returned to England to seek the necessary support.

Yet again he met with disappointment. Lack of funds prevented CMS or any other missionary society from coming to his assistance. When the Gardiner family settled in Brighton, however, he was able to present his case personally to several influential people. Now with support behind him, in 1844 a committee of eight men formed the Patagonian Mission, for the purpose of receiving money and sending out workers.

Funds were slow in coming in and there was only one man, Robert Hunt, a schoolmaster from Kendal, who volunteered for service. Gardiner wasted no time, and at his own expense sailed with Hunt for Patagonia in December. But their stay did not last long. Not only was there a Catholic presence in the area, but Wissale, the Hawanchi chief, turned out to be a man of changing moods, and made frequent and unreasonable demands upon the missionaries.

**Difficulties**

When the pair received news of an impending battle in the territory between Chile and Argentina, they felt it wiser to withdraw and return to England. Meanwhile, news of the exploits of these brave Englishmen had touched the public, and donations poured in for the missionary enterprise.

These journeys highlighted the difficulties Gardiner faced in seeking an entrance into South America. In addition to the obvious physical demands of travel and dangers from the natives, his attempts were continually thwarted by the presence of Roman priests and Catholic governments who opposed his Protestant mission.

Frustrated by these failures, the Brighton committee considered abandoning the idea. But not so Gardiner. While Hunt left the Mission to become ordained, Gardiner determined to carry on. He realised that he must concentrate his search for a region where the Catholics made no such restrictions and where there would be freedom of evangelism.

Between 1845 and 1848 Gardiner made further expeditions to South America. He explored the Gran Chaco, an area which straddled the borders of Chile, Bolivia, Paraguay and Argentina, for centuries under the domination of Spain. The British consul in Bolivia, however, advised against the plan, as the Catholic hold in the region was strong.

It was in 1848 that Gardiner finally decided on Tierra del Fuego, the southern-most tip of South America, as the right place to begin work. He also decided that his mission must operate from a ship. In this way the missionaries could withdraw from the land in time of danger. Two launches were built and enough supplies assembled to keep a group of seven men for six months while they established a mission.

There was no problem this time in finding enough volunteers:

Gardiner chose three Cornish fishermen, a waiter, a doctor, and one who had been a ship's carpenter on a previous trip. (This man volunteered because of his immense admiration for Captain Gardiner. 'It's like heaven on earth to be with him – he's such a man of prayer.') The party left Liverpool on 7 September 1850 and reached their destination in the December. Their provisions were unloaded onto the beach and the supply ship bade them farewell.

From the outset, nothing seemed to go well: the cask of gunpowder was nowhere to be found (which meant no fresh food until the supply ship returned), one of the launches was damaged beyond repair, and the natives made continued threats on their lives. And without a knowledge of the language, it was impossible to attempt any evangelism.

## Desperate

By the following June the Antarctic winter had set in. Despite rationing, supplies eventually began to run out and the men became weaker. Things looked desperate unless the supply ship could find them in time. But there was no ship available to carry new stores from the Falklands, a mere 400 miles away.

One by one death overtook the missionaries. Gardiner kept a journal – as he did on all his previous journeys – which gave a moving account of the men's last days. There was no note of regret or doubting God's guidance; in fact, his days were full of thankfulness to God.

His last entry, on 6 September 1851, was written in broken phrases, and declared '... the Almighty to sing the praises ... I neither hunger nor thirst .... though days without water.' With almost his last strength, he wrote letters to his wife, daughter and son.

Four months later, in January 1852, a search party found the missionaries' bodies on the beach. News did not reach England until the following April. *The Times* carried a blistering attack on the Patagonian Mission, deploring the (supposed) waste of lives and money on hordes of savages on the other side of the world.

In 1854, a schooner named the *Allen Gardiner* sailed from Bristol with a team of missionaries. Its aim was to implement the Missionary Memoranda Gardiner had written shortly before he died. A missionary base was set up on the Falkland Islands, and in 1859 the first missionary landed in Patagonia.

The work of Allen Gardiner was not in vain, for the gospel has been

## CHURCH GROWTH IN SOUTH AMERICA

In 1900 the population of South America was almost entirely Catholic, with fewer than half a million evangelical Christians. A deep spiritual awakening has been taking place, however, especially among the poor and lower middle classes, and there is now an estimated 51 million evangelical believers. These are mainly from Pentecostal and Baptist churches, though some have remained within the Catholic Church.

The onset of the charismatic movement and a renewed emphasis on Bible reading have been largely responsible for this dramatic change. Many have been brought to faith through the work of small home groups set up for Bible study and prayer, and women from the slums are being trained to share their faith with friends and neighbours.

One development over the past 30 years has been the attempt by the Church to deal with the problem of poverty. Some priests in the Catholic Church began to teach 'liberation theology', dealing with the question of social justice for the poor. It gave birth to a new type of church known as 'Base Community'. The movement started in the 1970s and spread rapidly, so that there are now over 120,000 of these 'house churches' in Brazil alone.

Protestant philosophy is to preach the gospel and bring people into a new life experience through Jesus; as individuals are renewed and families strengthened, a basis is provided for a new way of living. But practical help is also needed to help the poor overcome their immediate problems, so that they become self-reliant and self-sufficient. SAMS is one of a number of Christian missions responding to this need, and operates in Argentina, Brazil, Bolivia and Uruguay.

openly preached and churches planted in the countries where his toil was greatest and his sufferings the worst.

As he recorded in his diary shortly before his death, 'Great and marvellous are the loving kindnesses of my gracious God.'

In 1867 the Patagonian Mission took the new name of South American Missionary Society[1]. Since the last century the work has expanded, and now there are over 100 staff operating in seven South American countries, as well as in Spain and Portugal. Independent branches of SAMS exist now in Ireland, Canada, USA, Australia and New Zealand.

1. In 1996, the Society will change its name to emphasise its changing role in line with the above-mentioned objectives. It will be known as the South American Mission Society.

As one of the eleven mission agencies of the Church of England, its special task is to further the proclamation of the gospel in word and works, and to promote partnership between the churches of South America and the Iberian Peninsula and other churches in the Anglican Communion.

To do this, it seeks to respond positively to the requests it receives from the dioceses in South America in their mission within and beyond their own national boundaries.

The bishops of the Anglican Council of South America stated several years ago, 'We are determined that South America should not remain the neglected continent. Its doors are still open ... We must not fail in partnership together to present the living Christ to its peoples.'

The South American church will be figuring much more in world Christianity as we enter the Third Millennium.

## MISSION STATEMENT OF
## THE SOUTH AMERICAN MISSION SOCIETY

The South American Mission Society, a voluntary Anglican agency, exists to promote partnership in the proclamation of the gospel of the Lord Jesus Christ in Word and Works, between the churches in Latin America and the Iberian Peninsula, and other churches of the Anglican Communion. It is linked to the structures of the Church of England, whereby mutual sharing of prayer, information, resources and personnel is facilitated.

1. We seek to be an agent of multi-way mission.

2. We seek to shift our focus away from sending missionaries to supporting national mission.

3. We seek to represent the Church of South America to the Church in the UK.

4. We seek to take appropriate initiatives in partnership with other mission agencies.

## 17. TRANS WORLD RADIO (1952)
### Dr Paul Freed (born 1918)

The audio and video revolution of the 20th century has created an entirely new means of communicating the gospel. While great mountain ranges and dense tropical jungles have rendered many regions inaccessible to missionaries, and hostile governments have closed their borders, the powerful medium of radio has overcome all these barriers. Now, as a result of Christian radio programmes, the Word of God has reached regions previously closed to the message of salvation, and millions of listeners have heard the gospel for the first time.

Missionary radio was pioneered by Clarence Jones and Reuben Larson, who founded World Radio Missionary in 1931. In the late 1920s Jones was a producer for the first radio station opened in Chicago, when he had the vision of using radio for preaching the gospel. Looking around for somewhere to set up a radio station, the Lord led him to South America where he teamed up with Larson, then serving with the Christian and Missionary Alliance in Ecuador.

In Quito, high up in the Andes mountains, a 250-watt transmitter with an antenna wire was rigged up in a sheep shed. A Christmas programme was broadcast in Spanish to a total of just 13 receiving sets, and missionary radio was born. With the call sign HCJB – 'Heralding Christ Jesus' Blessings' – both local and international short wave ministries were established.

Today HCJB broadcasts the gospel in many major languages around the world, whilst World Radio's ministry has widened to include television, health care, literature and technical services.

Since then, the revolution in broadcasting has continued to develop and grow, and Christian broadcasting companies have been established in other parts of the world.

The most powerful Christian missionary radio broadcasting complex is Trans World Radio (TWR), which began broadcasting from Tangier, Morocco, in 1954. It was founded by Paul Freed, a 36-year-old Youth for Christ Director from North Carolina (USA) and the son of missionary parents.

## Example

From his boyhood days, Paul Freed had a real desire to win people to Christ. His enthusiasm was inspired by the prayers of his mother and the example of his father, who served with the Christian and Missionary Alliance. Based in the town of Dera'a in southern Syria, they also worked across the border among the peoples of what were then called Palestine and Transjordan. They were the only missionaries for some 300 villages, and kept open house for any Arab who cared to drop in.

When he was only eight years old, young Paul Freed had the joy of leading his ten-year-old Arab friend, Thani, to Christ. It was this experience that awakened in him a concern for the needs of other people. He was able to tell Thani, who was staying in their home, that there was only one who could forgive his sin, and that was Jesus. He explained how the Lord could come into his heart and give him a new one, as he had done for Paul.

The Arab boy responded, and a few days later confessed the happiness he had known since receiving Jesus. But he was concerned for his family, and wanted to tell them the good news. With his few belongings, Thani set off for his home village. As a result of his witness, the gospel gained an entrance into the village and a church was founded.

Often Paul accompanied his parents on missionary trips around the Arab villages. These occasions gave him the opportunity to learn Arabic customs and the language. When they stopped in a village, the natives were curious about the visitors and wanted to hear what they had to say. In the evening, they would gather together around a little fire, drinking black coffee and asking questions. This provided Paul's father the opportunity to speak to them of Jesus.

## Limitations

Watching his father at work, however, Paul began to realise the limitations of witnessing to just the ones and twos as they visited the remote villages. The question, 'What about all the others who have never had a chance?', often troubled his young mind.

Occasionally, some of the Arabs resented the gospel message. But those who did understand and respond, gave themselves to the Lord. It altered their whole pattern of living, so that they gave up lying, cheating, stealing and polygamy. It made such an impression on the youngster, that he never forgot it.

Whilst his evangelistic drive was to undergo a refining and maturing, it never swerved from the main course set during his childhood. His greatest heritage, he acknowledged, was the life of his parents which demonstrated the Lord Jesus Christ to him through the everyday evidences of their love.

Freed remained true to his youthful ambition to be a missionary. After studying in the United States at Wheaton College and then Nyack Missionary College, New York, he graduated from Columbia University with a Master's degree.

For a while he was pastor to a new church in North Carolina. During that time, after a brief courtship of seven weeks, he married Betty Jane Sewell, whose father was an outstanding Christian attorney. His stay at the church was short-lived, however, as he left the pastorate to join the recently-founded Youth For Christ movement (YFC) as its Director at Greensboro.

The founder of YFC, Torrey Johnson, influenced the young evangelist's thinking, and encouraged him always to move ahead in faith to accomplish the thing that appeared so inspired in a moment of clarity.

In 1948, Johnson prevailed upon Freed to attend an international YFC conference at Beatenberg, Switzerland. 'Paul, I believe God would have you go to Europe,' he urged. Although Freed had no thought of leaving the popular youth organization, the visit led him to a completely new avenue of service.

### Spain
Persuaded by two Spanish conference delegates to visit Spain en route for home, he finally relented. Their plea was for someone to help them bear the massive burden of reaching their 30 million countrymen with the gospel. As Freed travelled around the country, visiting groups of Christians and speaking in their churches, he became aware that here was a mission field waiting to hear the gospel.

Before he left, he knew without doubt that the Lord had linked his heart to Spain, and the idea of using radio to reach the nation increasingly impressed itself upon his mind. He had no money, and did not know what was the next step to take. But there was no doubt about his call.

He resigned his position with YFC and announced his availability as an evangelist. With no salary, he began living by faith, as he had seen his parents do when a child, and started to make preparations and arouse interest in the project. Then, believing he should move as indicated by

God, he felt it right to take a job, and to put aside what money he could for his future ministry. He set up in business designing and building trailers, and later, homes.

When he again felt the time right, he gave up his business and returned to Spain, to make further investigations for beginning his ministry. Considering where to begin, he was startled by a suggestion from his Spanish interpreter that it would be better to locate his radio station in Tangier, Morocco, rather than on the Spanish mainland.

The idea appeared a threat to his ministry, which was to Spanish people, and not to Arabs. So why should God want to move him to Africa? When, however, he heard that there were Spanish Christians in Tangier praying about a radio ministry to Spain, he began to understand. As it was, the move really was of the Lord. For he realised there was freedom to build in Tangier, where there might not necessarily be the same opportunity in Spain.

Before he returned home, Freed had acquired the promise at a knock-down price of a mission property – delightfully situated, overlooking the Straits of Gibraltar – that could be used as a radio station. Now all that was needed was the money. For two and a half months, Freed and his wife toured the States, stirring up interest in their radio project. On 11 February 1952 Freed founded the organisation that would one day be known as Trans World Radio.

**Groundwork**
In 1953 Freed returned to Tangier to lay the groundwork for the station. It was not long, however, before he had to admit that he did not have any expert knowledge of radio, or the technical know-how. He realised that his first step would be to get the necessary permit from the government, which he appreciated could take some time, before making a start on the station.

The answer to all his problems was met in one fell swoop, when an American in Tangier offered to construct the station for him. Using his own permit, his engineers would erect the transmitters and antennas, and he would then lease the whole package back to Freed. Such an arrangement enabled Freed to have all the technical problems dealt with by knowledgeable people.

So, within a relatively short space of time, Freed had the necessary permit, a building, plus an agreement for a 2.5 kilowatt transmitter, complete with an engineering crew. Now he needed the best possible man to be placed in charge of the station, and came to the conclusion that his father would be the right one. Although the elder Freed had just accepted a position as president of a Bible school in Canada, he felt this was God's call for him. At 61, he gave up his new-found honour to return to the mission field.

There was little in interest at this time among the Christians of Europe in Christian broadcasting. Freed put down the indifference to the fact that all radio in Europe was government-controlled, except Luxembourg and Monte Carlo. There were no sponsored religious programmes and no suggestion that an evangelist or Bible teacher could have access to broadcast time. One Christian leader told him, 'Radio just isn't our line. We understand they do that in America, but it's not just our way.'

As preparations for the new station went ahead, Freed hitchhiked around America in a further effort to encourage interest, but money was slow to come in. At one point, his father declared, 'If we don't get some real encouragement, some real help this week, I've made arrangements to give up the broadcasting business and return home.' The following day, a church with no knowledge of the predicament, volunteered to be responsible for the full support of Freed's parents. The work was back on course.

**Voice of Tangier**
The new radio station began broadcasting as 'The Voice of Tangier' in February 1954. The first programmes were devised for Spain by Spanish-speaking nationals. Soon, other language broadcasts were added – in German, Serbo-Croat and Romanian.

In 1956, two more powerful transmitters were set up in Tangier, enabling programmes to be beamed to almost every country in Europe, North Africa, the Middle East and beyond what was then the 'Iron Curtain'. By this time, the staff had grown from two to 26 workers, and the station was broadcasting in 24 languages.

Planning ahead, however, Freed grew restless about Tangier and started to think about finding a site on the continent of Europe. Because there was no state radio at Monte Carlo, Monaco, it seemed a possible alternative site.

For two years, exploratory talks took place with Radio Monte Carlo, though there were no decisions. But the situation changed dramatically

## FEBC

In December 1945 three young men – John Broger, Robert Bowman and William Roberts – pooled their resources, totalling $1,000, to form the Far East Broadcasting Company, for the purpose of broadcasting the gospel to the Orient.

Permission was received to establish a broadcasting station in the Philippines. (This was around the time the Philippines gained its independence from America.) Christian Radio City, as it became known, made its first broadcast at 6pm on 14 April 1948, from a 1,000-watt shortwave transmitter that reached the capital Manila and the surrounding area. Before long, letters began reaching the station, indicating that the gospel was being received.

Other transmitters were set up, enabling FEBC to reach listeners throughout the Philippines and much of the Far East: Communist China and Russia, Japan, Burma, India, Arabia and East Africa. The Communists attempted to 'jam' the broadcasts with a deafening high-pitched screech, though they were only 50% successful.

A more recent development has been FEBA Radio, which is the British arm of FEBC. Aimed initially at India, it began broadcasting from the Seychelles in 1970. The work expanded to take in other parts of south Asia and Arab countries of the Middle East. To date, broadcasts are made in over 40 languages.

Several auxiliary organizations have been formed, in Germany, Canada, New Zealand and other countries, to work as support agencies. They are all linked together under the banner of FEB Radio International, and co-operate with HCJB, TWR and ELWA to avoid duplication of effort and to maximise studios and transmitters worldwide.

when Morocco gained its independence from France. All radio in the country was to be nationalised by the end of the year 1959. As there was no gospel radio on the Continent, Freed expected God to do something. He prayed, 'Lord, if you're closing this door, show us what you have for us next.'

The delay proved to be God's timing. Although there was no tangible assurance of anything developing at Monte Carlo, the feeling was that God would open another broadcasting opportunity. Following fresh discussions with Radio Monte Carlo, an agreement was reached in April of that year to build a new station with a 100 kilowatt transmitter.

The cost involved was enormous: $500,000 to be paid over 12 months, with a first instalment of $83,000. Whilst thrilled at the possibility of the new location, Freed was overawed at the prospect of even raising the first instalment. Few people knew of the secret negotiations, and much time was given to prayer. But one of those who had learned of the contract – a shipping magnate from Norway – paid the first instalment. The way the rest of the money came in convinced all concerned that God's hand was upon this work, as the exact payments were made on time, at the very last moment.

## Volunteers

Broadcasting from Tangier ended 31 December 1959, though the building continued in use as a production studio. TWR Monte Carlo went on the air in October 1960. News of the new station stirred a number of people in the United States and Canada to offer themselves to TWR for missionary service. Volunteers needed to be highly-trained specialised workers, showing the highest spiritual standards and a genuine calling from God. The number of staff increased to meet the expanding workload, from 26 in Tangier to 35 in Monte Carlo.

DR PAUL E FREED

TWR Monte Carlo is on the top of Mount Agel, overlooking the Mediterranean, and housed in a building which Hitler had built for sending out Nazi propaganda. With a more powerful transmitter and a vastly superior system of antennas, it was possible to target eight specific areas for broadcasting, and to do it more effectively.

Europe was the main target area for TWR, and programmes were produced by indigenous staff in each of the interested countries, for transmission to their own language speakers. The Middle East was also high on their list of priorities, and though Freed had a burden for the Arabs, there was also a concern for Israel.

As the broadcasts went out, results began to show up immediately. During the first year, the station received 18,000 letters, with 800 requests for spiritual help. There were countless testimonies from listeners who had responded to the gospel and become Christians.

Many of the targeted countries agreed to take an interest in TWR's work, and some of them became responsible for setting up their own production units. Messages, church services and choirs were all recorded in their own country and the tapes sent to TWR for inclusion in their programmes.

The strain of these past years, when Freed had worked really hard – and he enjoyed hard work – resulted in a heart attack in 1961. Believing he was about to die, Freed asked his wife to bring in their children, so that he could say goodbye. In an oxygen tent for three days, then flat on his back for one whole month, the 42-year-old missionary began to improve.

It was a time of heart-searching and learning from God. He saw that God could carry on the work without him, and that he needed to yield control of his life and work to the Lord. He emerged a more tolerant man, aware of other people's capacities and gifts, and their decisions.

The time of enforced rest gave Freed the opportunity to think and pray about the future. Experts told him that in order to reach more people, another station was needed, and that the Caribbean area was the best location. Although he was still recuperating, he pressed ahead with the scheme.

## Bonaire

The outcome was a station on the island of Bonaire, in the Netherlands' Antilles Islands (off the coast of Venezuela), equipped with a 500,000 watt AM transmitter, the most powerful transmitter in the western hemisphere. By August 1964 the new station was on air, with responses coming in from Canada in the north, to Tierra del Fuego at the southernmost tip of South America.

TWR has continued to advance in its campaign to reach the world with the gospel. Further stations have opened, in Cyprus (1974), Swaziland (1974), Guam (1975), Sri Lanka (1978), Uruguay (1981), Albania (1992), Russia (1992), and Johannesburg (1994). In addition to ten primary transmission sites, TWR also broadcasts from ALAS (the first Christian radio satellite network in Latin America) to local AM and FM stations in Latin America's cities; and from ASTRA, Europe's most popular direct broadcast satellite.

TWR broadcasts gospel programming in more than 100 languages each week and has a worldwide staff of over 1,000 serving at its transmitting sites, studios, and offices in more than 30 countries.

From the international headquarters in the USA, Dr Freed wrote, 'We praise God that he is using superpower missionary radio to touch lives around the world, bringing many to Christ and helping them to grow spiritually.'

## MISSION STATEMENT OF TRANS WORLD RADIO

The purpose of Trans World Radio is to assist the Church to fulfil the command of Jesus Christ to make disciples of all peoples, and to do so by using and making available mass media to:

proclaim the gospel of salvation to as many people as possible.

instruct believers in Biblical doctrine and daily Christ-like living.

model our message through our corporate and cooperative relationships.

## 18. YOUTH WITH A MISSION (1960)
### Loren Cunningham (born 1935)

The revival of Pentecostal Christianity at the end of the 19th century brought a new awareness of the ways in which God makes his purposes known to his people. One form of revelation is that of visions, in which God speaks to individuals through supernaturally-given pictures.

Visions are not a new phenomenon. They have been known from Old Testament times when they were a recognised form of divine communication in which God revealed his prophetic will. The New Testament also confirms the same experience in the early Church. At crucial moments God spoke to both Peter and Paul in visions, while the apostle John wrote of a number of revelations given him by God while on the island of Patmos.

When Loren Cunningham was a 21-year-old American Bible College student, he had a similar experience in which God showed him something of his purposes for the future.

Cunningham was not unused to supernatural happenings, for he had been raised in a godly home. From his boyhood he had learned from his parents that God answers prayer, and that he reveals his will to his children in a variety of wonderful ways.

As a member of an Assemblies of God gospel singing quartet, Cunningham visited the Bahamas in 1956. It was here that he had a revelation from God that was ultimately to set the course of his life. Talking with some of the missionaries in Nassau, he heard of a group of young people who had visited the island, totally on their own, to do missionary work.

Impressed by their initiative, he retired one evening to pray in his bedroom with this thought on his mind. When he opened his Bible and asked God to speak to him, a map of the world appeared on the wall of his room. What followed was a sort of 'mental movie', for the picture was alive. In the picture he saw waves crashing onto the five continents until they covered all the nations. As he watched, the waves became young people of different races; they were witnessing to men and women in their homes and on street corners, and caring for people everywhere. Soon the scene was gone and the white wall was quite blank.

Not sure what to make of it, his first reaction was to ask, 'Was that really you, Lord?' He wondered what God was trying to say to him, and was his future to be in some way linked to the waves of young people? What an idea, he thought – young people going out as missionaries! If this strange picture really had come from God, there must be a way to harness youthful energies in the cause of the gospel.

One thing, he determined, was certain: he would tell no-one about the vision until he understood what it meant.

## Ordained

Cunningham completed his college course and became an ordained minister in the Assemblies of God Church. His first appointment was as a leader of youth activities in the Los Angeles area, the city where he had grown up. Though he enjoyed the work, he felt restless and had to admit that most of the activities he planned were empty – they held no challenge.

Remembering the strange vision he had had four years previously, he felt the time had come for him to do something. He began by taking a group of 106 of his young people to Hawaii on a missionary trip. It was here that he learned a vital lesson, that it was not possible to mix sightseeing with the single-minded purpose of evangelism.

As the vision of the waves continued to haunt him, he decided that the best way forward would be to scout out the possibilities overseas. To do this, he took a round-the-world tour; he sold his car, took leave of absence, and set out.

Believing that God was calling him to some kind of missionary service, he had the idea of sending out young people for a short period of mission straight after leaving high school. Preferably, they would be vocational volunteers who had a skill to offer. Drawn from all denominations, they would pay their own way and would be attached to a mission station where they could be properly supervised.

The trouble with the system as it stood, was that intending missionaries were expected to have years of schooling behind them before they were accepted as candidates. Cunningham wanted to channel the real enthusiasm he had met into mission work before they lost their zeal.

## Volunteers

Aided and encouraged by two friends, Bob and Lorraine Theetge, he decided to press ahead with the idea. In responding to God's vision, he was giving up the chance to be part of a multimillion dollar family business, but he knew that his calling was 'to the world'.

The three of them gave the new venture a nickname, 'Youth With a Mission' (YWAM). It was December 1960 when they set about looking for their first volunteers. Immediately, they had an enthusiastic response, more than they had expected.

At his Dad's suggestion, Cunningham took his ideas to the missionary committee of his denomination, who were not so sure about his plan. They pointed out the problems of sending inexperienced young people to countries with vastly different cultures, where there might be dangers from political unrest as well as from diseases.

But one committee member stood with him : 'If you were to send out vocational volunteers, to a compound where they could be properly supervised ... I'd stand on a chair and cheer you on!' This was the breakthrough he had wanted.

Within a short time, Cunningham learned of a need in Liberia, West Africa, for heavy equipment operators to build a road through the jungle to a leprosy colony. Two of Cunningham's volunteers exactly fitted the bill, and after consulting their pastors decided to accept the assignment. The first two YWAMers were on their way. The young men spent a year in West Africa, building a road and visiting villages to speak about 'the great God who made us all'.

By now Cunningham was a married man. His wife, Darlene Scratch of San Francisco, had had a call to be a missionary since the age of nine, but had neglected to fulfil it. After their honeymoon, Darlene realised she had to get her role as Loren's wife sorted out. She felt she did not just fit in to the YWAM scene.

She brought it before the Lord; when she read the story of David and Abigail, God spoke to her. 'That's my ministry,' she decided. 'I'm to be a servant – a footwasher.' Her crisis was resolved, and her husband recognised her as the first of many who would be called full-time to YWAM.

## Love in Action

Over the first two years YWAM sent out only 10 volunteers. In 1964, however, Cunningham was able to return to the Bahamas with a team of 146 young people for a two month evangelistic campaign. During their stay, the volunteers were excited to see so many people won to Christ, but their visit was marred by a violent hurricane which killed 138 of the inhabitants.

LOREN AND DARLENE CUNNINGHAM

Surveying the devastation, Cunningham began to realise that he was in danger of presenting only one aspect of the gospel. He saw that it was equally essential to put the love of God into action. The disaster changed his thinking, and the idea came to his mind of using a ship filled with volunteers willing to go where people needed help.

During the early years, YWAM was slow to attract full-time workers, though each summer Cunningham was able to send out hundreds of short-term volunteers. Following his resignation as an Assemblies of God minister, he was able to concentrate on organising the mission and build it up on an interdenominational basis.

On a visit to New Zealand to recruit volunteers for a YWAM outreach into the South Pacific, he felt led to spend some days in fasting and prayer. It proved a decisive time in his own walk with God, as well as a turning point in the work of the mission.

From then on, YWAM began to take off; more full-time workers volunteered, and other major developments soon followed. As the number of workers increased, the need for training facilities became more essential, and over the years YWAM developed its own training programme.

A School of Evangelism, located in a former rundown hotel near Lausanne, Switzerland, was founded in 1969, offering short-term courses. The emphasis was not on academic study but on increasing faith in God and learning of his character.

The first intake consisted of 36 young people from five nations, and at the end of their course they were sent out to various parts of the globe on an evangelistic mission. As a result, many of these students either joined the YWAM staff or stayed with other related missionary work.

## M/V Anastasis

It was some years before Cunningham began to reconsider the idea of a ship, but it seemed clearly the voice of God. The problems of such a project, he appreciated, would be enormous, though it would enable them to fulfil their twin aims of loving God and caring for people.

In 1973 a New Zealand ship came up for sale that seemed to offer exactly the kind of accommodation they required. Negotiations started well, but the Lord showed them that they had to let the plan die and wait until he resurrected it.

Some six years later another suitable ship came on

### MERCY SHIPS

Mercy Ships is the maritime arm of YWAM. It is a non-profit Christian relief agency taking medical care and development assistance to impoverished nations around the world. With a vision for a fleet of 10 ships, there are at present four relief vessels in operation which sail to areas of natural disaster or chronic need. Since 1978 Mercy Ships has provided needed surgeries, dental care, medical supplies, clothing, food, seeds, construction materials, development projects and a message of hope to over 60 port areas worldwide.

The four international crews represent over 30 nations, all major denominations and many professions. All crew members are volunteers and are responsible for raising their own financial support. This allows Mercy Ships' finances to go directly to helping the needy. Whereas most commercial shipping companies spend £200-£250 per crew member per day operating their vessels, Mercy Ships are able to run on less than £10 per crew member, which includes food, fuel, supplies and vessel maintenance.

*Anastasis* ('Resurrection') is the fleet's flagship and is the world's largest non-government hospital ship afloat. It contains three fully-equipped operating theatres, dental clinic, laboratory, and X-ray unit, while its hold has a cargo capacity of 1,500 tons. The *Island Mercy*, formerly called *The Good Samaritan,* is based in New Zealand and serves the South Pacific. *The Pacific Ruby*, donated to Mercy Ships in 1990, operates around the South Pacific islands, and *Caribbean Mercy* (bought in 1994) serves the Greater Caribbean Basin.

Writing of YWAM's ministry, Ronald Reagan, former President of the United States, stated, 'Your Organisation's founding and growth is an inspiring story of men and women with a vision of compassion and concern for others throughout the world...Thank you for all the good you do.'

the market and this time they were able to go ahead with its purchase. Named the *MV Anastasis* (Greek for 'resurrection') the vessel fulfils YWAM's threefold purpose, of evangelism, training and mercy ministry.

Its first mission of mercy was to the Boat People of Hong Kong, who had escaped from Vietnam. Using the ship as a base, a team of young people, each one paying their own way, was sent into one of the refugee camps to clean up the terrible mess no one else would do. They also opened a school and held Bible studies. As word of this work spread around, a stream of other volunteers were encouraged to join YWAM.

Now a second ship, *The Good Samaritan*, has been commissioned, to assist in bringing help to many of the world's poorer nations.

About this time another cherished project, to train Asian and Pacific islanders, became a reality. So far the gospel had mainly been communicated in a 'religious' context, but the secular world used different means of reaching the public: the arts, entertainment, family, education and so on.

In 1980 YWAM opened the Pacific and Asian Christian University (PACU) on the island of Hawaii, to teach these very skills. The students live together in the village lifestyle of Asia, with the emphasis on learning through doing. As well as biblical studies, the course includes paramedical training, science and technology geared to Third World needs.

YWAM has succeeded in capturing the imagination of thousands of young Christians. Each year over 220,000 of them from different denominations and nationalities are involved in short-term YWAM ministries. The number of full-time staff members has increased to around 9,000, making it the largest of all missionary societies.

Perhaps more than any other missionary organisation, YWAM has grown extremely fast, and the scope of its ministry is truly tremendous. Throughout the world, in desperate inner cities and developing countries, on university and college campuses, with refugees, drug addicts and orphans, these young people proclaim the gospel in both word and deed.

## MISSION STATEMENT OF YOUTH WITH A MISSION

Our goal is to help the Church equip and mobilise a generation of Christians, who can demonstrate the love of God to others wherever they are

# 2

# LITERATURE

# 19. BIBLE SOCIETY
## (1804)

One of the main objects in Protestant missionary work has been the distribution of the Scriptures. In recent centuries an increasing number of agencies have been set up to circulate the Word of God to whoever would receive a copy. As a result, peoples and tribes around the world have access to portions of the Bible, if not the whole book, signalling one of the most fruitful achievements of the modern missionary movement.

The oldest British society to engage in the distribution of Christian literature is the Anglican mission, the Society for the Promotion of Christian Knowledge (SPCK). Founded in 1689 by the Rev Thomas Bray, Rector of Sheldon (Warwickshire), to encourage the building of charity schools, the SPCK also distributed Bibles and tracts with the idea of promoting Christian knowledge.

A similar evangelical work, though on a non-sectarian basis, was done by the Religious Tract Society (RTS). Its aim was to bring cheap Christian literature, subsidised by subscriptions, to the general public.

Founded in London in 1799, it started with a series of pamphlets called Cheap Repository Tracts, written by Hannah More. Sold at one or one and a half pence each, they consisted of ballads, Sunday readings and stories, some in serial form, and were often illustrated by woodcuts. One of the Society's most popular tracts was called *The Dairyman's Daughter*, which sold over four million copies and was translated into 19 languages.

But there was a great need for Bibles as well, which were in short supply. The reason for this was partly one of expense, but it also reflected a greater demand for copies of the Scriptures. When, in 1802, the London Missionary Society decided to print a New Testament edition in French, they turned to the RTS for help. As others were also pressing their case for more Bibles, the society – which did not regard the distribution of Bibles as part of its work – was forced to consider what could be done.

In December 1802, the Rev Thomas Charles, a Methodist minister of Bala, North Wales, was invited to address a committee meeting of the Religious Tract Society. Charles had given up his church to travel throughout the Principality in order to encourage the formation of

Sunday Schools. In the course of his journeys he had discovered a serious lack of Bibles in Welsh.

As far back as 1787 he had received letters from clergymen asking for more Bibles. There had been 'great complaining among the poor for want of Bibles; and that there was none to be had for money'. The SPCK had endeavoured to help, but abandoned the idea for lack of funds. An edition finally published in 1799 was immediately taken up.

As the need was still pressing, Charles had come to London to plead with the RTS for the production of a cheap Welsh Bible. During the discussion that followed, Charles proposed a society devoted solely to the purpose of supplying Bibles in Welsh.

The Rev Joseph Hughes, secretary to the Society, aware of other requests for Bibles for missions in France and Italy, countered with the suggestion, 'If for Wales, why not also for the kingdom and the world?'

**Home and Abroad**

The idea of a separate society was greeted with enthusiasm, and they arranged a series of meetings to explore the possibilities. At the next, larger committee meeting, Joseph Hughes, formerly a professor at the Baptist College, Bristol, delivered a memorable paper on 'The Excellence of the Holy Scriptures: an Argument for their more general dispersion at Home and Abroad'. The thrust of his argument carried the day.

He envisaged a society that would survey the world's needs for the Scriptures, arouse interest both at home and overseas, collect funds in a businesslike manner, and 'demolish the invidious wall of partition, cut off the occasions of theological hostilities and invite Christians in general to associate for the more extensive propagation of their common faith'.

During these preliminary meetings two other important decisions were reached. One was to limit translations to those which avoided any criticism of publishing 'popish' or heretical texts. The other was that the new society should be composed of an equal number of Anglicans and Dissenters (i.e. Nonconformists), enabling the inclusion of laymen on the committee.

In order to further the cause, Hughes' paper was circulated to a number of men of distinguished reputation, including members of the Clapham Sect. This was a group of wealthy evangelical Anglicans, so-called because they lived around the village of Clapham, south west of

London, and worshipped at the parish church. Between 1785 and 1830 their influence on the affairs of Church and State was out of all proportion to their numbers, and they did much to revive the Church's witness.

The most influential member was William Wilberforce, MP for Yorkshire, who was a fervent supporter of a wide variety of Christian causes and a close friend of the Prime Minister, Pitt the Younger. Wilberforce was the first of this group to be approached. It was some little while before he agreed to support the project, until he realised how admirably the new society would complement the work of the Clapham Saints.

Other notable members included Lord Teignmouth, recently returned from India, Henry Thornton, a city banker, and Granville Sharp, the slave-trade abolitionist, all of whom gave themselves wholeheartedly to the cause. From then on, the Clapham Sect took the new society under its wing, and it was largely Wilberforce's persuasion that a formal decision was made by the RTS to form a Bible Society.

## Unity

An inaugural meeting was held in March 1804, when a gathering of 300 people of all denominations met at the London Tavern. Doctrinal differences were set aside in a way 'never exhibited before the public since Christians had begun to organise among each other the strife of separation'. The aim of the new society was simple: to encourage the wider circulation of the Holy Scriptures, without note or comment, at a price affordable to all.

Resolutions moved by the Rev John Owen, chaplain to the Bishop of London, were adopted with 'unanimous demonstrations of cordiality and joy', and £700 subscribed towards the work. A general committee was chosen that reflected the breadth of the Society's appeal, with 15 Anglicans, 15 Nonconformists and six 'foreigners' (i.e. from the continent of Europe). Lord Teignmouth was elected President, and six of the committee were members of the Clapham Sect, all of which reflected the strength of their interest in the work.

From the beginning, certain principles were laid down in order to make it clear that the British and Foreign Bible Society (to give its full title, suggested by Joseph Hughes) was not confined to any one party within the Church. The intention of the society was not to interpret Scripture or to propagate any doctrine about the Bible. Its concern was first to produce accurate and readable versions of the Bible in all languages, and then to make copies available to those who would read it. In this way, the Society would be 'the servant of the servants of God in supplying the indispensable weapon of their warfare'.

Steps were also taken to ensure that the society should not be identified with any particular church or party. For example, the society's public meetings were held on neutral ground at the London Tavern, and religious acts, such as prayers, hymns and sermons, were not allowed.

**Immediate Beginning**

The task of providing the Scriptures began immediately. In 1804 there were Bibles or portions of Scriptures in only some 70 languages, and the society began to print those editions that were needed. Within a year, 20,000 Welsh Bibles and 5,000 New Testaments had been made available for Wales. Moves were also made to produce Scriptures in Irish, Gaelic and Manx, while a new edition in French was planned for the Channel Islands. By 1806 consignments of the Spanish New Testament had reached Buenos Aires, and a year later the West Indies.

In its first 13 years the society printed over a million and a half books in 18 languages, of which all but five were non-European. From 1806, it contributed at least £1,000 a year to William Carey's translation work in India, a sum which was doubled from 1810. A further £10,000 was provided for Robert Morrison over a period of years as he worked on a translation of the Bible into Chinese.

The value of such work can be appreciated from a report by Carey that several Brahmins and others of high caste had 'obtained the knowledge of the truth, and met for worship on the Lord's Day, before they had any intercourse with the missionaries, simply by reading the Scriptures.'

The society's efforts were backed by a number of auxiliary societies which began to appear throughout Britain soon after 1804. These included London and Glasgow (1805), Birmingham and Dublin (1806), and Edinburgh and Norwich (1809). Further support came from the colonies, with auxiliaries in Canada (1807), Australia (1817) and New Zealand (1837).

In addition to raising funds, they worked to promote the circulation of the Scriptures in their own localities.

## BIBLE SOCIETIES IN SCOTLAND

From the Reformation onwards, the Scots had a strong traditional attachment to the Bible as a book which people should own, read and take to church. When the BFBS was founded in London, it received a warm welcome from Scottish Christians, who in 1806 provided 46 per cent of that Society's income.

The first permanent Bible Society in Scotland was formed in Edinburgh in 1809, followed a few days later by the Scottish Bible Society (SBS). Other societies sprang up around Scotland, some of which were auxiliaries to the BFBS while others operated separately. The main aim of the Bible Societies in Scotland was the supply of Scriptures to Ireland, England, the Highlands (the Gaelic-speaking areas) and overseas. The Edinburgh and Glasgow societies – each the focal point of smaller societies – distributed Scriptures among French, Danish and Dutch prisoners of war held in Scotland. The Edinburgh Society also regularly supported a number of missionary agencies, especially William Carey's Serampore Press in India.

Among the many ministers who supported the new societies was Thomas Chalmers of Kilmany, Fife, who regarded them as 'the most magnificent scheme that ever was instituted for bettering the moral condition of the species.' A large proportion of the contributions towards the societies' work came from ordinary people, through a system of regular penny a week donations.

## MISSION STATEMENT OF THE
## NATIONAL BIBLE SOCIETY OF SCOTLAND

The NBSS exists to promote the Bible as God's Word for today, and to make it available to all peoples in appropriate and relevant forms, so as to help churches fulfil their mission and to increase the number of people who own, use and share the Scriptures.

Other areas of the world were also covered by BFBS's agencies. At the inaugural meeting in 1804, the Rev Carl Steinkopf, minister of the German Lutheran Church in the Savoy, London, drew attention to the scarcity of Bibles in Europe. As a result, the first Society to be founded outside Britain was at Nuremberg, in Germany.

The St Petersburg (or Russian) Bible Society was started (in 1813) at the suggestion of the Minister for Foreign Creeds, Prince Galitzin, to Tsar Alexander 1, who happily agreed. It attracted the support of clergy both of the Greek and Roman Churches, and was soon established across the whole of Siberia.

## Europe

Encouraged by this development, two BFBS agents were despatched to Europe to seek further openings. Robert Pinkerton established committees in Amsterdam, Elberfeld, Hanover, Berlin and Dresden; John Paterson set up societies in Norway, Sweden and Denmark.

### The Bible in Spain

George Borrow had a genius for languages. In 1833 he was appointed by the Bible Society to journey to Russia and see through the press a translation of the New Testament into the Manchu-Tartar language.

He set out in the July, and by 1835 had completed his task and returned to England in search of another commission. Borrow spent the next seven years circulating the Scriptures in Spain and Portugal.

His chief aim was to discover whether or not the people were prepared to receive the truth of the gospel. He began by learning the language, then received permission from the Spanish government to print 5,000 copies of an edition of the New Testament.

From Madrid he travelled to Granada, where he spent some time living with the gypsies. Back in Madrid he opened a shop for the sale of his Testaments, together with his own translation of St Luke in the gypsy dialect. His advertisements of the Scriptures offended the authorities and in January 1838 he was arrested and thrown into prison.

Released, Borrow took to the road with the sale of his books and tracts. For a further three years he travelled the Iberian peninsula, meeting with beggars, brigands and barbarians. He was arrested on other occasions and feared for his life, that he might meet 'the fate of St Stephen'.

Always he found his sturdiest supporters among the peasantry, despite their token commitment to Rome.

On his return in 1842 he set out the story of his adventures in a book, *The Bible in Spain*, which went through several reprintings.

## APOCRYPHA CONTROVERSY

Between 1823 and 1826 a controversy arose which threatened to disrupt the BFBS cause in Scotland. It concerned the publication of the Apocrypha, sometimes known as the 'deutero-canonical books', which were 12 books found in the Greek version of the Old Testament but not included in the Hebrew Bible. The Edinburgh Bible Society took the view that publishing Bibles with the Apocrypha was in breach of the constitution. (A request by the Church of Scotland to have an edition which contained the metrical version of the Psalms had been refused.)

When churches on the Continent began requesting that the Apocrypha be included in their Bibles, BFBS left the decision to their foreign societies, provided they were printed without note or comment. (In effect, this permitted the printing of the Apocrypha.) Scotsman Robert Haldane accidentally discovered this practice, and was further dismayed to learn that an edition he had largely financed had contained these books.

A decision by the Society to grant £500 towards a German edition with the Apocrypha hardened the Scottish position and in 1826 the Edinburgh Society (followed by Glasgow) intimated its intention to withdraw its support. Even though the following year BFBS decided 'not to print or circulate the Apocryphal books', it came too late for Scotland and the idea of a national Bible Society was conceived. However, it was not until 1861 that the National Bible Society of Scotland was formed, taking in Edinburgh, Glasgow and a number of smaller societies. The Scottish Bible Society did not merge with the National Bible Socierty of Scotland until 1985.

Meanwhile an American Bible Society was formed in 1816, which was an amalgamation of earlier committees set up since 1808.

The usual method of selling the books was by colporteurs, first employed around 1830 in France. These men, who were in effect missionaries, peddled their wares in the streets and markets of many countries throughout the world – China, Japan, Korea, Malaya, India, even Nepal and Tibet, and in Muslim countries such as Morocco and Algeria.

Despite the sense of unity, albeit on a rather narrow basis, there were controversies which led to groups of members withdrawing their support. One involved a request to include the Apocrypha in Bibles printed for the Continent. Because of the Society's loosely-worded response, a number of continental editions included the non-canonical books. It took two annual general meetings to rectify the matter.

Then around the same time, a second dispute was reaching its climax. Charges were made by Robert Haldane, a Scot who gave considerable financial support to the Society, that some auxiliaries were governed by heretical Arian and Socinian (i.e. Unitarian) groups.

In 1831 BFBS decided not to adopt a doctrinal test, for it was argued that under such a ruling any number of groups might be excluded. A number of members left the society and formed the Trinitarian Bible Society, based 'upon scriptural principles'.

Throughout the century, however, the work continued to grow. By 1906 there were some 5,800 auxiliaries in Britain, and the following year BFBS reported that since its founding 203,931,768 Bibles and other Scripture portions had been distributed.

The Society greatly aided the work of the Sunday School Movement, sent out large quantities of Bibles in native languages to some of the first missionaries in India, supported the Emancipation Act of 1833 by sending copies of the New Testament to freed slaves, and brought Christians together on a non-sectarian basis.

Incorporated by Royal Charter in 1948, the BFBS continues in its task of enabling Christian churches to make the Bible more available, and to find ways of encouraging people to read and use it. Along with sister Societies in Scotland and Ireland, it is facing unprecedented opportunities opening up in the former Soviet Union, among refugees in Africa and in the remote corners of the Far East.

More than ever before, the Bible Societies are looking to the Christian public for support to ensure that everybody has access to the Bible for themselves.

## OBJECT AND PURPOSE OF THE BIBLE SOCIETY

The principal object of the BFBS according to its Royal Charter is: 'to encourage the wider circulation and use of the Holy Scripture'.

Its purpose statement is: 'Enabling the Church, through the use of the Bible, to engage more effectively in God's mission within contemporary cultures'.

## 20. CHRISTIAN HERALD Weekly Newspaper
### Rev Michael Baxter (1834-1910)

'Reading Christians will be knowing Christians,' asserted John Wesley. He believed it was essential that his followers should be informed as well as edified, and he paid strict attention to the provision of suitable reading material for them. His 50-volume Christian Library of abridged spiritual classics and his monthly *Arminian Magazine* were specially designed to establish the reading habit among his local preachers.

A similar philosophy led the Rev Michael Paget Baxter to found the monthly *Signs of Our Times* magazine, in May 1866. Intended to teach its readers about the imminent return of Christ, it was subsequently re-introduced on a wider basis as the *Christian Herald* and was soon established as the most popular weekly religious newspaper of its day.

Around this time the number of newspapers in England was rapidly increasing, and rose from under 500 to more than 2,300 by the turn of the century. One daily newspaper, the *Daily Telegraph*, reached record sales of 250,000 copies a day.

Religious magazines and newspapers also became more and more popular. By the year 1900 all the major denominations were represented in print, together with a variety of undenominational publications.

### Mass Circulation
Popular newspapers were an invention of the 18th century. One of the first national newspapers to be established was *The Times* (1785) at a cost of 7d, but when the notorious newspaper stamp duty was finally abolished in 1855 the price was reduced to 3d. The *Daily Telegraph*, founded two weeks after the stamp duty was revoked, cost only 1d. So the era of the mass circulation newspaper gathered momentum.

For the religious press, one of the earliest regular publications was John Wesley's monthly *Arminian Magazine*, founded in 1778. Other denominational publications included the *Record* (1828), the earliest Anglican newspaper to appear. It quickly acquired a reputation for being aggressive, especially towards Church leaders. In 1863 the Anglo-Catholics brought out the *Church Times* and, nearer the end of the century the *Church of England Newspaper* (1894) was founded.

Among the other denominations, there was the *Baptist Magazine* (1809) and *The Freeman*, which later changed its name to the *Baptist*

*Times.* The *Methodist Recorder* appeared in 1861, and the Quakers published *The Friend,* in 1893. At the opposite end of the religious spectrum, the Catholics introduced both the *Universe* and the *Catholic Times* in 1860.

Of the undenominational publications, one of the most popular was the *Revival.* First published in 1859, its intention – as its title suggests – was that of keeping aglow the fires of the new revival movement lately spread from across the Atlantic. However, regarded by Nonconformists as the most outstanding periodical was the *British Weekly,* a Journal of Christian and Social Progress, founded in 1886 under the editorship of Robertson Nicoll.

## SECULAR NEWSPAPERS

Although printing had been invented in the middle of the 15th century, the origins of the newspaper only go back to the early years of the 17th century, when many news sheets and pamphlets became available to the public.

In England, the publication of news was assumed to be a royal prerogative, though the position had to be clarified in 1680 by the courts. It was declared that 'to print and publish any news books or pamphlets of news whatsoever is illegal'. (This ruling was not often enforced.)

The development of a postal service at the beginning of the 1600s greatly assisted the circulation of news publications, though the first substantial paper – the *Daily Courant* – was not established until 1702.

Inadequate printing techniques made the publication of a large print run difficult, and the prohibition on reporting parliamentary debates and the imposition of a heavy stamp duty (1712) further hindered progress. By the middle of the 18th century, newspapers included most features found today, with the exception of illustrations. After 1771, when the right to publish debates was finally conceded, the size of papers increased from one to as many as four pages.

One of the first national papers to be established was *The Times* (1785) at a cost of 7d, but when the stamp duty was finally abolished (1855) the price was reduced to 3d. The *Sunday Observer,* the *Manchester Guardian* and the *Daily News* were among the next papers to be published. The *Daily Telegraph,* founded two weeks after the stamp duty was revoked, cost only 2d. As the mass circulation of newspapers gathered momentum, the *Daily Mail* (1896), the *Daily Express* (1900) and the *Daily Mirror* (1903) also began publication.

But despite the diversity of the competition, the *Christian Herald*, under its owner, the Rev Michael Baxter, set out to achieve new standards in journalism. It did not take long for it to become one of the leading Christian newspapers of the day.

## Evangelical Tradition

Michael Paget Baxter was born in 1834 into a middle class Christian family. His father, Robert Baxter (a descendant of the famous Dissenter, Richard Baxter) was a lawyer who practised in Doncaster (South Yorkshire), and his mother, Joanna Marie Paget, was the daughter of a Tamworth banker. They were active in several Christian missions, particularly the Church Missionary Society and the British and Foreign Bible Society.

Together with Lord Radstock, Robert Baxter helped found the Open-Air Mission (1853), the Evangelization Society (1864), the Christian Community and the Soldiers' Homes.

When he took up an appointment in London as head of an eminent firm of solicitors, the family went to live at 28 Queen Anne's Gate. In the capital, the Baxters moved among upper class Evangelicals and became further involved in mission activities, including the Ragged School Union and the Religious Tract Society.

It was while studying at Trinity College, Cambridge, that Michael Baxter was converted to Christ. Although born of godly parents and reared in the evangelical tradition, it was not until he reached the age of 20 that he came to a knowledge of salvation. It was the preaching of the Rev Samuel Martin at Westminster Chapel in London that brought him to faith.

From that moment his life was changed. At Trinity he had been reading law, but now he felt called to preach the gospel. He abandoned the idea of entering the legal profession and went up to Oxford to prepare for the Anglican ministry.

In 1859 he paid a visit to North America, staying first in the United States before moving to Canada, where he made a name as an itinerant preacher. Whilst in Canada his preaching impressed the Bishop of Huron, who ordained him into the Anglican Church, then presented him with the living of Onondaga (Ontario).

**Prophecy**

During his stay he became gripped by his reading of prophecy. He realised that not only were the masses of people living without a concern for their spiritual well-being, but that Christians also were ignorant with regard to the Lord's coming. It was not long before he felt impelled to give up his church and travel from place to place, speaking of the things he had learned concerning the advent of Christ.

To make his message more powerful, Baxter acquired a lantern and set of slides with which to illustrate his sermons. As a result of his prophetic studies, he published several books on the subject. The first, entitled *Louis Napoleon, the Destined Monarch of the World*, sold 50,000 copies in a short space of time. His more famous book, *Forty Coming Wonders*, sold over 100,000 copies.

On his return to England in 1863, he again began lecturing on prophecy, but decided he could reach a wider audience using the printed word. Around 1866 he started a monthly prophetic magazine, *Signs of Our Times*, which published articles by ministers and others concerning the return of Christ. Though well-received it was of limited interest, and he realised that a monthly magazine for Christians was unsuitable for an approach to the unconverted.

In the 1870s he made a bold move. During the winter of 1873-74 Baxter attended Moody and Sankey's Glasgow mission. The two American evangelists had made an unpromising start to their tour of Britain, but by the time they reached Scotland they were proving a great attraction.

Inspired by the spiritually hungry crowds, Baxter recognised the interest and enthusiasm people were showing for the meetings. It was then that he conceived the idea of reporting the mission services and some of the sermons for the benefit of those unable to attend.

**New Formula**

He remodelled the *Signs of Our Times* magazine, switching from monthly to weekly publication, giving greater coverage to evangelism. Also significantly, he set about improving the dull image that all religious newspapers had at that time.

About 1876 he introduced a new title, *The Christian Herald and Signs of Our Times*, incorporating the monthly magazine into the weekly newspaper. He changed from quarto to tabloid format and spent money lavishly on the use of more pictures and drawings. Weekly sermons by popular preachers such as Spurgeon and Moody were included, as well as news items of interest to the Christian public. Through the columns of his paper he encouraged evangelism; even small missions were reported and periodically he offered free gospel literature to readers.

The new formula was an immediate success and appealed to a much wider readership. The *Herald's* circulation began to grow and at its peak reached over 300,000 per week.

As Baxter's biographer commented about the transformation: 'It fell upon the eager supporters of Moody's mission everywhere with refreshing influence. At once Scotland accepted it, and while it floated into popularity upon the Revival, it also tended to deepen its flood and extend its Nile-like blessings.

'The newspaper asserted and applied the truths concerning the Cross, the essential doctrines that were emphasised at the Reformation, with a touch of the enthusiastic interest of Wesley and Whitefield. Moreover, it was careful to keep in mind the average reader, not using

Michael Baxter

inflated language but only the speech of ordinary people. It was at all times loyal to the authority of the Lord Jesus Christ and magnifying him as a Saviour.'

In 1877 Baxter sent two of his staff to the United States, where they started an American edition of the *Christian Herald*. For some years it was published in unison with the London edition, and with gratifying success. But as the paper was becoming established, the rapidly increasing pressure of business in London forced Baxter to sell the American *Herald* in 1890.

## Gifted Wife

Throughout their life together, Baxter was ably supported by his gifted wife, Elizabeth. The couple met at Mildmay and were married in 1868. Mrs Baxter became a regular contributor to the *Herald* from its early days. As well as writing weekly notes for the Sunday School Lesson, she also edited a monthly magazine entitled *The Eleventh Hour*.

A man of intellect and vigour, Baxter spent much of his considerable energies in pursuing a number of other gospel causes. In 1882 he launched the Gospel Union, which consisted of a chain of undenominational missions in towns throughout England and Scotland. Although organised on the evangelistic lines of the Salvation Army, they did not imitate the Army's military-style approach.

His attention was next drawn to the needs of people in lands dominated by Roman Catholicism. For many weekends in the year, Baxter travelled parts of the Continent, distributing copies of the Scriptures. He also employed a Rev Joshua Jaye to continue the work, going from house to house. In this way, he estimated that they had distributed between two and three million gospels and tracts.

Among his other works was the establishment of the Willow Street Mission, which provided free food and lodging for out of work men and women. And during a period of high unemployment in 1905 he organised a daily distribution of dole money for a thousand men from the *Herald*'s City offices.

In recent years, *Christian Herald* backed the launch of *Christian Woman* (now *Woman Alive*, one of the UK's most popular evangelistic monthlies) and *Christian Music* (now *Deo*).

Michael Baxter died in 1910, one of the evangelical world's lesser-known worthies. Judged by some to be eccentric, he was a man of immense generosity and many poor families received of his bounty. His contribution to Christian journalism was invaluable, and marked a turning point in the evolution of the religious press.

The paper was taken over by his wife Elizabeth and son Paget, who maintained the traditions built up since 1866 and continued the charitable works associated with the paper. Elizabeth died in 1926 and eventually the editorship passed to Rev Percy Hicks, and then to the founder's great-granddaughter, Elizabeth.

In the mid 70's the role of editor passed to Dr T Wilkinson Riddle, a Baptist preacher and a popular leader-writer since 1938. The editorial and management team had grown very elderly (Dr Riddle was in the Guinness Book of Records as the world's oldest working editor, aged 94), when a group of concerned Christians asked to take over the paper in 1979.

As a result, Herald House was formed and, under Colin Reeves, produced the first issue for the new decade. The new team re-established the early principles, gave the paper a renewed evangelical emphasis, introduced news and mission reports, and set about making it better known.

For over 125 years the *Christian Herald* has sought to bring its readers a varied fare of good things that encourage faith, build up the believer and keep them informed about the Christian scene.

It is a paper steeped in history and has a record of evangelical life for over a century. Looking back over past copies – all editions except the very earliest are in the archive – fills the reader with awe, a sense of 'treading on holy ground'.

## MISSION STATEMENT OF HERALD HOUSE

1) To make and nurture disciples
2) primarily through the printed word
3) while maintaining good stewardship
and striving for excellence

## 21. CHRISTIAN LITERATURE CRUSADE (1941)
### Kenneth (1914-1985) and Bessie (1908-1986) Adams

There can be no doubt that one of the greatest inventions of the modern world is that of printing. Whereas previously books had been copied by hand, when Johann Gutenberg (c1397-1468) invented movable type in c1449 he made it possible for hundreds of copies to be made in one print run. His invention remained a secret for only a few years; in 1467 it was known in Rome, and William Caxton set up a printing press at Westminster in 1476. By the end of the century nearly 40,000 titles had been published throughout Europe.

The first full-length book to be printed was the Bible (in Latin) in 1456, later known as the Mazarin Bible. Before long, large numbers of Bibles were made available to the public, as were other types of literature. With books more readily available and relatively cheap to buy, there was an increasing demand for literature of all kinds. But like the invention of gunpowder, printing had great potential for good and for evil, and history has shown that there is tremendous power in the printed word.

Early the following century, the knowledge of Luther's challenge to the Roman Church (in 1517) was disseminated throughout Christendom and the reformer's ideas quickly spread abroad in printed form. One of his books, *Beneficio di Christo*, sold 40,000 copies in Venice alone. A timely invention, printing significantly contributed towards the progress of the Reformation and the spread of the gospel.

### False Ideologies
Yet Protestants have been slow to appreciate the importance of getting across the message by the written word, as well as by preaching. It has taken, among other things, the threat of false ideologies to awaken the Church to the opportunities presented by literature.

During the 20th century the greatest enemy of the Church has been Communism, which came to power following the 1917 revolution in Russia. The Communists laid stress on the printed word, and they deliberately set out to spread their propaganda by leaflets and books. Yet the Church still lagged behind. As Gandhi's nephew once wryly remarked, 'The missionaries have taught us to read, but the Communists have given us the literature.'

In many parts of the world, enthusiastic Communist party members distributed their books and magazines, supplying atheistic propaganda to millions of young people. Nearer home, Mormon and Jehovah's Witness missionaries peddled their publications from door to door under the guise of spreading biblical truth.

The problem was highlighted in a *Daily Mirror* report on 2 October 1950. Attention was drawn to the distribution of literature by Communists into the hands of the newly-literate people of Nigeria. 'The buyers are not Communists, but intelligent people anxious to improve their world knowledge. And therein lies the danger to the cause of Britain and the United Nations', the report concluded. (And to the Church, we might add.)

### Evangelical Literature

Increasingly aware of the power of the written word and keen to get good literature into the hands of Christian people, Ken and Bessie Adams founded Christian Literature Crusade in 1941. It was 'for the specific purpose of spreading evangelical literature over the widest possible area in the shortest time'. For nearly 50 years they pioneered the Christian literature cause at a time when the world literacy explosion was bringing a new challenge to the Church.

From his teenage years Ken's two chief concerns were for evangelism and literature. At the age of 20, he opened his own bookshop in Westcliff-on-Sea (Essex), with money loaned by his mother and friends. But it was not long before he felt God wanted him to train for missionary service. He found someone to take over the stock and began studies at the Faith Mission Bible College, Edinburgh.

When he married Bessie Miners in 1938, they linked up with the Friends Evangelistic Band (FEB) – not a Quaker group – and began village evangelism in rural East Anglia, holding tent meetings and visiting homes.

As they made their visits, they often discovered that Jehovah's Witnesses had been there before them. Many villagers were impressed by the Witnesses' ability to quote Scripture, and had bought books and magazines unaware that they were opening their doors to false teachings.

Adams declared, 'I cannot stand by and watch the spread of so much dangerous propaganda and not do something about spreading the truths of the gospel.' So he and Bessie began visiting armed with good Christian literature.

## Evangelical Publishers

Despite today's technological revolution, the printed word is still in great demand. Not only Bibles and books, but a range of other helps to faith such as magazines and newspapers are available to the Christian public. To provide for them, over the last 50 years or so a number of new evangelical publishers have emerged, each one with its own special emphasis.

One of the oldest evangelical publishing houses, set up in 1868 by M H Hodder and T W Stoughton, had already served the Christian public for many years. Their aim was to produce and distribute books which would help spread the Christian gospel. In that same year, Scripture Union (then called CSSM) was founded, and shortly began producing material for work with children and young people.

In 1936 Inter-Varsity Press (IVP) was founded to counter liberal thinking in the church by producing high-quality works of biblical scholarship for students, books which would once again emphasise the importance of the Word of God.

The Banner of Truth Trust began publishing books in 1957. They have made available again many of the works of past centuries, including the writings of the Reformers and the Puritans.

To maintain this evangelical thrust, since 1967 the Evangelical Press has endeavoured to produce books that present biblical truths in such a way as to be readily understood by the majority of Christians.

When Lion Publishing started in 1971, its aim was to produce attractively-presented Christian books for the general reader, books which could be displayed alongside the best that secular publishers had to offer. Others have followed Lion's lead, resulting in the production of a wide range of delightfully-illustrated publications.

Kingsway Publications came to birth in the mid-1970s, to provide literature at a fairly popular level. It has a reputation for publishing books for the charismatic movement.

In 1983 Christian Focus Publications began publishing quality books for children. They also produce adult books, mainly at a popular level. Other publishers from that decade include Highland Books (1984) and Monarch (1988).

At his suggestion, FEB agreed in October 1939 to develop its own literature programme. They rented two upstairs rooms in Sir Isaac's Walk, Colchester, and bought a small stock of books with money loaned by friends. The Adamses knew that God had called them to a life of faith, with no regular salary, and they felt that this should remain a mark of their future service.

## Restrictions

After eight months, the Adamses found alternative premises to rent, and they had their first 'real' shop in St John's Street, which they named The Evangelical Publishing House. All this happened when war-time government restrictions severely limited publishing and the opening of bookshops.

After a sluggish start, sales began to pick up, but in 1941 links with the FEB were severed. Unsure about their future, the Adamses wondered why the Lord had landed them with a book centre when their hearts were in evangelism. Thinking they might join WEC International as area representatives, they offered themselves to WEC 'on condition that the book centre be maintained'.

Norman Grubb, the WEC General Secretary, began to capture something of their vision for literature work. He recalls that God gave him inspiration: 'Why shouldn't the bookshop come too?' he suggested. 'We could begin scattering "spiritual Woolworths" around the country and then worldwide!'

WEC had already considered the possibility of starting a literature ministry and this seemed like the way forward. For the Adamses, the prospect was an exciting one as they recognised the potential of a chain of book centres not only in Britain, but throughout the English-speaking world.

Even though they felt it right to go ahead, the idea was that they should set up a new organisation to work alongside WEC. So first they felt it essential to discuss WEC's basic principles with their new partners. Known as 'The Four Pillars of WEC', they consisted of Faith, Sacrifice, Holiness and Fellowship, the chief of which was faith. (More recently, suggestions have been made that there have always been seven pillars, which included Love, Vision and Prayer.)

The way of faith was eventually re-affirmed and it was accepted that CLC staff would not receive a regular salary, but would live on what the

Lord provided. They also decided that candidates would have to spend some time in training at WEC headquarters, after which they would be transferred to the literature ministry.

### Service Agency

While the two societies would be linked in fellowship, the new organisation would be independent and responsible for its own finances. It would not be the publishing arm of WEC. The function of the Evangelical Publishing House would be to act as a service agency to other missionary societies, as well as providing retail outlets for Christian literature.

Equally important, like WEC, it was to be a missionary society, dedicated to spreading the gospel. The name Christian Literature Crusade was adopted later, to indicate more precisely the nature of its work.

The Adamses determined not to let doctrinal differences hinder the work from serving all denominations with their literature needs. 'Our position,' Ken affirmed, 'is to be uncompromisingly evangelical so that purchasers feel quite sure that all they see and buy will build up readers or point the unconverted to the Saviour.'

Norman Grubb announced the new society in the October 1941 issue of WEC's *World Conquest* magazine. He boldly stated that the aim was to open 200 'spiritual Woolworths' throughout the British Isles. It caused the Adamses a certain alarm, but the article produced results, in that there were several enquiries from prospective workers.

While the work continued to operate from Colchester, much prayer went up about where they should open their next centre. In January two new staff were designated to spearhead this advance. Then a telephone call from a businessman and WEC supporter in Leicester turned out to be God's answer. As a result, permission was rather miraculously given by the Board of Trade to open the first CLC branch.

This was followed by Stockport (1942) and Chatham (1943). Despite war-time restrictions, by 1945 there were five book centres in England and one in Dundee, Scotland.

## London

It was in 1944 that the CLC staff began to talk in terms of the probability one day of establishing their main base in the capital, the hub of the British publishing world. On a visit to London, Ken noticed a 'To Let' sign on three dilapidated buildings on Ludgate Hill, below St Paul's Cathedral.

Enquiries revealed that the buildings had been bombed and a surveyor's report proved discouraging. The matter was dropped, until a letter was received nine months later asking if CLC was still interested. This time an agreement was possible; the vendor accepted responsibility for the 365 repair jobs that needed to be done, and a contract was signed for a 14-year lease.

By the summer of 1946 all was ready for CLC to move into no. 39 Ludgate Hill. A number of Christian publishers came to their aid, and the showrooms were stocked with £10,000-worth of books. The new CLC headquarters were ready for opening. The building had six floors and a basement, with two sales floors and the Mail Order Department below.

KENNETH AND BESSIE ADAMS

One outstanding feature of the shop was the high standard of window dressing, which frequently attracted the attention of passers-by, and was an unusual means of presenting the gospel. A window cleaner working at the shop was so convicted by one display that he went inside and asked how to be saved.

Considerable time and effort went into creating displays of new book titles, and the results were so effective that several publishers asked CLC to make displays for them.

### Floodtide

The year 1946 was important for another reason, for it was in January that year that CLC's magazine *Floodtide* was first published. It had begun under its editor, Miriam Booth, as a newsletter, but this new glossy magazine with a two-colour cover was acclaimed as something which really met a need, and with which folks were just thrilled.

Miriam had asked the Lord about a title, and the choice of *Floodtide* linked up with Isaiah 11:9, 'for the earth will be full of the knowledge of the LORD as the waters cover the sea.'

Since 1944, when Phil and Miriam Booth (later of Radio Worldwide, a branch of WEC International) joined the team, the possibility of expanding the work overseas had always been in mind. Phil was placed in charge of the 'foreign department', and after the war links with the Continent were established.

It was through the promptings of an RAF chaplain, who had read in *Floodtide* of the plan to open centres abroad, that a work was begun in Germany. Prayer was made for £1,000 with which to open a bookshop, and within a few days a cheque for that amount was received from an anonymous donor, earmarked 'for literature in Germany'. It was this experience that set the pattern and standard for the future: 'Discover God's will, then seek by faith his provision to fulfil it.'

Canada was already opening up a work, and in 1947 Norman Grubb and Kenneth Adams attended a WEC conference in Chicago, USA. The outcome was that for a limited period Kenneth and Bessie Adams were released to North America, where they established a permanent base for CLC.

**Requests**

The work grew, not by planning, but by Christians catching the vision and approaching CLC for help. Requests came in from other continents, and book centres were opened in Australia, Africa and South America. In 1949 Ken went to Japan for two months' investigations. Though initially 'the picture was not bright', the next year plans for a shop began to materialise.

Because of the developments, it became necessary to build a new administrative block at Fort Washington, USA. That same year, 1961, Ken was confirmed as CLC's International Secretary, and he and his wife took out US citizenship.

Always ready to pioneer new ministries, an important development was the introduction of bookmobiles, used to reach isolated communities in rural areas of remote mountainous regions.

The work of CLC has grown rapidly. In 1950 there were book centres in eight countries spread over five continents; by 1962, CLC was at work in 36 countries. There are now over 150 book centres operating in more than 50 countries, with publishing and printing services as well.

But what of the future? The backdrop to the whole CLC scene during the 1980s and 90s was a worldwide economic recession which inevitably affected the bookselling business. But many CLC workers are optimistic, and they report that in Africa, Indonesia and Far East Asia opportunities for literature work are continually opening up. Other regions also have plans for more book centres, and there are centres in several former Communist countries in Central and Eastern Europe.

After Kenneth Adams died in 1985 one of his daughters wrote, 'Dad was a man with a burning heart, with the desire for the world to be reached with the gospel; a man constantly on the move to see this desire accomplished.' In fact, one of his greatest joys was to send cheques to overseas fields and to hear of new advances.

CLC's bookshops around the world are a fine tribute to the faith and obedience of Ken and Bettie Adams. And the work is still growing.

## MISSION STATEMENT OF
## CHRISTIAN LITERATURE CRUSADE

'CLC's Goal is to make evangelical literature available to all the nations, so that people may come to faith and maturity in the Lord Jesus Christ.'
We seek to achieve this goal by:

*Operating effective retail centres in strategic locations throughout the U.K.

*Constantly and energetically seeking to reach out from these centres through Bookstalls, Book Parties, Mail Order, etc. in order to attract those who do not frequent Christian bookshops.

*Providing funds for overseas development and support, through the careful management of resources.

*Praying for revival and spiritual renewal, and actively promoting books on these topics.

*Cooperating with similar organisations to actively encourage the reading of the Bible and Christian books.

*Continuing to develop our wholesale operation and encouraging others in retail distribution.

*Encouraging others into full-time Christian service through deputation and mission promotion.

*Producing and distributing *Floodtide* Magazine to inform and challenge the Church and encourage the widespread use of Christian literature.

Working in: Europe, India, Far East, North America, South America, West Indies, Australasia.

## 22. THE GIDEONS INTERNATIONAL (1899)
### John Nicholson (b 1859), Samuel Hill (b 1867)
### and Will Knights (b 1853)

The Gideons International is an association of Christian business and professional men and their wives who believe the message of the Bible to be relevant to people in all walks of life today. Their aim is to place Bibles or New Testaments, free of charge, where people may be in special need and have the opportunity to give time to reading God's Word. As a result, thousands of people who have not previously known the gospel or entered a church have encountered God through reading a Gideon Bible.

The Gideon story goes back to 14 September 1898, and to one of those 'God-opportunities' that believers experience as they serve the Lord.

Paper salesman John Nicholson had had a tiring day lugging his case of samples around various firms in Boscobel, Wisconsin, in the USA. It was nine o'clock at night when he attempted to book into his usual hotel, only to be told there were no rooms left.

But there was a paint salesman by the name of Hill who had a spare bed in his twin room. Perhaps, the clerk suggested, he could be persuaded to allow Nicholson to share? Hill was sitting in the hotel lobby writing up his orders for the day. As Nicholson thought he was a clean-looking chap (in contrast to some of the other guests, who were either playing cards or were the worse for drink) he approached Hill who agreed to share the room. Nicholson left him to finish his orders, and retired upstairs.

Placing his Bible at his bedside, Nicholson then wrote out his orders and finished the day's correspondence. Before going to sleep, he wanted to spend time reading his Bible and praying. This was a practice he had followed since making a promise at the age of 13 to his dying mother.

He asked his room-mate, 'Pardon me if I keep the light on a little longer, because I always make it a practice to read the Word of God and have a little chat with him before I retire.'

Hill jumped up in bed, obviously delighted at the discovery. 'Read it aloud,' he insisted. 'Let me join you, for I'm a Christian as well.'

The two of them read John 15, then knelt and prayed together. After that, they talked until around 2 o'clock in the morning, both of them excited at the thrill of meeting another believer.

Among the many things they said, they agreed it would be a good idea to have an association of Christian travelling men. They could have an emblem by which they would recognise each other and enable them to have fellowship.

## By Chance

The two men parted the following morning without making any further reference to the matter. Nothing became of the scheme until some eight months later, when 'by chance' the two of them met again as Hill was hurrying on his way to a railway station.

During the few minutes they spent together on the street, they decided on a plan of action and agreed to hold a meeting in a month's time. This would be at the YMCA in Nicholson's home town of Janesville, also in Wisconsin. It was their intention to form an association as they had previously discussed. The meeting was fixed for Sunday afternoon, 1 July 1899.

Although both men had approached a number of their colleagues about the venture, when they met at the YMCA that July day only one other man joined them. He was Will Knights, a grocery salesman whom Nicholson had met the previous year. Undeterred, the three of them prayed and agreed to go ahead with the idea. Hill was chosen as

Mr. Samuel E. Hill
President (1899)

Mr. William J. Knights
Vice-President (1899)

Mr. John H. Nicholson
Secretary (1899)

President, Knights became Vicepresident and Nicholson, who did the organising, was Secretary.

Membership, they decided, would be open to commercial travellers who openly acknowledged their faith in Christ and believed that the Bible was true – 'all of it'. Their aim was to bring together Christian salesmen for mutual encouragement and to witness for the Lord as they went about their business. Being prepared to speak to other men about the Lord was an essential qualification, making each member a living testimony to their faith.

When the question of a name arose, they prayed again and at the end Knights rose to his feet and said, 'I have it – we'll be Gideons.' He read out the sixth and seventh chapters of the Book of Judges, and they determined to be 'modern Gideons', a small band of men witnessing for the Lord.

By the time they held their first business meeting a month later, nine men had been recruited. The matter of a badge was raised, needed in order to assist them to recognise each other. One member had a suggestion, an idea based on the story of Gideon. He proposed a circular badge with a white pitcher on a blue background, with a red flame, representing the torches, coming out of the top, and an outer gold circle representing the trumpets. The emblem was accepted, and has continued in use ever since.

Despite the few members, the founders' faith was soon rewarded, for within 12 months, by the time they held their first convention, 600 men had joined the new movement. There were 37 members present at that convention to hear Samuel Hill declare, 'Who dare predict the future and what it has in store for us? But however large and powerful the army of Gideon may become, I shall always thank God that he permitted me to have some part in its beginning, for already I feel the fulfilment of Zechariah's prophecy when he said, "Who shall despise the day of small things, for they shall rejoice."'

As the membership increased it became necessary to employ a full-time secretary and to rent an office, opened in Chicago in 1905.

## Bibles

Interestingly, the idea of distributing Bibles did not originate in America, but Britain. It came about when Fred Woodcock of the Chicago branch of Gideons paid a visit to England in 1903. He discovered Bibles and other books of 'wholesome reading' placed in hotels by The Commercial Travellers Christian Association, a group formed some thirty years earlier.

Woodcock reported back to headquarters: 'They are doing a great work by putting Bibles in all the rooms of different hotels,' suggesting they ought to adopt the same practice in the USA. 'They do not hold their meetings in churches, as we do ... and do personal work on the road amongst their fellow travellers,' he reported.

It was not until the Louisville convention of 1908, however, that the association voted in favour of the plan to distribute Bibles. No arrangements were made by which to finance the project, but from among themselves they donated $700 as a starter.

In September of that year, a group of pastors at Cedar Rapids, Iowa, heard a report of the work and decided to raise funds with which to purchase Bibles for the hotels in their town. This was the first occasion in which churches co-operated in the scheme, and the link has been maintained ever since.

One difficulty they encountered was that strangers to the Bible had no idea where to start reading. It was this realisation that led them to insert a page inside the front cover of each Bible, making some suggestions and giving the address of the headquarters.

With such a large distribution of Bibles, however, it seemed more sensible to have the Bibles printed with the insert already in place. As the American Bible Society (like its British counterpart) was obliged to print Bibles 'entirely without note or comment', it eventually became necessary for The Gideons to become their own publisher.

From the beginning, God's hand was evidently upon the association and news began to come in of people whose lives had been transformed by reading a Bible placed by The Gideons.

As interest in the work increased, it was decided to broaden the basis of its membership by inviting to join them business and professional men whose work entailed much travelling.

**Britain**

It was some while before the idea was taken up in other countries, and in 1911 Canada was the first one outside the USA to open a branch. And although Bibles had been placed in countries such as Japan and Java, Sweden and Syria, it was felt essential to expand the work still further.

After the Second World War, in 1947, The Gideons' International Extension Committee was formed to establish centres abroad, beginning with Britain. It was realised that opening up the work in Britain would not be so easy, for it was felt the British were cautious of anything from across the Atlantic. The association approached the matter sensitively, by asking a Canadian member to make an initial survey in the UK.

It was ultimately decided to seek the help of a sympathetic organisation, the Scripture Gift Mission, to help them get the scheme off the ground. So it was that in 1948 Mr Montague ('Monty') H Knott of London was seconded by SGM to help out the Americans. After spending some time in the States and Canada to see how the association worked, he returned full of enthusiasm for his new task.

The campaign was finally begun in November 1949. Initially there was some discouragement, as the number of members did not fulfil expectations. Assisted by Fred Bradbury, a retired civil servant, visits were made to various parts of the UK, lunches held to launch the scheme, and the aims, privileges and responsibilities explained.

It was a little while before the first branch was opened, at Portsmouth; this was followed by others in Essex and London. But by 1952 there were still only 412 Gideons enrolled, and 49 of them were from overseas.

**Coronation Year**
It may well have been the coronation of Queen Elizabeth II, however, that put The Gideons on the map. Supported by the mother association, a plan to distribute 50,000 Bibles in British hotels during 1953 was put into operation. Most of the hoteliers responded well, and by the end of the year the 30 Gideon branches had placed 55,000 Bibles throughout the UK.

Travellers and tourists for the first time became aware of the name of The Gideons, which was now an established name on the Christian scene in Britain. Things went increasingly well, as branches reported monthly meetings, funds raised and new recruits enrolled.

The work broadened; not only hotels, but prisons, schools, hospitals and residential homes received Bibles. They were even placed in the cabins of passenger liners and, today, on oil rigs.

It was around this time that the Auxiliary was formed, whereby the enthusiastic support of thousands of women was brought into use.

Although the Americans had encouraged the help of women from as far back as the days when inserts were first placed in the Bibles, it had still remained a male preserve in Britain. From 1956, when the Auxiliary was founded, wives of Gideons enrolled on the basis of faith, like their husbands. They have given the movement an extra impetus, and have proved how invaluable their contribution can be.

The movement has now spread to many parts of the world, and more recently to a number of former Communist countries.

There are now about 270 branches in the British Isles. Each year they distribute about 830,000 Bibles and Testaments, including around 650,000 New Testaments and Psalms to young people. By 1995 they had presented over 25 million copies in the British Isles.

In Britain, the Scriptures are available both in the New International and Authorised Versions. They specially feature a Bible reading aid system that directs readers' attention to passages relating to a wide range of life issues. These notes are greatly appreciated. Letters are received daily at the Gideons' headquarters telling of the help, comfort and inspiration that people have experienced through reading God's Word.

As one member remarked about the movement, 'It is wonderful to realise that so few Gideons have been able to distribute so many portions of Scripture. I am thrilled to be associated with such a work of God.'

## MISSION STATEMENT OF
## THE GIDEONS INTERNATIONAL

The Gideons International has one simple and clearly defined aim, to win men, women and young people for the Lord Jesus Christ. Our strategy for achieving this is threefold:

1. Fellowship and mutual encouragement by meeting with other Christian business and professional men and their wives.

2. Personal testimony and personal work by members.

3. Placing and presenting God's Word in the mainstreams of life.

The Gideons is currently working in more than 170 countries, distributing over 40 million Bibles and New Testaments per annum.

## 23. SCRIPTURE GIFT MISSION INTERNATIONAL (1888)
### William Walters (1845-1907)

Towards the end of the 17th century a reawakening of evangelical fervour broke out in Germany. It reached Britain the following century and before long revitalised all the Protestant denominations. The first stirrings were felt within the Anglican Church, where groups of 'serious men' formed new societies for religious and social purposes. Among the first of these was the Society for Promoting Christian Knowledge.

Founded in 1698 by a group of clergy and laymen under the leadership of Dr Thomas Bray, rector of a parish in Warwickshire and then in London, its primary aim was to encourage the building of charity schools. But its secondary purpose was to distribute Bibles and tracts, the first society to begin such a work. It still operates today and has its own publishing house in London.

It was not until over a century later that the need to make the Scriptures more readily available was recognised, and further societies were established. The earliest foundation was the Naval and Military Bible Society (1779), soon to be followed by the British and Foreign Bible Society (1804).

These inspired the formation of other similar local groups throughout the United Kingdom. Within a matter of years, a succession of Bible societies had been set up throughout the British Empire and across Europe and America, supported by Protestants, Catholics and Unitarians.

With the growth of the missionary movement at the end of the 18th century, a number of Christians began to appreciate the value of the Scriptures as a powerful tool for evangelism. Both George Müller and C H Spurgeon formed organisations for selling Bibles and New Testaments at low cost. And in 1874 the Christian Colportage Association was founded to introduce the Scriptures into homes by door-to-door sales.

William Walters, however, who was also persuaded of the need to encourage ordinary people to read the Bible, went one step further. He founded the Scripture Gift Mission (SGM) for the purpose of offering New Testaments and Bibles as a free gift to those who would receive one.

As a young man, Walters inherited his father's spiritual and artistic gifts. He had a profound love for the Scriptures, and often longed to share this treasure with others. Every day before breakfast he set time aside for study, and in summer he would read his Bible in a secluded spot in the garden.

Born in Wolverhampton, Walters was apprenticed to a printer, then later set up his own business in Birmingham. In addition to printing, he also published the writings of such notable Brethren authors as J N Darby, William Kelly and C H Macintosh. But he was aware that there were millions of people in Britain who were strangers to the Bible. And although many families had a Bible in the home, it was rarely read.

## Visions

Approaching his fortieth birthday, Walters felt that he had done so little of vital service for the Lord. He began to see visions of what could be done to bring a little beauty into the lives of the unreached millions in his city.

Walters gradually became convinced that God wanted him to use his skill and knowledge to reach people with God's Word. But Bibles in those days were produced in an unattractive format; Walters wanted copies of the Scriptures that would appeal to ordinary people and encourage them to read it. Why, he asked himself, should they not have beautiful pictures that bring the Bible to life?

His decision to give up his printing work may have been quickened by the unusual events of that year, which convinced him of the deep need for people to know the Word of God. A great fire that destroyed the centre of Birmingham had excited the rumour that the end of the world was to come that year. This was followed in July by some exceptional weather, with heavy snow and then five days of the 'thickest fog ever known'. Gloom and apprehension filled the hearts of the people.

Encouraged by his wife, he took a step of faith in 1885 and finally decided, 'I will devote my energies to the dissemination of the Scriptures.' His resolve was soon confirmed by a gift, totally unexpected, given specifically for that purpose.

The publication of the Brethren material was passed to another, thereby cutting off a substantial source of revenue (and from some with whom he had previously had fellowship and shared 'the deep things of God'). The publishing side of his business was sold; he moved to London and opened an office at Paternoster Row, near to St Paul's Cathedral.

According to records, the work of SGM actually commenced in February 1888 under the title of Scripture Text Mission, and was established 'for the free distribution of Scripture texts and Gospel books.' It was some months before the title, Scripture Gift Mission, was finally settled.

The first printed statement concerning the aim of the mission was as follows: 'The object of the Scripture Gift Mission is to print and publish portions of the Word of God in an attractive and acceptable form, and to enable Christian workers at home, and missionaries abroad, to circulate them freely and gratuitously in their respective districts.'

**Illustrations**

It was Walters who pioneered the use of colour and illustrations in Bibles, 'to catch the eye in order to win the heart'. Anxious to improve the presentation of his publications, he conceived the idea of illustrating them with true Eastern scenes rather than the imaginary Bible story pictures then in vogue.

He was fortunate in securing the services of two well-known artists to execute the work – Henry Harper, a landscape painter who was later to become art tutor to Queen Alexandra, and James Clark whose paintings proved to be so true to life.

He maintained the two artists during the time they were working for him in Palestine. Between them, they produced some 200 illustrations of Eastern life, replacing the illustrations by an earlier artist used by Walters. Eventually the original pictures were framed and hung on the four walls of his office. News of this unusual art gallery soon circulated, bringing many distinguished visitors to see them.

For the first three years Walters confined his publishing to copies of the four Gospels in English. But an ostrich farmer with an interest in missionary work among the Muslims of North Africa enquired about the possibility of printing the Gospel of John in Arabic.

Responding to the challenge, Walters purchased a fount of Arabic characters. One of his staff set himself the task of learning sufficient of the alphabet and vowel marks to enable him to follow the copy and compose the type.

This edition was followed by Gospels of John in Spanish and Portuguese, Luke in French and Mark in Italian. Missionaries who saw the five attractive booklets requested further foreign language editions, and this side of the work grew quickly. By December 1895 SGM had printed over two million copies of the Gospels, half of them in the five foreign languages.

That year it was felt necessary to place the business on a more official footing, and an advisory council of eight members was formed. Walters also invited 18 prominent evangelical Christians, including three bishops, to become patrons. He started a monthly magazine, *The Word of Life*, to keep supporters informed of the gospel work at home and abroad.

Walters adopted the policy of giving the Scripture portions free of charge right from the beginning. His action was based partly on biblical teaching, but also on the realisation that anyone reading the Scriptures, even without human aid, could be soundly converted.

This policy was not generally accepted in some Christian circles, on the basis that 'People value what they pay for'. A controversy arose in the columns of certain daily newspapers, strongly criticising the free distribution of the Holy Scriptures. Walters' only response was to print a dignified justification of his policy in his monthly magazine. The SGM had witnessed tremendous blessing by its ministry, which continued unchanged.

## Faith Basis

Obviously, this work placed a great financial burden on Walters, though he was supported by gifts from the Christian public. From 1888 to 1933 the mission's income was procured by appeals, advertisements, campaigns and inter-society finance. Although some members doubted the rightness of appealing for funds, the Chairman of the Council, the Rev Prebendary Webb-Peploe felt it appropriate to use this method. At the annual meeting in 1899, at the Mildmay Conference Hall, he had no hesitation in asking his hearers to give financial support to the mission.

However, when a further grave financial situation arose in 1903, SGM was forced to sell off some of its most treasured possessions, the Palestine Pictures, though Walters always retained the right of reproduction. But in 1933 the council became convinced that this was not God's way, and that such activities should be dropped.

Since 1934 the mission has abandoned appeals and advertisements, and each year contributions have continued to increase. The mission now works solely on a faith basis.

Despite financial restraints, Walters went ahead with the publication of several special editions to meet national occasions. In 1899, at the start of the Boer War, he prepared a pocket edition called *The Soldier's New Testament*, with a newly-designed cover. The Commander-in-

Chief, Lord Wolsley, gave his support for the project and provided a commendatory preface, and Queen Victoria also expressed her thanks.

When King Edward VII came to the throne in 1901 and invited thousands of poor people to a coronation dinner, SGM was able to provide a Gospel of Mark with a commemorative cover for all the 'guests'.

Queen Alexandra requested Mr Walters to wait upon her at Marlborough House, to speak to her about the Palestine edition of the New Testament, and she ordered copies which she personally presented to members of the Court. Walters received great satisfaction in having royal approval of his production of the complete illustrated New Testament.

Now his ambition was to see a similar edition of the whole Bible, though the cost would have been considerable. Yet an opportunity arose when the Oxford University Press saw possibilities in the issue of one or more of their editions of the complete Bible with a set of the pictures.

## Illustrated Edition

Following a public subscription towards the project, a start was made on an illustrated edition. It contained 40 coloured pictures and 72 sepia engravings. Sales were beyond expectations, and OUP realised that this Bible was being received with favour. It resulted in two further editions being published, of different size Bibles.

WILLIAM WALTERS

For ten years Walters had suffered from angina pectoris. His first attack was in his office in St Paul's Churchyard, where his son found him lying on the floor in great pain. There were further attacks, which meant that the eldest son had to relieve his father of much of the business. Shortly after a family holiday on the Isle of Wight, in May 1907, he unexpectedly passed away.

Walters' death left behind a record hardly equalled by

any other man or woman of faith. In the short space of 20 years this remarkable man had sent out 10 million portions of Scriptures, published in 22 languages and circulated in 50 countries. Like his great predecessor of 400 years, William Caxton, he had used the power of the press to spread the gospel of his Lord and Saviour.

In 1920 SGM launched out in a new direction, producing a wide variety of publications, beginning with smaller compilations of Scripture verses. There is now a range of about 60 booklets and leaflets in English, all in the words of the Bible. Some are for evangelism or teaching, while others are designed to meet different needs, such as the old, the sick and the bereaved.

Each year some 17 million publications are sent as free supplies to about 20,000 Christians in more than 150 countries. They are printed in around 350 languages, though altogether SGM has published Scripture portions in nearly 800 languages.

The Mission is also involved in translation work and every year publishes 'pioneer editions', which are the first ever printed portions of Scripture in a particular language. Since 1888, SGM has produced 146 'pioneers'. Each year the mission publishes the first Scripture in one or two of the world's languages which have no part of the Bible in print.

In the early nineties SGM developed its international strategy significantly, making its nine overseas offices more autonomous. This move was reflected both in the new name, SGM International, and in the change of logo.

## MISSION STATEMENT OF SCRIPTURE GIFT MISSION INTERNATIONAL

Scripture Gift Mission exists to publish and distribute the Word of God throughout the world so that people may come to know Jesus Christ as Saviour and Lord. The Mission's quality publications in many languages are designed to be given, without charge, to those who will use them with care in their prayerful personal witness. The Mission looks to God to provide its financial needs without solicitation and encourages the prayerful support of Christians everywhere.

## 24. SCRIPTURE UNION (1867)
### Josiah Spiers (1837-1909) and Tom Bishop (1840-1920)

One outcome of the Evangelical Revival which began in the 18th century was that greater attention was given to the needs of poor children. Although initially concern was directed towards providing for their social necessities, this was invariably accompanied by attempts to meet their spiritual needs. It was during this era that the Sunday School Movement was founded, so that working children could be given an elementary education and receive simple Bible teaching.

Little thought was given, however, to the religious instruction of children from the homes of better-off families. It was customary in Victorian times for children 'to be seen and not heard', and this was no more evident than in church. Dressed in their 'Sunday best', children accompanied their parents to church, where they sat through a long sermon designed for the likes of adults.

Although Sunday Schools were an established feature of church life, those from wealthier families did not usually mix with working class children. Their religious upbringing tended to be of a rather more formal kind, with attendance at family prayers and confirmation (or similar) classes where they were taught the catechism.

The idea of enjoying church was quite foreign to them. That is, until Josiah Spiers and Tom Bishop founded the Children's Special Service Mission (CSSM) in 1867. Its purpose was to cater specifically for the spiritual needs of the young and to make religion more meaningful to them.

Spiers called into question a well-established view that children could not understand enough theology to be saved. Through the work of CSSM he awakened in children an interest in the gospel that had long been suppressed by formal religion, and many were consequently won to Christ at an early age.

### Informal Methods
The origin of the Mission can be traced back to a children's meeting Spiers attended one summer evening in 1867. He took a group from his north London Sunday School to a special children's service at John Street Baptist Chapel in the West End. The pastor of the chapel was the aged Rev. Baptist Noel, but the meeting was conducted by Payson Hammond, a young American who had trained in Scotland to become

a missionary. Hammond had come to the realisation, in contrast to what was then current opinion, that young children were able to understand enough of the gospel to have a living relationship with Christ.

That evening the church was packed with over 1,000 people. Instead of being tucked away in the gallery, as was usually the case, the seating arrangement was reversed – children were in the main body of the church and adults in the gallery. The whole service was geared to the young congregation. The hymns had simple words and were set to bright and cheerful tunes. Prayers were short, couched in language children could understand and in which they could join.

The preacher's informal methods caught the children's interest, as he spoke to them simply of the gospel and he encouraged them to enjoy themselves. Abandoning the pulpit, Hammond stood on a platform to speak to his young audience. He told stories that were interesting, even amusing; he also asked them questions, making the Bible teaching clear and appealing.

After the last hymn, he invited children to stay behind for counselling – another innovation – and many of them that evening professed faith in Christ.

Josiah  Spiers

Some of the adults were critical of his methods, believing that it was dangerous to encourage children to make a decision they felt they could not understand. Others accused him of 'playing on the emotions of children' and of 'sensationalism'.

Nevertheless, during the four evenings Hammond preached at the church, hundreds of children made decisions for Christ. Spiers was impressed with the lively approach and the call for a response, and recognised the possibilities of the evangelist's ideas.

That week Spiers teamed up with an artist friend, Thomas Hughes, and on the following Sunday started a children's meeting in his home on similar lines. The experiment was a success, and as numbers increased they combined with another group at the Rev William Pennefather's church of St Jude's, Mildmay, in the East End. By the time of the first annual meeting in July 1868, an average of 300 children were coming to Spiers' weekly services, and he had 687 names on the register.

Concerning the work, the Mission's report announced: 'Many of the children have given decided evidence of conversion, and of others we are very hopeful.' Five years later, it was agreed: 'There is no doubt that a deep interest has been awakened all over the country in regard to the conversion of children.'

**Auxiliary Force**

Hammond's meetings had triggered off a similar work at Surrey Chapel, south of the Thames, under a young civil servant called Thomas Bishop. Spiers and Bishop met in April 1868 and decided to join forces. Bishop's main gifts were as a writer and organiser, whereas Spiers proved to be a magnetic preacher. The two men worked together for 42 years, building CSSM and later Scripture Union into a national and international auxiliary force alongside the Church.

Spiers and Bishop formed a committee and adopted the title Children's Special Service Mission for their new organization. The choice of the unusual title was very deliberate, for it described the work accurately. It was probably influenced by events in parliament, where a Special Services Act had recently been passed. Under the act, Anglican churches were allowed on certain occasions to use services not in the Prayer Book.

For a while CSSM remained as a little-known local society, but following Spiers' summer holiday in August that year it became a national institution. As he walked along the beach at Llandudno, he watched children of well-to-do parents playing in the sand, making a 'garden' with pebbles and seaweed. (Working class families had not yet reached the stage of affording a seaside holiday.) It occurred to Spiers that instead of making a garden, the children could be making a text of Scripture with their pebbles.

He hurriedly purchased a ball of string and some pegs, and ran back to the beach. 'Who'll help me write a text?' he called to the nearest group. A crowd of children soon gathered around him for the activity, which he followed up by telling Bible stories. For the rest of the week Spiers kept his daily tryst with the children, which culminated on the Sunday with a special service attended by nearly 400 people.

The beach services proved a major step forward. They gave CSSM useful publicity and, more important, provided a way of reaching the wealthier sections of society.

Spiers turned out to be a gifted speaker with both children and adults. A small legacy from his father enabled him to resign his job and devote the remainder of his life to being an evangelist. For the next 40 years, until his death, he gave his time and services to CSSM without pay.

**Around the Country**

Beach services in summer were a regular feature of Spiers' ministry. Often they were an opportunity to contact the children of upper class families who would otherwise never have attended Sunday School. Adults, too, heard the message. On one occasion, Spiers preached on the promenade at Eastbourne, when a young society débutante, Grace Josephine Wakefield, responded to the gospel. She sold her jewels and set out to follow her new Lord. Becoming a Mildmay deaconess, she served in the Mildmay Mission Hospital before going out to a hospital in north-west China.

Spiers received invitations from around the country to hold missions in numerous towns and villages. This was the pattern of his ministry throughout the rest of his life. Equipped with a carpet bag bulging with hymn sheets and leaflets, Spiers would leave London on a Monday morning to start a mission. He was usually back in the capital by the following weekend in order to be at St Jude's on the Sunday.

Great care was taken over arrangements for his meetings, which were held in public buildings in keeping with the non-sectarian nature of the mission. His methods were based on those he had learned from Hammond, so that his services were always bright and cheerful. But his ministry was to rich and poor children alike. With money collected from well-to-do families he provided hot soup and dumplings for poor children from ragged schools, which he followed up with hymns and stories.

For the children of better-off parents who did not attend Sunday School he held drawing-room meetings. Each service closed with a Conversational Meeting, 'the most important feature of the work'. In this way, teachers were able to speak personally to children about the way of salvation. Spiers put great emphasis on individual attention and pastoral care, and always urged workers to keep a careful watch over young believers.

The invention of steam-driven printing presses and advances in education made it possible for CSSM to develop a literature pro-gramme. It began with tracts written specially for children, which were soon translated into other languages for use on the Continent. But it was the provision of a Bible reading list that was to have the greatest impact.

It took CSSM two years to awaken to the plan, suggested by Annie Marston of Keswick, who wanted to encourage her Sunday School pupils to read their Bibles every day. Bishop was at first sceptical about expecting children to make this kind of commitment, but both he and Spiers eventually warmed to the idea.

Launched on 1st April 1879, the scheme initially covered the four Gospels, but a regular four-year course was drawn up to operate from the following January. The Bible portions were printed on a card folded in three, and members had to agree to read and pray every day. If they were unable to keep up the practice, they were expected to return the card. Six thousand cards were issued, but by July membership had risen to 30,000 in over 400 branches.

The following October CSSM issued the first monthly edition of *Our Own Magazine* for children, which included articles illustrating or explaining the current Bible readings. It was an immediate success and soon reached a circulation of 62,000.

Separate cards were issued for schoolboys in preparatory and public schools, and for young people, though the list of readings was always identical. In 1885 cards were made available for adults, and were simply headed The Scripture Union. Notes to accompany the Bible readings, however, were not produced until 1886, when they were published in *Our Boys' Magazine*. They were not issued as a separate booklet until 1923, following the resignation of Tom Bishop after 52 years' service with the mission.

## Wider Circle

The work of CSSM and SU soon spread far beyond the shores of Britain, to countries as far apart as Jamaica and Japan. In Canada, a branch was started among the emigrant boys of one of Annie Macpherson's homes. Groups sprang up in the USA; across Europe, from Holland to Russia, branches were begun using their own language; and a 14-year-old girl started a branch in Japan for adults. In Britain, CSSM adapted its methods to reach a wider circle, while continuing to serve as a nursery of the Church.

The Caravan Mission to Village Children was founded in 1876, camps for school boys were started in 1892, and Crusaders was formed in 1906 to reach boys not linked to a Sunday School. Beach missions and camps were staffed by volunteers from the universities, many of whom later went into full-time Christian work.

Despite the assaults of liberal theology towards the end of the century, CSSM remained true to its biblical foundation and its twin aims of evangelism and teaching. The rapid growth of SU during the early years was to a large extent due to its link with CSSM, an already widely-known and respected organization. At the same time, the foundation of the SU work greatly assisted the advance of CSSM, because of its scriptural basis.

When Spiers died at the age of 72, the movement could justly claim to have changed the nature of British Christianity and to have brought a new awareness of the value of the child. Further, it greatly enhanced the Christian life of the universities, by its 'robust manliness', its allegiance to the Bible and the non-denominational character of its work.

Scripture Union, which incorporates the work of CSSM, operates in over 100 countries. It continues to be innovative in communicating God's love for children and young people, and works through a diversity of activities. In addition to promoting evangelism and publishing Bible reading notes, SU works in schools alongside teachers and pupils, and produces materials to resource and train Christians to work with children.

Although it no longer runs bookshops in England, SU continues to publish a wide range of books and audio visuals for people of all ages. It also works with families, in urban mission, through Bible ministries and in other aspects of training.

There is no doubt that the need for SU's imaginative, responsible, biblical evangelism and nurture is as great as ever. As long as SU continues 'showing love in an age of loneliness ... giving witness in an age lacking standards ... (and) speaking simply of a wonderful Lord in an age that lacks a Master', then God will be able to use SU to bring his Word to a young world.

## AIMS OF SCRIPTURE UNION

Working with the churches, Scripture Union aims

(a) to make God's Good News known to children, young people and families
(b) to encourage people of all ages to meet God daily through the Bible and prayer

so that they may

come to personal faith in our Lord Jesus Christ
grow in Christian maturity and
become both committed church members and servants of a world in need.

*Scripture Union pursues these aims through a variety of specialist ministries around the world in obedience to our Lord Jesus Christ and in reliance on the Holy Spirit.*

## 25. WYCLIFFE BIBLE TRANSLATORS (1942)
## & SUMMER INSTITUTE OF LINGUISTICS (1936)
### W Cameron Townsend (1896-1982)

The last hundred years have witnessed a tremendous upsurge in Bible translation, unparalleled in the previous centuries of the Church's history.

At the time of the Reformation there were only 24 languages with Bibles, or portions of it. By 1600 this figure had risen to 30. In 1900 the total stood at 118 languages with a complete translation of the Bible, and 517 with at least one book.

Today there are 342 complete translations, the New Testament is available in 823 languages, while in another 957 languages there is at least one book of the Bible. This brings the total of 2,122 languages where there is some portion of Scripture.

This recent growth is due to the work of groups such as the United Bible Societies, the Scripture Gift Mission and the Trinitarian Bible Society. A number of Roman Catholic Bibles and New Testaments have also appeared. But by far the greatest contribution has been made by Wycliffe Bible Translators, founded by W Cameron Townsend.

The Great Commission, to 'Go and make disciples of all nations', was burned into the bones of Cam Townsend, a young college student from California. When he discovered that the Bible House of Los Angeles wanted Bible salesmen for South America, he recognised that here was his opportunity to respond to the call. He had studied Spanish at High School and college, and decided to take time off to use his talent in the service of the gospel. His intention was to spend a year selling Bibles before returning to college to complete his studies.

Assigned to Guatemala in Central America, he left the States in August 1917, accompanied by his good friend Robby. After an initial period of orientation with missionaries from the Central American Mission, the young men set off to sell their Bibles.

On his journey, Townsend was accompanied by an Indian friend, Frisco, who was a believer. It was from Frisco that he soon learned of the plight of the Cakchiquel Indians, and how they lived under oppression from their witch doctors, the Spanish-speaking peoples, and even the clergy. No one paid any attention to their real needs. They had no schools, the men worked in a forced labour system and they were generally a despised people.

Not even the evangelical missions had attempted to reach them with the gospel, added Frisco, for the missionaries did not speak their language. Straightway, Townsend realised that he was following in their footsteps, for his Bibles were in Spanish, and so far he had only gone to Spanish-speaking people.

## Challenge

As the awareness of this sunk in, Frisco challenged Townsend: 'No one evangelizes the Indian in his own tongue. Why don't you come and be our missionary?'

'But I don't know Spanish well, much less Cakchiquel,' he protested.

'We'll teach you,' Frisco promised.

In the silence that followed it dawned on Townsend that if he learned the language, then he would be able to translate the Bible into it. But how could he do it, with no special training? The thought troubled him. By the middle of the next month, however, the conflict was resolved. He decided that this was what the Lord wanted him to do, whatever the problems.

It was 1919 when Townsend and his newlywed wife, Elvira, of Moody Church, Chicago, who was a missionary whom he met on the field, decided to go and live among the Cakchiquel Indians in the small town of San Antonio. The couple went as members of the Central America Mission, which had given him much support since his arrival in Guatemala.

To the delight of the Indians, Townsend immediately began a study of the Indians' language and culture. The task was quite new to him, and he found great difficulty in getting to grips with the intricacies of the grammar. Despite this problem, he became involved in the life of the people and set up a number of projects.

Accompanied by Frisco, he spent some of his time on evangelistic treks to neighbouring villages. He also started a 'school of the prophets' for Bible teaching and practical training, aimed at establishing a group of Indian evangelists and pastors. As the work developed and churches were founded, he opened a Bible institute for students from the surrounding tribes. Deeply concerned for their physical and material needs as well, Townsend kept his promise by opening a day school for the children of believers, held in a room loaned by the village chief. In time, he was able to erect a school building, and open a clinic and a home for needy Indian children.

## New Testament

All the time Townsend was extending his knowledge of the Cakchiquel language and adding to his list of words and phrases. But the problem of analysing the grammar continued to confound him. The key to the solution was provided for him by a visiting American archaeologist.

'Young man,' he said, 'I suspect you've been trying to force Cakchiquel into the Latin mould. Dr Sapir, the University of Chicago linguist, stresses the importance of a truly descriptive approach.'

It occurred to Townsend that each language had its own pattern and logical development. From then on, he started to look at the language from a Cakchiquel point of view. This advice had turned him in the right direction, and slowly the pieces of the puzzle gradually fitted together.

Although his grasp of the language was still imperfect, he began by translating the Gospel of Mark. Because of his many other commitments, however, it took 10 years of dedicated work to complete the whole New Testament in Cakchiquel. When it was published, he arranged a dedication ceremony, attended by the President of Guatemala who was given a leather-bound copy of the book.

As a result of his efforts, lives were changed and great improvements made in the Indians' standards of living. But he wondered whether he should let the Cakchiquels take over the work so that he could move on elsewhere. Other missionaries wanted him to stay, but he felt the Lord had given him a word to go after 'the one lost sheep'.

His mind meanwhile turned towards other literacy projects, in the belief that God would send more young men and women to plant his Word in every language. His chief concern at that time was for the Indian tribes of the vast Amazonian basin of Brazil.

But a missionary friend, L L Legters, pointed out that there was a mission field much closer, that of Mexico, where there were nearly 50 Indian tribes without a Bible in their own language. The way forward was opened up by a chance meeting with an eminent Mexican educator, Dr Moises Saenz, who was studying Indian problems in Guatemala. Townsend explained his aims to Dr Saenz: the need for people to be able to read in their mother tongue, and for them to have a Bible to set them free from vice and superstition.

Impressed with his ideas, the professor wrote to Townsend inviting him to transfer his efforts to Mexico. Two years later, in 1933, Townsend and Legters drove to Mexico in the hope of carrying out a survey. Even though they travelled as linguists rather than missionaries, they were refused entrance. It was only on production of Dr Saenz's letter that they were eventually allowed into the country. Nevertheless, they were warned not to preach or study Indian languages, or else they would be expelled!

## Summer School

Townsend was beginning to realise that the task of reaching so many tribes without a Bible in their own language was too big for him. 'We need to start a summer training school where young pioneers from all missions can come and rough it, and learn how to reduce a language to writing and translate the Scriptures,' he concluded.

After their return from Mexico, he organised their first annual summer school for training translators. Only two students turned up, but with each succeeding year the number increased. The course included phonetics, how to analyse a language, anthropology, missionary policy and how to live the victorious life.

Gradually they built up a corps of dedicated workers, trained to live with a tribe, write down their unwritten language and then begin Bible translation.

In 1936 the need for an office and to put the work on an official footing meant they had to reconsider their position. The school had initially been known as Camp Wycliffe; now they adopted the title 'Summer Institute of Linguistics' (SIL). There was a committee with a constitution and an annual business conference; the work, however, was to be directed by the missionaries out on the field.

Townsend was elected Director, though he proposed he should operate under the executive committee. He believed it was dangerous for one man to have too much control.

From 1936 to 1944 Cameron and Elvira Townsend returned to Mexico and lived in the town of Tetelcingo, said to be the most backward Aztec settlement in the state of Morelos. His experience of Cakchiquel made learning Aztec easier and, as in Guatemala, he became thoroughly involved in the life of the people.

To learn their language and gain their trust, he felt that as far as possible he must become one of them. He planted fruit trees and flowers, and grew vegetables. A co-operative store was started to enable the Indians to sell their produce, he brought in more teachers for the school, and water was piped from a spring to the plaza.

News of his achievements reached the ears of the President, who one day turned up unannounced at the town to see the work for himself. The visit marked the beginning of a lifelong friendship between the two men, and of staunch support for the work of SIL. It was as a result of this friendship that Townsend learned the value of working through local governments, identifying and co-operating with them rather than competing.

With increased responsibilities as Director of SIL, Townsend began to spend less time in Mexico. Two new missionaries offered to take over his work, which left him free to move around more. But as the number of workers increased – there were 37 translators working in 18 tribes – it became necessary to set up a second organisation to co-ordinate their affairs back home.

In 1942 Wycliffe Bible Translators (WBT) was founded, with Townsend as Director of the twin organisations. WBT was to be responsible for making financial arrangements, publicising the work and assisting evangelical missionaries to get special linguistic training.

## Peru

It was the work of linguistics that opened the door for SIL to begin operations in South America. This came about following an approach to Peru, Bolivia and Ecuador, with an offer to help solve some linguistic problems in the Quechua language.

The entrance to Peru aptly illustrates Townsend's philosophy of co-operating with national governments, by way of a personal approach. It was an invitation to the Peruvian Minister of Education to have dinner with him and his wife that led to the founding of a bilingual school system in Peru.

CAMERON TOWNSEND

SIL trained specially selected young men, using Spanish and their own tribal language. The students in turn taught what they had learned to their Indian tribes. In 1945, as a result of this plan, Townsend was able to draw up a contract with the government of Peru which allowed SIL to operate within that country. This development was of strategic importance, for it also opened up the way for a move into the vast Amazonian area of Brazil and its neighbouring countries.

During these years Townsend set up two further projects in support of Wycliffe's work, to further benefit the work of SIL. A jungle training camp was started in 1945, set in southern Mexico, to give young people the chance to learn how to cope with pioneer living in a jungle setting. And his long-standing vision for Wycliffe's own aviation service finally came true in 1949, when Jungle Aviation and Radio Service (JAARS) started flights in Peru.

## JAARS

As early as 1926 Cam Townsend had the vision of an aviation service to support his missionary enterprises. But it was many years before his dream became a reality.

When invited by the minister of education in 1945 to work among the Indians of Peru, he recognised that a small plane would be invaluable for reaching jungle tribes. By this time the American MAF had been formed, and they were able to help.

An amphibious plane was purchased. MAF sent Betty Greene, an experienced pilot and former member of WASP (Women's Air-Force Service Pilot) who had ferried aircraft across the Atlantic during the war, to fly the plane. But as she was also flying for other missions in Peru, she could only help on a part-time basis.

However, as MAF did not agree with the idea of flying for the Peruvian government, Townsend was even more convinced that Wycliffe needed its own planes and support services. By 1949 the $40,000 needed to start the service had been donated, and he was able to go ahead with the scheme. It was called Jungle Aviation and Radio Service (JAARS).

In 1951 a Catalina flying boat was dedicated at a ceremony at Mexico City Airport. The plane was then flown to Lima, the capital of Peru, to take up its duties in support of WBT.

Townsend's work was not without controversy, both at home and abroad, and it took all his tact and diplomatic skill to repair potential breaches that could otherwise have damaged Wycliffe's progress. In 1949 criticism was made against Wycliffe through the Interdenominational Foreign Missions Association (IFMA) concerning their alleged co-operation with Catholics. Around the same time, some of Townsend's own colleagues were bothered about the acceptance of Pentecostals and the matter of speaking in tongues. Some years later further trouble was sparked off by anonymous critics who charged Wycliffe with being scientific and cultural, and not spiritual; also they used their planes to help the Catholic Church.

These were real problems that threatened Wycliffe's financial position and standing. Though Townsend managed to mount a defence, it finally led to Wycliffe's withdrawal from the IFMA. But it did not hinder the work, and Wycliffe continued to grow and serve other missions as before.

The Wycliffe story is quite remarkable, and to the end of his life Townsend continually pioneered new ventures. Affectionately known throughout Wycliffe as 'Uncle Cam', he was a man of great faith. His constantly re-affirmed belief, that 'nothing was impossible to God', was frequently evidenced by the tremendous obstacles that he over-came.

With incredible singleness of mind, Townsend would not be satis-fied until the very last group of people had received the Word of God in their own language. He spent 65 years in pursuit of this aim.

---

### MISSION STATEMENT OF
### WYCLIFFE BIBLE TRANSLATORS (UK)

In obedience to God:
1. To enable people groups worldwide to encounter the good news of Jesus through the ministry of Bible translation and literacy.

2. To mobilise and facilitate the involvement of churches and individuals in the UK in the provision of people, funds and prayer to this end.

## WYCLIFFE BIBLE TRANSLATORS
## TRANSLATION PROCESS

It takes between 8 and 34 years, depending on local circumstances, for Wycliffe personnel to produce a translation of the New Testament. There are many complex stages to be completed, involving a team of workers with different gifts and responsibilities, in which educated mother-tongue speakers play a major role, assisted by Wycliffe project advisors. Below are some of those stages, assuming an area where there is already a church/mother-tongue translator(s) :

*Preparation*
* Team members learn to speak language and understand local culture
* Analyse sounds, grammar; if language unwritten, develop/test writing system
* Work with the church leaders, forming an organising committee, selecting and training local translators

*Beginning Translation*
* Study Bible text, research exegetical/textual/translation/cross-cultural problems
* Make first draft translation

*First Draft Stage*
* Check translation with project advisor/team members
* Test translation with other individuals/groups
* Make a 'back translation' – a speaker of the language translates the draft literally back into English or a common language
* Check translation verse by verse with consultant; revise, making second draft

*Second Draft Stage*
* Proofread, check corrections
* Send copies to reviewers from different churches/dialects for comments
* Prepare/distribute trial copies for testing; revise, make third draft

*Third Draft Stage*
* Many checks necessary: for consistency, spelling/capital letters/punctuation, illustrations, chapter/verse numbers, layout/format, accuracy of translation (inaccuracies may have crept in during revisions)
* Decide final design/appearance of book
* Final approval from consultant/branch director

# 3

# SUPPORT AGENCIES

## 26. EVANGELICAL ALLIANCE
## (1846)

The term 'evangelical' has been in use since the post Reformation era, and means simply 'of the gospel'. It was applied to certain churches during the 16th and 17th century, but came to prominence in the 18th century revival when it was increasingly employed to describe those men and women who had undergone a conversion experience and had accepted the fundamental truths of the gospel.

Both the Anglican and Nonconformist churches were permeated by the revival, and there arose a movement across the mainstream denominations of Protestantism that became known as 'Evangelicalism'. Today, over a third of all churchgoers in Britain belong to the evangelical tradition.

The roots of the evangelical movement can be traced back to Holland and Germany towards the end of the 17th century. A professor at Leyden University, Johannes Cocceius (1603-1669), began to expound theology on a purely biblical basis, and taught that religion was a covenant between God and man.

This return to a more personal faith was taken up by a Lutheran pastor, Philipp Spener (1635-1705) of Frankfurt. He operated by holding twice weekly meetings in his home for prayer and Bible study, known as *collegia pietatis*. The ensuing movement, termed Pietism, made rapid progress; it led to the foundation of the University of Halle (1694) which became a pietist stronghold.

A move began next among the Moravian Brethren under their leader, Count von Zinzendorf (1700-1760), at Herrenhut, a village east of Dresden. When the spiritual life of the Brethren was revitalised in 1727, it resulted in a wave of missionary zeal. Foreign missions, almost unknown among Reformed Churches, were set up from Greenland to Africa.

Some of the Moravians emigrated to America, where they founded settlements in Pennsylvania and North Carolina. In doing so they provided a link between them and the British and American revivals.

### Low Ebb
Christianity in Britain at the turn of the 17th century was at a low ebb. Not only were there few churches being built, but many Nonconform-

ists had lost much of the fervour that had characterised their dissenting forebears. A number of Presbyterian and General Baptist churches had gone over to the Unitarians where they adopted Arian views (which denied the true divinity of Christ).

Nor did the Church of England fare any better, for its services were often formal and meaningless, while the clergy gave more time to sport, politics and entertainment than attending to their flock.

From the 1730s there began a movement of the Spirit of God in revival, which transformed the Church and made a great impact on British society.

It started in Wales when Howel Harris (1714-1773), a school master from near Brecon, came to faith. Shortly afterwards, Daniel Rowland (1714-1790), a curate from Llangeitho, Cardiganshire, also underwent a conversion experience. Forbidden to preach in church, both men began to proclaim the gospel in the open-air, and hundreds throughout the Principality were brought to Christ.

Around the same time in England, George Whitefield (1714-1770) also came to a saving faith in Christ, followed three years later by John Wesley (1703-1791). Both men, ordained into the Church of England, attracted large crowds to the churches where they preached.

In 1739, first Whitefield and then Wesley began to follow Harris' example by preaching in the open-air, despite earning the contempt of other clergymen for their 'enthusiasm'. Large numbers of working class people were won to Christ, and were then formed into religious societies to support and encourage their faith.

### Growth

Throughout much of the century the new societies – known as Methodists – continued to grow. The movement permeated the Anglican Church as well as the other denominations, reaching even to the upper classes of society, including nobility. By the beginning of the next century it was noted that there had been a moral improvement in the nation, and – according to the historian Lecky – England had been saved from the sort of revolution that in 1789 had erupted in France.

Evangelicals from all denominations now had a common cause and found themselves coming together in order to further the gospel. In 1795 the London Missionary Society was founded on a non-denominational basis (though it later became a Congregational work) to promote Christianity among the heathen. Four years later the Religious Tract Society was similarly set up to publish tracts and other evangelical literature, while the Bible Society was established in 1804 to publish the Scriptures.

By the beginning of the 19th century Evangelicals were a recognised and established group on the Christian scene, though all was not well. Before long, a new generation of Christians arose which signalled a change of direction in Evangelicalism. Anglicans and Dissenters were taken up with their differing concerns and a breach appeared between the two groups that two or three decades earlier would not have been considered possible.

One other factor has to be taken into consideration when examining the progress of Evangelicalism. So far, Roman Catholicism in Britain had not constituted a threat to mainstream Christianity. But the Catholic Emancipation Act (1829) brought about a revival of Catholic life in England. Further support came from Italy, when a number of missioners of the Fathers of Charity were sent over, to stir up the Catholics by their preaching and ministry.

There was also an Anglo-Catholic revival within the Church of England, when the Oxford Movement emerged in an attempt to restore High Church principles to Anglicanism. Under Keble, Newman and Pusey, it gained influential support and a number of their members were converted to Rome.

### Plea For Unity

It was against this background that the first feelers were put out in an attempt to arrest deteriorating relationships between Evangelicals. One of the first to make a plea for unity was Andrew Reed, the Congregational minister from Wycliffe Chapel, East London. Reed corresponded with a number of European Protestants about the possibility of some kind of Evangelical union, though a conference in 1839 failed to produce any tangible results.

In the provinces, John Angell James, a leading evangelical pastor in Birmingham, received a letter on the matter from Dr Patton of New York. In it, it was suggested that a conference of delegates from different denominations should be convened in London to draw up a statement of truths upon which Evangelicals were agreed.

There was also considerable support for the idea in Scotland. John Henderson, a wealthy merchant from Glasgow, had published in 1843

## EVANGELICALISM

In his excellent study, *Evangelicalism in Modern Britain: A History from the 1730s to the 1980s*, David Bebbington identifies four main characteristics that help define evangelical Christianity. Though each generation has given them different emphases or formulated them in different terms, these four traits have continued as the basis of Evangelical faith.

### 1. The Bible
Evangelicals accept the Bible as the Word of God, and contend that God has specially revealed himself through his Word. They claim the Bible is God-breathed (i.e. by the Holy Spirit), and is the sole authority for Christian belief.

### 2. The Death of Christ
The crucifixion is the very essence of Christianity. It is God's provision, by which sinful man can approach a holy God. It is usually expressed in the Bible as an atonement for sin, a reconciliation between God and Man, a ransom, the only way of salvation or an expression of the love of God.

### 3. Conversion
Evangelicals stress the need for a conversion experience, known as the new birth. Preachers of the gospel urge their hearers to make a 'decision for Christ' and surrender their life to him. Such an act leads to a new way of living in which the believer endeavours to please his Lord.

### 4. Action
Those who have been born again find their aims and attitudes change, so that their wish is to share their new faith with others. They become involved in mission and in various forms of social concern.

The evangelical tradition crosses all Protestant denominational boundaries, uniting together many believers who would otherwise be separated by ecclesiastical differences. It has manifested itself throughout Church history, and according to John Stott 'the evangelical faith is original, biblical, apostolic Christianity'.

a series of papers by leading ministers who favoured unity, under the title, *Essays on Christian Union*. The wind of change was beginning to blow in Europe as well, led by Dr Merle D'Aubigné of Switzerland, who invited continental ministers to form a confederation.

The time was now felt ripe to bring the whole matter before the Christian public, and a meeting was arranged for the Exeter Hall, Strand, in June 1843. The demand for tickets was overwhelming and thousands had to be refused. The main speakers on that occasion were Dr James Hamilton (Presbyterian), the Hon and Rev Baptist Noel (Anglican) and the Rev John Angell James (Congregational), all leading Evangelicals of the day.

It was clear that not only Christian leaders were anxious for such a step forward, but also large numbers of other evangelicals. Further meetings in Liverpool, Manchester, Belfast and Dublin confirmed the suggestion, and it was resolved that a general conference be held in London.

**Remarkable Spirit**

In August 1846 nearly 1,000 delegates from every mainstream denomination around the British Isles, plus 80 from America and 60 from Europe, in all representing 52 Christian bodies. Assembled in the Freemasons' Hall, the leaders included Kinnaird, Binney, Angell James, Leifchild, Baptist Noel, D'Aubigné and Adolphe Monod, to mention a few. The chair was taken by Sir Culling Eardley, Bart., and his firm but kindly guidance contributed much to the success of the assembly.

From the beginning there was a remarkable spirit of harmony among the delegates, which seemed to some to be a foretaste of heaven! On the second day a resolution was passed forming a confederation on the basis of the great evangelical principles held in common by them ... under the name of the 'Evangelical Alliance'. This done, there was a two minute silence, and the matter was sealed by everyone shaking hands with those round about them.

Time was given to considering a doctrinal basis, proposed by the Rev Edward Bickersteth (Anglican), and a statement of nine points was drawn up to which members would have to subscribe. Dr Thomas Chalmers (Free Church of Scotland) brought the assembly down to earth when he expressed himself afraid of a 'union without work', which led the conference to define the work it set itself. The decisions taken became known as 'The Practical Resolutions', and were consequently read at every succeeding general conference of the Alliance.

The Alliance's great object was to be the promotion of Christian unity, and its areas of concern included support for Christians suffering persecution, the promotion of evangelical Protestantism, defence of the Lord's Day, and opposition to Romanism and other errors.

Towards the end of the conference, one issue was raised which could quite easily have split the Alliance. Some British members wished a resolution preventing any slave-holder from becoming a member. Whilst most of the Americans sympathised with the motion, they asked that it be withdrawn as it was felt this would prevent some American churches from joining. After considerable debate it was decided to let individuals follow the dictates of their conscience. (As a result, it was some years before an Alliance was formed in the States.)

### Critics

Though the conference ended in an atmosphere of thanksgiving and joy, it was not without its critics. Archbishop Whately of Dublin thought it would produce 'more dissension than union', and it was attacked in *The Christian Witness* as a movement that hoped 'to achieve impossibilities'. Andrew Reed, one of its earliest supporters, expressed disappointment, in that he distrusted the Alliance's aggressively Protestant sectarianism.

Once established, the Alliance quickly began to take root abroad. Branches were formed in France, Belgium and French Switzerland, followed by Canada (1846), Germany and Sweden (1847), India (1849), Turkey (1855), Spain and Portugal, and the United States (1867).

Its progress was monitored by a number of 'great and inspiring' conferences, held in some of the capital cities of Europe, and in America. The first International Conference of the Alliance was held in the Roman Catholic country of France, where – it was noted – some three hundred years previously had occurred the massacre of St Bartholomew (when large numbers of Huguenots were put to death).

Recognition of the Alliance was accorded by heads of governments, as well as by several crowned heads of Europe and the President of the United States. From the outset, the Alliance was true to its intentions and, as a consequence of its wide achievements, attracted much respect throughout the Christian world.

## Religious Liberty

From the beginning, one of the Alliance's chief objectives was to support the cause of religious liberty. Soon after it was formed, a religious crisis arose in the canton of Vaud (Switzerland), where the Council of State forbade the holding of any assemblies for religious purposes, except those of the state churches. It was some time before freedom of worship was granted.

Another task was to make representations on behalf of Protestants persecuted for their faith. In Turkey, there was an appeal to the Sultan on behalf of Christian minorities who were suffering from ill-treatment by Muslims, and who were threatened with death for changing their religion. In Italy, a family was imprisoned for reading the Bible, while in Spain 34 Protestants were imprisoned for changing their faith.

Although not a missionary society, the Alliance lent its support to societies and individuals engaged in mission and other evangelistic causes. At home, services were sponsored in the Exeter Hall, London, throughout the winter of 1855-56, when every Sunday for three months gospel

CLIVE CALVER (LEFT), CURRENT DIRECTOR GENERAL OF THE EVANGELICAL ALLIANCE, WITH JOSEF TSON OF THE ROMANIAN EVANGELICAL ALLIANCE.

## THE LORD'S DAY

When the emperor Constantine (in 321) designated the first day of the week as 'the Day of the Sun' and proclaimed it a public holiday, Christians reinterpreted the name as implying 'Sun of Righteousness'. Later emperors and Church councils were much occupied with questions of Sunday observance, and there were frequent attempts to identify Sunday with the Jewish Sabbath.

After the Reformation, Protestants such as Luther and Calvin could not identify the Christian Sunday with the Jewish Sabbath. There were attempts by Cromwell and the Puritans, for example, to enforce a more legalistic approach to the day, and one outcome of the 18th century Evangelical Revival was to make Sunday observance more strict.

In the early 19th century there was an increasing concern about the neglect of the Lord's Day. The Rev Daniel Wilson, Vicar of Islington (later, Bishop of Calcutta) founded an association in Islington (June 1830) 'for the better observance of the Lord's Day'. But it was his cousin, Joseph Wilson of Clapham, an influential businessman who was the prime mover of the Sunday observance campaign.

Believing the very soul of the nation to be at stake, he called together a number of prominent clergy and laymen in February 1831. At a meeting in London 'The Society for the due Observance of the Lord's Day' was founded – 'to diffuse information as widely as possible on the subject ... to lead to a due observance of the Lord's Day by such measures as are consistent with scriptural principles ... and to promote the enactment of such laws as may be necessary for repressing the open violation of the Lord's Day.'

Sunday observance became one of the chief concerns of the Evangelical Alliance, and a number of lively controversies ensued. Among them were the question of Sunday railway travel, and the opening of the Crystal Palace and the British Museum on Sunday afternoons. It was 20 years before any legislative result came from the debate.

meetings attracted a capacity congregation (with an estimated two-thirds of them not usually to be found in church). The missions of Moody and Sankey, together with lesser-known events, were actively encouraged.

Abroad, evangelism was fostered in India and China, and – nearer to home – in Europe and Russia, where Dr Baedeker toured prisons, and visited German Baptist churches and evangelical churches in Armenia.

The Universal Week of Prayer dates from 1860, though from the Alliance's inception the need for prayer had been constantly stressed. Each year there was an appeal for members to engage in united prayer for the Alliance, to be held during the first week of the year. A group of missionaries in Ludhiana, north India, wrote to the Council, suggesting that the call to prayer should be extended to all parts of the world, and the universal week has remained a permanent fixture.

## Projects

In more recent times, the Alliance has initiated a wide variety of projects. In 1951 it was instrumental in setting up the World Evangelical Fellowship, and in 1958 established the Evangelical Missionary Alliance. The purpose of this missionary body is to encourage co-operation, and provide co-ordination between missionary societies, churches and colleges.

Some of the Alliance's aims highlighted in 1846 are still being pursued. It has continued to campaign on behalf of persecuted Christians around the world, including Africa, Turkey and Russia, has promoted visits by the evangelists Billy Graham and Luis Palau, and has played a leading role in fighting attempts to introduce unlimited Sunday trading.

Its most recent outstanding achievement has been the founding of what has become one of Britain's foremost relief agencies – TEAR Fund. The origin goes back to the World Refugee Year in 1960, when gifts for the campaign began to arrive in the Alliance office. Donations continued to arrive during the succeeding years, until in 1967 Morgan Derham (the General Secretary) recognised the need for a separate agency to deal with the funds.

The outcome was The Evangelical Alliance Relief Fund (TEAR Fund), set up the following year under the direction of George Hoffman, a man of vision and compassion. Since then, giving to the Fund has soared from £34,000 in 1968 to over £20 million today.

The Alliance acts as a representative body for over one million evangelical Christians in the UK. It works through a wide network of member societies in areas of social, moral and spiritual concern, and speaks nationally to the government, the media and to other church bodies.

As someone once remarked, 'If the Alliance did not exist today, we would have to invent it.'

## EVANGELICAL ALLIANCE (UK) MISSION STATEMENT

Evangelical Alliance's purpose is to promote evangelical unity and truth and to represent evangelical concerns to the wider world of church, state and society.

a. By fostering evangelical co-operation, working through our members locally, regionally, nationally and internationally.
b. By advocating evangelical perspectives to government, media and the wider church.
c. By defending religious liberties and human rights worldwide.
d. By initiating consultation and reconciliation in areas of disagreement.
e. By proclaiming and explaining Biblical truth.
f. By encouraging united evangelical action in evangelism, prayer, mission, and in the pursuit of justice and responsibility.

The Evangelical Alliance is a partnership of individuals, local churches and denominational members of all races and cultures who share its Doctrinal Basis and desire to co-operate together.

## 27. KESTON INSTITUTE (1970)
### Michael Bourdeaux (born 1934)

The Bolshevik revolution of 1917 signalled the beginning of an official policy in Russia of opposition to religion. Its ultimate aim was to wipe out the Church and establish a Marxist state based on atheism.

During the 70 years of Communist rule, extended after 1945 to include much of Eastern Europe, millions of Christians and opponents of the State were either imprisoned or killed. Thousands of churches were confiscated and secularised, or even razed to the ground. Probably because of its association with the Tsarist regime, the Russian Orthodox Church was the Communists' first target.

Lenin declared the separation of Church and State, yet placed many stringent limitations on Soviet citizens' right of worship. Propaganda attacks in 1918 led to raids on churches and monasteries, which were ransacked and over two thousand priests killed. All church treasures were appropriated by the government.

Religious minorities, such as the Baptists (a term which came to include all Evangelicals), however, escaped attention, perhaps because of their low profile. For ten years or so the Baptists were free to evangelize, but it was only the lull before the storm.

A Law on Religious Associations was passed in 1928, which gave the Communists virtually any excuse for arresting believers. 'Prayer houses' had to be registered and the appointment of church officials rested with a government committee. Religious classes for children, young people and women were forbidden and restrictions placed on the clergy's ministry.

### Reign of Terror

With Stalin's promotion to Premier in 1929 (he was already the Party Secretary), the Church in Russia began to experience an even more brutal reign of terror under the new law. Thousands of church leaders were imprisoned and more churches closed. This time Evangelicals were included, and ordinary Christians were subjected to grievous suffering, torture and even martyrdom. The number of forced labour camps was increased, and thousands of believers met their death.

Russia entered the Second World War in 1941, when the persecution was halted in order to encourage support from church leaders. In the peace negotiations that followed, the Communists were allowed by the Allies to retain control over the nations of Eastern Europe. As in Soviet Russia, freedom of worship was lost and anti-Christian measures were implemented.

When Khrushchev came to power in 1956, Christians hoped that persecution might become a thing of the past. But a new wave of attacks started in 1959, when old laws were once more rigidly enforced. In order to survive, many believers found it necessary to go 'underground', and unregistered Christian meetings were held in homes and other secret locations.

Despite a determined appeal by the Baptists (1965) to a leading party official, Leonid Brezhnev, and Russia's signature of the Helsinki Agreement (1975) guaranteeing human rights, believers continued to be persecuted. In some instances they managed to escape, bringing news of the persecution of Christians behind the Iron Curtain.

As people in the West gradually began to appreciate the terrible situation existing under Communist regimes, a number of agencies were set up to provide support for the oppressed Church and to draw the world's attention to their plight.

Among these was Keston College, today renamed Keston Institute and based in Oxford, founded by the Rev Michael Bourdeaux, an Anglican clergyman.

## Plight of Christians

Michael Bourdeaux's concern for the plight of Christians behind the Iron Curtain began in 1959 when, as a postgraduate student at Moscow University, he learned of the persecution of the Church in Russia. His determination to 'Tell the West' the truth led eventually to his founding Keston College as a centre for the study of religion and Communism in the Soviet Union and Eastern Europe.

Two events, some five years apart, set Bourdeaux's life on a course apparently determined by God. Already qualified in French and German, he was sent for training as a Russian linguist while on National Service with the RAF. He decided to pursue this new interest at Oxford where he acquired a degree in Russian and French, and a further degree in Theology at Wycliffe Hall.

In 1959 he was one of the first British exchange students to study at Moscow University. His arrival in the Russian capital coincided with

MICHAEL  BOURDEAUX

the beginning of a new wave of persecution against the churches by the Khrushchev government, which aimed at eradicating all religion by the year 1980. The government-controlled press began fresh attacks on church leaders, and the full might of the law was used against believers. Despite the difficulties, Bourdeaux managed to worship in many of the capital's churches and made a number of friends, both Christian and atheist.

On his return home, he was ordained as a priest in the Church of England and was appointed curate to a parish in Enfield, North London. It was during his time in Moscow that Bourdeaux began to appreciate the extent of the persecution to which Christians were subject under the Khrushchev regime. He felt that somehow he ought to use this knowledge and his linguistic gifts to serve God.

A trip to Moscow the following year revealed nothing new about the Church's position. It was only afterwards when he received a copy of a letter written by two women from the Ukraine that he realised the situation was worsening. In this letter, the women recounted a number of disturbing persecutions, and begged someone to intervene with the Soviet government on their behalf.

Bourdeaux determined to discover the truth of the situation for himself, and in 1964 paid a further visit to the USSR. He started by searching out the church where he had worshipped as a student, but was horrified to find that the building had been reduced to rubble and the site surrounded by a fence.

## Be Our Voice

As he surveyed the scene, bewildered by the destruction, he noticed two women there. They were also apparently investigating what had happened to the church. When he was later able to speak with them privately, he was amazed to discover that they were the very same two

women who had written the appeal he had received some months
earlier! They had travelled 1,300 kilometres from the Ukraine to
Moscow in order to make a further attempt to find help, and their visit
to the church coincided with his.

It was this second happening, and their heart-rending appeal to 'Be
our voice', that set the seal upon the realisation he had to find some way
of serving the suffering Church. As there was no existing organisation
devoted to this cause, it meant launching out on his own. This would
really be an act of faith when he considered that he now had to provide
for a wife and family as well.

As an initial step he accepted a position as Soviet researcher with the
Geneva-based *Centre de Recherches*, which was investigating religious
affairs in Communist countries. When the work was disbanded, he
decided to set up his own group to replace it. He gave it the name,
'Centre for the Study of Religion and Communism'. This was in 1970.

For some time Bourdeaux used his home as a base, but the need to

---

*'Reconciliation between East and West
is only possible when based on truth'*
Michael Bourdeaux.

---

expand led to his first financial appeal. The response enabled him to
recruit more staff and to purchase a disused primary school as his
headquarters. Situated on the southern outskirts of London, Keston
College was opened in 1974 as a listening post for monitoring the
struggle for religious freedom in Eastern Europe.

As the College's work became more widely known, it became
possible to take on more researchers to cover both the Soviet Union and
Eastern Europe. In recent years, however, a drop in funding has meant
the loss of staff, though gaps are now being filled from the expertise
available at Oxford University.

**Public Informed**

From its early days, Keston has given high priority to keeping the public informed of news and developments from behind the Iron Curtain. Its first periodical was a quarterly academic journal, *Religion in Communist Lands*. Later this was supplemented by the fortnightly *Keston News Service*, published to provide news and information for churches, individuals and the media.

As the scope of the work widened, these two publications were replaced by two others. A quarterly newsletter, *The Right to Believe*,

## COLLAPSE OF COMMUNISM

While the collapse of Communism in 1991 provided a welcome opening for the gospel, it also gave an entrance to the cults, such as Jehovah's Witnesses, Moonies and Hare Krishna devotees, and to fundamentalist Muslims. Although many years of persecution had left the Church slimmer but stronger, 70 years of atheistic Communism had also created a spiritual vacuum throughout the land.

Prior to 1991 agencies such as Open Doors, Child Evangelism Fellowship, Keston Institute and the Bible Society had maintained contact with the persecuted Church. Now it is not only possible to take in Bibles and other kinds of Christian literature, but there is freedom to openly engage in evangelism. Mass evangelistic meetings have attracted huge crowds and have been given prime time on television. Local churches are being encouraged to reach out to their neighbourhood, and even schools are requesting Christian literature to help fill the moral and spiritual vacuum.

A number of ventures have been set up to reach out to Jewish people and many thousands of them have come to faith in their Messiah. *Hear O Israel Ministries* of America, for example, has endeavoured to draw these new believers into local Messianic fellowships and to attend short-term Bible schools. Meanwhile the Exodus Project (of Operation Eastern Europe) has been helping thousands of Jewish people return to their homeland of Israel.

In 1990 the Russian Congress of People's Deputies attempted to restrict the activities of foreign missionaries, but President Yeltsin refused to sign the amendment. The possibility of another clampdown is still a serious threat and Christians are hastening to make best use of the time that is left.

was produced from 1976. Then a bi-monthly glossy magazine, *Frontier*, was also launched to give a more accessible overview of the current religious situation in Eastern Europe.

More recently, responding to the new situation in the former USSR and Eastern Europe, *Religion in Communist Lands* was retitled *Religion, State and Society*. It monitors the experiences of religious communities in Communist and former Communist countries throughout the world and provides important analysis by international experts.

Within the span of its brief existence, the Institute has built up a worldwide reputation as the leading authority on religion in the USSR and Eastern Europe. Now relocated in Oxford, Keston has space for housing its extensive archive material.

Information has been documented, analysed and recorded, based on letters, newspaper reports, cassettes, photographs, typewritten *samizdat* (unofficial publications), prayers, poems and paintings. One of the most treasured possessions in the Keston archives is a bundle of folded cloth containing the entire transcript of the trial of Aida Skripnikova in 1968, noted down word for word in the court room by fellow-believers.

**Assistance**
As well as gathering reports, Keston has also assisted numerous groups and individual Christians suffering persecution or imprisonment, or seeking to emigrate. When Georgi Vins, the Baptist leader, was exiled to America in 1979, Michael Bourdeaux was called on to join him as soon as possible to ease his sudden transition from a concentration camp to the West.

In 1978 members of two Pentecostal families, later dubbed the 'Siberian Seven', made a successful dash for the American Embassy in Moscow with a request for asylum. Their plight was taken up by Keston and *Buzz* magazine, and in 1983 they were finally allowed to leave the country.

That same year, a Russian Christian rock singer, Valeri Barinov, was arrested and interned in a psychiatric hospital. Keston immediately informed the religious and secular press, and the news received wide publicity. One week later the singer was released; his family believe it was a direct result of prayer and publicity in the West.

When Bourdeaux received the Templeton Prize for Progress in Religion in 1984, it put Keston truly on the map and streams of enquiries began to pour in. Although the Iron Curtain has now been drawn back and *glasnost* is in the air, Keston still continues to monitor the religious situation and brings theological students and church leaders to the UK to help them develop their special interests.

In the former USSR, doors have opened that until a few years ago seemed impossibly shut. Michael Bourdeaux has played no small part in bringing religious freedom to nearly 200 million people formerly living under Communist rule.

## MISSION STATEMENT OF KESTON INSTITUTE

*Purpose*
1. To collect, study and disseminate, by publication and other means, information and informed comment on religion, state and society in Central and Eastern Europe.

2. To maintain for the benefit of scholars and researchers an archive of historical and current material on the state of religion in those areas which were under the domination of the communist regimes of Eastern Europe.

3. To foster contact, co-operation, mutual knowledge, understanding and practical help between religious groups and organisations East and West.

*Means*
In carrying out its work Keston aims to
1. Maintain the highest standards of accuracy and scholarship;

2. Collect and study information from a wide variety of sources and provide facts together with well-informed comment and reliable analysis.

# 28. LEAGUE OF PRAYER (1891)
## Reader Harris KC (1847-1909)

The holiness movement that arose during the latter part of the 19th century exerted a tremendous influence on evangelical Christianity. Many believers had an experience of the Holy Spirit, often referred to as a 'second blessing' or 'full salvation', which revolutionised their lives and spread revival through the churches. There was a quickening of missionary endeavour and evangelism as Christians offered themselves for full-time service, and from around 1870 the Church in Britain began to recover its evangelical witness.

It was Wesley's teaching on Christian perfection that prepared the way for the modern holiness movement. Based on the text, 'Be ye therefore perfect...' (Matthew 5:48), Wesley called his Methodist people to a life of 'entire sanctification'. Taking Jesus' words literally, he contended that perfection was attainable on earth. It was brought about, he suggested, by the reign of 'perfect love' in the heart of the believer. Thus he believed it possible to 'love God with all our hearts ... and our neighbours as ourselves'.

His teaching continued to influence Christians into the following century. It was affirmed by various Methodist denominations, and was known among some Brethren and Anglican believers. The Salvation Army, an offshoot of Methodism, also held to the holiness teaching, which was said to be one of its major strengths.

Across the Atlantic, Charles G Finney, President of Oberlin College and the leading revivalist of his day, was one of the early contributors to the movement. Phoebe Palmer, an influential Methodist proponent of the teaching, taught a 'shorter way' to holiness, claiming that it was to be had simply by accepting a 'second moment of grace'.

A number of Americans, among them Robert and Hannah Pearsall Smith, visited England in the 1870s to promote the teaching. Holiness meetings held at Oxford and Brighton in 1874 led directly to the founding of the Keswick Convention the following year, formed for the sole purpose of 'helping men to be holy'.

A variety of groups sprang up outside the denominations, aimed at promoting the teaching. In Britain, the movement found its focal point in the annual Keswick Convention. But among the several other groups set up with a similar aim was the Pentecostal League of Prayer, conceived by Reader Harris KC.

**Agnostic**

Reader Harris was born into a devout Anglican family, but while yet a boy the first seeds of agnostic thought were implanted in his young mind. His great aunt, when one day teaching him the Shorter Catechism, explained that not even the grace of God could enable a man to fully obey him. Reader argued with himself that if a grown-up could not obey God, a little boy ought not to be expected to obey his great aunt. An ensuing misdemeanour, however, caused him much suffering!

A second incident some few years later raised further doubts in his mind. When being prepared for confirmation by his vicar, Harris asked the meaning of Jesus' words, 'Be ye therefore perfect, even as your heavenly Father is perfect.' The vicar replied that the whole Sermon on the Mount was an ideal every believer should endeavour to reach, but it was unobtainable in this life.

To the 14-year-old boy, the idea of aiming at something without hope of attaining it seemed rather strange. It was at that point that he took another step on the downward path of unbelief.

In 1868, while working in London as a railway engineer, Harris heard a talk given by a well-known atheist, Charles Bradlaugh, President of the London Secular Society. During the course of his address,

READER HARRIS

Bradlaugh denounced Christians for not believing the Bible and for failing to live up to the Sermon on the Mount. He explained that his Society had been formed specifically to put the ideals of Christ's sermon into practice.

Captivated by Bradlaugh's thinking, Harris became a regular attender at the Hall of Science, and before long had abandoned his religious beliefs and become an agnostic.

It was some years before Harris was converted to Christ and restored to the Anglican Church. The journey began in 1878. When working as an engineer in Bolivia he had an escape from death and was forced to ask himself why God had spared him. He was also led gently along the path to faith by his wife, Mary Bristow, whom he married in 1880.

**Conviction**
Following her example, he began to read the Bible and attend church. He even engaged in preaching, but had no assurance of salvation. Under the conviction of the Holy Spirit, Harris eventually expressed a desire to be saved, but did not know what to do.

One day while travelling to Ealing by train, he read some words of Jesus spoken to his disciples, 'Receive ye the Holy Spirit'. While seated in his railway carriage, he prayed for and received the Holy Spirit – and missed his station in the process! Now he knew what it was to be born again, and realised that the foundation for his future work had been laid down.

During the years 1884 to 1890, Harris immersed himself in a variety of Christian activities. He was also increasingly occupied with his legal duties as a newly-qualified barrister and, later, as a King's Counsellor. Both he and his wife were involved in Moody and Sankey's London campaign in 1884, where they caught a vision for evangelism.

They started a special mission at Speke Road Hall, Battersea, south London. The building had previously been a Theatre of Varieties, and had seats for 1,400 people. He subsequently bought the hall, for which his wife sold most of her jewellery to help meet the cost. It was opened as a mission to reach the people who never attended church or chapel.

Harris himself conducted the services, and the Sunday evening meetings were invariably full. They formed a Mission Band of new converts, not only for the purposes of evangelism but also to visit homes and public houses where they were able to help people in need.

Other activities included a thriving Sunday School, Bible Classes for young people, a Mothers' Club and a lending library.

## Turning Point

The turning point in Harris' Christian life came in 1890, at a series of meetings at which two Americans preached. Their theme was 'holiness and the right of every believer to be baptised with the Holy Spirit'. Both Reader and Mary Harris were convicted by the message, and together made 'a complete surrender to God'. After that, God's seal rested on their work in a new way.

Hundreds of others entered into the same experience at Speke Hall, which became a powerhouse from where blessings spread out to many parts of the country. Within two years mission halls had been opened in a number of centres, including Croydon, Hampstead, Bristol and Hull, 'to spread scriptural holiness by unsectarian methods'. He also founded his own magazine, *Tongues of Fire*, to further this teaching.

At this point, Harris was faced with a problem: should he go on opening further mission halls for 'revived Christians', or should he encourage believers to stay in their own churches and spread the message there?

To arouse believers to seek an outpouring of the Spirit, he decided to form a prayer union. The purpose would be to pray for the filling of the Holy Spirit, the revival of the churches and the spread of Christian holiness. Known as the Pentecostal League of Prayer, it was not associated with any denomination, but was rather a ministry to the whole body of Christ.

The work of the Pentecostal League grew rapidly and over 3,000 people attended the first annual general meeting, held at Exeter Hall in the Strand. Branches were established in America, Australia and Japan, and by the end of the century the total membership numbered over 17,000.

## Oswald Chambers

Harris and his wife made regular tours around the country, speaking at services and conventions, where churches held united meetings to promote the work. They were assisted by other holiness evangelists, including Oswald Chambers, who was later to become renowned as a Bible teacher and evangelist.

## KESWICK CONVENTION

A renewed emphasis on holiness in the life of the Christian arose in the 1870s, largely under the influence of American preachers. While Charles G Finney of Oberlin College helped prepare the soil, the movement was pioneered in Britain by Mrs Phoebe Palmer, W E Boardman, and Robert and Hannah Pearsall Smith, and was advocated by D L Moody on his 1873-75 tour. Whilst Mrs Palmer introduced William and Catherine Booth to the teaching – at the time they were still in the Methodist New Connexion – the Pearsall Smiths set up a number of meetings for ministers and others which led in 1875 to the founding of the Keswick Convention.

Pearsall Smith came to Britain in 1873 and with Boardman held a long series of meetings, at Curzon Street Chapel in the West End and later moving to Cambridge. The Smiths were friends with Lord Mount-Temple, the Earl of Shaftesbury's brother-in-law, who invited them the following year to hold a conference at Broadlands, on his estate near Romsey (Hampshire), for the purpose of considering 'the scriptural possibilities of faith in the life of the Christian in the daily walk ... (with God)'. It was followed by larger conferences at Oxford and Brighton, where one of the members was Canon Harford-Battersby, Vicar of St John's, Keswick.

One month later, in conjunction with Robert Wilson of Broughton Grange, Battersby organised a 'convention for the promotion of practical holiness', held at Keswick in June 1875. Among the chief leaders were Theodore Monod, Andrew Murray, Dr A T Pierson, F B Meyer, and H C G Moule. As one advocate wrote, 'The Keswick Convention has set up no new school of theology, it has instituted no new sect, it has not even formed a society, but exists for the sole purpose of helping men to be holy.'

Despite Pearsall Smith's fall from grace, the convention survived, and by the 1880s had become an established element of the evangelical scene.

Chambers had a few years earlier entered 'years of heaven on earth' through the baptism of the Holy Spirit, and consequently in his messages emphasised 'the mighty efficacy of the Holy Ghost'.

It was in 1905 that Chambers first attended the May meetings of the League at Exeter Hall, as a delegate from Perth. He was immediately taken by Reader Harris, 'that man of God', and immersed himself in the League's work.

Frequently called upon to speak at conventions and missions under the auspices of the League of Prayer, he made a special impact on Scotland where, he felt, both people and ministers had for the first time in Scottish religious history been doubting the Bible.

When Harris was suddenly called home in March 1909, it was Chambers who was the leading speaker at the memorial service held in Queen's Hall, in the West End. At the close of the meeting, hundreds of

OSWALD CHAMBERS

men and women rose to signify their determination to carry on the work which Harris had started in uniting believers in prayer. At a council meeting the following day Chambers pledged his services to help carry on the work.

Chambers' time was largely taken up with ministry at Speke Hall, where he took over the leadership of the League. He regularly conducted services and supervised the Bible School correspondence classes, one of the main features of his activities.

During these years, he married Gertrude Hobbs at the Eltham Park Wesleyan Church, south east London, and they spent part of their honeymoon touring America where he spoke at various camp meetings.

It had been felt for some time that there was a real need for a training college, where practical holiness and effective soul-winning could be taught and demonstrated. Plans were set in motion and an ideal house found on the North Side of Clapham Common, not far from Speke Hall.

Chambers, formerly a theological tutor at Dunoon College, was appointed Principal of the Bible Training College, which opened in

January 1911. A number of well-known names were associated with the
college, including Dinsdale Young and Campbell Morgan.

He continued in charge of the college until 1915, when he volunteered as a chaplain to the British troops in Egypt. Mrs Harris replaced
him as principal and continued to be involved in the League. When
Chambers died suddenly while on active service, she took his place as
leader of the work and editor of the magazine. She continued in this
capacity until her death in 1922.

## MISSION STATEMENT OF THE LEAGUE OF PRAYER

The League of Prayer is an inter-denominational union of Christian
people who, conscious of their own need, would join in prayer

* For the Filling of the Holy Spirit for all believers;
* For Revival in the Churches
* For the spread of Scriptural holiness.

## 29. MISSION AVIATION FELLOWSHIP (1945)
## Murray Kendon (born 1917)

Since the beginning of the modern missionary movement at the end of the 18th century, the task of taking the gospel into inaccessible mountainous areas and jungles has entailed immense hardships and sacrifices. As well as the threat of hostile peoples and dangers to health and well-being, missionaries have been further handicapped by primitive living conditions, lack of backup services and adequate means of communication.

The risk of being killed by tribesmen, either as a result of ignorance or superstition, or by rebels for political or religious reasons, still prevails. Missionaries, by the very nature of their work, are vulnerable to all kinds of attacks. They need whatever support the Church can give, both in practical terms and in prayer. It was an attempt to meet some of these needs that led to the foundation of Missionary Aviation Fellowship (MAF).

### Vision

Towards the end of World War II a group of Christian airmen caught the vision of using small aircraft to advance the cause of the gospel. When the advantages of using small planes was recognised in other parts of the

---

**Wings of Mercy**

Betty Guthrie lay desperately ill at a remote missionary station in southern Sudan. Without medical help she would die, and the nearest accessible hospital was 500 miles away in Khartoum. When her husband Chuck discussed the situation with Sam Burns, the missionary in charge, it was decided she would have to be got out. A rough stretcher was made for Betty and her baby, and tribesmen helped carry it through swamps to the River Nile, 180 miles away. Remarkably, she and the baby survived the gruelling journey.

The final 25 miles to the river were by truck. After a two day wait, a journey by paddle steamer and then by train eventually brought them to Khartoum. It had taken ten arduous days' travel to reach the hospital, during which time Chuck had also been taken ill. With treatment, they both recovered, but it was six months before they were able to return to their station. Later, Betty was again taken seriously ill. But by then Mission Aviation Fellowship had begun operations in the Sudan. The MAF plane was summoned and in a matter of four hours the patient was safely delivered to hospital. Already the 'wings of mercy' were providing a life-support line for isolated missionaries.

---

world, it looked as though the dream could come true.

Murray Kendon was a New Zealand pilot based in England with RAF Coastal Command. The long hours spent patrolling over the grey waters of the Atlantic gave him time to ponder the more serious matters of life. During these periods he often asked himself, 'If aircraft can be so effective in war and destruction, why can't they be used to spread the gospel of peace?'

Brought up in a Christian home, Kendon had a concern for the millions of deprived people around the world who lived in isolated places, unable to hear the gospel or to enjoy a more abundant life. Something should be done to reach them, he concluded, and he believed that planes could be used for that purpose.

In 1944, shortly before his demobilization, he explained his ideas to Dr Thomas Cochrane of the Mildmay Movement. Cochrane, formerly a medical missionary in China, was a man of vision. He had founded the Mildmay Movement to encourage fresh initiatives in Christian outreach all over the world. When he heard Kendon's ideas he became quite enthusiastic, and envisaged a force of 1,000 planes around the world. But his response took the New Zealander by surprise. 'What would be the chance of your coming to start this at once?' he asked. 'It will be a full-time job for someone. Is that someone you?'

JACK HEMMINGS (pilot), STUART KING (in rear),
and MURRAY KENDON (closing aircraft).

For some time Kendon thought and prayed about the matter, for he had expected to return to New Zealand when he left the RAF. Eventually he realised that this was what God wanted him to do. He moved to the Mildmay Centre with his young English wife, and began work.

Searching around for a name for the new organization, he decided to call it 'Missionary Aviation Fellowship', which soon became known simply as MAF.

## Africa

Other Christian airmen were thinking along the same lines, and were attracted to MAF. First to join him in the venture was Stuart King, an RAF engineer officer. After him came Jack Hemmings, an RAF pilot who had won the Air Force Cross in India.

The next step was to stir the interest of the Christian public, and to encourage prayer and practical support from the churches. To that end they wrote articles, spoke at meetings and made contact with as many people as they could.

A temporary MAF Advisory Council was formed, consisting of six Christian pilots and twenty well-known Christian leaders. The first chairman of the council was Mr John Laing, head of the well-known construction company. One of their immediate tasks was to decide where to begin work. Many places, even China, were considered by the council. In the end it was agreed to start with Africa.

Questionnaires were then sent out to more than a hundred mission stations across central Africa, but it was recognised that it was necessary to have specific and exact information. To do this meant making an exploratory visit by plane, to carry out an on-the-spot survey. However, it was two years before enough money was raised to purchase an aircraft, a small twin engined Miles Gemini.

It was around this time they heard from Steve Stevens DFC, a South African Air Force pilot. At the end of World War II when ferrying troops from Cairo back to South Africa, Stevens had met leaders of the Sudan Interior Mission in Khartoum.

They had informed him of the desperate need of a plane for their missionaries working in the swampy southern Sudan. During the long rainy season, which made roads impassable for many months of the year, this region became one of the most isolated parts of the world.

Steve Stevens and his bride Kay determined to do something to help the Sudan Interior Mission's desperate situation, planning to set up an air service on their own if necessary. However, when Steve heard about the new organization he contacted MAF in London, asking that their air survey of Central Africa should begin with the Sudan. The Stevens went further, and offered to devote their lives to the opening up of an air service for missions in the Sudan.

On 13 January 1948 King and Hemmings took off from Croydon Airport en route for Central Africa. After first visiting the Sudan, where they recognized was a great need for an air service, their itinerary went on to include modern day Uganda, Kenya, Tanzania, Ruanda, Zaire and the Central African Republic.

**Disaster**

Towards the end of the tour whilst en route for Nairobi, disaster struck in Burundi. Their underpowered Gemini was caught in the fierce down-current of a wind as they endeavoured to clear a mountain. The plane crashed into the mountainside, and though the Gemini was a total wreck, the two men climbed out unhurt.

Despite the comfort and sympathy of missionaries from a nearby station, they were left shocked and dispirited. The survey had to be completed by road. In spite of the accident, they were able to take back to England a most comprehensive report concerning the opportunities for aviation.

Looking back at the accident, the airmen were able to consider all the other flying problems they had encountered on the tour. These lessons stood them in good stead for their future flying programme in Africa and enabled them to develop special flying techniques. Most of the missionaries they had met and talked to about an air service welcomed the prospect, but there were some with reservations. A number of missionaries had access by car or lorry to medical and supply centres, and could manage as they were. For others, their hesitation was mainly because of the high cost factor and the question of safety.

The most serious needs were those in the Sudan, where many missionaries were locked away in inaccessible stations and were far away from any semblance of civilization. Here, the two men recognised, was the greatest need.

Back home, Kendon read their report and queried whether in fact MAF was really needed after all. The facts did not seem to bear out their original contention. It almost appeared that MAF might be doomed before it had even commenced operation. But although King and Hemmings were convinced the scheme had great potential, the evidence seemed to be against them.

## Way Forward

As MAF worked under the umbrella of the Mildmay Movement, they met together with the council to consider the way forward. Insurance money from the Gemini crash made it possible to purchase a replacement plane, so that problem was resolved. Another call from a missionary in south Sudan confirmed that this was where God wanted the work to begin in the African continent.

But the council was reluctant. The first plane had been lost, they argued, would another fare any better? Suddenly the chairman pronounced, 'I think that if these two young men feel God is calling MAF to the Sudan we should let them go.' No one challenged him, and the purchase of a De Havilland Rapide was approved. MAF was reprieved and given a chance to prove its worth.

In the meanwhile Stevens had set about obtaining his Air Transport Pilot's Licence, and resigned his Air Force commission in preparation for joining MAF. He and his wife Kay, already a pioneer who had lived on a mission station in the remotest parts of Zambia, took their three children and began work with MAF in the Sudan.

Jack Hemmings, with Stuart King as engineer, flew the Rapide to the Sudan and they started negotiations with the government for permission to operate an air service. And though Hemmings had to return to England, King was joined by Steve Stevens, and in the September of 1950 they were able to begin regular flights. A network of routes and landing strips covering South Sudan was soon established, bringing missionaries the prospect of a lifeline.

Sadly, three years later Stevens developed a detached retina and had to give up flying. He was quickly replaced by a lifelong friend, Gordon Marshall, also a South African Air Force Pilot. The Stevens family moved to the UK where he became the Home Director, with the task of making MAF known throughout Britain.

In the early 1950s MAF became an independent organization, while other British and South African workers joined the team. Over the next ten years MAF was able to provide an air-arm for missionaries and assist the growing Sudanese Church during its difficult formative years. The work in the Sudan proved crucial for MAF in that it formed a launching pad for its entry into other African countries.

In 1964 civil war in the Sudan put the mission in jeopardy. Islamic fundamentalists wanted the Christians out of the country, so the Muslim government eventually decreed that all missions were to be expelled. Although MAF was later allowed to return for a while, operations were finally suspended in 1983.

## Expansion

MAF is now a global organisation, with over 300 pilots working in nearly 30 Third World countries across four continents. While the British branch was launched to serve Africa, MAF USA (founded in 1945) moved into Central and South America, whilst operating in Africa and Indonesia as well.

Since 1950 MAF Europe has expanded its services to cover a wide area of Central Africa. Tanzania is now its largest sphere of operation, where it has worked alongside national churches, reaching and nurturing remote groups.

In partnership with the Lutheran Church, monthly evangelistic and medical safaris have been made to the nomadic Masai in the north; and doctors from the Christoffel Blindenmission have been enabled to reach areas where many people are suffering from eye diseases. For the Anglican Church, the air services have helped support pastors in distant corners of the land, covering over a thousand congregations.

An entry was gained into the mountainous kingdom of Ethiopia in 1960, where MAF support has enabled missionaries and national churches to contact the previously unreached Mesengo people, one of the country's lost tribes. A military coup in 1974, however, led to a Marxist style government. Restrictions made the work increasingly difficult, and in 1977 MAF was forced to withdraw from the country.

The MAF programme in Chad started in 1966, and despite persecution and war it has seen the Church grow rapidly. When the country was hit by famine, MAF came to the rescue. On one occasion it carried out an extensive spraying operation to save the harvest, as well as saving an estimated 55,000 lives.

Kenya, Uganda, Madagascar, Zaire and Namibia are also areas of MAF ministry. Angola, where millions have suffered through years of violent conflict, is a MAF Canada activity.

Plans are going ahead for opening up a new front in Asia in the hope of one day setting up work in Mongolia where little is known of the gospel. The Australian and New Zealand MAF, founded in 1947, set up bases in Papua New Guinea and the Australian outback, where they support the Aborigine community.

Other MAF home entities have been started in South Africa, Canada and throughout Europe. Within MAF Europe there are eight national groups, some of which operate on a resource or support only basis.

Since MAF's foundation in the mid-1940s, countries which had been subject to colonial rule have become independent and new governments come to power. Churches have also undergone a quiet revolution, and have become self-governing and self-supporting. In addition to working in partnership with missions and national churches, MAF also supports hospitals, relief and development agencies, and assists government departments in times of emergency.

During these years the demand for MAF's services in Africa has increased rather than diminished. New governments have not had the available capital for a road maintenance programme, or for replacing bridges washed away by floods or destroyed by rebel forces. Faced with these road transport problems, the services provided by MAF have become more vital and the need for planes is urgent.

Over the years MAF's aim has been to demonstrate the love of God in meeting practical needs, especially in countries where the gospel is not welcome. Its commitment to supporting missionaries on the field has won a reputation for a sure and reliable transport service. No longer need missionaries fear the prospect of operating in remote areas, for help is just a radio call away.

## MISSION STATEMENT OF
## MISSION AVIATION FELLOWSHIP

### Centred in Jesus Christ

A part of his Church, we actively seek to proclaim the gospel of Christ and extend his kingdom worldwide through aviation and related ministries, by providing mobility to the church and by strategically positioning our staff for ministry and witness.

# 30. THE NAVIGATORS (1933)
## Dawson Trotman (1906-1956)

Mass evangelism has been a feature of evangelical Christianity for over 250 years. The 18th century evangelists, George Whitefield and John Wesley, attracted huge crowds to hear the gospel, and thousands of people were converted. Whilst the two men occasionally prayed with individuals requesting spiritual help, others who responded to the gospel were encouraged to join one of the newly-formed religious societies set up around the country.

Beginning in the second half of the following century, a more personal approach evolved, designed to assist anyone seeking to know the way of salvation. The first stage was the introduction of the 'inquiry room' or 'after-meeting', where counselling and prayer was offered to individual seekers. Later, steps were taken to disciple the new converts and watch over them during the early period of their Christian life.

It would seem the practice of using an inquiry room started in America and was widely used by D L Moody during the course of his first mission to Britain in 1873-74. But Moody was not the first to use the method in Britain. Credit must go to another American evangelist, Payson Hammond, who had conducted revival meetings in Scotland and had held special meetings for children.

### Innovations

In the summer of 1867 Hammond held services in London especially for children when he introduced a number of innovations. Among them was that of a Children's Inquiry Meeting at the close of a service, whereby any child might stay behind to ask questions and seek help. (It was as a result of seeing Hammond at work that inspired Joseph Spiers to found the Children's Special Service Mission.)

Moody made use of the inquiry room in his work in Chicago, though the idea was quite novel in England. But it was not new to Edinburgh, where it was claimed that Moody had picked it up during a previous visit in 1867. However, many ministers held this method in suspect, believing it to be an emotional forcing-house or even a threat to the doctrine of free will.

For Moody, it was crucial to his evangelistic work, for it enabled his 'personal workers' to counsel enquirers and lead them to Christ. Whilst at first there was a tendency to involve ministers and theological students, it quickly became an opportunity for laymen to make use of their gifts. Despite some initial reserve, the inquiry room was a success, and has remained an essential feature of evangelistic campaigns ever since.

Even so, there was still room for improving the procedure; it was not until the 1940s, when Dawson Trotman of the Navigators began to draw attention to the problem, that Christians started to reconsider their methods. The next stage of development had to wait until 1951, when the American evangelist Billy Graham invited Trotman to devise a follow-up scheme for one of his crusades. Trotman was able to introduce some of his ideas, and began the principle of personal discipling.

## Popular

At the age of 14 Dawson Trotman joined his local Presbyterian church in Lomita, a small town on the outskirts of Los Angeles, California. He became a keen member of the Christian Endeavour and regularly attended the midweek Fun and Study Class. He was a popular and successful student at school, and was recognised as a born leader.

But behind this facade, there was another boy – a persistent liar and given to stealing, even though he had made a profession of faith. As he grew up, he gradually drifted from church and became a man of the world; he spent Sundays on the beach, took to drinking and gambling, and began to fill his diary with the names of all the girls he had dated.

Until he came to his senses. Though he detested himself for his bad habits, he could do nothing about them. But arrested by the police, he vowed to God, 'Lord, if you will get me out of this trouble, I will go to church next Sunday.' He kept his promise and it proved to be the turning point in his life.

That Sunday evening the young people were having a competition, and one way to gain points for your team was to memorise verses of Scripture. Trotman accepted a list of ten scriptures on salvation and memorised them for his return visit the following Sunday.

After three weeks he had 20 verses of Scripture committed to memory. As he was walking to work at the lumberyard, one of the verses (John 5:24) impressed itself on his mind : 'He that heareth my word, and believeth on him that sent me, hath everlasting life.'

Overwhelmed with the prospect of eternal life, he prayed to God to

receive it. Immediately, another verse (John 1:12) came to mind : 'But
as many as received him, to them gave he power to become the sons of
God, even to them that believe on his name.' Now he knew he had passed
from death to life, and it was a new Dawson Trotman that went to the
lumberyard that June day in 1926.

He was amazed at his changed outlook, and the whole town (pop.
3,500) knew it as well. Although some of his old habits persisted for a
time, he began consciously to live a Christian life. Determined to get to
know the Bible, he joined study groups, took notes on his pastor's
sermons and listened to radio talks.

## Witness

From the beginning, he used every opportunity to witness to his faith.
He also vowed to speak to at least one person a day about the Lord. One
evening he even got out of bed when he realised he had not kept his word.
He drove his car for a few miles and offered a lift to a man carrying a
briefcase. When he explained the reason for his action, the stranger told him
that he had been looking for God for 20 years, and now he had found him.

Every day Trotman learned a verse of Scripture, often as he was

DAWSON TROTMAN

driving his truck around the harbour area of Los Angeles. In three years he had memorised 1,000 verses! He found verses of Scripture invaluable in sharing the gospel; to him, every verse was an arrow pointed at someone's heart.

Keen to lead boys to Christ, he became involved in Sunday School work, a Junior Fishermens Club and a Prospectors Club, using graded lessons and memory materials to teach the Bible. All the time he encouraged the boys to memorise verses and witness for Christ.

Always seeking new ideas with which to put over the message to his boys, he was given the idea of a wheel, denoting forward motion. The Word, prayer, witness and living the Christian life (obedience) were all spokes of The Wheel, with Christ as the hub. The Wheel, with its four spokes connecting the Christian to his source of life and power, was a model of the kind of disciple God wanted.

As a young Christian, Trotman was determined to keep his spiritual life vital, and to cultivate the practice of prayer. Once he joined a friend to pray for two hours daily over a period of six weeks. On the basis of Jeremiah 33:3, they prayed for the salvation of young men, for cities and for the world. It was this experience that proved to be the beginning of Navigators.

His compelling drive to spend much time in prayer was motivated by the conviction that God worked only in response to prayer. And he fervently wished to be a usable instrument in 'the Lord's work – that wonderful work of winning souls'. Looking back later, he had no doubt that his disciplined practice of prayer during the first five years of his Christian life laid the foundation for all his subsequent ministry.

Over a period of two years he began to realise that God was calling him to work with young men. His commissioning came in 1931, at a time when his boys' clubs were thriving; but it was his motto not to do what another could or would do, when there was much else to be done. So he gathered a team of young Christians around him to work under the International Fishermen Club. They travelled around Southern California, evangelising young men, and through the Fishermen Clubs built them up as disciples.

### Navy
One of his contacts was US navy man, Lester Spencer, who had been a Christian from the age of eleven. This eager young man had joined the

navy to save enough money to go to theological college and become a minister. Trotman saw a young man who was like-minded and open to learn. At his request, Trotman took him aside and taught him how to memorise verses and to use his Bible in witnessing.

Before long, Spencer met a young Christian who wanted to grow but didn't know how. When he took him to Trotman for training, the reply was, 'Why don't you teach him?' When the navy man replied that he was not competent enough, Trotman's response was, 'If you can't teach him what I have taught you, then I'm going to keep on with you until you can teach him what I have taught you!'

Through Spencer his contacts with sailors increased, and he and his newly-wed wife, Lila, decided to move home nearer to the harbour. By this time, Trotman was in contact with a large group of sailors, who regularly came to his home for study. It was not long, however, before two of the leading men suggested to Trotman that he should come out as a full-time missionary to the fleet.

It was a big step of faith, but they made it. They moved nearer to San Pedro, where once again they were able to welcome sailors to their home. In fact, he and his wife seldom ate breakfast or evening meal alone. He was later able to claim that he had led sailors to the Lord from every one of the states of the USA. The year was 1933 when Navigators was born, though the name was not adopted until a year later.

One great disappointment to Trotman was his meeting with a former 'convert' who showed no evidence of life. He believed that God had intended him to see a man through to discipleship, and he decided to contact again as many as he could of those he had led to the Lord. He started a card-file system and began a campaign of letter writing, to encourage them to go on with the Lord.

The thought occurred to him that he ought to spend more time in helping young Christians to grow. One lesson he realised he had learned with Les Spencer, was that it was better to spend time in depth with one person than to scatter the seed widely; for he expected his pupils to go out and share with others what they had learned.

As he started to get alongside individual believers, teaching them how to study the Word and how to evangelise, more sailors became Christians, for his 'students' had learned how to win other men to Christ.

Memorising Scripture was one of the pillars of Trotman's spiritual life, and he encouraged others to do the same. He devised a Topical

Memory System, with 105 key verses from the Bible, which gave practical help for the growing Christian. This system pioneered the concept of learning relevant verses for specific personal use.

He had them printed in a booklet that would easily fit into a purse or pocket. The idea was to learn by heart both the verse and its biblical reference, quoting it both at the beginning and the end of the verse, providing a quick method of referral when sharing the Scriptures with someone else. He used his TMS among the sailors on the USA battleships in Los Angeles Bay, though with varying success.

**Disappointed**

After several weeks he contacted a hundred of the people who had asked for his booklet, to see how they had got on. He was greatly disappointed to discover that only one person had memorised a third of the verses. Getting started, it seemed, was the biggest obstacle to progress; but Trotman was also aware that many of them needed someone to help them press on.

Undeterred, he continued with the system. But as he nurtured his 'spiritual babes' he realised that the Church also needed to pay more attention to discipling young Christians. Trotman and his wife felt like voices crying in the wilderness. Even though he was invited to speak at denominational meetings across the States, his ideas on discipling were not taken seriously.

In 1935 the idea took shape of a gospel team tour across the USA, with a singing quartet (something unusual in those days). The aim was partly to contact servicemen, but also to challenge other young people to the possibility of enjoying a dynamic Christian life. There was the additional thought that they might establish more Navigator bases.

The tour was a memorable one, not least because it confirmed the young organisation's name. Trotman had already made use of the name the previous year, and had had it printed on their stationery, bearing the subtitle, 'To Know Christ and to Make Him Known'. But the sailors were unenthusiastic, perhaps associating it with the former Navigator clubs for small boys. However, the quartet had a most unwieldy name; the name Navigators was re-considered and finally adopted. Its parallels to spiritual navigation were evidently recognised.

The work of Navigators continued throughout the years of the Second World War, with more servicemen's centres opened and training courses and conferences held. By now, the Navigators were also ministering to Army men, and in 1942 it noted that they were in contact with more Army camps than ships.

## Follow-up

In 1944 the evangelist Jack Wyrtzen was holding a series of Word of Life rallies in New York, and he contacted Trotman for advice about follow-up procedures. Usually each enquirer was led in a prayer of commitment and was then given a Gospel of John. Now Wyrtzen, as a result of his discussions with Trotman, gradually began to put Navigator ideas into practice. But it was his work with Billy Graham that finally brought his method of personal discipling to the attention of the Christian public

At a conference in Trotman's home in 1946, a group of Youth For Christ leaders – including Billy Graham – faced the question, 'How many of the hundreds who had made a decision for Christ at their rallies had gone on to become active, growing Christians?' The question troubled Graham, and he came to the conclusion that 'the most important phase (of a crusade) is the follow-up'.

Anxious to ensure that enquirers were more soundly established, Graham turned to the Navigators for help and asked Trotman to be Director of Counsellor Training. Trotman at first refused, protesting that the work was really a new field for him, and he was more concerned for individuals. But aided by his chief lieutenant Lorne Sanny, he took a team to the Shreveport (Louisiana) crusade in April 1951. The scheme collapsed, largely because the local chairman had not prepared the counsellors.

Realising that it was necessary to start with training the counsellors, Trotman tried again (at Memphis, May-June 1951). Having learned a few lessons at the previous crusade, this time he insisted on local counsellors, and that they should be selected, not taken on simply because they volunteered. Training classes were held emphasising the idea of personal follow-up, and counsellors learned how to interview enquirers and to nurture them during the difficult early days of their new life.

By 1952-53 the chief elements of the counselling and follow-up system had been laid down. But, as Lorne Sanny remarked, 'far more important was the growing conviction that God can use laymen'. Soon it was obvious that never before had so many converts been passed on to the churches.

As Trotman's work expanded around the world, more and more Christian organisations turned to Navigators for help. Staff members were frequently lent for training purposes to other groups such as MAF, Wycliffe and the Moody Institute of Science. Trotman believed it was their duty to serve other branches of the Church, for 'they were all on the King's business'.

The Navigators started work in Britain in the early 1950s, though it was not until the 1954 Greater London Crusade that its full impact was experienced. Trotman and a team of Navigators led the counselling training classes at Harringay, and then again at Wembley the following year.

Whilst enjoying a break in the Adirondack Mountains, north east of New York, in 1955, Trotman was drowned in a boating accident on Schroon Lake. He died as he had lived – for others, endeavouring to save the life of a non-swimmer.

The world mourned the loss of a remarkable pioneer. For more than anyone else 'Daws' brought back into focus fundamental Bible truths about the follow-up of new converts.

## VISION OF THE NAVIGATORS INTERNATIONAL

### Knowing ... and growing in Christ

This is our passion. The Navigator vision is to nurture this longing in each heart ... from one life to another, building relationships around the world.

We believe God has called us. He expects us to be – and to make – disciples who follow Jesus Christ. He requires us to serve and equip others for his service. He deserves our joyful and passionate obedience to this call.

From the beginning, we have been giving ourselves to this vision. Our history began in 1933 when Californian Dawson Trotman helped a spiritually hungry friend:

* *to apply the truth of Scripture to his daily life;*
* *to pass on what he was learning to others;*
* *to help them, in turn, find ways to repeat this process.*

# 31. THE SUNDAY SCHOOL MOVEMENT (1780)
## Robert Raikes (1735-1811)

The Sunday School Movement owed much of its early success to Robert Raikes, an Anglican layman and wealthy newspaper proprietor from Gloucester. Although often portrayed as the 'founder of Sunday Schools', the movement had already taken root when he opened his first school in 1780. Yet it was due to his untiring efforts and the considerable publicity he put out through the columns of his newspaper that the movement spread rapidly throughout the country, and was ultimately recognised as the beginning of universal education.

Although children received informal religious instruction in the catechism in some early Christian communities, it was often neglected by the clergy. Not until the early 16th century, when Martin Luther and John Knox opened their catechetical schools, was the practice resumed on a more regular basis. Even then, it was mostly children of wealthy parents who benefited.

In England, attempts to provide religious education for the children of working class parents date from the seventeenth century. The earliest known Sunday School was started by the Rev Joseph Alleine, a dissenting minister from Bath. Despite being imprisoned for flouting the Act of Uniformity in 1662, he afterwards gathered a group of some 60 to 70 children to give them religious instruction on Sundays.

It was not until the following century, however, that the movement really got under way. A Sunday School was started in Berkshire as early as 1710, there was one for around 100 boys at Catterick (1764), and another at Bedale (1765). The idea was also taken up in Scotland (1760) and Ireland (1770).

## Methodist Societies

In most cases the schools were to be found among the new Methodist societies, and may therefore owe their inspiration to John Wesley. When Wesley was a minister in Savannah, America (1735), it was his custom to meet with the children before the Sunday evening meeting and teach them to recite the catechism.

The idea was later taken up by other Methodists. Most important among them was Hannah Ball from High Wycombe, regarded by some as the more likely founder of Sunday Schools. From 1769 she met with children on Sunday and again on Monday, 'earnestly desiring to
268

promote the interest of the Church of Christ'.

In Gloucester, a young Methodist woman, Sophia Cook, started a Sunday School in 1777. With the help of her sister, she gathered together a group of children who worked at her uncle's pin factory and, after teaching them, took them to a service conducted by the Rev Thomas Stock, Headmaster of the Cathedral School.

Later, Sophia Cook is said to have marched through the streets of Gloucester with Raikes when

ROBERT RAIKES

he led his first band of poor children to Sunday School. It was she, it has been suggested, who gave Raikes the idea.

## Compassion

In 1757 Raikes inherited his father's printing business and became the owner and editor, reporter and proofreader, of one of the country's two greatest provincial newspapers. Like his father before him, he brought a high moral tone to his reporting. He showed compassion for the poor and oppressed, and developed a concern for prisoners harshly treated under the severity of English law.

It was during the 1760s that he began to take an interest in the condition of prisoners in Gloucester gaol. He became a prison visitor, and was involved in attending to their welfare. He publicised the plight of prisoners to his readers, and acted as an agent to receive and distribute gifts of charity to them. When the prison reformer John Howard visited the gaol in 1773 he praised Raikes' endeavours.

The idea of starting a Sunday School came to Raikes one day as he visited one of Gloucester's lower class suburbs. There was a place near the river known as St Catherine's Meadows, and Raikes had gone there in order to hire a gardener. While waiting for the man to return home, his attention was taken by a noisy group of ragged children at play. He lamented their 'misery and idleness' to the gardener's wife, who agreed.

In the conversation that followed, the woman told him that the situation on a Sunday, when many children enjoyed their one day of freedom from work, was far worse. He would be shocked, she informed him, by the 'noise and riot, and cursing and swearing of these wretches'. They behaved in a manner 'so as to convey to any serious mind an idea of hell rather than any other place', while their parents made no effort to restrain them.

Raikes, already aware of the 'extreme annoyance of all decent people' to this nuisance, immediately began to formulate a plan for a Sunday School (which suggests he already had some knowledge of the idea). He visited the Rev Stock, an experienced teacher and a man with great sympathy for the poor, who agreed to help.

They selected four lady teachers who were 'decent, well-disposed women (and) who kept schools for teaching to read'. With Stock, he visited the children's homes and persuaded parents to send their children to Sunday School. A list was drawn up of some 90 children, aged 5-14 years, including many of the worst cases he could find.

## Clean Hands
No one would be refused admission because of their ragged clothes or poor behaviour, but they had to attend with clean hands and faces, and with their hair combed (for which he gave each pupil a comb). 'If you have no clean shirt, come in that you have on,' he urged.

There were initially four classes, held in different locations. One was started in St Catherine's Street, in the house of a Mr King, steward to the city's MP, in July of that year, 1780. Another was held in Sooty Alley, an area near the city gaol in which chimney sweeps lived.

Each class was divided into four groups with a monitor, usually the 'best' boy or girl, who helped the other pupils. The children were taught to read and spell, but in common with other Sunday Schools no attention was given to writing. (This was possibly because of the extra demands it would have made on the teachers.) Pupils learned the catechism and memorised collects, Bible passages and hymns.

Social training was of special importance to Raikes, as he believed that Sunday Schools should bring about a reformation in their pupils' character. Cursing and swearing were forbidden, pupils were exhorted to be kind to each other and to be dutiful to their parents, and quarrels and fights were settled 'by sound common-sense approaches'. 'It was,' he avowed, 'that part of our Saviour's character which I aim at imitating ... (who) went about doing good.'

## Church Service

The pattern for each Sunday was laid down by Raikes: morning school from 10 until 12, afternoons from 2 until 5.30. The programme included a visit to a church service, though he would not inflict a long sermon on his pupils. Afterwards, the children were instructed to go home without making a noise or playing in the streets.

Not surprisingly, some children went to Sunday School under duress, and Raikes and Stock found it necessary to visit the schools to support the teachers in maintaining order.

Raikes, who appears generally to have been well-liked by the children, used a system of rewards and punishments to encourage good attendance and behaviour. These could be small monetary gifts or even a pair of shoes for the 'good' ones, while boys who caused trouble were sometimes caned. Those able to recite the catechism from memory received a number of tickets towards the prize of a prayer book.

In the early days of the movement, Sunday Schools were a separate institution from the Church and were privately financed. Meetings were usually held in the teachers' home, and books and all other resources were paid for by benefactors or from other charitable sources. Raikes and Stock covered their own expenses, and paid their teachers one shilling each Sunday.

To raise funds, charity sermons were preached and were published in Raikes' newspaper. The collections and sales were devoted to Sunday School work until the churches increasingly started their own schools.

## Good Influence

Raikes was the leading advocate in his day of the Sunday School Movement, and he used the columns of his *Gloucester Journal* to spread news of the movement's success. His first announcement appeared on 3 November 1783, with a report that a number of clergy in different parts of the country had established Sunday Schools, 'attempting a reform among the children of the lower class'.

In 1786, when two Sunday Schools were opened at Wotton-under-Edge, he urged the poor inhabitants of the parish to avail themselves of the advantages for their children. To gain acceptance for the work by the public, he publicised the good influence Sunday Schools had on children's behaviour.

While at first the Church hesitated to support the movement, by 1786 Raikes found approval coming from a number of prominent people.

These included the Rev Dr Kay, Almoner to the Queen, the Bishop of Chester, Jonas Hanway (inventor of the umbrella and champion of poor children) and even Adam Smith, the renowned economist and author.

While visiting some relations at Windsor at Christmas 1787, Raikes had the honour of speaking about the work with Queen Charlotte, wife of George III. Hearing he was in the neighbourhood, the Queen sent for him and enquired about the benefits of Sunday Schools for the poor, and especially their influence upon their behaviour. After this interview the Queen continued to take a lively interest in the movement.

## Spread

Moved by Raikes' success, in 1785 a Sunday School Society was founded by William Fox, a prosperous businessman, to further promote the movement. Then in 1803 the Sunday School Union was founded to produce materials for the use of teachers and pupils. By 1818 there were around half a million children in Sunday Schools; in 1851 it had risen to two and a half million, and by 1898 there were seven and a half million.

The Sunday School movement was quick to take hold throughout the English-speaking world, especially in North America. Efforts to establish it on the Continent met with only limited success, and it was not until renewed attempts were made in the 1860s that it spread to many European countries.

A number of organizations were founded to support the work of Sunday Schools. In the United States, the nondenominational Sunday School Society was set up in Philadelphia, in 1791. This was later followed by several denominational organizations, to supervise and extend the work within their own churches.

In Britain, the Sunday School Union, founded in 1803, served as the parent body to the British movement. Classes for both children and adults were encouraged. Lesson notes were published and, later, examinations held for pupils; the practice of paying teachers soon gave way to a volunteer system.

Since 1882, under the auspices of the Union, the International Bible Reading Association has provided Bible study notes for adults. The Sunday School Union is now known as the National Christian Education Council; the work has spread to all five continents, ministering to children, young people and adults alike.

## CHILD EVANGELISM FELLOWSHIP (CEF)

Sunday Schools were not started as an attempt at overt evangelism, for it was not until towards the end of the 19th century that it was recognised that children were able to respond to the gospel and make a genuine commitment. The idea was rather to introduce them to the Bible, what today might be termed 'pre-evangelism'. It was an American, evangelist Payson Hammond, who in the 1860s first held special meetings for children in London, that drew attention to children's ability to understand the way of salvation. As a result, many Sunday School meetings were transformed by the new informal methods.

CEF is an interdenominational, international organisation dedicated to the task of presenting the gospel to the large number of children whom no one else is able to reach. It was founded in 1935 by J Irvin Overholtzer who was brought up in California, USA. Although he went to Sunday School, his denomination did not believe that a child could understand enough of the gospel to be saved. As a teenager he rebelled against the church, but was later saved and became a pastor.

Overholtzer was encouraged to begin his work among children by some words of Spurgeon, who wrote, 'A child of five, if properly instructed, can as readily believe and be regenerated as anyone.' This statement stirred Overholtzer to action, and he began a Bible class for boys and girls. His desire was to tell them how to be forgiven for their sins, which no one would tell him when he was a boy.

CEF operates in over 130 countries and has over 1,500 national and mission workers. In Britain, it runs Good News clubs throughout the winter, when meetings are held in homes to attract those who would not consider attending a church. During the summer months, workers run holiday Bible camps and hold teacher training courses.

## Potential

Although Raikes had not originally anticipated such a tremendous response, he later began to realise the movement's potential. Apart from a revival of religious teaching among the poor, Sunday Schools were responsible for providing working class children with a basic education they would not otherwise have received.

The movement also stimulated the development of weekday schools, such as the 'schools of industry' started for children not in employment, and the older type charity school which catered for the children of poor families which were slightly better-off.

With the onset of compulsory education in 1870, however, when children no longer needed to go to Sunday School to receive an education, attendance began to decline.

The significance of Raikes' work is not that he founded the Sunday School movement, but that he encouraged its development and thereby laid the foundation on which our day school system was built.

More than that, Sunday Schools served as a means of introducing thousands of children to the message of the gospel. Not only did they learn Bible passages, but they were also taught to read, enabling them to read the Scriptures for themselves. Sunday Schools were a form of pre-evangelism, and many children were able in later life to respond to the claims of Christ.

When Raikes started his first Sunday School in 1780, he responded to what he believed to be a Divine call, when God put the thought into his heart. Years later, when in retirement, he was visited by a young Quaker named Joseph Lancaster. Raikes took the young man to the back streets of Gloucester, where he held his first Sunday School.

Uncovering his head, and with his eyes full of tears, he explained, 'This is the spot on which I stood when I saw the destitution of the children, and the desecration of the Sabbath by the inhabitants of the city. As I asked "Can nothing be done?" a voice answered "Try". I did try, and see what God has wrought!'

### NATIONAL CHRISTIAN EDUCATION COUNCIL MISSION STATEMENT

1. NCEC's task is to help churches and other Christian groups in developing the faith and releasing the gifts of children, young people and adults, as individuals and together in the community. It does so by providing training, producing learning and resource materials, and by offering individuals and churches opportunities to reflect on the task of Christian education.

2. NCEC is motivated by a call to serve God and to respond to God's love in Jesus Christ.

3. NCEC tries to express the Christian faith through its relationships among staff and with those we serve. Working for NCEC and having dealings with NCEC should be a positive experience.

4. NCEC values people and therefore seeks to avoid discrimination on the grounds of race, sex or age.

5. NCEC aims to offer a service which is efficient and effective. It seeks to establish appropriate systems for delivering training, publications, helps and advice.

6. NCEC embraces change positively. It reviews its work in order to meet altering needs.

7. NCEC seeks to work in partnership with individuals and organisations which share the same goals.

8. NCEC attempts to exercise good stewardship of its resources - human, material and financial.

# 4

# YOUNG PEOPLE

## 32. THE BOYS' BRIGADE (1883)
### Sir William Smith (1854-1914)

Until more recent times children from poor families have been forced to go out to work as soon as they were old enough. This was especially the case during the years of the Industrial Revolution when many of them worked up to 16 hours a day in factories, coal mines or other disagreeable occupations. Even better-off young people who were employed as office clerks or shop assistants found themselves labouring equally long hours. For many of them there was hardly time for adequate sleep, let alone an opportunity for relaxation.

Thus in the earlier part of the 19th century the idea of providing leisure-time interests for young people would have seemed unnecessary. But as the century progressed and reforms were introduced limiting the hours worked by young people, the opportunity arose for them to take part in an increasing variety of spare time activities. Christians began to appreciate that children and teenagers had educational and recreational needs, and churches, chapels and other agencies stepped in to fill the gap.

A small beginning was made towards the end of the 18th century by Robert Raikes, who pioneered Sunday School work in Gloucester, while in 1818 John Pounds opened the first ragged school in Portsmouth. The Band of Hope's mid-week clubs for children were started in the 1840s, and later for older boys and girls as well. Although these classes were primarily educational, they also served as a form of recreation.

At the turn of the century, from as early as 1806, 'mutual improvement' societies were formed to cater for the more mature teenager. In the 1820s and 30s David Nasmith, founder of the London City Mission, founded two such societies, in Glasgow and in London. And George Williams started the Young Mens Christian Association (1844) for young men who worked in the offices and shops of the city of London.

A number of 'institutes' were also set up by missions and individual Christians to provide evening recreational and educational programmes. These institutes, formed by many of the missions, were the chief means of providing leisure-time activities for working class boys and girls.

Perhaps the most famous institute was Quintin Hogg's Youths' Christian Institute (1879) at Long Acre School. Hogg realised that the boys needed more than simply Bible study and elementary education;

at his institute they were also taught practical subjects in preparation for taking up a trade. The institute later became the Regent Street Polytechnic.

## Practical Holiness

American evangelist Dwight L Moody, who had a heart for 'practical holiness', gave much support to a wide variety of social projects. He frequently stressed his conviction that teenage years were of vital importance, and young people needed help and direction at this crucial time. As a result of his links in his early Christian life with the YMCA, a powerhouse of evangelism, Moody made it his concern to encourage the formation of YMCA branches in all the cities and towns he visited.

During his tours of Britain he especially encouraged Christians to become involved in working on behalf of the poor and among young people. This is nowhere better illustrated than on his visit to Glasgow in 1874. As a result of his urging, the United Evangelistic Committee set up to organize his meetings was afterwards re-constituted as the Glasgow Evangelistic Association. It was devoted to both evangelism and philanthropic works, and started – among others – Poor Children's Day Refuges, a temperance work, the Cripple Girls' League and the Glasgow Christian Institute.

It was under his ministry in Glasgow that 19-year-old William Smith was converted to Christ and inspired to begin his work among boys. This in turn led to the formation of the Boys' Brigade, which became a worldwide organization, active in over 60 countries.

In the spring of 1874 Moody and the singer Ira D Sankey reached Glasgow on their tour of Britain. Their meetings were held in the Crystal Palace, a building of glass, crowded every night with 5,000 people from all parts of Scotland. At every meeting there were up to 200 inquirers, resulting in over 3,000 decisions for Christ.

A regular churchgoer, Smith had for some time faced the challenge to follow Christ. Yet he had refused to make what he thought to be a hasty or emotional decision, believing the matter required serious consideration and prayer.

He went to hear Moody soon after the campaign opened and was again faced with an invitation to accept Christ. 'Why not tonight?', the evangelist challenged the assembled crowd. Smith felt that to delay was disloyal, cowardly and self-indulgent, and so decided that night to devote his life to the service of his Saviour.

### Involved

Already attending Free College Church, he was accepted into membership and became actively involved in the life of the church. He became a Sunday School teacher at the North Woodside Mission, and a member of the Young Men's Society, formed under the banner of the Woodside Morning Branch, YMCA (also attended by the young James Moffatt, later famous for his translation of the Old and New Testaments). He also joined an Evening Meeting for young men, of which he became president.

As a Sunday School teacher his aim was to win boys to Christ, and he persisted in his attempts to reach the hearts of boys who came unwillingly to his classes. With a genuine love for his pupils, his teaching was characterised by enthusiasm and thoroughness, but he was not satisfied with the results. Despite all his efforts there was little response from his pupils, and he was disappointed by his failure to keep their attention and persuade them to attend regularly.

After struggling with the problem for some years, he one day shared his concern with his business partner. Back came the reply, 'Can't you make some use of your Volunteer methods in the Sunday School?'

Sir William Smith

## Military Methods

This remark was a reference to Smith's military background. Both his father and grandfather had been regular soldiers and William Smith had hoped to follow in their footsteps. At the age of 18 he joined the 1st Lanarkshire Rifle Volunteers (the equivalent of our modern day Territorial Army), and was eventually commissioned as an officer. Regarded by his men as an ideal officer, he was a stickler for discipline, correctness and smart uniform.

When his business partner suggested the use of military methods with the boys, the thought immediately struck Smith and he began to turn it over in his mind. 'Why should it be so easy,' he asked himself, 'for a man to control a hundred other men on a Saturday afternoon, and so difficult to control a handful of boys on the Sunday?'

He was aware that boys were often full of high spirits and needed to have their energies properly directed. 'What they need is discipline and esprit de corps,' he thought to himself. 'If I can help control these activities and direct them into right channels, the boys will enjoy themselves far more than when running wild. And instead of becoming mere hooligans and loafers, they will gain manliness and, more than that, they may be led to the service of their Master.'

To do this would mean bringing them together with a common interest, with a distinctive title, badge or uniform to mark it as their own. As they were, they were passive attenders – albeit sometimes irregular – and engaged in no form of work or play in which teamwork was called for action.

He drew up plans for banding together the Sunday School boys over the age of 12 into a 'Brigade'. During the week they would be taught elementary drill, physical exercises, obedience to words of command, punctuality and cleanliness. He hoped they would become so proud of their Brigade that they would be ashamed to bring any discredit upon it. This, he felt, would create a spirit resulting in discipline and order in the Sunday School.

## Into God's Hands

Here was the germ of an idea that was to revolutionize Sunday School methods, by giving boys an outlet for their tremendous energies. Smith gained the interest of two brothers, James and John Hill, who taught at the Sunday School and were also members of the Volunteers. The three of them met together on many evenings in the summer of 1883, to talk things over. As they prayed, Smith told his two colleagues, 'This is going to be a great thing – let us put it into God's hands.'

Reluctantly, the Mission gave them permission for the scheme to go ahead. The three young men met several times together, to pray and plan every detail before the inaugural date. They decided a name: The Boys Brigade. It would have a crest, which was to be an anchor with the words 'Steadfast and Sure'; and with a motto, 'Remember now thy Creator in the days of thy youth.'

The aim was to be 'the advancement of Christ's kingdom among boys, and the promotion of habits of reverence, discipline, self-respect and all that tends towards true Christian manliness.' (The word 'obedience' was added later, in 1893.)

A constitution was drawn up in which the Brigade was stated to be open for boys between the ages of 12 and 17. They had to fill in an application form, agreeing to abide by the rules of the Brigade and expressing a desire to be true to Christ. For the officers, it was decided to have only captains and lieutenants, who were to wear a small red rosette pinned to the lapel of their jacket.

The Boys Brigade was formally launched on 4 October 1883 in the Free College Church Mission, North Woodside Road, Glasgow. There were three officers and 28 boys. Smith was the Captain, and the two Hill brothers were his Lieutenants. After three weeks, 59 boys had been accepted for enrolment.

**Strict Discipline**

From the start, strict discipline was enforced: no boy could fall-in on parade even if only one minute late, and no one was allowed to miss two consecutive drills without a satisfactory reason. The idea of punctuality was a novelty to the boys, but it greatly enhanced the importance of the Brigade to others and did much to foster a right spirit.

In December an examination for promotion was held: first a practical examination in drill open to all boys over 14, then a written paper for the 12 boys who were highest in the practical. Marks were added by the officers according to the boys' conduct, character and suitability to hold office. Two sergeants were appointed, two corporals and two lance-corporals.

Despite initial bouts of jeers and taunts, the boys stood firm. At their first inspection on 24 March, 1884, a large crowd gathered to watch as Captain H A Kerr, 1st Lanarkshire Rifle Volunteers, reviewed the Brigade and commended the boys for their smart turn-out.

Over the next two years the Brigade went from strength to strength and Smith was able to make further developments. In December 1884, the Sunday morning Bible class began, and Smith encouraged the boys to write essays on scriptural topics which they read out at the meeting. Two rooms were made available each weeknight at the mission for games and reading. Activities such as gymnastics and swimming were also added to the company programme.

The first Brigade camp, in July 1886, was held on the Kyles of Bute and led by the Captain and his young wife Amelia (who shared her husband's love for the boys). It was a tremendous success. Camping holidays for boys was quite unknown at that time, though that same year Dr Wilfred Grenfell took a small group of East End boys camping in Dorset. The idea caught on and within ten years hundreds of boys were enjoying similar country or seaside holidays, and were the forerunners of the hugely successful camping programmes laid on today by a wide variety of Christian organizations.

## Controversy

One matter that caused some controversy was the introduction of dummy rifles, made of wood. They were intended to lend additional interest to the boys' drill sessions, and to promote good carriage and bearing. Smith had already been accused of teaching boys the art of war, but the success of the Brigade tended to quieten the opposition. However, he did suggest to new companies that rifles were not essential and they might find they could do without them.

During the second year of its existence the Brigade introduced the now familiar uniform, which was a number of separate items worn by the boys over their ordinary clothes. Simple and inexpensive, costing less than two shillings, it consisted of a brown leather waist-belt with the BB crest on the buckle, a white haversack slung over the right shoulder, and a small, round, dark-blue cap, encircled by two narrow rings of white braid and worn with a military tilt. Officers wore a civilian suit, with a glencarry cap, gloves and cane.

Another popular innovation was the introduction of a flute band, and the use of music has continued as an important feature of Brigade life.

One occasion eagerly awaited by the boys was the Saturday evening 'at homes' laid on by the Captain and Mrs Smith. Each squad was invited in turn to attend these informal gatherings, which enabled the Smiths to get to know the boys and helped forge a bond between them. The officers also visited the boys in their homes and established vital links with the parents.

## Vision

As a result of the Smiths' efforts, discipline in Sunday School was no longer a problem and boys were won to Christ. Other Christian leaders also caught the vision, and by the beginning of 1885 there were five companies in formation, including one in Edinburgh.

Smith saw the time had now come to organise the work on a national basis. A meeting of officers was held in October of that year when Major Carfrae Alston of the 1st LRV, an influential citizen, was elected President and Smith accepted the position of Secretary.

Enquiries were received from more than 20 towns in England and Scotland regarding the Boys Brigade, and as the movement spread the Secretary's workload increased. It was decided to employ a full-time Secretary, and Smith agreed to give up his business and concentrate his energies in building up the Brigade.

By 1891 there were 418 companies in England and Scotland, and the first company in Ireland joined in 1895. Under the influence of Professor Henry Drummond, one of the Boys Brigade's keenest supporters, companies were founded in the USA and Canada, and the movement soon spread to New Zealand, Australia and South Africa. Within three years, there were over 300 companies in the USA and 70 in Canada.

The valuable contribution made by the Boys Brigade to the life of the Church and the nation was widely recognised, both in the religious press and by a number of prominent people. Sunday School superintendents were especially glowing in their remarks concerning the benefits it brought to their work, and some companies found that employers were particularly anxious to have Brigade boys to fill vacancies in their employment.

In 1898 the Duke of York became the Boys Brigade's patron (today, it is the Queen) and in honour of his achievement Smith was awarded a knighthood, which brought great joy throughout the whole Brigade.

Inspired by Smith's success, other religious bodies formed similar

### Jewish Lads' Brigade

By the end of the 19th century an increasing number of Jewish immigrants from Russia and Poland had settled in Britain – in Manchester and Leeds, but most of them in the East End of London. There was a total of nearly 200,000 Jewish people in the land, including some 110,000 in the London area. Fearful that many of their people might lose their Jewish identity, an attempt was made to help the youth retain their heritage whilst at the same time enabling them to fit into the social and cultural background of their new homeland.

Following the early success of the BB, it was felt that a similar organisation would benefit Jewish boys in the East End. This came as a result of a plea by a Colonel Albert Goldsmid, who in 1894 called upon Jews to find 'the best means of ameliorating the physical conditions of our East End co-religionists.' (Goldsmid was born of Jewish parents who had been baptised as Christians, but he and his wife had converted to Judaism.)

A meeting was held at the Jews' Free School, Bell Lane, in April 1895, which led to the foundation of the Jewish Lads' Brigade. Initially, 120 boys, 'undersized but of good appearance', were enrolled, though the numbers increased until the First World War. The aim was 'to cultivate the sound spirit which marked the well-trained soldier' and to 'instil ... habits of orderliness, cleanliness and honour, so that in learning to respect themselves they will do credit to their community.'

The introduction of a simple uniform, military ranks and parades helped build up a form of muscular Judaism combined with British patriotism. Whilst numbers fluctuated, the decision to admit girls in 1963 gave added strength to the Brigade.

organizations. The Church Lads Brigade (1890) was quickly followed by the Catholic Boys' Brigade and the Jewish Lads' Brigade. In 1899 Dr Paton of Nottingham, who was not enthused by the Boys Brigade's military image, started the Boys' Life Brigade, and in 1908 Major-General Baden Powell (a BB supporter) founded the Boy Scouts.

The Boys Brigade now caters for a wider age-range of boys, from six to 18 years. There are companies in about 3,000 churches throughout Great Britain and Ireland, north and south, and the movement has spread to over 60 countries.

Cliff Richard, one of the Brigade's honorary Vice-presidents, says of the Boys Brigade: 'I've seen it at work and been impressed. It stands for important values and challenging activities, and is up front and unashamed in commending Christ.'

## MISSION STATEMENT OF THE BOYS' BRIGADE

By the year 2000, The Boys' Brigade will be known for its leading Christian Youth Work which cares and challenges young people for life.

BB will consolidate its position as regards membership, by maintaining and improving its penetration level in the pool of young people in its age range.

BB will seek to provide greater opportunity for disadvantaged and disabled young people to become full and active members. It will encourage the provision of equal opportunity for all, provided that its principal objective – The Advancement of Christ's Kingdom amongst Boys – is in no way compromised.

BB will keep under review its position regarding work with girls in conjunction with other uniformed youth organisations, particularly those only for girls.

BB will seek to enhance its position within the Churches by consulting closely with Church youth and children's work departments, by offering an informed opinion and by widening the range of Christian Churches using its methods either directly or indirectly.

BB will seek to improve the quality of its leadership by continually improving its training methods. It will introduce better training for leaders, and consider carefully what levels of training are appropriate for the various types of leader. It will also consider the use of external training agencies where appropriate.

BB pledges itself to widen the opportunities for leadership within the organisation, and to ensure that the decision making process reflects all age groups. It will take positive steps to ensure that young people are actively involved at all levels of government of the organisation.

The Boys' Brigade will maintain its position in seeking to inculcate Christian moral and spiritual values in its membership in an increasingly secular world. It will seek to provide guidance and succour to young people in their struggle against the pressures of the world.

# 33. THE GIRLS' BRIGADE (1893)

The Girls' Brigade is an amalgamation of three originally separate and thriving girls' Christian organisations, formed around the beginning of this century. In 1965, nearly 40 years after the idea had first been proposed, the Girls' Brigade of Ireland (1893), the Girls' Guildry of Scotland (1900) and the Girls' Life Brigade of England (1902) finally combined to form the Girls' Brigade. The move was intended to strengthen their work and witness amongst girls, and to promote a greater caring and sharing with overseas Companies.

Provision for the recreational needs of girls and young women in the 19th century was slower to develop than that for the boys. The movement was influenced by the success of the Boys' Brigade, founded in 1883, though the need for girls' clubs seemed less urgent. Many girls were employed in domestic service, with hardly any time off for leisure activities. Others were employed in shops or factories which often involved working late into the evening.

Among the first clubs formed for recreational activities were those for mill girls in Liverpool and Manchester in the 1860s, and the YWCA also opened girls' clubs in the East End of London. Others were started by individuals. In 1876 Fanny Guinness (a daughter of Grattan Guinness) started a night school at Harley Hall for the match girls of the Bryant and May factory, and there were other similar ventures. By the 1880s the YWCA had gradually established itself as the country's leading organisation for young women.

Several independent girls' institutes were established around the same time, some as a result of the Moody campaign of 1873-1875, while others were linked to churches or missions. Of the other religious bodies involved in providing for girls, the Wesleyans and the Quakers were to the fore.

The idea of a girls' organisation in England and Wales along the lines of the Boys' Brigade took some time to germinate, and it was the turn of the century before it got started. The impetus for it came indirectly from the Rev J B Paton (1830-1911), a Congregational minister in Nottingham and founder of the Boys' Life Brigade (BLB). He was involved in a number of philanthropic activities, but had a special interest in young people.

## England

Paton gave much thought to the failure of Sunday Schools to keep their pupils after the day school leaving age of 13. He believed William Smith's Boys' Brigade (BB) might be a remedy, though he was unhappy about the BB's military image. When he founded the BLB in 1889 he retained some of the features of the BB, but placed an emphasis on different aspects of 'life-saving'.

Launched under the auspices of the Sunday School Union, the BLB had a great impact on both the bearing of the boys and their Sunday School attendance. But, as Paton pointed out, Sunday Schools have girls as well as boys, and they too have their adolescent period. Ever since his visit to the Deaconess Institute at Kaiserwerth, Germany, he had become more aware that girls needed their own organisation and began to campaign on their behalf.

The Sunday School Union took up the issue. In March 1901 the Council minutes recorded that a 'Mr Witchell gave notice of a motion that a branch of the BLB to be called the Girls' Life Brigade (GLB) be arranged'. The Council elected a women's group to advise on the work, to draw up rules and consider a uniform. By the following year the idea had taken definite shape, and a handbook was sent out to all Sunday School branches.

In January 1903 the first company, based at Beckington Baptist Church, near Bath, was received into membership. At the end of its ten years, the GLB could boast of 101 companies with 3,414 girls, and 347 officers and staff sergeants. It was established as a weeknight activity, in the hope that girls would remain in the Sunday School through their teens and eventually graduate into the church.

Its aim was to raise 'the physical, mental and spiritual standards of the girlhood of the nation', and took as its motto the words, 'To save life'. Like the BLB, it was helpful in keeping girls attached to Sunday School, and later in introducing them into full church membership.

Leaders devised a wide range of activities designed to appeal specifically to girls and help in their development. As with the BB, there was an emphasis on drill and marching, but the girls also enjoyed first aid lessons, home nursing instruction and work for displays and exhibitions. In addition, there was either opening or closing devotions, conducted whenever possible by the chaplain of the company.

The GLB continued to increase in strength and from 1925 began to expand overseas. As the movement grew, it was widely recognised that the GLB had a valuable part to play in the work of the Church and in leading girls to Christ.

### Scotland

The Girls' Guildry in Scotland was founded by Dr W F Somerville (1858-1926) two years earlier than the GLB. Somerville was born and brought up in Glasgow, son of the minister of Anderston Free Church.

After qualifying in medicine, he undertook postgraduate studies in Vienna and Stockholm before returning to his native city. It was during these years that he developed his ideas about the value of physical exercises as an antidote to illness and an aid to personal well-being.

In the church of his childhood days he was appointed superintendent of the girls' Sunday School. Before long he began to experience the problem of teenagers 'dropping out' rather than going on to church membership.

His mind turned to the achievement of his friend, William Smith. Smith, through the formation of the BB, had effectively halted the slide and had even boosted recruitment to his Sunday School. Sympathetic women from Somerville's church kept urging him, 'Why don't you do something like this for the girls? You could do it.'

Somerville finally decided to act. One Sunday morning, early in 1900, he invited the older girls in his Sunday School to a midweek meeting in the church hall, at which he spoke of his plans for a new club. It was to include training similar to that given to the BB, plus other activities such as first aid, sewing and nursing, which were considered more appropriate for girls.

Somerville was a man of boundless and infectious energy, and was supported by a band of enthusiastic women. During its first brief session, from February to May of that year, the new movement quickly lost its Sunday School image. Its programme included drill classes and physical exercises (as practised in Sweden), and each meeting began and ended with prayers. Despite its critics – some said it was 'unwomanly and unladylike' – it obviously appealed to the girls, and the Anderston company began to grow and flourish.

Almost from the beginning it became a uniformed organisation, which helped bridge the gap between middle and working class members of the companies. In addition, there was a badge on which was enshrined a lamp with the motto: 'Wise unto that which is good'.

The vision was soon caught by other churches in Glasgow and the idea began to spread. By the following year there were five companies established in the city: three connected with the United Free Church, two from the Established Church of Scotland, including the Cathedral. It not only showed the non-denominational basis of the Guildry, but also united churches which had not previously enjoyed fellowship.

By the time of the first annual report, a constitution had been drawn up and the movement placed on a firm foundation. Its name was to be the Girls' Guildry, while its aim was 'to induce girls to become followers of the Lord Jesus Christ, and to develop in them capacities of womanly helpfulness'. Each company had to be linked to a church or mission. They were to be supervised by a 'Guardian' and the members were to be known as 'Maids'.

In three years the Guildry spread throughout Scotland, and soon moved into England and Ireland as well. Further activities were introduced to encourage the girls and to promote the work: annual camps, displays, music festivals and rallies all contributed towards building up Guildry loyalty.

After the First World War the Guildry spread beyond the British Isles. In the 1920s further companies were formed in Jamaica and other parts of the Commonwealth, usually under the direction of missionaries.

Throughout these years Dr Somerville maintained a practice in the West End of Glasgow, ran a private nursing home and pioneered the use of X-rays. With the exception of a brief absence during the war years, he remained an official of the Guildry until shortly before his death. He left behind a flourishing movement that had not only made a useful contribution towards female emancipation, but had provided healthy activities of body, mind and spirit for thousands of the rising generation of Christian young women.

## Ireland

Although the Girls' Brigade of Ireland started in 1893, it did not become an official organisation until 1908. It began when the girls of Sandymount Presbyterian Church in Dublin met for a Saturday singing practice in preparation for their annual Sabbath School Meeting.

The girls seemed to be feeling the cold that rather chilly October day. Their conductor, Miss Margaret Lyttle, thought that some physical drill would warm them up. The effect was immediate. Stimulated by the exercise, the girls asked that drill should be a regular part of their Saturday programme.

When one of the girls suggested they should call themselves the Girls' Brigade – many of their brothers were in the Boys' Brigade – a new worldwide organisation was born. The movement did not take off immediately, and it was not until three years later that another company was formed. When the girls of Sandymount visited Rutland Square Presbyterian Church (now known as the Abbey Presbyterian Church) with one of its drill displays, it led to the founding of another company. Other churches soon followed their example, and the clergy gave them splendid support.

The growth was mostly in the north side of the city, where over the next ten years or so churches and mission halls formed their own groups. At this stage there was no attempt to co-ordinate their activities, and they went under different names; sometimes they called themselves 'Girls' Brigades' or simply 'Drill Classes'. But as numbers grew it was eventually decided the time had arrived for them to unite into one organisation.

Under the inspired leadership of the Rev E H C Lewis-Crosby (later to become the greatly admired Dean of Christ Church Cathedral), the Girls' Brigade gained official recognition. A meeting was called for 2 October 1908, to establish the Girls' Brigade on the same organisational lines as those of the Boys' Brigade.

A resolution was passed which read, 'We adopt the scheme of the Boys' Brigade as far as is applicable to girls and call our organisation the Girls' Brigade'. Each company was to be attached to a church or church hall, thus keeping the organisation within the framework of the Church.

A further meeting was held to draft a constitution and rules, and later it adopted the motto 'Onward and upward', with its aim: 'The advancement of Christ's kingdom among girls, and the promotion of habits of obedience, reverence, discipline and self-respect and all that leads towards a true Christian girlhood.' There was a simple uniform, together with a badge which was a Celtic cross, surrounded by the motto and the title, The Girls' Brigade.

From the beginning, the twin pillars of the Girls' Brigade were the Bible Class and physical training, both of which form the backbone of its programme today. A weekly company Bible Class was held for the study of the Scriptures, and time was devoted to a variety of physical exercises that obviously improved the girls' health and well-being, and proved extremely popular.

Although founded in the south, the movement is now more widely-established in Northern Ireland.

Several attempts were made over the years to unite the Girls' Brigade and the Girls' Life Brigade. In 1964 the Girls' Guildry of Scotland also expressed an interest, and talks were begun with a view to an amalgamation. Agreement was reached that year in principle, which also included the affiliated Commonwealth countries.

The emergence of the new united organisation was at a Brigade rally at the Albert Hall, London, in May 1965, when the badges of the three organisations were laid down, to be replaced by the new one.

The modern Girls' Brigade has separate national councils for England and Wales, Scotland, and Ireland. It is an interdenominational movement which, at the time of the union, had a total membership of over 163,000. But like many other similar movements, it has to work hard to retain its members while adhering to its foundational principles.

With the aim 'to help girls to become followers of the Lord Jesus Christ', and the motto, 'Seek, Serve and follow Christ', members are constantly reminded of their high calling.

# AIM & PRINCIPLES OF THE GIRLS' BRIGADE

*Aim*
The aim of The Girls' Brigade, being a Christian organisation, international and interdenominational, shall be: To help girls become followers of the Lord Jesus Christ, and through self-control, reverence and a sense of responsibility, to find true enrichment of life.

*Objectives*
The work of the Brigade shall be conducted through Companies, controlled by a Captain, each of which shall be connected with a Church or Mission of an approved Christian denomination, and every member shall be encouraged to attend Church, Bible Class or Sunday School or other place of worship which may be approved by the National Board.

The Brigade shall provide activities designed to help girls to attain physical, mental and spiritual maturity and shall encourage girls to employ their knowledge in practical service in the home, the community and the Church.

There shall be an approved Badge of the Brigade and an approved Uniform.

*Principles*
The Brigade acknowledges Jesus Christ as Saviour and Lord according to the Scriptures and seeks to fulfil its aim to the glory of One God, Father, Son and Holy Spirit.

The Brigade witnesses to the standard set by Jesus Christ and gives positive teaching on the Christian attitude to life.

The Brigade promotes a just society where all people are equally valued.

*Motto*
Seek, serve and follow Christ.

## 34. HOPE UK (1847)
### Mrs Ann Jane Carlile (1775-1864) and
### Rev Jabez Tunnicliffe (1808-1864)

Drunkenness was the recognised national vice of all classes of English-men during the 18th century. It was one of the chief causes of crime and the ruination of the family, and constituted one of the major evils of city life. For the working classes, with little time or opportunity for leisure, drinking broke up the monotony of the long working day and provided an escape from the extreme poverty in which most of them lived. Between 1720-50 the problem worsened, when the availability of cheap gin led to a rise in the death rate in London.

In the following century there was an estimated 100,000 public houses and taverns in the capital, and every fifth shop in the East End was a gin shop. These places were open every day until midnight, and served adults, young people and children alike. With nowhere else to go for entertainment or relaxation, the public house – with all its attendant temptations – became a major attraction for the poorer classes. Often the wages of craftsmen and domestic workers were paid out at the public house, and many clubs held their meetings on their premises.

Gradually the appalling social consequences of drinking brought home the need for action to the more enlightened members of the public. Increasing concern about the harmful effects of alcohol on individuals and families led to the publication of pamphlets decrying the evil. Protests were raised and suggestions made that the drink trade should be closely controlled by law.

The Temperance Movement was a response to this situation, and owes its origins to the evangelical revival of the 18th century and the writings of John Wesley. Wesley condemned drink as a national disaster and advised Methodist people to avoid the use of 'spirituous liquors'. His powerful tract, *A Word to a Drunkard*, described people given to such habits as 'enemies of God and of Christ', and they were to be expelled from church membership.

Wesley's work inspired a number of Primitive Methodists and Quakers in the 1820s to form temperance societies, mainly in the North of England and the Midlands. Their motives were not so much religious as moral, for they recognised the harmful effects of alcohol upon the individual and society. They encouraged their members to 'sign the pledge' and abstain from drink for a given period. Later, the movement was to adopt a religious approach, and the idea of 'gospel temperance' was introduced.

## America

The arrival in Britain of two temperance societies from America further influenced the movement, and the idea of abstinence was carried a step further. Branches were opened around the country which advocated the practice of total abstinence, combined with that of mutual assistance to one another.

By the middle of the 19th century the move towards temperance was well-established, and many well-known Evangelicals were supporters of the work. Despite the advances made by the movement, two more societies were started to promote further developments. The United Kingdom Alliance (1853) was a pressure group, founded to persuade the government to pass legislation prohibiting the sale of liquor.

Three years later the National Temperance League was formed to co-ordinate the work of local societies and organise lectures for teaching the public about the effects of alcohol on the body. It was especially influential in encouraging city missionaries and other social workers to make temperance a matter of urgent concern in their ministry.

During the second half of the century, the American influence on the British movement increased as J B Gough of Washington introduced the idea of 'gospel temperance', linking total abstinence to conversion. And D L Moody included temperance as an element of his preaching on his British tours.

In the early stages, the movement aimed to encourage moderation in drinking (i.e. temperance), but it soon began to advocate total abstinence, or 'tee-totalism'. This was a word first coined in America, when the initial 't' was emphasised to convey the idea of complete restraint. As a public sign of allegiance to the movement, Americans began the practice (in the 1870s) of wearing a blue ribbon on the coat lapel, which soon became a familiar sight in England.

## Children Drunk

Whilst the temperance movement was initially aimcd at adults, supporters soon realised that alcohol education was equally essential for younger people, as they often acquired a taste for drink early in life. It was not uncommon to see children drunk in the streets, a sight that persuaded Mrs Ann Jane Carlile to wage a crusade against alcohol abuse.

Mrs Carlile, the widow of an Irish Presbyterian minister, at the age of 72 determined to start a temperance work among children. She began a series of tours of the British Isles, urging churches to take up the anti-drink cause on behalf of children. On her third visit to Britain, in 1847, she met a young Baptist minister in Leeds who was enthused by her ideas. He was concerned about the children in the city who were suffering from the effects of drink-related problems.

The Rev Jabez Tunnicliffe had already proposed the idea of meetings for children to the Leeds Temperance Society, and Mrs Carlile's visit set a seal on the proposal. They formed a ladies' committee to start 'a special organisation for children', which proved to be the first society of its kind in Britain. Before long the idea had spread throughout the country.

Tunnicliffe visited the local schools and issued invitations to children to attend the weekly meetings of a new club. The meetings were held, not in a church, but in a rented room on the third floor of a building in the centre of the city. Children responded to the idea, and each week the number of children increased. Eventually, when the total reached 400, they were forced to look for extra accommodation and decided to split them into three separate groups.

**Unusual Title**
Almost from the beginning they adopted the unusual title, Band of Hope. There are at least two different explanations for the origin of the name. One gives the credit to Mrs Carlile who, surveying the children from the platform at the first meeting remarked, '...children are our hope for the future' and that her group made '...a happy band ... I think we ought to call the present meeting a Band of Hope.'

The other version suggests that Mr Tunnicliffe used the phrase in a hymn he composed for that first meeting. He had written the first verse and was singing it over to himself when he exclaimed, 'I have it!' He then added, 'The Band of Hope shall be our name, the Temperance star our guide.' Apparently, he then went to the next committee meeting with the name, which was accepted.

The weekly meetings were primarily to educate the children about the dangers of alcohol. But they also included a lot of hymn singing, some of them composed by Tunnicliffe who adapted them to popular and lively airs. One of them, Come All Ye Children, Sing a Song, became the Band of Hope's theme song.

After the meetings at Leeds were established, Mrs Carlile continued

## Coffee House

In the 17th and 18th centuries the London coffee house was the centre of social life and a place where journalism news could be obtained. It was a haven of rest from the public house and the severe drinking habits of the time, for alcohol was not served on the premises. At one point there were 3,000 of these coffee houses in the capital, popular with middle class men such as merchants, writers, lawyers and clergymen. By the 19th century these houses had either become clubs or eating houses for the more well-to-do, or had fallen into a state of disrepute.

With the advent of the temperance movement there was nowhere for the working classes to find refreshment, except in the public house. It was not until the 1850s that coffee houses were opened to offer cheap meals and non-alcoholic drinks, often with a room for reading and games, to the poor. The first one was opened in Dundee and another in Edinburgh, followed by a third in Barnet under the direction of the Rev William Pennefather.

Mobile coffee stalls and vans supplied coffee and tea for navvies building the new railways, for factory workers and dockers. Coffee palaces and taverns began to appear, such as the Edinburgh Castle (formerly a gin palace) opened in the East End by Dr Barnardo in 1873.

In 1867 a temperance establishment was opened in Leeds in an old public house. It offered working people the chance of non-alcoholic drinks and cheap meals in warm and comfortable surroundings. The idea proved successful and spread to other provincial towns and cities.

'People's Cafes' were opened in London in 1874. Cheap and clean, they served non-alcoholic drinks and meals. Some provision was made for women in an upstairs room. The YWCA also opened two restaurants for office girls.

By the end of the century, there was widespread provision of establishments offering non-alcoholic drinks and cheap meals, catering for both men and women. They were the forerunners of the teashops and cafes that we know today.

her tour of the British Isles and encouraged others to set up similar groups. The movement gained in popularity and spread rapidly, particularly in the North of England and in the capital, where John Esterbrooke emerged as the leader.

## London

Esterbrooke, like Mrs Carlile, had been drawn into the temperance movement after seeing drunken children in the street. In 1848, he started a Band of Hope in Walworth, south London, and within a few years had founded a further 92 groups.

The most famous Band was at the Pear Street Mission Hall, Westminster, once visited by the Earl of Shaftesbury. In those days, Westminster was not the pleasant suburb that might have been expected. Within the shadow of the Houses of Parliament, only recently rebuilt, were slums that housed 'undernourished, and verminous and illiterate wisps of humanity'.

As well as a weekly club for children, Esterbrooke organised a Sunday open-air meeting at the pump in Broadway. He encountered a lot of opposition from the drink trade, and publicans stirred up draymen to attack him. Once he was imprisoned for causing a disturbance when assaulted after speaking at a meeting.

By 1855 there was an urgent need to bring together the Bands of Hope around the metropolis in some form of union. A meeting that year at St. Martin's Hall, under the chairmanship of the Earl of Shaftesbury and addressed by the American J B Gough, brought matters to a head. Under the leadership of Stephen Shirley, a group of interested workers met together early one morning at 14 Hanover Street, Long Acre, in what is now a part of the West End, and agreed to set up a Band of Hope Union for fellowship and co-operation.

From the beginning, the members had a strong missionary spirit. They worked to build up the movement by articles in the religious press, visits to Sunday and day schools, public meetings and even magic lantern shows. Within two years they were able to send representatives to nine or ten counties, from Hampshire to Yorkshire, and Unions were formed all over the country, supported by churches from every denomination.

By the end of the century there were over 26,000 Bands with more than three million juvenile members. In 1909 the Church of England Temperance Society claimed 639,233 members, of whom 141,444 were pledged to total abstinence.

A number of prominent people lent their support to the Union, and its first Patron was Lord Robert Grosvenor. Other supporters included Lord Kinnaird, George Cruikshank, the famous illustrator of Dickens' work, Thomas Cook, founder of the travel agency that began as a day train excursion to a Temperance outing, and Sir George Williams, founder of the YMCA.

From among those more intimately involved in social work, who witnessed the disastrous results from close quarters, were General Booth and Dr Barnardo in the East End, and Agnes Weston and Elise Sandes, founders of Homes for servicemen. And, of course, there was the Earl of Shaftesbury.

### Changes
It is impossible to say exactly what changes the gospel temperance brought about, but many people were influenced for the better. Laws eventually limited the sale of alcohol to adults only and kept children out of public houses. Drunkenness among children was reduced and the

quality of life in poor people's homes improved. Many people could testify to the help they had from the Band of Hope, and also from Christian missions which provided coffee houses and other alternative attractions to the public house.

As the country began to forget the social problems caused by alcohol and drinking became accepted by many as a normal, social activity, the Band of Hope's membership dropped. The Second World War dealt what could have been a death blow to the movement, as it completely disrupted the children's work in the cities. Recovery seemed an impossible dream.

From the 1950s through to the 70s the movement declined. Its affiliated organizations either ceased to exist or became committees rather than bodies which controlled active work.

Since the 1970s, however, the Band of Hope – now called Hope UK – has undergone a transformation. Recognising that it still had an essential role to play in teaching children and young people about alcohol, it began to produce helpful and attractive literature for schools. This, combined with the increasing attention being given to drug education, has resulted in gaining a higher profile.

At national level, Hope UK has responded strongly to a recent government initiative, pointing out the value of the voluntary sector and emphasising primary preventative work. It has also broadened its brief to include all forms of drug education, providing resources and an important information service for churches, schools, parents and young people's organisations. It holds training weekends, and works in partnership with Oasis Trust and the Salvation Army.

The days of the Band of Hope children's clubs and signing the pledge are gone, but the task of encouraging young people to live fulfilled lives remains.

### VISION OF HOPE UK

As a Christian educational charity we will work with our affiliated groups, members and any other group or individual to effectively reduce alcohol and other drug-related harm in the United Kingdom. Working for children and young people we aim to achieve this by positive health promotion methods including peer-led activities, promoting 'drug-free' lifestyles, the provision of high quality resources and training events.

## 35. NCH ACTION FOR CHILDREN (1869)
### Dr Thomas Bowman Stephenson (1839-1912)

The onset of the Industrial Revolution towards the end of the 18th century was accompanied by a sharp increase in the population of Britain. It rose from nine million in 1801 to 37 million in less than a hundred years.

People living in the country streamed into the towns in search of low-paid jobs in the factories. Dwellings, hastily erected to shelter the new workers, usually resulted in crowding large families into single rooms. Lacking proper sanitation and adequate water supplies, the new housing developments degenerated into slums.

Among the first casualties were the children, who in many cases were abandoned by their parents. Thousands were thrown out of the family home and left to fend for themselves. They died of exposure or starvation, and many even committed suicide. As yet there was no effective state provision for destitute children.

The first attempt to care for them was made during the reign of Elizabeth I. Under the Poor Law of 1601 each parish was held responsible for its poor. One of the clauses provided for orphan children to be apprenticed to a trade, girls until the age of 21 and boys until 24. But by the 19th century this system had clearly broken down. Destitute children were usually confined to a workhouse, without training or employment. Rather than enter an institution, many of them preferred to take to the streets and depend upon their own resources.

The plight of these children was brought to public knowledge through the reports of the ragged schools and other Christian missions, and by the works of authors such as Charles Dickens and Charles Kingsley. As often the case, however, it was left to private individuals to take the first steps in grappling with the problem.

A small beginning had been made the previous century to care for children abandoned by their parents. But as the number of destitute children increased, a band of Christian men and women responded to the need. Of the great orphanages, the first to be established was in 1836 at Bristol under the direction of George Müller.

In London, where thousands of homeless children roamed the streets of the East End, further homes were opened. While many of them were independent of any church or mission, others had denominational links.

In addition to Roman Catholic and Church of England orphanages, one of the best known was started by a Wesleyan minister, the Rev Thomas Bowman Stephenson.

Stephenson was a son of the manse, for his father was a Methodist minister who had also served as a missionary in the West Indies. Following the usual Methodist practice, his father moved on every three years to another church.

Brought up in a motley of industrial towns, Stephenson was accustomed to the grime and soot of the factories and the sight of thin, hungry children. Talk of revolution and change was in the air, and the Earl of Shaftesbury was campaigning for better conditions for children in factories and mines.

It was while living in Dudley that Bowman decided for Christ, and at Wesley's College, Sheffield, that he determined to become a lawyer. But when a wave of revival swept through the college, he realised that he had an urge to preach. Later, while preaching as a supply in a Tyneside village, the conviction came to him that his future lay in the pulpit and not at the Bar.

From the beginning of his ministry at the age of 21, Stephenson had the hallmark of a pioneer. He was not only a fine preacher, but also an innovator, quick to recognise the needs of a situation and to respond to it. He was often criticised by some of the more staid members of his congregations, yet with his fine singing voice and his common touch, he appealed to the ordinary people and his meetings were often crowded.

**Popular Services**

Trained at Richmond College, in 1860 he was posted to his first church, at Norwich. Throughout that first winter he took over a theatre on Sunday evenings; he conducted a series of popular services which attracted many people who would not normally have attended church. One evening he held a public debate with Charles Bradlaugh, a well-known atheist, and ran out the acknowledged winner.

In accordance with Methodist practice, he was moved on to another church, and spent six years in Manchester and Bolton. He felt more at home in Lancashire, among the working classes, for he had grown up among such people. There was a good congregation at Bolton, and a large Sunday School, where there was an openness to experiment.

His enthusiasm knew no bounds, and new ideas were quickly put to the test. For three winters he organised Saturday evening soirées, as he called them, which offered the poor an alternative to the public house. Despite an entrance fee of 2d, which included a free coffee and bun, around 500 people crowded the hall every week. The mill workers were offered a programme of music, and lectures by leading politicians, writers, artists and scientists of the day. Over the New Year holiday he organised an exhibition of models, embroidery and drawings which drew in large crowds. He opened a Savings Bank, started adult literacy classes and edited a monthly magazine.

Above all, Stephenson was an evangelist and he wanted to see both adults and children won to Christ. He held open-air services, began cottage meetings and started a mission that soon had 70 members and 200 children in the Sunday School. Always he encouraged converts to become involved in 'works of service', and founded a Union of Christian Work which brought evangelism and service together. He even employed a lady worker, on the grounds that there were needs that could only be dealt with by a woman. Some of these experiments in working-class Bolton later found expression in his Order of Sisters of the Children's Home and the Deaconess Order.

During this time his ideas began to germinate and take root, so that by the time the Methodist Conference posted him to Lambeth in south London, in 1868, he was already thinking about starting a work among children.

**Tough Area**

The Methodist chapel was in Waterloo Road, a stone's throw from the River Thames and across the bridge from the Strand. When Stephenson and his wife Ellen moved there, they were not prepared for the squalid slums, poverty, crime and vice that faced them.

Evangelism was ever his first concern, and it was for this reason that the Conference had called him to this position. It was a tough area, needing new methods and a deep commitment to communicating the gospel. One of his first innovations was to build a preaching platform in a space outside the church, where open-air meetings could be held. On Sundays the road outside the church became a market, lined with stalls and barrows. 'It was no use waiting for the people to come inside,' he argued. 'We've got to go to where they are.'

On arrival at Lambeth he was immediately struck by the plight of the children he encountered. Their faces were pinched with hunger and their bodies marked by the beatings they received from drunken parents. They were ragged, filthy and shoeless. And many of them were completely homeless.

It was a meeting with two young men, Francis Horner and Alfred Mager, both of them dedicated to serving the Lord, that determined Stephenson to set up a boys' home in one of the roughest areas of Lambeth. Known as 'the Mint', it was the haunt of pickpockets, prostitutes and criminals, an area usually avoided by the police.

Stephenson was a practical man as well as a visionary, and he took the main responsibility for the project. He rented a costermonger's cottage in Church Street, just off Waterloo Road, which consisted of a loft and a downstairs room, plus a stable. He cleaned and renovated the buildings himself. A week later, on 9 July 1869, the first two boys were received into care.

## Children's Home

From the beginning, the three men decided to open a home rather than an institution. Houseparents were appointed and, to create a true family atmosphere, they planned as soon as possible to accept girls as well. This principle was reflected in their choice of name, fixed on the outside of the building. It was to be known simply as The Children's Home.

In the early days it looked as though the venture might collapse. Not all the members of his chapel supported his work and they were critical of his efforts; for one thing, he was always wanting money. Even an ex-President of the Conference expressed his doubts and poured scorn on the project. Nor did the boys easily take to the idea of discipline and the ordered life of a home; they often fought with each other and the place was in danger of being wrecked. But as a routine was established, the boys responded to Stephenson's warm personality and accepted him as their friend.

Eventually, it became possible to take over the house next door, allowing for further expansion. By 1871 there were 29 boys in the home and it became necessary to look for even larger premises.

When the Methodist Conference moved Stephenson across the river to Bethnal Green, he found a small, disused factory in Bonner Road that suited their purposes. He made it ready, dividing the quarters into four separate houses, including one for girls.

**Praying and Working**

While at Bethnal Green, Stephenson established an Order of Sisters, later to become the Wesley Deaconess Order of the Methodist Church. His ideas had been influenced by reading a book, *Praying and Working*, by an Irishman called Fleming Stevenson. The book included an account of the work of two German pioneers in Christian social concern, Dr Immanuel Wichern and Pastor Theodore Fliedner.

Wichern had opened a home for destitute boys in Hamburg, and also trained women to undertake social work among the city's down-and-outs. At Kaiserwerth, near Düsseldorf, Fliedner and his wife had founded an order of deaconesses, to care for the sick and to meet other social needs.

Inspired by this work, Stephenson began an Order of Sisters at Bethnal Green, to train women in working with the children in his home. By 1893 there were 43 deaconesses and probationers, three training houses and a residential deaconesses' home in Salford. The scheme grew until, in 1901, it was taken over by the Methodist Conference. It became the Wesley Deaconess Order, with Stephenson as its Warden.

The work of the Children's Home continued to expand when in 1873 James Barlow, a wealthy businessman, gave them a disused public house and barn, once a venue for cockfighting, at Edgeworth, high up

THOMAS STEPHENSON AND BOYS

## Kaiserwerth

The Kaiserwerth Institution, near Düsseldorf, Germany, was founded in the mid-1830s by Pastor Theodore Fliedner (1800-1864) and his wife to train deaconesses as nurses, and to undertake other forms of social work.

Concerned for the men of the nearby Düsseldorf prison, in 1826 Fliedner founded the first Prison Society in Germany. When, in 1833, a discharged female prisoner came for help, he and his wife set up a home for her in a hut in their garden. As others were also found to be in need, a larger building had to be found for them.

Around the same time, a disused factory was taken over and opened as a hospital with one patient. A deaconess order was established to train nurses for the work. The women were simple working-class people, at least 25 years old, industrious, conscientious and clean, with a desire to serve God. They were instructed by Mrs Fliedner, whose lecture notes became the standard text for nurses at that time.

Other concerns were shortly added: an infant school, an orphanage, a training centre for school teachers and a reform school, as well as a home for retired deaconesses.

Kaiserwerth's influence spread far, especially to England. Elizabeth Fry visited the Institution in 1840, and set up her own order of nurses the following year. Catherine Pennefather, of the Mildmay Institution, started a deaconess order in 1866, based on similar principles. And Florence Nightingale trained at Kaiserwerth in 1851, and it was from here that she received her inspiration for her life's work.

on the Lancashire moors. It was soon to become the home for 24 London cockney boys who had never before left the capital.

In the mid 70s an industrial school was opened at Gravesend, to cater for the needs of children too old to go to school but unfit for normal life. This was followed by further homes on the Isle of Man (1880) and in Birmingham (1882), and a convalescent home at Alverstoke, Hampshire (1887).

## Recognition

In 1873 the Methodist Conference recognised the importance of Stephenson's work and released him from his circuit responsibilities to become Principal of the Children's Home.

Free to undertake other activities, he supported the Moody and Sankey mission at the Agricultural Hall in Islington (he even stood in for Sankey when the singer had a sore throat), started an emigration scheme to Canada and in 1874 established a training school for lay men and women who had a vocation to work among children.

Despite his success, there were constant pressures: the problem of finance, criticism from within his Church, an attack upon the reputation of his

Canadian home (cleared only after a government investigation), and the death of his wife, all of which took their toll. He had a serious breakdown in health and a vice-principal was appointed to give him added support. In 1900, he was forced to resign under medical advice.

Conference posted him to Ilkley, a quiet country circuit in West Yorkshire where, with his second wife Ella, he was re-invigorated by the clear atmosphere of the Yorkshire dales.

When Stephenson was made the Warden of the Wesley Deaconess Order, rather than move back to London, he raised the money to establish a training college at Ilkley. It was opened in 1902, and he remained there until he finally retired in 1907. He eventually moved back to London, where in 1912 he died at the age of 73.

In his funeral address, the Rev William Bradfield said of him, 'It seems to me that, as the years recede, the towering greatness of the man and of his work will become more and more apparent, till perhaps future generations will wonder if we ever realised what a giant we had among us.'

The NCH Action For Children runs over 200 projects throughout Britain, helping over 11,000 children and their families each year. Whilst its main emphasis is on preventative work, it also offers counselling through its Careline, Drugline and Touchline services, runs residential schools for handicapped youngsters and has a support unit for young offenders.

Whilst Stephenson looked forward to the time when there would be no further need for the Children's Home, he would doubtless be impressed by the wide array of services offered today by its successor.

## AIMS OF NCH ACTION FOR CHILDREN

NCH Action For Children, founded in 1869, is one of the country's largest child care organisations, with 235 projects looking after 16,000 children in need nationwide.

NCH Action For Children continues to be responsive to the calls of the young and those in need, with quality services and unfailing commitment.

We will press for the right of all children to a decent life.

## 36. TEEN CHALLENGE (1958)
### David Wilkerson (born 1931)

Many diseases which once proved fatal can now be controlled or even eliminated by the use of drugs. By the same token, however, drugs which can cure illnesses and relieve suffering can, by their misuse, have harmful effects and cause premature death. Since 1908 laws have been passed in an effort to try and control the use of these dangerous substances, but the number of drug offences and addicts has continued to rise.

In Britain, a variety of agencies have been set up to deal with this disturbing trend. Among them are several Christian organisations which aim to educate the public about the dangers of drugs, offer addicts a message of hope and provide them with means of rehabilitation.

The American organisation Teen Challenge has an international ministry and operates in nearly 50 countries around the globe. Founded by David Wilkerson, an Assemblies of God pastor, it arose out of a Spirit-led mission to the gangs of New York in 1958. It is now the world's largest voluntary organisation fighting drug alcohol and solvent abuse.

Wilkerson was the pastor of a small Assembly of God church in Philipsburg, Pennsylvania, made up mostly of farmers and coal miners. Although he and his wife, Gwen, had the joy of seeing the numbers grow from 50 members to nearly 250, Wilkerson began to feel a spiritual discontent.

The thought occurred to him one day that instead of watching TV for two hours every night, what would be the result if he gave that time to prayer? The only one in the family who watched TV, he sold the set – and his life was radically changed. It was during one of these nightly trysts with God, from midnight to 2am, that his eye caught sight of a copy of *Life* magazine on his desk as he wandered around the room in meditation.

Supposed to be in prayer, he finally asked, 'Lord, is there something in there you want me to see?' As he scanned the pages of the magazine he came across a report of seven teenage boys on trial for murder. They were members of the Dragon gang, one of the many gangs that terrorised the ethnic neighbourhoods of New York. Bored and with nothing to do, the seven Spanish boys had set out one day intent on mischief. They came across a disabled boy named Michael Farmer; so they beat him up and stabbed him to death.

Tears began to stream down his face as he read the account and he felt the Lord wanted him to do something for them, though he did not know what. With the support of his congregation and believing he was on a divine errand, Wilkerson drove to New York, accompanied by Miles Hoover, the Youth Director from his church. His intention was to try and speak to the boys.

### Arrest

Prevented from reaching them, Wilkerson tried in desperation to speak to the trial judge – in the court room. Jumped on and arrested by armed police officers, he was released after the truth of his story had been verified. A report of the incident appeared in the newspapers, together with his photograph. His name and face received wide publicity, so that even gang members knew who he was. It was this incident more than anything else that gained him access to the gangs.

The New York gangs were mainly teenage boys – though some had their female counterpart – from unstable home backgrounds who joined together for mutual support and protection. Usually wanting excitement, the gangs were involved in muggings, drugs, rape and prostitution, and were often at war with other gangs. All the boys carried weapons and were not afraid to use them, so stabbings and murders were common occurrences. Any outsider who entered a gang's 'turf' did so at their peril.

Wilkerson found that his brush with the police had given him a certain notoriety among gang members, which provided him with an open door. Still unsure about what the Lord wanted him to do, for the next four months he continued travelling the 350 miles to New York each week, on his day off. His prayer was, 'Lord, if you have a work for me to do in this place, then teach me what it is.'

During these long journeys, from March to June in 1958, he walked the streets of the city, returning home after midnight. One drug addict, Maria, told him, 'If you want to see New York at its worst, just drive across Brooklyn Bridge to Bedford-Stuyvesant.' Formerly a home for middle-class families, it was now a ghetto for Blacks and Puerto Ricans. It was here that he discovered gang life at its lowest: after-school parties for drugs and sex, pornography, promiscuity, fighting and – above all – drug addiction.

He learned that basically he was dealing with kids who were lonely, which in turn led to their gang involvement and often to an early death. He visited police stations and talked with social workers and parole officers, who confirmed his impressions; so much so that he began to think of quitting.

It was at this point that God again stepped in. Driving back to Philipsburg, he found himself asking, 'Suppose you were to be granted one wish for these kids. What would be the best thing you could hope for?' And the answer came to him, that more than anything he wanted them to begin life all over again, with the fresh and innocent personalties of newborn children, surrounded by love instead of hate and fear.

## Miracle Wanted

Then he had a picture of a house where the kids could come, to be welcomed and loved. 'Lord,' he said aloud, 'what a wonderful dream this is! But it would take a miracle!' Remembering that it was impossible for anyone to enter the kingdom of God unless he was born again, he realised that he could not convert gang members; it was the work of the Holy Spirit who alone could convict these youngsters of the need of a Saviour.

Now he determined the time had come to speak to the gangs, trusting the Holy Spirit to reach them. He enquired about the toughest gangs in town, and was told of the Chaplains and the Mau Maus. Both of them were in Forte Green, Brooklyn. With a friend, Jimmy Stahl, he drove over Brooklyn Bridge and began his crusade.

On a street corner, Stahl played his trumpet lively and loud, and a crowd, curious to know what was going on, gathered around them. Unable to get people to listen to him, David bowed his head to seek the Lord's help; he asked God for a miracle, that lives would be changed.

There was a sudden silence, and speaking from John 3:16 he was able to tell them of God's love. When his brief message was finished, four gang members knelt down in the street to ask God to change their lives and make them 'new men in Christ'.

Watching this dramatic event were Israel and Nicky, leaders of the notorious Mau Mau gang. When Wilkerson attempted to speak to Nicky, the reply was, 'Go to hell, preacher. You come near me and I'll kill you.' And he meant it.

'You could do that,' agreed the preacher. 'You could cut me in a thousand pieces and lay them out in the street and every piece would love you.' And though he was thinking that no love on earth could reach Nicky, unknown to Wilkerson a work of God evidently began in the Mau Mau leader's heart.

## Youth Rally

Wilkerson's real breakthrough with the gangs came some weeks later, at a city-wide youth rally. Whilst walking through a street in Spanish Harlem one evening, he heard the sound of gospel singing. To his delight, he discovered an Assembly of God house church having a meeting. The pastor, Vincente Ortez, took Wilkerson in and with his church gave him much needed support, bringing together representatives from 65 city assemblies. It was from here that the idea of a youth rally, to which the gangs would be invited, took hold.

The rally was held in the July, at the 7,000 seater St Nicholas Arena where boxing events were staged. The attendances for the first four days were poor, and the fourth meeting was the worst; Wilkerson cut the meeting short and went home ready to give up. It was a casual remark

DAVID WILKERSON

from a homeless gang member he met on the street that brought him back to earth.

'Preach, you're trying too hard,' the boy told him. Wilkerson realised his mistake, and decided that from then on he would step aside and let the Spirit come through.

On the last night, not only was the attendance up, but several rival gangs, including the Mau Maus, turned up for the meeting. For a while the situation was tense, as gang members cheered, clapped and whistled. When he began to speak, he had constant interruptions as they responded to his message. Not knowing how to calm the youngsters or to proceed with the meeting, he bowed his head and prayed, for what seemed like an eternity. He asked the Holy Spirit to come and reach the hearts of the boys and girls.

Gradually the noise died down and he was able to speak. Many of the youngsters were obviously challenged by his words, and a sense of the presence of God swept over the arena. When afterwards he invited any who wanted to have their life changed to come forward, over 30 gang members stood up. Among them were Israel, the Mau Mau President, and Nicky, with 16 stabbings to his credit.

**Powerful Witness**

Of all the boys who came to Christ that night, Nicky's conversion was the most difficult to believe, as he was the toughest gang member Wilkerson had ever met. But it was real, and Nicky Cruz went on to become a powerful witness for the gospel. He was later responsible for founding Outreach for Youth, an organisation which set up Homes for youngsters rejected by their parents.

For the next six months or so Wilkerson concentrated his efforts on his parish in Philipsburg. But in August 1959 he felt the Lord was moving him on, though he was not sure where – possibly New York. He resigned his pastorate, and for a while accepted a number of invitations to speak in towns and cities across the States. Until a pastor in New Jersey told him, 'Dave, it seems to me that the churches need a full-time worker among the gangs in New York.'

The outcome was a meeting of pastors in New York, in the winter of 1960, from which was born a new ministry, Teen-Age Evangelism, with Wilkerson as the Director. It was February when the search began for a suitable building, and three rooms were rented on Staten Island. He started a literature distribution programme, aimed at high school pupils in the city's troubled areas. A series of TV programmes for teenagers was launched, with a very simple format. It consisted of 100 boys and girls who had been in trouble and found the way out; the kids sang, then one of the boys or girls told their story.

Of the many youngsters coming to Christ, some he linked to local churches; but Wilkerson recognised that those in serious trouble or without homes needed some kind of residential care. Once again, the old dream came back to his mind – a house located in the toughest part of the city. There would be a dozen or more dedicated full-time workers, each one specialising in a different work – one with gangs, another with addicts, and women workers with girl gang members. It would be a place where boys and girls could receive special help and live in an atmosphere of discipline and true Christian affection.

The Committee warmed to his idea, but as always there was a lack of funds. The new project would be expensive, and it would take time to raise the money.

'But you're going at this backward,' Gwen Wilkerson told her husband. 'If you're doing this in faith, you should commit yourself to the Centre first, then raise the money for it.'

So it was agreed to go ahead and find a property before attempting to raise the money. Again the Committee decided to follow Wilkerson's leading, to enquire along Clinton Avenue, Brooklyn, where a number of properties were for sale, and a street impressed upon his mind as he prayed. Several houses seemed to offer suitable accommodation, but it was the most expensive house they visited that appeared to be the right choice.

## Mansion

It was a stately red brick Georgian mansion, empty for two years and had been allowed to deteriorate. One of the pastors looked around and declared, 'This is the place God wants for us.' The asking price was $65,000, but the owner agreed on the knockdown price of $42,000. A deposit of 10 per cent was needed within one week, and exactly the right amount came in; the rest of the money was donated exactly on time, all in answer to prayer, and the building was theirs.

An army of young people – decorators, carpenters and plumbers – moved in and Teen Challenge Centre opened in the spring of 1961. And what had started as an essentially Assemblies of God project, ended with an interdenominational flavour, with helpers from a wide variety of churches.

Enough young people volunteered as workers for Wilkerson to be able to select the 20 he needed. They were later joined by Nicky Cruz and his wife Gloria, who stayed for three years before leaving to start their own Home for teenagers and children.

The workers spent every morning in prayer and Bible study. After lunch they went onto the streets in twos, keeping their eyes open for teenage drug addicts, alcoholics and prostitutes. They were not to convert people – that was God's responsibility – but to try and meet their needs. Most of the youngsters they contacted were put in touch with a minister near their home; only a few were brought back to the Centre for special help.

One thing that Wilkerson discovered about the boys he met on the streets was that most of them had no real home, and were lonely. But when they came to the Centre, as one boy explained, they felt 'a strange sensation of warmth as they walked through the doors.'

It was Nicky Cruz who saw the heart of the problem when he told Wilkerson, 'What I want is to work not just with kids, but with their parents as well. What's the good of helping a boy if he's got to go home to a miserable family situation?'

Many miracles were witnessed at the Centre as gang members received the baptism of the Holy Spirit. Lives were changed and drug addicts came painlessly off drugs, though not all of them experienced immediate release. And young believers learned to grow in faith as they saw God answering their prayers and supplying their needs.

**Faith**

On one occasion there was no food for breakfast. When Wilkerson arrived at the Centre from his home he was greeted by a cynic who told him, 'Your prayers didn't work this time, did they, Dave?'

Silently, he asked the Lord to teach them a lesson in faith, and then led them all down to the chapel for prayer. As they prayed and thanked God for the food they were to receive, a lady called at the Centre with a gift of $32, enough to purchase food for the whole day.

As the work developed, other Teen Challenge centres were opened, first in Chicago, then in Philadelphia and other cities across the States and Canada. In 1964 a Teen Challenge coffee house was opened at The Hague, Holland, and a Euro-Asian project was set up with headquarters at Wiesbaden, Germany. Now Teen Challenge is a worldwide network of interlocking fellowships.

## Britain

The work in Britain was slow to build up, but following the appointment in 1980 of John Macey as National Director, the Teen Challenge ministry began to make an impact on the British drug scene. John Macey was formerly a pastor in Aberdare, South Wales – a centre for drug distribution – where his church opened a coffee house primarily to reach young people involved in drugs. Under his leadership, Teen Challenge operates a programme of preventative work through education in schools, and also through street and coffee house evangelism.

Help centres have been established around the country, and there are ten Coffee Houses where people are able to drop in for counselling, help or simply friendship. There are also three rehabilitation centres where young male ex-drug addicts can be introduced to a Christian lifestyle. The aim is to provide them with personal disciplines and character strengths which will enable them to live a normal and useful life.

David Wilkerson is now pastor of a thriving church on Times Square, New York, amid the hustle and bustle of Broadway's theatres and cinemas. He handed over responsibility for Teen Challenge some 25 years ago, though his book, *The Cross and the Switchblade*, is a continual testimony to the power of the Holy Spirit, and shows what God is able to do with one dedicated man.

### PURPOSE OF TEEN CHALLENGE (UK)

To win lost youth to Jesus Christ and train these new converts to become fruitful disciples for Christ. The ultimate goal is to see that those who are reached for Christ become established in local churches. When it is necessary, Teen Challenge will seek to establish one in co-operation with the local national churches. To accomplish this purpose Teen Challenge utilizes basic aspects of ministry; evangelism and discipleship; prevention; rehabilitation; worker training; Turning Point; Eastern Europe Outreach; and Macedonian Mission.

# 37. YOUNG MEN'S CHRISTIAN ASSOCIATION (1844)
## Sir George Williams (1821-1905)

Concern for the welfare of children and young people was one of the outstanding features of 19th century evangelical Christianity. Among the many institutions established for young men were the 'mutual improvement' societies, which gained momentum during the 1820s and 30s. The most famous of these was the Young Men's Christian Association (YMCA), which today has an international reputation and operates in 130 countries.

Possibly the earliest of these societies was the Society of Contending Brethren, pioneered in 1806 by the Rev Andrew Reed, founder of the Royal Hospital for Neuro-disability at Putney. The purpose was to awaken the religious interests of young men, but their discussions also covered social and political issues. Ten years later, in 1817, Thomas Binney set up a similar meeting for young men at a Presbyterian church in Newcastle-upon-Tyne 'for the purpose of prayer, Bible study and mutual religion'.

More influential, however, were the young men's societies started in Scotland by David Nasmith, founder of the London City Mission. In 1824 he formed the Glasgow Young Men's Society for Religious Improvement. It provided for young men between the ages of 14 and 35 who were 'of good moral character and professing no opinions subversive of evangelical principles'. When Nasmith settled in London in 1835, he continued to press the cause of young men, and formed the Metropolitan Young Men's Society. The society did not survive, and he planned to re-launch it as the Christian Young Men's Union, but died before it got off the ground.

It would seem that when Williams came to London and set up the YMCA, he was not aware of Nasmith's work. Even when he visited Scotland on business in 1848, he had no idea of the societies Nasmith had founded there before him. He made contact with the Young Men's Christian Institute, which seemed to be on its last legs, and suggested that it became a YMCA. It did so, and within a matter of a few years boasted some 1,350 members.

## Draper's Assistant

It was in 1841, two years after Nasmith's death, that the 20-year-old George Williams arrived in the capital from Dulverton, Somerset. He became a draper's assistant at Messrs Hitchcock & Rogers, formerly of Ludgate Hill, but now moved to St Paul's Churchyard.

Here was the centre of the retail trade before it was usurped by the West End. The shops took advantage of modern developments: they had large plate-glass windows allowing elegant displays, and gas lighting, fixed outside but which reflected the light onto the window displays.

As an apprentice in Bridgewater, Williams had been 'a careless, thoughtless, godless and swearing young fellow'. Although brought up an Anglican, he was soundly converted at the Congregational church at the age of 16. He remained a keen Evangelical for the rest of his life, a temperance advocate and an opponent of tobacco and gambling.

The drapery establishment of Hitchcock & Rogers had some 140 assistants, most of them under the age of 20. They lived on the premises and were provided with board and lodging. Accommodation was spartan; each bedroom contained two or three beds, and they had sitting rooms in which to relax. They worked long hours, from 7am to 9pm, with a break for meals; and as the doors were locked at 11pm there was little time for leisure.

Williams was an ambitious young man and the drapery trade offered him the prospect of promotion. His personal qualities were soon noted. By 1844 he was recognised as 'the most important man in the house, and buyer and manager of one of the largest departments' (there were 12 departments in all). When invited by Hitchcock to take up the position of buyer, he only did so after prayer and believing it to be God's will.

## Nonconformist

For about ten years he was a member of the Weigh House Congregational Chapel. This fashionable Nonconformist place of worship, which dated from the 17th century, was on Fish Street Hill, but a new building seating 1,500 people was erected in Duke Street (off Oxford Street).

It was a chapel for the well-to-do, and attracted many members of social and political standing. Among them were Samuel Morley, the manufacturer of shirts and stockings (reputed to be the richest commoner in the land), and Matthew Henry Hodder of the publishing family.

Williams devoted his spare time, what little there was, to evangelical and temperance work. For a while he also taught in two of the London City Mission's ragged schools.

As a young Christian he was influenced by the writings of Charles G Finney, the well-known American Congregational minister and revivalist. These emphasised the need for repentance and conversion, and stressed the value of small praying groups either in churches or in mutual improvement societies.

There were a number of other Christian young men at Hitchcock & Rogers, and from early in 1843 they began praying for individual friends and colleagues. Eventually they were given permission by Hitchcock to hold meetings on the premises. They started a regular Wednesday prayer meeting and Bible Class, and specifically prayed for the conversion of young men.

Their prayers were answered, for Mr Hitchcock himself was converted that year, and Rogers came to the Lord later. Henceforth, Hitchcock became an ally and a father in the movement, and he immediately informed the establishment that family prayers would be held every morning at 7 o'clock. Prayer meetings were also being held in other city houses close by, and the feeling grew among them that there ought to be a society for 'the spiritual improvement of young men'.

With this in mind, a meeting was held at Hitchcock's on Thursday, 6 June 1844. Though accounts of the occasion are somewhat confused, it would appear that 12 or 13 young men met in Williams' room, to form 'a society which should have for its object the arousing of converted men in the different drapery establishments of the Metropolis' to evangelise their colleagues. The group, drawn from four different denominations, was quite ecumenical in its composition, and the new society had the advantage of not being under the umbrella of any particular Church.

The question of who founded the society remains a vexed one. Obviously, any of the group who met that June evening could lay claim to being one of the founding fathers. Minutes of the meeting give little help on this matter, and accounts written later do not tally.

Williams wrote that he never claimed to be the founder, rather others claimed it for him. But he did agree that he was the first used by God in June 1844 to take the initial step. History seems to support him.

The Drapers' Evangelistic Association, as it was called, held further meetings, this time at George's Coffee House on Ludgate Hill. Twenty young men met, to draw up rules and make other arrangements. By November they had moved their meeting place to the comfort of Radley's Hotel, Blackfriars, which attracted increasingly larger gatherings. At their fifth meeting it was decided to adopt the new name of Young Men's Christian Association.

SIR GEORGE WILLIAMS

## New Emphasis

At first, the new association admitted to full membership only those who were converted and in church membership, as it was their concern to promote 'the Saviour's kingdom and the salvation of souls'. Within a few months its statement of purpose was amended to reflect the idea of 'mutual improvement'. Its aim was broadened to become 'the improvement of the spiritual and mental condition of young men'.

This introduced a new emphasis and signalled the beginning of an educational programme in the winter of 1845. Initially it consisted of a course of public lectures held at the Exeter Hall, in the Strand. They were delivered by the Rev Dr John Stoughton of Kensington Chapel, and proved extremely popular.

### The YMCA and Moody

As a result of the Great Exhibition (1851), the YMCA spread across the Atlantic to North America. It was in the United States that the YMCA achieved its greatest degree of success. By 1853 there were 27 YMCAs in the USA and Canada, the first in Montreal and then a week later the second in Boston (where the young D L Moody, newly arrived in that city, joined as a shoe-shop assistant). The associations came together the following year in a confederation. They were represented at the World Alliance held in Paris in 1855.

Catering for young men coming into the cities, the YMCAs were unhampered by tradition and soon developed a wide-ranging programme for the spiritual, intellectual, social and physical well-being of its members. Later they branched out into the colleges and universities, where they provided a platform for the students' voluntary religious activities. For many years they were most important centres for evangelism, and they helped to organise many union prayer services and revival meetings.

One of their most illustrious members was D L Moody, who gave up his job to become a full-time evangelist with the YMCA in Chicago. Known as 'Crazy Moody', during the Civil War (1861-1865) he ministered to the troops first at Camp Douglas, then at Elizabethtown, Kentucky. The YMCA also organised the provision of extra doctors, nurses and medical students to attend to the wounded.

When Moody and Sankey toured England in 1873-1875, it was the YMCA secretaries at Liverpool and York who helped them get started. Throughout the tour Moody encouraged the YMCAs in the towns where he preached, and helped raise new associations where none existed.

The movement spread rapidly, and by the beginning of 1845 other associations had been opened beyond the city, in provincial centres such as Leeds and Manchester. During the 1850s it expanded into Europe, where similar groups had already been started in Switzerland (1815) and Germany (1834), and to the United States.

This development was probably the result of a vast outreach campaign, mounted by the London YMCA on the occasion of the Great Exhibition of 1851. The capital was divided into 36 districts for the purpose of distributing tracts, and each Sunday 16,000 were to be given out to the crowds converging on Hyde Park. In all, nearly 350,000 tracts were distributed.

Overseas visitors who received them returned to their own countries enthused by the idea of the YMCA, and so further associations were established. As the number increased, the possibility of forming a world alliance was proposed by Henry Dunant (who later founded the Red Cross).

An international conference was called, which met in Paris in 1855. There were 99 representatives from nine countries. The British delegation was led by George Williams, whose contribution obviously carried great weight. It was decided to set up an international federation of affiliated societies.

The crucial issue was that of membership. Under the London association's Rule VII, membership was to depend on evidence of conversion, but at Paris a slightly more flexible basis was drawn up. This was in effect a simple summary of evangelical doctrine, afterwards known as the Paris Basis, to which members had to subscribe.

This basis remains in force today, but is not a condition of individual membership of the YMCA, which is left to the local association.

## Success

The 1850s were also years of personal success for Williams. His standing as a businessman continued to grow, and he travelled to Europe on behalf of Hitchcock & Rogers. In 1853 he married Hitchcock's daughter, Helen, and the firm changed its name to George Hitchcock, Williams & Co. When his father-in-law died, he became the sole principal of the firm.

It was about this time that Williams moved from Nonconformity to the Established Church, possibly because his in-laws were Anglicans.

He and his wife worshipped at Portman Chapel, now known as St Paul's, Portman Square. Already a centre of evangelical witness, it included among its incumbents Griffith Thomas (later principal of Wycliffe Hall, Oxford) and Evan Hopkins.

Throughout his years with the YMCA, Williams received the support of a wide variety of distinguished people. The Earl of Shaftesbury was president from 1851; Samuel Morley provided financial backing; and other patrons included several titled gentlemen.

In 1881 the lease of Exeter Hall, in the Strand, was purchased for £25,000. This was achieved by inviting four men each to contribute £5,000; the remaining £5,000 was donated by Williams. It was already recognised as 'the cathedral of evangelicalism', and hosted the May Meetings and a wide variety of other evangelical gatherings. Its future was assured and it became the new YMCA headquarters.

One room in the basement was furnished as a large gymnasium, which recognised the onset of a new development, that of providing recreational activities for members. Now the YMCA catered for the whole man, body as well as soul and spirit, a move which led to an increase in the number of provincial associations in the 1890s.

Throughout his life Williams held firm to his original conviction for his work. He summed it up thus in 1869: 'I have one great business in life left, and that is to extend the kingdom of our dear Lord all I can.'

As always, he was a generous man and willingly donated to evangelical philanthropic causes. He continued to be a temperance supporter all his life, and was president of the UK Band of Hope Alliance.

In 1894 he was knighted by Queen Victoria, but only accepted the accolade as an honour for the YMCA. He has the unique distinction of being buried in the crypt of St Paul's Cathedral, and having a window dedicated to him in Westminster Abbey, a double honour not given to anyone else.

The YMCA is truly a worldwide movement, with associations in Africa, India, South America, and even China and Japan. Since 1964 women and girls have been admitted into the YMCA ranks, and enjoy equal status with men and boys.

It is a serving movement, which also provides housing and hostel accommodation for young people. And Y-Care International, the World Development wing of the YMCAs of England, Scotland, Ireland and Wales, helps people in developing countries.

The YMCA continues its Christian tradition through its aims and purposes, which were adopted at the British Conference in 1971. At its centre are Christians who aim to make Jesus Christ known in all human relationships.

## AIMS AND PURPOSE OF THE YMCA

At the British YMCA Conference of 1971, the following statement of the aims and purpose of the Movement was adopted:

The YMCA is a Christian Movement. At its centre are Christians who, regarding Jesus Christ as Lord and Saviour, desire to share their faith with others and make Him known, believed, trusted, loved, served and exemplified in all human relationships. It welcomes into its fellowship persons of other religious faiths and of none.

**Accordingly the YMCA stands for:**
A world-wide fellowship based on the equal value of all persons. Respect and freedom for all, tolerance and understanding between people of different opinions. Active concern for the needs of the community. United effort by Christians of different traditions.

**The YMCA aims to:**
Provide a welcome to members for themselves, in a meeting place which is theirs to share, where friendships can be made and counsel sought.

Develop activities which stimulate and challenge its members in an environment that enables them to take responsibility and find a sense of achievement.

Involve all members in care and work for others.

Create opportunities for exchanging views, so that its members can improve their understanding of the world, of themselves and of one another.

# 38. YOUNG WOMEN'S CHRISTIAN ASSOCIATION (1850)
## Lady Mary Jane Kinnaird (1816-1888)
## and Miss Emma Robarts (1818-1877)

There were a number of remarkable Christian women during the course of the 19th century who played a prominent part in improving the social and environmental conditions of thousands of ordinary people. Some of these women came from the ranks of the middle or upper classes and were steeped in the evangelical tradition of the Anglican and Noncon-formist Churches.

With the advantage of position and wealth they could afford the time to become involved in philanthropic causes, and were consequently in the vanguard of women's emancipation. So despite the ethos of the day, which confined women to the home, the Church provided them with an opportunity to fulfil their Christian call.

This is nowhere better illustrated than in the founding of the Young Women's Christian Association (YWCA), which came into being as the result of the efforts of two young women.

In 1855 Mrs Mary Jane Kinnaird – later to become Lady Kinnaird when her husband succeeded to the family title – opened a home for Florence Nightingale's nurses returning from the Crimean War and working girls in London, while Emma Robarts started a prayer union in Barnet, north of London. But it was not until 1877 that the two groups merged to eventually become an international organisation that was to play an important part in advancing the kingdom of God.

## Upper Class Evangelicals

Mary Kinnaird (née Hoare), a member of a well-known banking family, possessed a firm evangelical faith. Her children relate how very deeply absorbed she was in her daily private prayers, so that she did not seem even to hear any disturbing sounds. When they were young she insisted that they attend prayer meetings, whether they enjoyed them or not, in order to encourage them to pray for others. 'What matters,' she told them, 'is that you should pray and get an answer.'

Her husband, later to become the 10th Baron, was a firm supporter of the Free Church of Scotland and treasurer of the London Missionary Society. For over 40 years he was a Scottish Liberal MP. The senior partner in Ransom, Bouverie and Co (which held the accounts of many evangelical societies), he owned estates in Perthshire and Kent, and a town house in Pall Mall, London.

The Kinnairds belonged to a circle of upper class evangelicals who devoted considerable time and energy to missions and other Christian causes. They opened their homes to a wide circle of people. Moody and Sankey when campaigning in London always stayed with them – Sankey with the Arthur Kinnairds (later the 11th Baron) and Moody with the Quintin Hoggs. The Kinnairds also set aside a room in their Pall Mall home for entertaining working class girls and for meetings with Christian workers.

By the middle of the 19th century a number of different organisations had been started for young men, but little had been done for the needs of young women. For some years before the early beginnings of the YWCA, Lady Kinnaird involved herself in several schemes set up to help working girls.

Encouraged by her uncle, the Hon and Rev Baptist Noel (an ardent supporter of the London City Mission and a founder of the Evangelical Alliance) she took an interest in overseas work, for the Protestants on the continent of Europe, for the slaves of Africa, and for the gospel in India. But whatever occupation to which she gave herself, she regarded it as her service for God, from keeping accounts to entertaining visitors.

But her first concern was for the needs of girls and young women in the capital. In 1841 she opened one of the earliest training homes for servants, St John's Training School at Westbourne Park. The girls were taught cooking and domestic duties; at the end of the course they were provided with suitable clothes and found employment.

With Lord Radstock she helped found the British Ladies' Female Emigration Society in 1849, which provided matrons on board ships to escort girls going to work overseas. Several societies were set up at the time to help young people and families start a new life in the colonies. Little was done to make adequate arrangements for them, and the societies fulfilled an important task in ensuring there was proper provision for the journey and possibly a job to go to at the other end.

## Nightingale Nurses

A more important development, one which was to have permanent consequences, was the establishment of a home for young women in Upper Charlotte Street, Fitzroy Square. At that time there was a steady flow of young women of 'good standing' in transit through London on their way to the Crimea. They were to become Florence Nightingale's nurses, and they needed accommodation in a Christian atmosphere – to satisfy their anxious parents – while waiting to set sail.

Together with Viscountess Strangford, Lady Kinnaird opened the home in 1855 and supervised the work until the end of the war. It was, of course, only a temporary need, but Lady Kinnaird realised that there was an increasing number of other young women coming to the capital in search of work. She took over the Nurses' Home and opened it to young women in business at a charge of half a guinea a week. This included the use of a lending library and other facilities.

Known as the North London Home, it was the first of its kind in London, if not in the world, and proved to be the forerunner of all the hostels set up by the YWCA. It was planned to develop it under the name of the United Association for the Christian and Domestic Improvement of Young Women, but as several other homes around London were opened they were finally called Young Women's Christian Association. No doubt the name was influenced by that of the YMCA, which already provided hostel accommodation for young men coming up from the provinces.

In its first report, issued in 1862, mention is made of an office at 118 Pall Mall, with a secretary and a resident missionary, a reminder that one of the YWCA's main aims was to win young women to Christ, though physical and intellectual needs were also provided for. At that time there were only three centres open, but in each succeeding year new homes were acquired.

By 1865 Lady Kinnaird had opened five homes in London, plus a Central Christian Institute, rather on the lines of a modern club, with a reading room and library. The idea caught on in the provinces and a number of similar establishments were started in the larger cities: Birmingham, Bristol, Liverpool, Manchester and Glasgow among others. Although some of them took the name of YWCA, they were quite independent of the London group.

One unusual development, in 1870, was the first restaurant for women only, at the Welbeck Street home. Committee members of the home had seen girls walking up and down the streets during the dinner hour, eating their lunch brought in bits of paper from their home that morning. The restaurant was a success and proved to be the first of a series, set up to offer City girls cheap, hot meals.

## Prayer Union

As these advances were taking place, a rather quieter work was going on in the country under the leadership of Miss Emma Robarts of Barnet, just north of London.

Emma Robarts lived with her father and four unmarried sisters, all of them given to charitable works, which included a school for girls held in one of their out-buildings. Their father was a retired merchant banker and a member of the first committee of the British and Foreign Bible Society.

Although anxious to serve God, she was unable to find an outlet for her energies until she began to appreciate the potential not simply of prayer, but of 'unity in prayer'. It was in 1855 that she drew together a group of her praying friends, including Catherine Pennefather (wife of the vicar of Christ Church, Barnet), who were like-minded in seeking the Christian support of young women.

They agreed to link themselves together 'in spirit' every Saturday evening – there was no fixed time – 'to plead for loved ones individually, and for young women as a class.' Each member was invited to write a quarterly report giving examples of answers to prayer and other encouragements, which were made known to the others. As it was felt necessary to give itself a title, it was called the Young Women's Christian Association. They saw themselves as the female counterpart to the YMCA which had a similar vision for evangelism.

After four years it was decided to widen the prayer circle by inviting other ladies 'who knew the power of prayer', especially those engaged in social work with young women, to join a Prayer Union. The first membership list of 23 names included Mrs Pennefather, Mrs Horatius Bonar (wife of the hymn writer) of Kelso, and George Müller's daughter who afterwards became Mrs Wright. There were others from Scotland, and from Ireland as well.

## Evangelism

Besides regular intercessory prayer and Bible study, it was expected that every member would take some personal share in evangelism, whether through Bible class, Sunday school teaching, prison and workhouse visiting or tract distribution.

Wherever possible, Miss Robarts united the partners in local prayer bands and sent them a packet of leaflets to get them started. She was not anxious for any undue publicity, as she felt that the spiritual nature of the work should be a private matter.

By 1867 she was able to report there were 34 branches, and within the next five years the total reached 130. At one point it was reported there were 8,000 names on the list, and it was still growing. Each branch held a monthly prayer meeting and their reports gave many examples of conversions.

Perhaps it should be added that the YWCA activities were not merely to attract girls without an interest in the gospel, or as bait to induce them to attend Bible classes. Rather they were intended as a help towards building up character and the right use of all powers of body, mind and spirit created by God.

Until the end of 1876, Emma Robarts worked single-handed as secretary of the association, when she was finally persuaded to consider sharing the burden of responsibility. It was around this time that Lady Kinnaird was considering the idea of a prayer union in support of her work in London, and it occurred to her that it would be better for the two associations to be united.

## United

A chance meeting between Lady Kinnaird and Miss Robarts – they had never met before – led to an agreement to amalgamate the two associations, though the union only applied to the centres in London. Over the following weeks details were worked out and plans made for the union. However, Miss Robarts was suddenly taken ill and died before the new association could be set up.

Under the guiding hand of Mrs Catherine Pennefather, the union went ahead. It took the title of the Young Women's Christian Association, with temporary offices at the Mildmay Institute, in the East End. (The Rev and Mrs Pennefather had moved in 1861 from Christ Church, Barnet, to St Jude's, Mildmay.) The motto adopted by the association – and mottoes were very much in favour in the 19th century – was Zechariah 4:6, 'Not by might, nor by power, but by my spirit, saith the Lord of Hosts.'

The next step was to extend the work to the rest of the country, and so the movement was thrown open to the other YWCAs. Two councils were set up to oversee the two areas: Lady Kinnaird took responsibility for the London work, and Mrs Pennefather that of the provinces. As

## HOW WE CARE

The YWCA ('Y') is dedicated to addressing the needs of women and young people in their own communities. When, back in the 60s, Youth and Community workers found that people with problems were reluctant to seek help in centres, it was the Y who went into the streets, developing the first detached youth project in the country. With the continuing need to find solutions for other problems, the search continues. Now, thousands of young women every year come to the Y for practical and emotional support.

In 1992 a members' conference identified homelessness and child care as priorities for action, and it is these two areas of concern on which attention is still focused. The Y provides a home for more than 3,500 single people on low incomes, most of whom are young women between the ages of 16 and 26. More than 60 houses around the country offer safe, affordable housing for women and young people at a time of need.

Family workshops in Devon have piloted a new project which helps teach parents and young children how to play and learn together. There is also accommodation for young women and babies, and provision is made for 16-year-old young women leaving care and in need of a secure home. All are offered vocational guidance, information, counselling and health advice, to give them the confidence to make their own choices and resolve their own difficulties.

often the case, Lord Shaftesbury was invited to become President.

The aims of the YWCA were to unite young women in prayer and evangelism, to provide Christian friendship and mutual help, and to promote the moral, social and cultural well-being of its members.

**Firm Foundation**

The work undertaken by Miss Robarts' prayer groups provided a firm foundation for the fledgling association, complementing the social concerns of Lady Kinnaird's homes. Already with Prayer Union branches in many parts of the British Isles, the new organisation continued to expand and put down roots. From the beginning, it was an interdenominational work, and though branches were sometimes affiliated with Anglican or Nonconformist churches, its basis remained essentially evangelical.

During the early years a number of developments widened the scope of the association's services and attempted to meet the needs of different young women. The first department to be set up was for evangelism, which immediately introduced two new ideas. One was to use the Prayer Union's February Week of Prayer (later moved to November) as a time for evangelism as well. The other was to focus attention for a week at a time on a town or city, and hold evangelistic meetings, conducted by lady missioners, for all classes of women and girls.

Foreign missions formed an integral part of the YWCA programme, and an 'own missionary' working with the Zenana Bible Mission was adopted. (This society worked solely among women and girls in India.) Later it was estimated that over 700 of the association's members had become missionaries and many of them had opened YWCA branches, in India, Japan, the Middle East, Africa and the West Indies.

Other departments were established that showed the wide range of concerns during those early days : Total Abstinence, Thrift, Convalescent and Holiday Homes, Education and Emigration. Travellers' Aid was set up to care for young girls arriving in the capital to look for work, and the Time and Talents Department helped educated girls cultivate their gifts and use them for the good of others.

There was a special concern for handicapped people, and girls were encouraged to care for the blind and the deaf. Branches were invited to adopt a blind member and provide Braille literature.

As early as 1857 Prayer Union groups and YWCAs had been formed among Protestant women in Switzerland and several other European countries. Obviously, the same kind of spiritual impulse being experienced in Britain was influencing women in other parts of the globe. No doubt there was some link here with the Awakening among the churches that had begun on the other side of the Atlantic.

## World YWCA

It does not seem surprising that the next significant development was the inauguration of the World YWCA in 1894. The first move came in 1882 when the association opened an Emigration Department, to continue the work begun some 30 years previously by Lady Kinnaird. As members were scattered abroad and new branches opened in foreign parts, the YWCA became a truly international organisation. Great Britain, the United States, Norway and Sweden were the founding members, but they were soon joined by many others.

In England, most of the YWCA branches opened an institute rather on the same lines as those set up by Lady Kinnaird. Before long there were 150 such centres where girls could enjoy their leisure-time, and where those working away from home could get the advice and help of an older Christian woman.

Over the years the YWCA has continued to adapt to the changing needs of the times. During the First World War this involved providing clubs, canteens and hostels; after the Second World War 'Y' teams engaged in relief work and caring for refugees. Today's concerns include victims of violence, homeless teenagers and ethnic groups.

Today 100,000 young people visit the YWCA

## GIRLS' FRIENDLY SOCIETY (GFS)

The GFS is an Anglican organisation founded in 1875 by Mary Townsend to offer friendship and help to working girls moving into large cities. Brought up an orphan, Mrs Townsend had a concern for young girls, especially those who went from a country home to work in domestic service in large town households. Hours were long, wages were low and living conditions tended to be primitive. Cut off from their families, the girls were ignorant and inexperienced of life in the unfamiliar surroundings.

Mrs Townsend was involved in organising rescue work among young girls in Winchester when she first began to realise the support these girls needed. The first Anglican organisation designed for and run by lay women, it was immediately successful. By the end of the year there were several branches to be found around England, and ten years later it boasted 821 branches in England and Wales, with several abroad (including the USA).

Arrangements were made to meet and care for new members arriving at railway stations; there were residential hostels, holiday homes and nursing homes. Several departments were set up to cater for members' needs : Factories, Business, Workhouse, Training, Literature (including libraries) and Homes of Rest.

Now active in 23 countries across five continents, the Society has adapted to modern social needs. Under the name of Platform, it continues to be involved in caring for young women, providing accommodation for single mothers with babies and for homeless girls, as well as caring for those with other personal problems.

every year in search of practical and emotional support. By addressing issues as wide ranging as homelessness, unemployment, single parenthood, drug addiction, sexual abuse and domestic violence, the YWCA offers a lifeline, providing a safe, secure environment in which young women can gain confidence and independence.

The YWCA has grown into the world's largest women's organisation, with branches in over 80 countries. In Britain, although the emphasis on evangelism is less prominent, the founders' tradition of caring is continued through the Y youth and community programmes, and Mrs Pennefather's motto, 'By love serve one another', is still as relevant as it was over a hundred years ago.

## YWCA's MISSION, PURPOSE AND AIMS

### Mission Statement

The YWCA of Great Britain, being part of the worldwide Christian movement, is open to all; works for the full participation of women and young people in society; believes in social justice and action; responds positively to local and national needs; welcomes into membership men who share its commitment to encourage and promote women in decision making and leadership.

### Statement of purpose

The YWCA of Great Britain is an informed and active membership movement. We work at local, national and international level to support and encourage women and young people to gain greater control over their own lives.

# 5

# NATIONAL MISSIONS

## 39. CHURCH ARMY (1882)
### Rev Prebendary Wilson Carlile (1847-1942)

The Church of England was slow to respond to the challenge presented by the Industrial Revolution in the 19th century, when the majority of working class people were untouched by the claims of the gospel. The problem for the Established Church of how to evangelize the masses remained unresolved until towards the end of the century, when the Rev (later Prebendary) Wilson Carlile founded the Church Army in 1882.

His great vision was to set up a working men's mission to working men, and to use laymen to reach 'the failures of life, the wastrels, the criminal classes and the unemployed'. Although the Salvation Army and other Christian social agencies had been operative in the East End for some years, Carlile's work began in west London, where there were also urgent needs. For 60 years he directed and inspired the Army's work, which is still the front line unit of the Church of England.

Wilson Carlile came from a long line of Scottish Presbyterians, who had moved to London and were eventually assimilated into the Church of England. On his father's side was a long and distinguished family history, marked by involvement in both business life and community service, backed by a strong Christian tradition. It would seem that from his mother he inherited a flair for languages (he could preach in French, German and Italian), and a musical ability that he put to good use in Christian work.

Born in Brixton, south London, the eldest of 12 children (three died in infancy), he was a delicate child and suffered from a spinal illness that often kept him laid up. He was educated at home, but later attended a day school in Brixton. In 1860 he transferred to the City of London School, followed by a year at a French school in Lille.

The family had successful business interests in the city, and when the 14-year-old Wilson left school he joined his grandfather's company in Cheapside. Already having a firm grasp of figures, he set himself the target of making a fortune of £20,000 by the age of 25. He ran or cycled (or even travelled on horseback) to his office, arrived early and worked late. His success in the commercial world was a result of his attention to organization and detail.

That he succeeded in making his fortune was due partly to his thrift as well as to his business acumen and determination. But in 1873 a series of bank failures in London and New York, in which many businessmen were ruined overnight, left him with a mere £1,500. The shock of the loss brought on his old spinal complaint and he was forced to take to his bed for six months.

## Changed Life

Carlile later admitted that his reduced circumstances enabled God to speak to him. 'God threw me on my back that I might look up to the better,' he once remarked.

It happened when an aunt of Brethren persuasion gave him a book entitled *Grace and Truth*, telling him; 'If ever you are worried about your soul, read this.' He read it, and it changed his life. As he later explained, 'Before I had got to the end of the first chapter, I had thrown myself at the feet of Christ and cried "My Lord and my God".'

When his health recovered he joined his father's business, but his heart was no longer set on making money. Instead he spent his spare time in evangelistic work among boys at Blackfriars, first with the Plymouth Brethren – who considered him a 'disorderly brother' – and then in the Church of England, at Holy Trinity Church, Richmond.

In 1870 Carlile married Flora Vickers, who eventually came to share his new faith and vision. She joined him in teaching classes of particularly rough boys at Blackfriars and Richmond. It was at this point that the two of them moved into the Anglican Church, and were confirmed at Clapham Parish Church by Bishop Thorold of Rochester.

The visit to London in 1875 of the American evangelists, Moody and Sankey, provided Carlile with the opportunity to become more involved in evangelism. He volunteered his help in the London campaigns, where his obvious musical talent was put to good use. He frequently accompanied the singing on the harmonium, and trained the London Evangelistic Choir which grew out of the meetings at Camberwell.

As a result of his experiences during the campaigns he learned some of the skills needed in evangelism, and especially the part music could play in winning people to Christ. But he was particularly impressed by the way Moody's associate, Professor Henry Drummond of Edinburgh, used ordinary young men in the meetings, who were invited to give their testimonies. The idea was effective, and Carlile determined to use the same method of presenting the gospel when the opportunity arose.

By 1878 Carlile felt called to be ordained, and spent two years in study at St John's College, Highbury. He was ordained to the curacy at St Mary Abbots, the busy parish church of Kensington, with special responsibilities at the daughter church of St Paul.

From the beginning, his main concern was to reach the poorer people, who rarely entered the doors of a church. He began to develop what were then considered to be unorthodox methods of evangelism, when he gathered around him a small group of working class laymen to assist in the preaching. Though his ideas were not always enthusiastically received by his fellow clergy, he gradually built up a group of young working class men who were able to speak to the people in their own language.

They held open-air meetings, street processions, Sunday evening services in the Vestry Hall and magic lantern services in a school hall. Often, they were attacked by gangs of roughs; and while the meetings were usually noisy, many ordinary men and women were converted to Christ.

The experience of using laymen for evangelism showed him again that 'the timid exhortation and humble testimonies of working people' attracted quite as much as did his own preaching. In fact, they seemed to produce an even deeper effect on their own class. By these methods, he was able to train the men for evangelism within the Church of England.

Around that time in the Anglican Church there were several experiments in methods of evangelism taking place, and Carlile was considerably influenced by the Rev Evan Hopkins of Holy Trinity, Richmond. Inspired by the work of William Booth, Hopkins had started what he called 'The Church Gospel Army'. A similar work at Oxford was in progress under the title of 'The Church Salvation Army' and at Bristol a 'Church Mission Army' had been set up.

The leaders of these three groups – Evan Hopkins, Canon Atherton and F S Webster – met with Carlile in 1882 and agreed to combine forces. Under the title of 'The Church Army', they were established as a branch of the Church Parochial Mission Society. Carlile resigned from the staff of St Mary Abbots and became director of the new organization.

## Warfare Against Sin

An advertisement in the Church Press called for 'Young men ... full of fire and hard work, ready to give up all for the Lord Jesus'. Each recruit had to be a Church communicant and a total abstainer; they had to have a clear testimony of conversion and be prepared 'to engage in a warfare against sin and ungodliness'.

Among the first recruits were tradesmen, blacksmiths, clerks and factory workers, who were sent to a new Training Home at Oxford for their preparation. On completion of the course, they were each accorded the rank of Captain and placed in charge of a corps.

With a small staff of working men and friends, he set an example by organising a Church Army mission at Walworth, south London. Around 50 friends from Kensington joined the mission, and helped with singing and by giving brief addresses. Like William Booth's mission before him, they were pelted with rotten eggs and fruit, but succeeded in drawing crowds to the mission hall.

The first Church Army station was opened at Richmond, under W W Cox, the first officer to be commissioned. Carlile wanted his officers to be parish-based, to engage in open air witness and evangelism, but always under the direction of the incumbent. Instead of inviting people to go to church, the Army was the Church going to the people.

The Church Army was deliberately modelled along the lines of the Salvation Army, to which it readily admitted its indebtedness. Like Booth's soldiers, they wore a uniform, held processions, often headed by a band, carried banners and had their own newspaper, *Battleaxe* (later called the *Gazette*).

The chief difference between the Armies was that while the Church Army remained under the umbrella of the Anglican Church, the Salvation Army continued as a nondenominational body.

**Opposition**
Despite criticisms from some Anglican clergymen, the Army was soon established not only in and around the capital, but in industrial towns of the Midlands and the North, and in rural centres as well. His concern for what he described as 'the most lost' led him to set up work in parishes where there was a great deal of poverty and families were living in appalling conditions. Within six months there were corps in places from Brighton to Manchester, Swansea to Kings Lynn.

After three years the Church Army had a complement of 65 officers and between four and five thousand 'soldiers'. In one year alone over 2,000 converts – mostly 'gathered from street corners and public houses' – attended adult confirmation classes.

Carlile himself often led Army campaigns and on several occasions received physical injuries from the 'Skeleton Army' and other hooligans, which once again revived his spinal weakness. At an open-air meeting in Battersea Park, a gang of youths pelted Carlile and his friends (including some women) with stones, resulting in serious head injuries to the leader.

The Army's policy of refusing to prosecute their attackers made them a regular target, but the policy paid off. Typical was one attacker who received a prison sentence following his assault on Carlile. Impressed by Carlile's attitude, the man became a Christian and later took an active part in mission work.

Clerical opposition to Carlile fell away after 1885, when the Convocations of Canterbury and York both warmly commended his work. This change of attitude was partly due to his principle of working in a parish only with the approval of the bishop and under the local incumbent. He was also prepared to modify his methods to suit parish circumstances and, if necessary, to give less emphasis to the military titles.

He acknowledged that the full Church Army organization was not suitable in every working class parish, and allowed officers to serve in parishes for short missions or longer periods without building up a corps.

There were two other important developments that strengthened his cause and made the Army a more powerful weapon for good. One was his decision in 1887 to make use of women volunteers, who were invited to offer for training as mission nurses. His sister, Marie Louise – who joined almost from the beginning – devoted her whole life to the Army. She became Head of the Women's Work and superintendent of the Sisters' Training Home in London.

## Social Action

Carlile had long realised that simply talking to the poor about the love of God carried little conviction; it had to be demonstrated by deeds. Stirred by reading an account of social work by a German pastor, he determined to find constructive ways of helping the destitute and the homeless to whom he preached the gospel.

It led him to start a programme of social action that transformed words into deeds. Consequently, an unprecedented volume of social as well as evangelistic work was undertaken during the Army's early years, when every avenue of service was explored.

He felt that the most constructive way of helping such men was to provide a setting where they could gain their self-respect by helping themselves. For men who were prepared to co-operate, he planned to provide a home and opportunity for work.

During the hard winter of 1889-90 he discovered that men attending a gospel meeting hall in Marylebone were cold, ragged and homeless, and were forced to spend their nights sleeping rough. He had a section of the mission hall converted into a simple home for half-a-dozen men, and opened what proved to be the first of a number of 'Labour Homes'. The homes not only provided accommodation and work but, equally important, were an attempt to offer 'a fair moral training against habits of idleness and drink'.

Lodging Homes were also opened, attached to the Labour Homes, as a form of 'move on' accommodation from the Labour Homes and in which single men who had a regular job could live in decent conditions. A 'work test' was used to decide which men genuinely wanted help. Those chosen stayed until they were able to fend completely for themselves.

When a Labour Home for women was set up, the scheme was not so satisfactory. It was modified, so that the women could be cared for in smaller homes of between 8 and 20 beds, and after a time of rehabilitation were found suitable work. Mission nurses did rescue work among 'women of the streets', and other homes were started for 'Inebriate Women'.

WILSON CARLILE, MARIE CARLILE, AND CAPTAIN SPENCER (THE MOST SENIOR OFFICIAL AT THE TIME) AT BUCKINGHAM PALACE.

## Responding to Needs

All the time the Army was seeking to respond to needs as they became evident. As the founder or one of his staff became aware of a situation, then every attempt was made to meet that demand. The Army's programme expanded considerably and new projects were constantly being brought into operation. Missions were extended to country areas and evangelists were set apart to work with particular groups, such as cabmen, residents of common lodging houses or the unemployed.

As the evangelistic task of winning working class people to Christ remained the overriding concern, missions were organised to hop pickers, navvies, gypsies and sailors, in army barrack rooms, in prisons, and in public houses. Flying Squadrons on 'chargers', (i.e. bicycles), horse-drawn caravans and even a boat on the Thames were used to penetrate some of the more remote areas.

A wide variety of new projects were constantly being brought into opera-

### ROYAL PATRONAGE

For over 50 years the Church Army has been proud to enjoy royal patronage, through its association with Her Majesty Queen Elizabeth the Queen Mother which extends over 70 years. As Lady Bowes-Lyon, she placed an order for the Church Army's Eros rose petals for her wedding in 1923. The petals were made at a Church Army disabled men's centre, and were used to heavily shower the Duke and Duchess of York as they left Westminster Abbey for Buckingham Palace. Since then, the Queen Mother has continued to maintain close links with the Army.

As the Duchess of York she concerned herself with many aspects of the Army's work – attending annual meetings, visiting Church Army hostels to see at first hand the work amongst the homeless and even attending a sale of work. In 1935 she opened a new Army shelter near Waterloo Station, which had previously been the White Hart public house. Following the coronation, in May 1938 she summoned the Church Army founder, Prebendary Carlile, to the Palace for the occasion of his eighth star award, which marked 56 years of service.

During the War years, Her Majesty paid informal visits to Church Army Services clubs and recreation huts. In 1943 King George VI and Queen Elizabeth were graciously pleased to be Patrons, placing a seal on what was already a happy association. Since then her interest has never waned. The Church Army's 90th anniversary was marked by a reception at St James' Palace, and in 1980 she visited Blackheath village to declare open the new Church Army Headquarters. In 1992, on the occasion of a Church Army conference of its nine worldwide organisations, she welcomed the leaders to a reception at Clarence House. She took pleasure in her duties, and once declared, 'I trust that God's richest blessing may rest upon the work of the Church Army.'

tion, such as coffee taverns providing inexpensive meals, a second-hand clothing department, a Church Army Bible Reading Union, the sale of Christian literature by colporteurs, an emigration scheme and prison evangelism.

The extensive social work programme involved raising a great deal of additional income, and the burden of this fell largely on Carlile. Some of his supporters preferred that the Army remain as an evangelistic body, but this was not Carlile's wish. The stress of the situation threatened his health, and for ten months he was appointed as Rector of the Parish of Netteswell in Essex. In January 1892, he left Nettleswell and returned to London to the living of St. Mary-at-Hill and was there until March 1926. He was always the Honorary Chief Secretary of Church Army and never drew a salary from the Society.

Whilst at Nettleswell he not only threw himself into village life, but his stay there gave him an insight into the opportunities for village evangelism. This eventually led him to establish a fleet of mobile mission caravans, the first of which was dedicated on 24 June 1892.

**The 20th Century**
There was much unemployment in the early years of the 20th century and thousands of men poured into London hoping to find work. Many were homeless and destitute, and were able to receive lodging in the Army's emergency night shelters.

During the First World War the Army provided canteens, recreation tents and even a complete war hospital. The work took them into the battle zones where 37 evangelists lost their lives.

Despite advancing years Carlile continued to direct the Church Army and was personally involved in many of its activities. He rarely enjoyed the comforts of home, and for many years frequently slept at the Men's Training Room where he had a tiny bedroom.

He made preaching tours to the United States and Canada in 1926 to help launch a North American branch of the Army, and branches were also started in Asia, Australasia, East Africa and the Caribbean.

Recognition of his achievements were rewarded by his appointment in 1906 as a Prebendary of St Paul's Cathedral. (A prebendary is a non-residential canon; the position does not carry a salary, but has certain privileges and responsibilities.)

Wilson Carlile died 24 September 1942, shortly after his successor (the Rev Hubert Treacher) had been appointed as General Secretary and Head. His funeral was held at St Paul's Cathedral and his body laid to rest in the crypt.

Once asked what he would do if he had a million pounds, Carlile replied, 'I would organise a mission which would be social as well as religious, for I believe that God is as keenly interested in seeing food in the cupboards of the poor and happiness in their homes, as he is in seeing them with Bibles and clean hearts.'

At the Lambeth conference in 1988, the Anglican bishops renewed their commitment to the gospel by declaring the closing ten years of the 20th century to be a 'Decade of Evangelism', calling on other Christians to join them in making Christ known to the world.

Over the years, the Church Army has won the approval of the country at large, and has often been commended by government reports for its social concern. But true to the vision their founder gave them, the Army has continued to mobilise lay Christians, to tell others of the change Jesus has made in their lives.

## MISSION STATEMENT OF CHURCH ARMY

Church Army is a Society of evangelists within the Anglican Communion which exists to enable people to come to a living faith in Jesus Christ.

To achieve our purpose we have established eight aims and these are not in any order of priority, but they are:

1. To train, enable and equip evangelists.
2. To present people with the claims of Christ in such a way that they can understand and respond.
3. To give practical help and care to people to whom we go with the good news.
4. To train and enable church members to engage in witness and evangelism.
5. To take the good news to those areas and people where the church has found its evangelistic outreach particularly difficult.
6. To inspire and mobilise the Church in its task of evangelism.
7. To recognise, acknowledge and communicate the activity of God in the world.
8. To so provide and organise the Society's human and other resources that it will be able to fulfil all of its aims and meet with challenges of the future.

# 40. HOME EVANGELISM (1874)
## Robert Paton (died 1893)

Since the end of the 18th century, the use of door-to-door visitation in the Church's ministry has steadily gained ground. It appears to have originally been employed by John Wesley in the 1780s when he formed Strangers' Friend Societies and sent out helpers to visit the working class in their homes. Although this was done to assess the needs of the poor so that relief might be properly administered, it proved to be the germ of an idea that was widely taken up by both social and missionary agencies.

Thomas Chalmers, while a minister in Glasgow (1815-1823), set up a system with a similar purpose in mind. He organised lay people to visit the homes of his inner-city parish. In 1825, the Christian Instruction Society began fortnightly visits to poor families in London. And when David Nasmith founded the London City Mission in 1835 he adopted the same method in the East End.

The great value of this approach was that it established a link between the Church and non-attenders. Whereas many people would hesitate to enter a church building, it was easier for the Church to go to the masses. This humanitarian approach often resulted in drawing people to church, though later in some sections of the Church social concern became an end in itself and resulted in a 'social gospel'.

It was soon appreciated that door-to-door visitation could also be a useful means of distributing the Scriptures. The idea was taken up around 1830 by three French men from Toulouse, brothers by the name of Courtois, who began a gospel work in the Pyrenees with the aid of 'colporteurs'.

Originally the word colporteur meant 'one who carried something around his neck', suggesting a pedlar or street hawker. The term was now applied to a band of Christian men who 'peddled' the Scriptures, in this case selling Bibles and Testaments. Such was the success of the scheme that by 1854 there were 500 colporteurs employed in the work. In frequent journeys, either on foot or on horseback, the task was an arduous one and demanded not only a constant faith, but also true grit and determination.

The Bible Society recognised the value of this method. From around 1830 it had colporteurs distributing Bibles over much of Europe, from

Russia and Scandinavia in the north to Greece and the Iberian peninsula in the south. A small work was also started in North Africa, and colporteurs ventured into the region at a time when missions had yet to take up the challenge among the Muslims.

## Peak

The colportage movement reached its peak just before the First World War, when in 1912 the Bible Society employed 1,200 men and sold five million Bibles or Scripture portions, which was half the Society's circulation. By now, motor vans were widely used, enabling a colporteur to sell more in a day than previously had been sold in a month.

It was not until the second half of the 19th century, however, that colporteurs began working in Britain. This was in 1866, when C H Spurgeon founded his Colportage Association. Spurgeon had been born and brought up in the rural backwaters of Essex, where there were few evangelical churches and no Christian bookshops.

Concerned that the poor had little chance of purchasing Bibles or good Christian books at low cost, he determined to do something about it. Dividing the country into areas, he gathered together a group of men who would visit the ordinary people in their homes with the offer of good Christian literature. They were not simply salesmen, however, but also evangelists, intent on sharing the gospel at every opportunity.

The men travelled the country, knocking on doors or selling their wares at country markets. They prayed with the sick and dying, held open-air meetings and pointed men and women to Christ. At one time there were 96 colporteurs, who in one year alone sold 23,000 Bibles.

Several years later a similar ministry, The Christian Colportage Association of England (CCA), was founded in East London by Robert Paton. Although aware of Spurgeon's Association, Paton felt it better to have a broader-based work rather than a denominational society, and CCA was firmly established on a nationwide basis.

## Costermonger

Robert Paton was a civil engineer lately retired from many years' service in India, though inspiration for the idea more probably belongs to Arthur Smith, a converted East End costermonger. Smith lived in Hoxton, a short distance from where David Nasmith started the LCM, and had been brought to Christ by John Farley, a city missioner.

As Smith knelt in prayer one day, the thought flashed through his mind, 'I am the son of a King! I can do something better than trundle a costermonger's barrow.' His friend Farley, aware of the value of Christian literature in evangelism, felt that Smith would make a good bookseller. He raised a few pounds from his friends and bought a number of Bibles and other Christian books, and launched Arthur Smith as a colporteur.

One of the homes Smith called at was that of Robert Paton in Highbury. The maid announced that there was a man selling books at the door, and wanted to see the master. 'What can a man want by bringing books to me?' Paton thought to himself. 'Surely, if I want books, I have only to go to the bookshop around the corner and get anything I require.'

Curious to see what the man had for sale, Paton invited Smith into his study. Before long he was delighted to realise that his visitor was really an evangelist, seeking to win men to Christ. After Smith left, Paton turned the matter over in his mind. 'If this man can get into my house with his books, is he not able to get into any house in London?' he thought.

Paton, a Scotsman, was a very practical man with intense energy. After his return from abroad, he settled in London and became a member of Park Church, Highbury. A man who always put God first, he is remembered as someone who threw himself into every kind of evangelistic work.

As he considered Arthur Smith's visit, he became more and more convinced that here was a way by which the whole country could be quietly and systematically evangelised. Immediately he set about seeing if he could turn the incident to good account.

He made enquiries and discovered that the Religious Tract Society of Scotland had an extensive colportage work in the North, and that Spurgeon had a similar association based in the Metropolitan Taber-nacle. After praying about the matter with his friend H D Brown, they felt that there was a need for a broader, interdenominational society which could take up colportage as its own special work, and not be added to another already in hand.

The two men committed the whole enterprise to God. Over the next months Paton endeavoured to interest a number of his friends in the scheme, and wrote or called upon several prominent Christians. The matter finally came to the attention of Lady Kinnaird, already heavily involved in many other Christian causes, who persuaded Quintin Hogg to open his home for a meeting to launch the work.

Held at Richmond Terrace, Whitehall, on 24 February 1874, the meeting was well-attended by leading evangelical Christians of the day, both Anglicans and Nonconformists. The first General Council was elected which included, among others, Lord Kinnaird as Treasurer, Lady Kinnaird, Sir Arthur Blackwood KCB, Sir William McArthur (later Lord Mayor of London), J G Barclay, R C L Bevan (of the Quaker-Anglican banking family), and the Rev Dr Henry Allon of Union Chapel.

The council represented every section of evangelical Christians in the land. The purpose of the new society was to establish a system of home visiting in order to sell Bibles, Testaments, Christian books and magazines, and to use the open doors for opportunities for evangelism

The use of the French word rather than an English term to describe the workers was an attempt to be more precise in defining their role. The men were not merely 'book hawkers', but evangelists. To have described them by such a term would have failed to show the distinctiveness of their work. Hence the word 'colporteur'. The title suggested was The Christian Colportage Association for England (CCA), which was readily adopted.

**Bookstalls**

The birth of the association coincided with two major Christian events which gave the work an initial boost. The Moody and Sankey campaign of 1873-75, when Paton was the chairman of the campaign committee, brought the association's work to the attention of the Christian public. Paton received permission to set up CCA bookstalls at all the London meetings, where large numbers of Bibles and books were sold. New converts and Christian workers, it seems, were glad of the opportunity to have ready literature to hand.

Then there was the Keswick Convention, founded in 1875 as an arm of the holiness movement. It had a remarkable influence on the spiritual life of the Church. Bookstalls run by the association became a regular feature of the convention, and were gradually accepted at a variety of other evangelical conferences.

Colporteurs were appointed in London where they were allocated to a specific area: the first operated the notorious Seven Dials district (now New Oxford Street), the next Notting Hill, then Mildmay Park and

ROBERT PATON

Victoria Docks. Within a year there were 20 colporteurs stationed in the capital. The association continued to expand until there were over 140 agents scattered around the country.

By the end of the 19th century there were more than 130 colporteurs working for the association, though there were still vast areas of the country yet to be evangelized. The Earl of Shaftesbury, the great Christian leader and reformer, was a keen supporter of the work until his death in 1885. He once remarked, 'England needs a thousand colporteurs, indeed ten thousand would not be too many.'

The evangelists were trained at the CCA Training Home at Hastings, where they stayed for between six and 12 weeks. As they worked their rounds, the men were easily recognisable. Always neatly dressed, they carried their books in a case with the association's address and the words 'Buy The Truth' clearly displayed.

The work, however, was physically demanding, and soon bicycles, tricycles and carts were employed to transport their heavy loads. The 'William Tyndale' Bible van, manned by three colporteurs, was used to serve the smaller towns and villages. By the turn of the century the CCA had sold over 20 million Bibles, Testaments and other pieces of Christian literature, and had distributed 14 million gospel tracts.

But equally important were the frequent opportunities afforded the colporteurs to share the gospel with people on their doorsteps or in their homes. The association's records abound with testimonies of people who have come to the Lord as the result of these visits. In addition to visiting homes, they made use of market stalls, called at gypsy encampments and army barracks, and held seaside missions.

### Changes
In recent years significant changes have taken place that have strengthened the work and opened up new areas of service. In 1956 the

Spurgeon's Colportage Association was incorporated into the CCA, considerably improving its effectiveness. The selling aspect of the mission's work was gradually phased out; the title 'colporteur' was dropped in favour of 'evangelist', though visiting from house to house continued, and Scriptures and Christian literature were given away rather than sold.

In the 70s, as more local churches began to look to the association for help in evangelism, the idea of a training programme gradually developed. This new direction was confirmed at the 1973 annual meeting, when Tom Houston of the Bible Society urged the evangelists 'not to multiply their work, but to multiply their ministry'.

The association's name was accordingly amended to 'CCA Mission for Home Evangelism'. The mission now works alongside churches to provide training in home evangelism. It produces its own training and resource aids 'to prepare God's people for works of service'. Under the new motto of 'An open Bible in every home', it was decided in 1990 to simplify the name of the mission to 'Home Evangelism', though the work remains essentially the same.

As the Chairman at that time, Peter Clarke, remarked, 'I firmly believe this (change) marked a significant step forward in advancing sensibly with the need of the times.'

Today, Home Evangelism, backed by over a hundred years of experience, is anxious to play an ever increasing part in winning men and women to Christ.

---

### AIMS OF HOME EVANGELISM

*Our object*
The winning of men and women for the Lord Jesus Christ.

*Our Motto*
An open Bible in every home.

*Our Method*
Calling from home to home in town, village and hamlet, accompanying personal witness to the saving power of the gospel with distribution of the Holy Scriptures and selected Christian literature. By this means we seek to reach with the gospel thousands of people who never attend a place of worship.

## 41. LONDON CITY MISSION (1835)
### David Nasmith (1799-1839)

One outcome of the Evangelical Revival of the 18th and 19th centuries was the use of laymen and women in furthering the work of the gospel. For centuries Church affairs had been controlled by the clergy, with the laity usually as 'onlookers'.

But the Reformation had signalled a return to biblical principles. Increasingly, ordinary Christian men and women were becoming involved in building the kingdom of God. From the 18th century, evangelical Christians were frequently to be found either working alongside ordained clergy, or engaging in social activities set up by churches, chapels and the newly-formed missions. Rather than waiting for people to come to church, the Church moved out into the streets to meet the people on their own doorstep.

Denominational churches became more involved in this kind of work, with the formation of domestic missions and home missionary societies, in a continued attempt to alleviate inner city social problems. Interdenominational city missions were also started, of which the largest and most successful was the London City Mission (LCM), founded by Scotsman David Nasmith in 1835.

Nasmith spent much of his short life forming missions and associations. By the time of his death at the early age of 39, he had started 45 city missions in Britain and 36 in the United States and Canada, in addition to a variety of other societies. Little of his work survives today, though the Glasgow and London City Missions remain as a memorial to his indefatigable spirit.

A native of Glasgow, Nasmith showed early signs of his organising ability. At the age of 14, though not yet a Christian, he and two of his school friends formed a society for the distribution of Bibles to the poor. When he reached the age of 16 he joined the Congregational Chapel in Nile Street, where his parents worshipped.

It was probably after taking up membership that there came a moment when the young Nasmith fully committed himself to the Lord. Writing in his diary he commented, 'There is nothing in the world I desire more than holiness of heart and an entire conformity to the will of Christ.' When he looked around to see how he could serve the Lord, his first act was to offer himself as a Sunday School teacher.

## Use of Laymen

The use of dedicated laymen was one of the features of Methodism. John Wesley developed a system of local (unpaid) preachers, and in 1780 formed the Strangers Friend Society for door-to-door visitation, to search out and assist the poor. A similar movement began within evangelical parishes of the Established Church, whereby voluntary workers visited the poor and the infirm in their homes.

When Thomas Chalmers – regarded as one of the founders of modern sociology – became minister of Tron Church, Glasgow (in 1815), he set out to visit every family in his parish, whether church members or not, even though his calls had to be brief. When he moved to another part of the city to become minister of St John's Church, he appointed deacons to undertake the work of visitation. The deacons systematically visited the parish area by area to assess what help was needed, for the needs to be met by the parish.

From around 1818, Pilgrim Homes (founded 1807) sent out visitors each month to those receiving a pension, to enquire of their spiritual and physical well-being. In 1821 this task was increasingly taken over by female visitors.

Following the publication of Chalmers' book *Christian and Civic Economy in Large Towns* (1821), the idea of visitation was taken up by others. The Christian Instruction Society, founded in London in 1825, used voluntary workers – mostly women – to call on families every two weeks.

But his hopes were set on becoming a missionary. Although his application to go to Africa was turned down, he found other ways of expressing his commitment. By the time he was 19 he had started a number of adult schools and, as a result of his prison visiting experience, was appointed secretary of the Bridewell Association.

Employed by a manufacturer as an accountant, in 1820 Nasmith applied for a job as a clerk, required to act as assistant secretary to the Glasgow Benevolent Institution. His organizational skills were fully stretched, for the work involved the oversight of 23 philanthropic societies, grouped together under one roof for the purpose of economy. His duties involved calling their meetings, recording minutes, keeping accounts, and generally watching over the societies' affairs.

## Mutual Improvement

Not only did Nasmith fulfil his responsibilities to everyone's satisfaction, he spent his spare time pursuing other good causes. On New Year's Day, 1824, the inaugural meeting was held of the first of several 'mutual improvement societies' formed by Nasmith (thus anticipating the YMCA movement by nearly 20 years). The societies were for young men between the ages of 14 and 35, 'whose principles and character (were) in accordance with evangelical Christianity'.

Later to become the Glasgow Young Men's Society for Religious Improvement, members met together each Sunday for religious purposes. The stated aim was to promote 'mutual religious improvement, by meeting every Sabbath and engaging in praise, prayer and other religious exercises'.

Members were also encouraged to reach out and help others more needy than themselves, especially the slum dwellers who lived near the docks. However, as most members were in full-time work and had little spare time for visiting, Nasmith felt it necessary to form a society which could employ suitable men to undertake these responsibilities.

In 1826 he founded the Glasgow City Mission, employing laymen who were able to meet the poor people at their own level, and communicate in terms they could understand. This was something new on the

DAVID NASMITH

Christian scene: a mission of laymen, without university training, who could present the gospel in everyday language.

Six of his members each undertook to raise the money to support one worker, and by the end of the year there were eight men supported by voluntary contributions. The mission was such a success that Nasmith wrote an account of it and sent copies to churches in Scotland, England, Ireland and France, as well as to Africa, Asia and America. His belief was that this method of reaching the poor in the cities could be used in other countries.

## Ireland

Nasmith received a number of encouraging responses to his letter, including an invitation to start a city mission in Dublin. As he had already resigned his position with the Benevolent Institution for health reasons, he and his young wife were free to move to Ireland. Here, he attached himself to York Street Congregational Church, from where he drew much of his support. Within 18 months he was able to report that some 13 or 14 men were employed as missionaries around the city.

After setting up the work, he felt it time to move on, and refused the position as general secretary to the mission. He believed that he would be 'eminently more useful to the cause of God by going to other cities, towns and villages in Ireland, for the purpose of establishing similar institutions'.

One point that struck him more forcibly while in Dublin was the need for city missions not linked to any one church or denomination, which became one of his guiding principles. Remaining in Ireland for a short time, Nasmith set up further societies and town missions before moving to the United States in 1830.

He landed in New York at a time when a revival was taking place under the ministry of evangelist Charles G Finney. Within three weeks Nasmith had founded the New York City Mission, with the full support of three missionaries guaranteed. Again, he did not stay long in any one place, and by the end of 1831 had visited over 120 towns in America and Canada. He founded 16 city missions as well as a number of other organisation societies: young men's societies, ethnic associations, matrons' societies and others on behalf of the poor.

Largely because of the deprivations his wife and child had to endure during these tours, they decided to settle in a home of their own. Despite the attraction of staying in New York at the time of a revival, they chose 'under God' to move to London. He was not still for long, visiting Paris and Le Havre to form city missions, before returning briefly to Ireland and Scotland. Eventually, he settled in London, in March 1835, where he wrote in his diary that he felt he would be 'more useful in London than in any other city'.

## London

The Nasmiths, financially impoverished, settled in a small terraced cottage by the Regents Canal at Hoxton, in the East End. They joined Maberley Congregational Chapel, in Balls Pond Road, off Kingsland Road, and made contact with a number of leading evangelicals of the day, both Nonconformist and Anglicans.

Nasmith's arrival in London was timely, for it coincided with a general awakening of the nation's social conscience, and with the publication of a letter in *The Times* from the Bishop of London. The letter drew attention to the needs of the hundreds of thousands of poor people in the capital, so many of them 'without God and without hope'.

Despite the need, there was considerable opposition to the idea of a city mission. His call to both Nonconformists and Anglicans to join him in forming a mission was discouraged on both sides. He was told that if he linked up with one group or the other, he might succeed, but not with both. There was too much friction at that time between Dissenters and Anglicans for them to support a joint venture.

Ignoring the advice, Nasmith went ahead with his plans. On 16 May 1835, at a simple ceremony, he knelt in prayer with two supporters at his cottage at 13 Canning Terrace. They laid 'the infant mission before the Lord, desiring that he would nurse and bless it, and make it a blessing to tens of thousands'.

For some months afterwards the three men continued to meet on average three times a week, at six o'clock in the morning, to pray, draw up a constitution and make other arrangements. A number of prominent churchmen encouraged the work, men such as Drs Leifchild and Morrison (Congregational ministers), and Sir Fowell Buxton MP (a member of the banking family) and the Hon and Rev Baptist Noel. The turning point came when Fowell Buxton agreed to become the Mission's treasurer; public confidence began to grow and contributions started to come in.

An inaugural meeting in December that year attracted so many people that several thousand had to be turned away. The future of the Mission seemed assured.

## Problems

However, two problems arose that threatened its very existence. In the first place, the Bishop of London publicised his dislike of Nasmith's missions, making it difficult for any Anglican clergyman to be involved. Not only was the employment of lay workers on an interdenominational basis a revolutionary idea for its time, but lay-preaching was particularly offensive to some Anglicans. Hence Anglican support for the Mission dwindled and later the Rev Baptist Noel resigned from the committee.

The other problem was of Nasmith's own doing, and was the consequence of his persistent habit of starting new societies. The Mission's headquarters was at 20 Red Lion Square, Holborn, which Nasmith in his position as honorary secretary used as the centre for all the other societies he continued to form. That same year he started a Metropolitan Young Men's Society, which failed because, as he later admitted, it had been founded on too broad a basis. He had not yet learned his lesson from previous foundations, which mixed converted men and others, and included Bible study and secular discussion.

Not content, he went on to set up a City and Town Missions (for the whole of the British Empire), a Metropolitan Tract Society, a British and Foreign Young Men's Association, a Reading Room, and an Adult School Society.

The committee protested with increasing anger, pointing out that the LCM was still in its infancy and needed his full time attention. Further, there were complaints that too high a proportion of the missionaries were Nonconformist, and as much of his financial support came from Anglicans then he needed to heed the warning.

Nasmith brushed aside these arguments, feeling it his duty towards God to pursue this path. The final showdown came when he formed the London Female Society, a rescue mission for prostitutes, with premises adjoining the LCM's offices, with a connecting door for convenience of administration.

A number of committee members resigned and public support diminished. Although he had committed no breach of trust, and those close to him were convinced of his integrity, Nasmith decided to resign his office to save the Mission. At a committee meeting on 17 March 1837, less than two years after its foundation, his resignation was accepted.

### Burned Out

Nasmith's zeal for forming societies continued unabated. Up to his death two years later, he travelled up and down the country promoting further missions, including Birmingham, Bristol, Dover, Manchester, Paisley and in many other towns.

In November 1839 he travelled to Guildford to set up the Guildford Town Mission, but was suddenly seized with chest and stomach pains. He died the following day, not yet 40 years old, doubtless burned out by his relentless life work. The funeral service was held at Wesley's Chapel, City Road, and he was buried in nearby Bunhill Fields.

Whilst most of Nasmith's societies no longer exist, his vision for the use of laymen revolutionised 19th century Christian missions. However, had he not resigned from the Mission it may well have ceased to exist. As it was, public confidence was restored and the Mission survived the crisis.

The Mission's main aim was 'to extend the knowledge of the gospel among the inhabitants of London and its vicinity (especially the poor).' Within a year of its foundation the LCM employed 41 full-time agents, the number rising to 330 some 20 years later, supported entirely by voluntary contributions.

But although the agents were evangelists, going round the slums from door-to-door with a pocket of tracts and a Bible, they were unable to ignore the poverty and squalor they encountered. Greeted at first with hostility and abuse, they were gradually accepted when people saw they really cared.

The first missionary, Lindsay Burfoot, struggled in Spitalfields for several months with little effect. Then one day he visited a home where a woman was suffering from the fever. As no one else would go near her, he carried the patient downstairs and took her to the workhouse. The kindness was much appreciated, and from then on doors were open to receive him.

Impressed by the valuable service of the ragged schools set up by the mission, Lord Ashley (later, the Earl of Shaftesbury) gave the LCM his full support. On one occasion he even stood in the House of Commons lobby, collecting money for a ragged school in Westminster. Years later, at the mission's Jubilee meeting, the earl averred, 'If the achievements of the London City Mission have not made London a city of saints, yet by the blessing of God they have undoubtedly saved it from becoming a city of devils.'

From 1844 the Mission began to assign missionaries to specific groups of people, first to cabmen, then to firemen, post office workers and busmen. Some were also attached to hospitals, where they were commended for the beneficial influence they exercised in the wards. The scheme was extended to include West End theatres, foreign seamen and many others.

Homelessness has been a problem that has concerned the mission throughout its history, and now there are over 30 day centres catering for these needs. The work expanded further in 1990, when the Mission merged with the London Embankment Mission (the story of which is described in the next chapter).

It is over 150 years now since the London City Mission first carried the gospel to some of the darkest corners of the capital. While some of the needs have changed, the spiritual hunger continues unabated.

## AIMS OF THE LONDON CITY MISSION

The London City Mission exists to make the gospel known to the inhabitants of London and its vicinity (especially the poor) without any reference to denominational distinctions or the peculiarities of Church government. In the words of David Nasmith: 'Let the glory of God and the salvation of souls be your chief, your only end'.

## 42. LONDON EMBANKMENT MISSION (1936)
### Ernest Walton-Lewsey (born 1914)

The years of Queen Victoria's reign were marked by a huge wave of philanthropic work, much of it carried out by Christians. One of the effects of this activity, early in the present century, was a keen debate on the issues of social reform and the gospel.

On the one side were those Christians who emphasised the importance of what came to be called 'the social gospel'. They laid great emphasis on the welfare of the needy and underprivileged. Undoubtedly, many were influenced by the increasing popularity of socialist ideas. But some who defended the social gospel seemed to be more interested in individual welfare than individual salvation.

Against them were those who resolutely believed that the key to a better society was a transformation of individual hearts through Christ. Improved social conditions, they argued, would follow.

Between the two world wars the debate shifted its emphasis. The key issue became the Bible: were the Scriptures infallible or not. And at the same time, evangelicals began to concentrate their energies on moral questions like drinking and gambling, and were less taken up with social issues such as unemployment and homelessness.

These debates form the background to the work of Ernest Walton-Lewsey, founder of the London Embankment Mission (LEM). He was determined not to engage simply in social work, however commendable, but first of all to present the claims of Christ upon the lives of lost men and women.

### Good Missionary

Walton-Lewsey was a young university student when he first hit upon the idea of a mission to the capital's down-and-outs. Walking home from college one evening, he noticed what appeared to be a bundle of rags in the doorway of a printer's warehouse, close to the Thames.

Startled to see the pile move, he took a closer look. It proved to be an old woman surrounded by her belongings, with a tea-can at her side. He thought to himself, 'Why should she have to sleep out while I have a comfortable bed to go home to? Surely God didn't mean her to be cold and dirty and hungry?' Feeling he should do something to help her, he went and found some refreshments. She beamed at his offer as he sat down beside her on the doorstep. 'Are you training to become a parson?' she enquired. When Walton-Lewsey shook his head, she went on, 'Well, you'd make a good missionary then, you would.'

It turned out that her name was Alice, and she began to tell him her story. She had once been an actress, but her marriage had ended in divorce, putting an end to her stage career. With the world seemingly against her, she took to the streets and became a vagrant.

The memory of that meeting stayed with him, and he wondered what he should do about it.

Some months later he experienced another encounter with a down-and-out. It happened one evening when he passed a man sprawled out on steps leading down to the river. The man called out to him: ''Ere mate, please help me,' and held out his bony hand in appeal.

The student turned to see what he could do. After pointing out to him the hardness of his way of life, he went on to speak to him of Jesus who had come to seek and to save the lost. As Walton-Lewsey prepared to leave him the man pleaded, 'Sir, don't go for a minute. You're the first clergyman that's ever told me about Jesus.'

Big Ben was sounding the first hour after midnight as Walton-Lewsey pressed a coin into the man's hand, and bent down to help him up to the pavement. He left him with the suggestion that he try and find a bed for the night. Plans now began to form in his mind. He believed that the man's outstretched hand was God's call.

Gathering together a few dedicated friends from his church, St Paul's of Portman Square, he discussed the possibilities with them. They turned their ideas to prayer, and asked God for premises which they could use for gospel services for down-and-outs.

As they prayed, however, they began to see the Lord wanted them to concentrate on outdoor work for the time being. So instead, they made preparations to set up an open-air canteen.

News of the new venture began to spread, and further voluntary help came from many young people from evangelical churches around the capital. They were supported by gifts of equipment, and people from many parts of the UK and from as far afield as the USA sent them money.

## Chief Tramp
In the early days the canteen was located on the Embankment, near to the Temple underground station, covering the section between Water-

ERNEST WALTON-LEWSEY

loo and Westminster bridge. The river police quickly became their friends, even boiling the water for their tea-urns.

The canteen became a rendezvous for vagrants ready for free tea and sandwiches. It attracted a motley crowd of needy men and women, including some who had been bank clerks, solicitors, doctors. Others had been in prison, but had been rejected when they tried to return home. There were a number who had been brought up in a Christian family, and a few had come to faith but had gone away from the Lord. Among them was a core of real hard cases, whereas others only needed a kindly hand to lift them over a difficult hurdle.

The workers determined that no one who came for refreshments should leave the stand without hearing something of the love of God and the way of salvation. Many responded to the gospel, but Walton-Lewsey knew that all he could do was to scatter the seed of the Word of God. It was left to the Lord to reap a harvest.

On occasions, Walton-Lewsey went out on midnight patrol, armed with a flask of tea and sandwiches. He even dressed as a tramp in order to meet the destitutes on their own ground. He discovered that to be able to live with vagrants, and to see what they could become by the grace of God, needed a special work of the Holy Spirit.

He recalls one night when he met an emaciated figure of a man walking slowly towards him. When Walton-Lewsey spoke to him, he discovered the sorrowful tale behind the man's destitution. At 65, partially blinded and invalided out of the army, he had no home or friends, and had been discharged from hospital with a then-considered incurable disease. 'Minutes ago,' he related, 'I was on the bridge thinking "Why not end it all now?"' But it seems that something – or someone – held him back. 'I felt strong arms around me ... and as the terror passed I groped my way to an empty seat.'

He was still trembling when the young missionary led him back to a seat. The one who had held him back, he pointed out, was God, who loved him and wanted to be his friend. The man agreed it must have been the Lord, who had sent this stranger at the right time of night. Slipping a coin into his hand, and leaving him with a gospel tract – for the man already had some idea of the Faith – Walton-Lewsey committed the man to God.

It was often the case that all he could do was to point such people to the Saviour, and offer them some form of temporary help. He wondered whether the time might come when he would have a mission hall, where he could provide them with a roof over their heads, with beds and a bath; perhaps there might even be a chapel.

Later, Walton-Lewsey became known as 'the Chief Tramp', a title he earned as the result of his many nocturnal excursions by the River Thames. In learning to be a tramp 'it was not only the sense of being homeless,' he once said, 'but also of holding lightly to material things in seeking to win for the Saviour those whom the world would see only as the lowest of the low, and for whom the world had proved too much.'

**Under the Arches**
Before long the mission obtained a centre underneath the arches in Hungerford Lane, below Charing Cross station. It consisted of two rooms which formed part of the basement of the Adelphi Hotel. The rooms allowed enough space for a canteen and a mission hall. It was here that Walton-Lewsey was given another title, 'Archbishop of the Gutter'.

As the work grew, Walton-Lewsey was for some years the presiding genius behind the organisation, as well as the general secretary. Though he was greatly helped by senior colleagues, referred to as missionaries, help also came from both official and voluntary workers, who assisted in the evangelistic and social work, as well as in the office.

With the beginning of the Second World War, the number of vagrants increased, and the mission began to pray for larger premises. A nearby disused garage became available, though it was over-run with rats and cats, and smelled of fish. When the Mission took it over, it appeared as though it would never be converted into a mission hall, but it was. It became the Garage Mission Hall, the scene of many crowded gospel services.

News of the new meeting-room spread along the vagrants' grape-vine, and the place was filled night after night, bringing hundreds within the sound of the gospel. Free food and hot drinks were always provided after the services.

During the blitz, a shelter directly opposite the garage was set aside especially for vagrants and destitutes, who were refused entry to other shelters. The LEM took over the responsibility for the shelter, which had 150 vagrants living in it. Needless to say, the place was filthy and the tramps were covered with lice. The walls were white-washed, and every Friday night the residents deloused and bathed (using a gift of 250 bars of Palmolive soap). The number in the shelter increased to around 200, and included a group of homeless women.

It was from here that the Mission conducted its work for the rest of the war. Services were held nightly, beginning at 7 o'clock. Hymn singing was followed by prayer and the message, often disrupted by comments and even snores. But the Holy Spirit convicted many, and they were brought to God.

Despite the good work being done and the transformed lives, the mission faced persistent problems. The most challenging one was that of alcoholism, which damaged many lives. Drinking bay rum was popular among one section of the vagrants, as well as paraffin, liquid metal polish and other harmful concoctions.

**Campaign**

During those years the Mission introduced a new venture in evangelism with the first ten-day campaign, in October 1943. A group of helpers spread out to Marble Arch, Leicester Square, Trafalgar Square and along the Embankment, inviting the homeless to meetings conducted by a team of ten young people.

The campaign proved a success and became an annual event until 1949, when it was decided to make a change. One of the campaign evangelists was Gypsy Ezekiel Smith, nephew of the famous Gypsy Smith. He attracted large crowds and many young people were converted under his preaching. 'It has humbled me greatly,' the evangelist confessed, 'to see people of the gutter fed and clothed by loving hands, but best of all to see them falling low at Christ's feet, crying "God be merciful to me, a sinner."'

However, the Mission never allowed itself to become complacent or get into a rut, and all the work was 'soaked in intercessions for the lost'. After the war this led to a number of other developments, designed to make their gospel outreach more effective.

In 1950 Walton-Lewsey was able to realise a plan that had been on his mind for some time. It was a gospel van, a church on wheels. The total cost of the vehicle was over £1,000, but the dealer let them have it for £850.

It was fitted out with a canteen section, space for a kitchen and a small sitting room, and even sleeping accommodation. Attractively furnished and with an amplifying system for open-air preaching, it proved very useful, especially in taking the church to people who would not normally darken its doors.

In 1961 the Mission's headquarters were moved to a derelict building behind the Old Vic theatre. After a break of 15 years, another ten day campaign was held, this time in the new chapel. Several well-known preachers spoke at the meetings, and on a number of occasions they experienced a definite visit of the Holy Spirit.

Some years later, in 1979, further hostel accommodation became available. A rehabilitation centre was opened in Upper Norwood, south London, enabling men to stay as part of a family while they learned to readjust to normal life. News of Walton-Lewsey's work spread overseas, and he was able to visit both the USA and Canada to help set up similar organisations. On 32 occasions he crossed the Atlantic to speak at the very large rescue missions of North America.

More recently, firmer links were established with the London City Mission. Like LEM, the City Mission was involved in meeting the spiritual and physical needs of vagrant men and women in central London. After several months of negotiations, the LEM was incorporated into the LCM on 1 January 1990.

There are several hundred people sleeping rough every night in the capital, many of whom are either in their teens or early 20s. They can be found every night in 'cardboard cities' at such places as the Waterloo Bullring, Euston Station, the Embankment Gardens, or in derelict buildings or on park benches.

With no money or anyone to care for them, they are in grave moral danger unless someone comes to their aid. The aim is to throw them a lifeline and to restore to them the dignity of living as children of God.

# 43. SOLDIERS' AND AIRMEN'S
## SCRIPTURE READERS ASSOCIATION (1838)

From Bible times there have been godly men who have served as soldiers, and have drawn strength from their trust in the God of Israel. In the Old Testament, men such as Joshua, Gideon and King David looked to God for help and guidance in their military responsibilities. And during the earthly ministry of Jesus and the days of the apostolic age, there were Roman centurions and soldiers who found the way to God through Christ.

In more recent times, men such as Major-General Sir Henry Havelock of India, General Gordon of Khartoum and Lieutenant General William Dobbie of Malta – whom Churchill described as 'that extraordinary man, the heroic defender of Malta' – have been an inspiration and example to all those serving under their command.

Though pursuing a military career, none of them recognised any conflict between their faith and their task as soldiers. In fact Dobbie once wrote a pamphlet on the subject, affirming that it was 'honourable' and 'well-fitting' for a Christian to serve as a soldier. Christians in the army were invariably known as men of high moral standing.

## Rough Lot
Yet there were times when soldiers were thought of as a 'rough lot', and little attention was paid to either their physical or spiritual well-being. It was not until the 18th century that anyone began to consider their needs. That the evangelical revival began to infiltrate even the ranks of the military can be evidenced from the fact that from 1744 small groups of 'Methodists' were known to exist in the army. In 1756, the Rev Samuel Walker ministered to one regiment in Truro. During the nine weeks they were billeted in the town around 200 soldiers turned to Christ.

Towards the end of the century, the Clapham Sect addressed the need by distributing Bibles to serving soldiers and sailors. John Thornton gave away large quantities of Bibles, many of them printed at his own expense. This led, in 1780, to the formation of the Bible Society by Thornton and Wilberforce, which circulated 25,000 Bibles in less than 25 years. After the British and Foreign Bible Society was founded in 1804, the name of the work was changed to the Naval and Military Bible Society.

The early years of the following century witnessed a continued interest in the gospel among soldiers. In the Peninsular War (1808-

1814), for example, there were numerous Christian officers and soldiers who met together for worship and mutual encouragement, either in the field or after a day's march. A token recognition of the need to cater for the men's spiritual needs was made with the provision of an authorised chaplain, but this was hardly adequate to serve the whole of the British Army in Spain.

The Duke of Wellington recognised the value of such provision, declaring that religious instruction was not only 'a moral necessity to every soul in the army', but also 'the greatest support and aid to military discipline'. In 1811 he pleaded with the authorities to send him more 'respectable clergymen' as chaplains, and it may have been in response to this plea that the Rev G C Smith went to serve for two years in a voluntary capacity.

As the century unfolded, there began a more permanent work among soldiers, a provision which is today a standard feature of the care the army offers its men. The most significant foundation was that of the Soldiers' Friend Society, now called the Soldiers' and Airmen's Scripture Readers Association (SASRA). The Association has no single founder, but there were three godly people who made key contributions towards its development.

## Woolwich

It was Sergeant William Rudd (1776-1861) of the Royal Artillery, stationed at Woolwich in south-east London, who more than anyone provided the original impetus for founding the work of the Association. As a result of his initiative, a work was started that was to last for 26 years, before many of the men were posted to the war front.

Rudd, a native of Arklow, Southern Ireland, was brought up as a devout member of the Church of England. In 1804, the 28-year-old Royal Artillery NCO was posted to Woolwich, where he 'fell into evil ways'. Through the prayers of a group of believing soldiers in the barracks, in 1816 he became a Christian. He joined the local Wesleyan Chapel in Meeting House Lane and was influential in leading many young recruits to faith in Christ.

Anxious to promote the gospel, Rudd posted a notice in the regimental guardroom, offering to loan a Bible or other Christian literature to any soldier in need of spiritual help. As his action was taken without permission, he was brought in front of his Commanding Officer, severely reprimanded for his action and threatened with an overseas posting.

These events came to the attention of a Christian officer, a Captain Maitland, who supported Rudd, and was also censured. As it happened, Maitland was the son of a senior serving officer who reported the affair to his superiors. The outcome was that a waggon-load of Bibles was sent to Woolwich, with orders that they be placed in the hospital and every guardroom in the garrison.

## Readers

It is thought that it was this incident which led to a decision in 1825 to issue a Bible and Prayer Book, at public expense, to all soldiers who wished to receive them. But most soldiers could not read, and so the Chaplain General, supported by several Christian officers, was allowed privately to employ Christian ex-servicemen to go into barrack-rooms and read the Scriptures to the troops. These men, in effect evangelists, were known as Scripture Readers, a title that has been retained to this day.

At Woolwich, Sergeant Rudd persisted in his efforts to care for the spiritual well-being of the troops. In 1830 he opened a Soldiers' Reading Room near to the barracks, to which 'godly men could go for reading, writing and devotional purposes'.

With advancing years and deteriorating health, however, Rudd was discharged in 1847 as 'medically unfit for further service'. With the help of another NCO he continued the work until 1855, when the Reading Room closed because the men who used it were posted to the Crimea.

The work of the Scripture Readers continued as a privately financed venture until 1838, when a group of Christian officers decided to put their work on a more permanent footing.

Known as the Soldiers' Friend Society, the new society was set up with two main objectives. First, to bring soldiers to a saving faith in Christ by means of personal evangelism in the barrack-rooms, and the distribution of Christian literature. Then to support believers by the provision of reading rooms, libraries and by setting up prayer groups. The Society was later renamed the Army Scripture Readers Society.

Thousands of men were contacted with the gospel and there were reports of many conversions. Soldiers shared their faith with their comrades and their influence spread to garrisons as far away as Canada and around the Mediterranean.

In 1856 the first War Office Charter was drawn up to regulate the work. Its emphasis was on permission to visit barrack rooms, hospital wards and detention barracks, and the work has continued since under this authority.

## India

At this time, events taking place thousands of miles away in India greatly influenced the work of the Society. A young officer was converted to Christ through the witness of a brother officer while en route for India with the Somerset Light Infantry in 1823.

Henry Havelock started Bible studies and prayer meetings at his garrison for all officers and soldiers who were 'well-disposed', and maintained his stand despite criticism from his fellow-officers. Soon it was acknowledged that the believing soldiers were among the best-behaved in the regiment, a factor which greatly impressed the Commanding Officer who readily supported Havelock's activities.

Whilst stationed at Agra, Havelock promoted a step which had far-reaching results. Aggrieved because the Articles of War only excused Roman Catholics from compulsory church parades, he petitioned that the same liberty should be extended to Dissenters. His representations were successful, and in 1839 Dissenters throughout the whole of the British Army were given freedom to withdraw from compulsory church parades.

As a soldier, he achieved considerable distinction while serving in India. Promoted to Major General and then knighted for his part in the relief of Lucknow (1857), he died shortly afterwards. His fine example served to strengthen the position of Christians in the army, so that it became possible 'to fear God as well as honour the Queen'. Havelock was described by Lord Hardinge as 'Every inch a soldier; and every inch a Christian'.

In 1859, the Soldiers' Friend Society amalgamated with the lesser known British Army Scripture Readers Society, an organisation which at that time did not enjoy the confidence of chaplains or military authorities. This union gave birth to the Army Scripture Readers Society (ASRS), which gained official recognition and under God increased the good work being done among soldiers.

The Scripture Readers proved themselves not only to be evangelists, but as non-combatants were also courageous men of God who took their place alongside the soldiers they served. They ministered to both British and French Protestant forces in the Crimean War, and one Russian-speaking Reader was able to witness to Russian prisoners-of-war.

Major-General Sir Henry Havelock (1795-1857) was born in Sunderland, son of a prosperous shipbuilder. It was to his mother that he owed his careful religious upbringing, though it was not until later that he came to faith. He was educated at Charterhouse, then entered the Middle Temple as a law student. Owing to a misunderstanding with his father, who had lost his fortune by unsuccessful speculation, he was thrown onto his own resources. He abandoned law as a profession and in 1815 entered the Army and was commissioned into the Rifle Brigade.

During his early years in the Army he made a study of military history and the art of war. With no prospect of active service, he volunteered for India. In preparation, he acquired a knowledge of the Persian and Hindustani languages, which were to be of value to him during his career.

On the long journey to India a brother officer, named James Gardner, spoke to Havelock about the Lord and showed him from the Bible why Christ had died for him. Havelock had never before realised the significance of Christ's death, and recognised that such an amazing love demanded a response. Having counted the cost of discipleship, especially in view of the possibility of being ostracised by his fellow officers, he decided for Christ.

He arrived in India a changed man and determined to dispel any suggestion that a Christian could not also be a soldier of valour. During the wars that followed, he became known as a fearless leader and was highly respected by his men. His most famous victory was the capture of Lucknow during the Indian Mutiny (1857). Four days later he was taken ill and died suddenly.

News of his death reached England and plunged the nation into mourning. A soldier of the old puritan type, he rendered service to God rather than to his superiors, yet was a popular hero among the people.

Two Readers accompanied the Abyssinian Expedition in 1868 and two others served in the Zululand campaign of 1879. The Reader who sailed up the Nile in 1884 with the relief force for Khartoum was said by the officer in charge to be worth two men in his boat.

When the First World War began in 1914, the number of Scripture Readers had risen to 64, of whom 36 were deployed in France and Belgium.

## Moody

The work of the ASRS was complemented by that of the Soldiers' Christian Association (SCA), founded in 1887 to link up soldiers converted during Moody's London mission in 1883. Its founder was a Miss Lucy Deacon, who came from a godly family of Christian bankers and was an enthusiastic supporter of Moody's evangelistic endeavours.

At the meetings in Exeter Hall, in the Strand, Moody noticed a number of soldiers in uniform who attended each night. As they sat in the front row, the evangelist's concern grew and he gave the matter prayerful consideration. He realised that, if any of them made a decision, then it would involve much opposition from their comrades. So in order to encourage any who appeared challenged by the message, he asked Miss Deacon to place herself close to where the men were sitting. Perhaps, he suggested, the gentle word of a woman might help them decide the issue.

Despite the social conventions of Victorian society, Lucy Deacon complied, and was a means of persuading scores of men to make their way into the enquiry room. Together with her cousin she was able to follow up those who came to faith. They called at the barrack gates, and handed in the list of those whom they wished to see, and waited until they were sent for. A parcel of books was given to each new convert. The two ladies started a small meeting for Bible study and prayer in the back room of a house in Vauxhall Bridge Road, from which the Soldiers' Christian Association originated.

Other people took up the idea and formed Bible study groups in garrisons in London, Windsor, Aldershot, Cork and other towns, where facilities were granted by the Sandes and Daniell Homes. Branches formed in India were given the use of the Prayer Rooms already established through the energetic work of W B Harington, a Public Works engineer.

Before long there were over 400 branches in existence, and the Association was equally active in times of peace and war. Its aim was to win soldiers to Christ and to build them up in the faith. Before long it was claimed that the best-taught believers were those involved with the SCA.

## Amalgamation

After the First World War, the growth and development of the Royal Air Force led the Association to extend its work. To recognise the new ministry, the name was changed in 1930 to the Soldiers' and Airman's Christian Association. But while ASRS worked within a charter laid down by the War Office, the newly-formed SACA had no official status.

Some of the leaders of the two societies began to see the wisdom of amalgamating the two groups, whose purpose and doctrine were almost identical and which had worked alongside each other for 52 years. After prayer, leaders took the decision to unite the two societies in September 1938. This was the centenary year of the original foundation, though the present title of SASRA was not adopted until 1950.

At the beginning of the Second World War there were 65 Scripture Readers ready for duty, a number which later increased to 183. Lady Readers were appointed in 1943. The readers were especially active in running rest rooms and homes for the troops, and frequently accompanied the men into the battle zone.

In recent years the association has linked up with Mrs Daniell's Soldiers' Homes, and has assumed responsibility for the running of the two organisations. Nevertheless, its chief aim continues to be the 'making and sustaining of Christians'.

---

### MISSION STATEMENT AND AIMS OF SASRA

The Association is established to befriend Service personnel with a view to their spiritual welfare, by introducing them to a practical experience of the Christian Faith, as the basis of their character and morale; and to promote inter-denominational fellowship through its branches.

AIMS
1. To present the claims of Christ to the men and women serving in HM forces, and to their families.
2. To promote inter-denominational Christian Fellowships at all Army Garrisons and RAF Stations, both at home and overseas.
3. To encourage serving Christians to witness to their comrades by their manner of life, and in their spoken testimony.

# 6

# SERVING
# THE
# COMMUNITY

# BETHNAL GREEN MEDICAL MISSION (1866)
## Annie Macpherson (1824-1904)

In the 19th century working class people who became ill had to cope with great difficulties. Apart from the totally inadequate provisions made under the 1601 Poor Law, the government's attitude was one of indifference. There were two kinds of hospital available for the poor: the workhouses, where sick paupers were expected to go, and voluntary hospitals, founded by charitable people from as early as the 16th century.

For anyone who had paid into a regular weekly medical scheme, which few could afford, help was available from a provident dispensary. Otherwise the sick had to rely on the Poor Law doctor or attend for free treatment at a hospital outpatients department. The benefits of both these options were dubious.

The voluntary hospitals were to be found both in London and the provinces, and were supported by the public through donations and subscriptions. Money was collected by the Sunday and Saturday Hospital Funds: Sundays through church offerings, and Saturday collections taken at sporting events and in the streets.

But it was difficult for the ordinary poor to gain access to the services of these institutions. The sick poor, usually left to fend for themselves and unable to pay for proper care, frequently died young from what would normally have been treatable diseases. At the turn of the 19th century two out of every five babies died before they reached the age of five, and in 1840 the average age of death was 29.

There were a number of common killer diseases that were feared by the masses, such as smallpox, typhoid, diptheria and tuberculosis. Outbreaks of cholera occurred regularly, and once 2,000 Londoners died from the disease during the course of one week. Mothers and babies were often at risk at the time of childbirth, and there were many orphans left with little chance of survival.

In 1841 the Edinburgh Medical Missionary Society (EMMS) was founded to train medical missionaries for service overseas. However, it was not long before it was realised that medical missions were needed for the poorer districts of Edinburgh and other large cities. Dr William Fairlie Clarke, a leading evangelical of his day, proposed setting up medical missions for the poor, to give them free advice and medicine.

But nothing appears to have been done until 1859, when Dr William Burns Thomson started a work in the Cowgate area of Edinburgh.

## Medical Missions

Dr Thomson, a student in training with EMMS, was visiting the slums of Edinburgh's Cowgate when he realised there was an urgent need here on his own doorstep. He decided to open a free dispensary, and rented a shop for this purpose in Cowgate. Known as the Edinburgh Medical Mission, the work was supported by medical men from the university, and Thomson used the opportunity to train medical missionaries for work in the slums of Britain's major cities.

The dispensary was open daily with a doctor and nurse at hand, and in the course of one year some 7,000 patients were treated. People too ill to attend the clinic were visited in their homes and, where necessary, arrangements made for the more urgent cases to be taken to hospital.

Soon Thomson was spending more and more time travelling around the country, encouraging the formation of similar missions. Liverpool, Aberdeen, Birmingham and other cities responded to his pleas. But the idea of medical missions was slow in reaching London. In 1869 a Dr George Saunders, encouraged by Thomson, started a medical mission in the St Giles district of London (now New Oxford Street). But it was not until Dr Thomson came to stay at the Mildmay Institute, in 1870, that the movement got off the ground and other missions were started around the capital.

Mildmay Institute, founded by the Rev William and Catherine Pennefather, was the centre for a variety of missions. For some years Mildmay deaconesses had been at work in the Bethnal Green area of the East End, and in 1877 William Pennefather was responsible for founding the Mildmay Hospital. The Mildmay Mission to the Jews, founded by John Wilkinson, also opened a medical mission, as did several of the denominations. By the last two decades of the century, medical mission work had become a regular part of Christian mission.

Two missions from this era have survived the 1948 National Health Service takeover: they are the Bethnal Green Medical Mission in east London, and the Bermondsey and Brook Lane Medical Mission (now called Mission Care) located in south London. Both missions have developed along quite different lines while still maintaining their Christian ethos.

## Home of Industry

Although the Bethnal Green Medical Mission began as a small medical work in 1901, its beginnings go back some 40 years. It really started with the work of Annie Macpherson, who opened a Home of Industry after the tragic cholera epidemic of 1866.

Annie Macpherson was a woman of great determination and vigour, with a longing to see ordinary men and women brought to Christ. Responsible for starting several evangelistic concerns in the East End, she also cooperated with a Mrs Meredith of Clapham to hold monthly meetings for social workers in the district, dealing with their problems and co-ordinating the work of specialists.

Before coming to London, Annie Macpherson had worked among the coprolite diggers of Cambridge, who produced the phosphate used in making artificial manure. At a conference in Shoreditch in 1861, Annie received a fresh vision of the work God was calling her to do. She wrote: 'That work was to bring souls into God's kingdom.'

In 1865, at the age of 40, she returned to London to live among the poor people of the East End. Struck by the conditions under which many of the children were forced to work, her heart ached for the 'child slaves', especially the match box makers. They were employed for up to 16 hours a day making boxes at two pence farthing a gross.

Determined to draw public attention to the conditions in which these children worked, she wrote a small booklet describing their plight. Her efforts were supported by R C Morgan, the editor of *The Christian* newspaper (formerly *The Revival*), who was instrumental in getting her ideas published.

## Warehouse

Determined to open a home for the poor match box makers, she searched around for a suitable building. Her attention was drawn to a disused warehouse on Commercial Street, Spitalfields, which had been used as a temporary shelter for cholera victims during the 1866 outbreak, and already had gas and water laid on. Visiting the building with her sister and brother-in-law and three other friends, she knelt down and prayed that one day God would give it to her.

With money provided almost entirely by readers of *The Christian*, she was eventually able to buy the building. It was to be another whole year before the building could be set up as a Home of Industry, to provide accommodation and training for poor children.

The home included a workshop where children could make match boxes under better conditions. There was provision for evening classes where they were taught to read and write, and she opened other training centres in Hackney for both boys and girls. Always looking for opportunities of service, she started an aged widows class and visited local lodging houses to offer whatever assistance she could to the down-and-outs. On Sundays she was involved in open-air work at Petticoat Lane's Bird Fair market (from 1874), from 1876 she worked with Catherine Pennefather who founded the Bible Flower Mission, and assisted with the Railway Gatekeepers' Mission (1882), all of which operated from the Hackney home.

Difficulty in finding permanent employment for many of her children prompted Annie to link up with Maria Rye, who was operating a scheme for sending children to begin a new life in Canada. In May 1870

## MISSION CARE

In 1904 Dr Selina Fox (1871-1958) of the Church Missionary Society felt called of God to open a medical mission in Bermondsey, close to where she had previously worked as medical officer at the CMS missionary school in Riley Street. A house was rented in Grange Road, and Dr Fox soon became a well-known figure in the district. She was in and out of houses working to relieve suffering, and helping in many other ways.

In the early years Dr Fox concentrated on women and children, as the mothers and daughters were often the breadwinners of the family. Food parcels were frequently supplied, which sometimes did more good than the medicine.

The mission survived during the black years of the First World War, and in 1921 a small hospital was opened. The work expanded and a new hospital built, opened in 1929 by HRH the Duchess of York (later the Queen Mother).

In the 1920s the London County Council re-housed some of the Bermondsey residents on the new Downham Estate, near Bromley, south-east London. But many of them continued to trek back to Bermondsey for their medical treatment, a journey of some 10 miles. After prayer, it seemed right under God to start a work in Downham. A Brethren Assembly, located on the edge of the Estate, offered free accommodation at Brook Lane Mission Hall, and a clinic was opened in March 1937.

The two missions amalgamated in 1982 to become the Bermondsey and Brook Lane Medical Mission, but is now known as Mission Care. All medical work was closed down in 1990 and attention is focused on six homes offering residential and nursing care for elderly people, including any who are frail or have a mental illness or a severe physical disability. The Mission also operates a Training Consortium, which provides training in care for its own homes and for 36 other homes as well.

she took her first batch of 100 boys to Ontario. It was around this time that Tom Barnardo was establishing his first children's home in nearby Stepney, and he helped Miss Macpherson train the first group of boys going out.

Despite opposition from various groups in Canada, who resented the idea of London's 'street arabs' being dumped on them, the venture proved a success. Each year two parties sailed for a new life in Canada, accompanied by their supervisor. Before long both Dr Barnardo and William Quarrier of Scotland decided to make use of her services and send some of their children across the Atlantic.

## Training Ground
As the work of the home expanded, the warehouse at 60 Commercial Street proved inadequate, and in 1887 the work was moved to Bethnal Green. A regular visitor when he returned to England was Hudson

### MISSION STATEMENT OF MISSION CARE

MISSION CARE is a Christian care organisation which aims to provide a range of the best quality residential care, nursing care and personal care services which are targeted to meet the identified needs of elderly people and people with disabilities.

VALUES STATEMENT
Christian beliefs will be reflected in the way we conduct ourselves. We will stand for these core values at all times:

Pioneering – we will be responsive to emerging needs.

Professional – we will pursue excellence in our work and have a commitment to recruiting quality staff and supporting their on-going development.

Caring – we will be compassionate and supportive towards and will listen and talk to our residents and staff.

This will result in the continuous pursuit of privacy, dignity, independence, choice, rights and fulfilment for those whom we serve.

VISION STATEMENT
By 2002, with local church involvement, we will be widely known for vibrant Christian distinctiveness centred on ten homes and the significant provision of respite and personal care services.

Taylor of the China Inland Mission, who often spoke at the home's monthly prayer meeting. The home provided a good training ground for those going to foreign mission fields, including CIM, and a number of candidates had their first experience of missionary work at the Home of Industry.

It was here, in 1901, that Annie was finally able to start a medical mission, with her nephew, Dr Merry, as the first doctor. A dispensary was opened which during the first eight months treated 2,700 patients. During the same period, the doctor and the nurses made over a thousand visits to people too ill to attend the surgery.

Annie Macpherson continued her work in the East End until 1902, when illness forced her to relinquish some of her responsibilities. She retired to Hove where she died in her 80th year, in 1904.

The work has flourished as a result of the foundations laid down by Miss Macpherson: it was based 'not upon a human being but upon Jesus Christ himself', and it relied entirely on God's provision. These two principles are those on which the mission has continued to work.

**Poverty**
The emigration scheme was finally discontinued in 1925 and was taken over by Barnardo's. And although, generally, social conditions in England had improved, there was still widespread poverty in the East End where the medical mission continued to meet a growing need.

From then on the emphasis of the mission was solely on medical work, but as the work grew new premises eventually became essential. An ideal building was found in nearby Cambridge Heath Road, though the owner was not willing to sell. It was not until nearly a year later that, hearing it was for the Lord's work, he finally decided 'for some reason I cannot explain I feel I must let you have it'. The following year (1926) the name of the work was changed to 'The Bethnal Green Medical Mission (The Annie Macpherson Home of Industry Inc.)'

Although essentially a medical mission, it also serves as a base for gospel outreach. Prayers are held for a short while every morning in the surgery. Patients seem almost invariably willing to join in, and often comment later on the message given. A number of new ventures have been started over the years, including Girl Covenanters, women's meetings, a Sunday School and a week night Bible Club. A party of Christian young people from the mission have been responsible for

services held in Bethnal Green Hospital, where patients have appreciated their ministry.

With the advent of the National Health Service in 1948, the future of
Christian medical work hung in the balance. The Mission opted to join
the National Health Service, and like Mildmay Hospital was able to
maintain its distinctive Christian foundation.

Since pre-war days there had been plans for another new building,
as the work had continued to grow. Plans were shelved in 1936 because
of lack of funds, and the war caused further delay. The estimated cost
of the new building was £35-40,000; the amount in the bank was
£14,000. But with their eyes upon God the council went ahead. Funds
came in, and the new building was opened in 1955 without incurring
any debt.

In Bethnal Green itself the work has become increasingly self-
supporting, both financially and as far as workers are concerned. The
leaders of many sections of the work are local people, who have grown
up in the fellowship of the mission.

Committed to working among East Enders, the mission operates a
group medical practice of four doctors and two nurses. There is a
bookroom that services the needs of local church and hospital book
stalls, and it is the home of an active Christian fellowship which takes
the gospel into the local community.

Annie Macpherson wrote in 1868, 'We wait patiently, believing our
government will yet turn her millions of drink revenue into improvement of the living conditions of the working class today.' Whilst much
has been done to improve standards of living, the message of the gospel
is still relevant for both rich and poor.

It was for this reason that the mission had erected on an outside wall
the words of Jesus, 'Come unto me and I will give you rest,' a rest needed
in a troubled world.

## MISSION STATEMENT OF
## BETHNAL GREEN MEDICAL MISSION

The society originated in the nineteenth century in order to provide
a home of Industry for the neighbourhood. It now promotes evangelical Christian teaching, and supports medical care in the community.

# JOHN GROOMS ASSOCIATION
# FOR DISABLED PEOPLE (1866)
## John Groom (1845-1919)

The 18th and 19th centuries saw medical science begin to replace what for hundreds of years had largely been superstitious and ancient practices in treating the sick. Hospitals, though primitive, introduced new discoveries such as anaesthetics, antiseptics and inoculations, which eventually led to further enormous advances. Outbreaks of cholera, typhoid and other diseases, which carried off hundreds of people, were investigated and steps taken to eradicate the causes.

These new techniques enabled doctors and surgeons to treat patients with a greater chance of success, and the average age of death steadily rose. Yet there was not the same sense of urgency applied to the needs of disabled people. Steps had already been taken to give assistance to the deaf and the blind, but those who were 'crippled' were often left to fend for themselves. This may have been because they were able to earn some kind of living – even if only as a beggar – but also because there was no known remedy for their condition.

Disabled children, however, attracted some sympathy because they needed protection from ruthless adults who would exploit them for financial gain. But there was hope for them, as they could be given the opportunity to mingle with healthy children and be trained in preparation for useful employment.

Evangelicals were among the first to care for disabled children, and they displayed a new love and compassion towards them. Their work stirred the public conscience and it led to several agencies being set up to provide for the spiritual, educational and vocational needs of these children.

Others, prompted by humanitarian motives, pioneered developments in medical help and occupational training. Between the two, provision was made for the entire health and well-being of the children.

A survey towards the end of the 19th century revealed that five out of every 1,000 school children were crippled, maimed or deformed, though this did not include those handicapped children unable to attend school. Begging was the only occupation for which they were thought to be fit, and they were sent onto the streets in the hope that the sight of a disabled child would touch the hearts and pockets of passers-by.

Other children earned a precarious form of living by selling a variety of wares from a small tray hung round their neck – matches, water cress, flowers, toffee apples or other cheap goods.

## Special Attention
One of the first to pay special attention to disabled children was John Pounds, recognised as the founder of the ragged school movement, who included several such children in his class. Later, a number of homes for disabled children were opened in London. The Winchmere Home for Girls (1851) in Marylebone Road and the Wright's Lane Boys' Home (1866) were among the first, and they encouraged others to follow their lead.

In 1877 a Mrs Giniver opened a Home at Kilburn where girls who had been refused entrance into other Homes were taught needlework and sewing. Dr Barnardo set up his Children's Fold for a hundred disabled children in 1887, and the following year the Waifs and Strays Society (now the Children's Society) also made special provision for these helpless children.

It was the work of John Groom, Superintendent of an East End mission, however, that brought the work into focus when he started a work among flower girls who attended his hall in Clerkenwell.

John Groom was born the third child of Christian parents who lived near St Paul's Cathedral. When his father died, the ten-year-old John was forced to take whatever work he could to help support the family. For him there was neither school nor play; often cold and tired, he grew up among the street-sellers, errand boys and beggars. It was here that he learned at first hand about poverty and hardship, and saw around him hundreds of children who were in a far worse plight then he was.

By the age of 16 he was already teaching in Sunday School. He was apprenticed as a silver engraver, and before long was successful enough to start his own business as a metal engraver and toolmaker.

## Home Visiting
About the age of 18 he was invited to share in the work of the London City Mission, and he engaged in open-air preaching and Bible teaching at cottage meetings. Accompanied by a City Missioner friend, Groom began visiting the homes near to the Mission, and soon discovered that there were more disabled children than he had realised, as many of them

were forced to stay indoors by the nature of their condition.

Some two years later he was asked to become the Superintendent of the Farringdon Mission in the City of London, and it was from here that he began his life's work.

Although never physically strong – two or three times he came near to death – he gave himself enthusiastically to his calling. He preached on the streets, in halls and schools; he gained the confidence of the criminal fraternity, winning their confidence and respect. But his main concern was for the children – and especially the disabled – to get them to Sunday School where he could share the gospel with them.

With the support of a few friends and relations, he raised enough funds to be able to launch his first venture in practical care. Not far from the Mission were two of London's great markets – the flower market at Covent Garden and the vegetable market at Farringdon. Here, early each morning, there gathered groups of poor children, some of them disabled, hoping to buy cheap left-overs of watercress and flowers for selling in the streets.

**Flower Girls**

It was among the flower girls that Groom opened his Mission. Aided by a band of willing helpers, which included two missioners and two Bible women, he hired a hall near the markets. Each morning at five o'clock he went out to invite the watercress and flower girls to breakfast. During winter, the most needy children were also provided with lunch. As they enjoyed the warmth of the room and their food, Groom read suitable verses of Scripture to them and spoke of God's love.

The work gradually expanded; more rooms were hired, and a soup kitchen, clothing club, boot and blanket clubs were formed. The more desperate cases of need were followed up by the Bible women, who also visited the neighbourhood to see how they could help families with food and fuel.

In 1866 the work was placed on a proper footing; a committee was formed to exercise some form of control, and the work was named the Watercress and Flower Girls' Mission. As its field of activity was enlarged to include Smithfield, St Giles and even the West End, the first permanent centre for the work was opened in Harp Alley, near Smithfield.

A chance meeting one day with the Earl of Shaftesbury led to an expansion of the work. A flower seller in Piccadilly Circus had broken

JOHN GROOM

her crutch and Groom had gone to her assistance when he received a summons to a carriage nearby. The Earl had witnessed the incident and wanted to know more about Groom.

When he learned of the Watercress and Flower Girls' Mission, the Earl offered to become their first President, and afterwards gave it much support and encouragement. It was the Earl's influence that helped provide more funds that led to the founding of what became known as John Groom's Crippleage. The support of other prominent people followed, including Samuel Morley, Baroness Burdett-Coutts and F A Bevan, all of them associated with other philanthropic causes in the capital.

The Mission had a great impact on the area around the markets, doing a tremendous amount of good. During the winter months 5,000 meals were served each week, and one year the annual total reached 100,000. Missionaries and deaconesses visited the homes, nursing sisters tended the sick, providing them with food and clothing where necessary, and tickets for bread, groceries and coal were distributed.

All the time the Mission's work continued to expand and various organisations were formed as part of the main work. There were other centres opened in Bermondsey, Chelsea, Holborn, St Pancras and

Westminster. A loan fund started by the Earl of Shaftesbury helped finance loans to flower girls, and a Penny Bank encouraged thrift.

A Flower Girls' Brigade was started in 1878 for girls unable to be trained for domestic service, especially those who were disabled. They were trained to take orders, make them up and deliver them for dinner tables, weddings and concerts. But Groom also had long-term plans for the girls. These included annual holidays by the sea; a training centre where girls could learn to do other kinds of work; plus homes, and care and meaningful work for disabled people.

## Artificial Flowers

It was possible in some areas of London for some disabled children to receive training from an early age through to their teens. However, they could not find work unless they had been brought up in a children's home, as there was no one to act on their behalf. So Groom began by preparing some of his strongest girls for domestic service. For the majority, however, they needed some other work.

At that time, artificial flowers were becoming fashionable; they were handmade, and usually imported from France and Germany. Groom felt this was the kind of work his disabled girls could do, and no other charity was engaged in this kind of work. The work would be light and colourful, and would enable the girls to develop their creative skills. He set up his mission hall as a 'factory' and persuaded his brothers to join in operating the machine that stamped out the flower petals.

An Industrial Training Home was opened, where the girls were cared for and trained free of charge. Only simple flowers were made at first, good lifelike copies of natural flowers, made in cloth by hand. As they became more experienced, the work became more ambitious, with dahlias, carnations and orchids. In the early days there were between 60 and 70 girls employed in the factory, but at the height of the demand the figure rose to around 300.

Groom was able to find a ready market for their products; the Flower Mission became quite famous and their flowers were often in demand. Hotels and ballrooms were their chief customers, but they were once invited to decorate the Guildhall for the Lord Mayor's banquet, and in 1912 they supplied the roses for the very first Queen Alexandra Rose Day collection.

## Accommodation

In order to bring the girls out of the slum conditions in which they lived, Groom launched an appeal for funds so that he could rent some accommodation. He had noticed that there were seven empty houses in Sekforde Street where he lived, and discovered he was able to rent all seven of them.

He had them furnished, and each house was supervised by a housemother who was able to take in 12 girls. Despite the drawback of being built on three floors – the disabled girls had to work their way up the stairs from a sitting position – they provided a healthier environment than anything the girls had previously known.

It is interesting to note the chief disabilities and deformities from which the girls suffered. Most of them had diseases of the spine, bones and joints, almost entirely caused by tuberculosis; others were without a limb or were blind, and others suffered from congenital deformities. Obviously, to succeed as a flower-maker required considerable determination and dexterity on the part of some of the girls.

It wasn't only the flower girls that needed a home, however; there were many other homeless children roaming the streets who had escaped the attentions of such men as Dr Barnardo and Dr Bowman Stephenson (of the National Children's Home). John Groom was determined to do something for these children as well. With a donation of £1,000 he bought and furnished a house at Clacton-on-Sea (Essex) where, he believed, the orphans would be able to live healthy and happy lives.

Further homes were later built on the same site, and included a small hospital, a sanatorium, a convalescent home and a holiday home for the flower girls. As all the houses were named after a flower, the local people quickly nicknamed it the 'Flower Village'.

## Pastor

In addition to the heavy workload of running the Mission, Groom was also a pastor and still had a heart for evangelism. When his mission hall was burned down, the work was moved to Woodbridge Chapel and re-opened on the first Sunday in 1895. There was plenty of space here for the many weeknight activities usually associated with an evangelical mission, including a mother's club, Christian Endeavour and a Band of Hope.

## CARE FOR DISABLED PEOPLE

Here are two quite contrasting (and more recently formed) Christian groups which offer practical support:

(1) *The Disabled Christians Fellowship*, based at Bristol, was founded in 1959 by Mrs Frances Pool, herself a multiple sclerosis sufferer. Recognising the advantages of linking together people with physical handicaps, she formed a small committee to launch the work. There are now around 80 branches of DCF in Britain and Northern Ireland, where many disabled Christians have found fellowship with other believers, some have discovered an avenue of service, while others have themselves come to know the Lord.

The DCF Centre in Bristol is a day centre and is opened to disabled people between the ages of 16-64. It offers a wide range of facilities for training programmes, as well as education and leisure opportunities. Members are linked together through a monthly magazine and audio cassettes, and many correspond with penfriends. Summer holidays are arranged, and a new holiday home has been opened at Newcastle, Co Down (Northern Ireland).

(2) *Christian Home for the Physically Handicapped* is a small charity set up in 1981. Ron Albon had failed to find a suitable home which could offer round-the-clock care for his 21-year-old disabled daughter. The few residential homes had long waiting lists, and fewer still had a true Christian atmosphere.

He formed a committee and began to make plans for residential accommodation that would provide 24-hour care. A plot of land has been purchased at Dagenham (Essex), and money is now coming in for the building. The idea is to provide 16 ground floor places, plus 11 flats on the first floor for disabled people to live wholly or partially independent with a carer or family, with 24-hour facilities. Residents will normally be teenagers or above, and will be cared for by a Christian staff.

The services each Sunday were packed with around 800 people, there was a 40-strong brass band and an organ to accompany the singing, and the gospel was preached. His sermons were urgent, simple and always Bible-based; and the local people loved him.

After 52 active years of service, in the summer of 1918 Groom finally felt it time to relinquish the work into other hands. He spent his post-retirement days in one of the Clacton Homes, where he died the following year, aged 74.

The funeral service was held at Woodbridge Chapel, which was crowded for the occasion. Former street-sellers, blind, lame and orphans all gathered to pay their last respects to the man they loved. There were masses of flowers around the chapel, tributes not from the great, but from ordinary folk whom he had helped.

Flower production continued to flourish and it was necessary to open up more centres. But in the early 1930s the leases on some of the properties were due to expire, and rather than pay higher rents it was decided to plan a new purpose-built estate. In 1932 the whole work was moved out of London and was transferred to Edgware, Middlesex, just north west of the capital.

## Adults with Disabilities

Over the years the work of John Grooms Association has changed and broadened. No longer caring for children, its emphasis is on meeting the needs of adults with disabilities. Artificial flowers are no longer produced, and a range of purposeful activities designed to meet individual needs have been introduced.

Residential care is an important feature of the Association's work. John Grooms has been at the forefront of the provision of residential and nursing care in the UK. Today, it provides specialist care for over 180 disabled people in locations as far afield as Norwich, Southend, Colchester and North London.

The John Grooms Housing Association was formed in 1976 to provide purpose-built flats in different parts of England for people requiring the use of a wheel-chair. There is hotel and self-catering holiday accommodation in various parts of the country, and a flagship hotel has been opened in South Wales.

In the 19th century, Christians introduced a love and compassion for disabled children and adults that was previously unknown. Today, John Grooms maintains the pattern of tradition laid down by its founder 130 years ago. And though times have changed, the call to care is essentially the same.

---

### MISSION STATEMENT OF
### JOHN GROOMS ASSOCIATION FOR DISABLED PEOPLE

Underlying all Grooms' work is the conviction that disabled people are PEOPLE first. People who have the right to privacy and choice. People who deserve the same dignity and right to self respect as anyone else; the right to be consulted and informed and to make choices about their lifestyle and how they spend their disposable income.

The ultimate fulfilment of our mission is to see each person with whom we work attaining a level of independence equal to his or her personal potential.

# LANGLEY HOUSE TRUST (1958)
## John Dodd (1916-1987)

Prisons have existed in some form or other from biblical times, and possibly earlier. For centuries they were used only as a means of punishment and torture, with no attempt to consider the prisoners' needs.

In 19th century England, a different approach was pioneered by Elizabeth Fry (1780-1845) with her work among the women in Newgate prison, London. Her idea was to reform the prisoner by improving conditions and providing constructive activities for them to do while serving their sentence.

Other changes in official attitudes towards prisoners were also being adopted about this time. Prison chaplains, known to have been employed since at least the 18th century, were to be appointed to every prison under an 1814 Act of Parliament. At first they were all Anglicans, and it was not until the end of the century that Nonconformist chaplains were allowed to enter prisons.

Towards the end of the 18th century, some prison authorities began to appreciate the need to make provision for discharged prisoners. In 1792 public funds were for the first time used to help them get started upon release.

Ten years later, in 1802, the first Discharged Prisoners' Aid Society was set up, to befriend discharged prisoners and assist them find work. It was not until 1862, however, that these societies received statutory recognition. By 1887 similar societies operated in most UK prisons.

Unfortunately the system never worked properly, and prisoners often failed to receive support when they completed their sentence. To deal with this problem a number of prison refuges were opened, usually by evangelical Christians, whereby the prisoner was met upon release with an offer of accommodation.

Despite various attempts over the years by parliament to make provision for discharged prisoners, after-care is still a fundamental weakness of our prison system. Prisoners are sometimes released with the minimum preparation for the return to outside life.

With no-one to support them after what may have been a long sentence, possibly rejected by families and with no job prospects, it is difficult for them to readjust to society. Without anyone to care for them, some return to crime and soon find themselves back inside.

### Prison After-care

Elizabeth Fry was one of the first to open a refuge for women prisoners, outside Tothill Fields prison, Westminster.

Later in the century a Mrs Susannah Meredith of Clapham carried on the work started by Fry, by providing after-care and also attempting to provide some form of rehabilitation. Already well-known for her medical mission in Brixton, she started a Prison Mission outside Tothill Fields in 1867.

Mrs Meredith rented a room in a house near the prison gate. She met women on their release with the offer of breakfast and advice concerning their future. She also provided employment for any who were anxious to reform. Placing them in lodgings rather than crowding them into a refuge, she found work for them in a laundry, and was able to observe those who were more likely to make a success of their freedom.

Such was her success that the following year the mission was made a recognised Discharged Prisoners' Aid Society, and prisons were able to send women to her direct from jail.

Her ideas spread to the Continent, and the Queen of Sweden sent one of her ladies-in-waiting to inspect the work, with a view to starting a similar project over there.

Many other prison gate missions, as they were known, were set up, but it led to competition between them.

Mrs Meredith eventually closed down her mission, and by the end of the century only a few of them remained.

It was this lack of care that alerted John Dodd to the need for a home for ex-prisoners, a place that offered them the security of a family environment. In 1958 Dodd set up the Langley House Trust (LHT). (Langley House was the name of the first house he attempted to buy for the Trust. The deal fell through, but he kept the name.)

## Changi Prison

At the beginning of the Second World War John Dodd was an airman, stationed in Singapore. When the city was over-run by the Japanese army he managed to get away on an overcrowded ship heading for the island of Java.

The ship was attacked by enemy aircraft, when Dodd had the first of several remarkable escapes. Whilst sheltering from machine gun fire, his mate under cover close-by was killed, but he was unscathed. When he was eventually captured on the island of Java, instead of being shot, as he expected, he was taken in for questioning.

Suspected of being a spy, he was interrogated by the Kempei Tai, the Japanese  equivalent of the Gestapo. For three days he was beaten almost nonstop in an effort to make him reveal the vital information they believed he possessed, but he had nothing to give. In the end his captors relented, and Dodd finally woke up in a prisoner of war hospital.

The Dutch doctors did their best for him, stitching up his legs, his head and the gaping wound near his right eye. Because he was young and healthy he survived the brutal treatment and began to recover.

Transferred first of all to Batavia, he was then returned to Singapore, where until the end of the war he was kept in the infamous Changi prison camp. For almost three years he struggled to survive, involving himself in all kinds of activities designed to win through.

But his mental and physical condition deteriorated. In 1944 he was again seriously ill and near to death, though he managed to hang on. Once a strapping young man over six feet tall and weighing 13 stone, he was now a mere skeleton of six and a half stones. When the war ended he was classified as partially disabled, with a small pension for the rest of his life.

It was inevitable that those who survived such places as Changi should be left with spiritual and mental scars, and John Dodd was no exception. But in his case, by the grace of God, his prison experience was turned to advantage.

After the war Dodd returned to the Isle of Wight, to live with his parents. His aim was to make up for all that he had missed during the five years he was in the RAF. Instead of settling down, he went in for girls, gambling and fast cars.

Totally without interest in religion, though his mother was a devout Christian, he came to faith through the prayerful concern of Alyson, the Christian girlfriend whom he later married. He described his conversion as 'the most exciting thing that had ever happened to him'.

### Prison Visiting
Near to the Dodds' home on the Isle of Wight was Parkhurst, a prison for men serving a long-term sentence for serious crime. When Dodd became a prison visitor in 1952, he discovered that many of the men had been unloved and rejected when they were children. Often, it was these factors that lay behind their criminal careers.

Dodd took his work seriously, visiting the prison twice a week. In the beginning he received a mixed reception from the men, and was at times ignored and rebuffed. But his persistence and jovial personality won through, and he began to strike up good relationships with a few of them. As a Christian, he saw that their only hope was to come to faith in Jesus.

When some of the men responded to his message, he followed them up after they left prison. It was not long before he realised the huge problems some of them faced when trying to return to normal life.

It was about this time that Dodd met up with Christian Teamwork, a voluntary organisation of professional men and women which helped believers put worthwhile ideas into practice. With them, plans were made to do something for discharged prisoners with nowhere to go. His background and temperament ideally fitted him for the job, and he responded to the challenge as a call from God.

He and Alyson found a small hotel called Elderfield at Otterbourne, near Winchester, which could house 17 residents. Opened for ex-prisoners in June 1959, it proved to be the first in a chain of 'halfway homes' for discharged offenders in need of family-type support.

A Salvation Army couple were engaged as houseparents, and Alyson agreed to do the office work (as well as bringing up their three children). This left Dodd free to run the house and concentrate on caring for the well-being of the men.

JOHN AND ALYSON DODD

**Going Straight**

The first residents were all men he had known at Parkhurst and had made a Christian commitment. These, he felt, had the best chance of going straight. But as no one had ever tried to do this kind of work before, he had no one to show him where he was going wrong.

Despite a claim to faith, the men did not always get on with each other, and filling a house with old lags turned out to be a potentially explosive situation. In the early days, life seemed to go from one crisis to another, but he learned from his mistakes as he went along.

Dodd soon found that the six or so weeks he had reckoned on for the men to readjust to life outside was not long enough for the majority of them. One man for whom he found lodgings and a job was caught stealing. He was only saved from a return to prison by Dodd's willingness to take him back to Elderfield. The man stayed for a year before it was felt he could manage on his own without getting into any more trouble.

Attracting the right kind of people to act as houseparents was another problem. The first couple at Elderfield were kindly people who were concerned about the men's well-being, and were prepared to work hard. But the constant strain of living alongside a difficult bunch of ex-criminals, who quarrelled and complained almost without stopping, was too much for them. They left after three months.

For a while, Dodd's elderly mother took over the responsibility of being the houseparent. The men rallied round her, and for over three months she kept the place going.

The next couple he chose had a different approach to the job, and were better suited to the work. But the problem became not how to find staff, but how to keep them, for the pressures of the work put a great strain upon couples.

**Changes**

As a result of his experiences with the first batch of men, Dodd was forced to make two important changes. In his efforts to make a home for the men, Dodd had allowed them their freedom. But he realised that if Elderfield was truly to become a family home, then he would have to introduce the discipline and control necessary for this to happen. So he placed a number of restrictions upon the men, relieving the pressure put on the houseparents.

Then he decided to be more selective of those he accepted into the home. Some of the men at Elderfield needed a different kind of attention to that which he could give them. He dropped the policy of taking 'Christians only', and decided to take men on the basis of their need, not their religion. In addition, he determined to admit no more than two serious offenders at a time, and not to accept men who were disturbed or handicapped.

Faced with so many problems during the first six months, many lesser men would have given up. But not John Dodd. Firmly convinced his work was the will of God, he put right his mistakes and carried on. Before long, chaplains all over the country were wanting to place men under the care of Langley House Trust.

The success of this first home also became known in a number of churches, and Langley began to build up a band of prayer partners and supporters. An elderly lady in Bradford who admired Dodd's work bought a second Langley house, called Box Tree Cottage. It opened in 1961 as another half-way home.

**Developments**
As residents began to find a new reason for living and lead a more useful life, reports of this success reached the Home Office. Langley was acknowledged for its good work, and in 1966 was recommended by the Advisory Council on the Treatment of Offenders for a Home Office grant.

Gifts and donations began to come in, enabling Langley to widen its scope and cater for ex-offenders with special needs. In 1969 the Methodist Church, one of Dodd's most generous supporters, helped him buy a small farm at Wing (Buckinghamshire). It was opened as a sheltered community home, where damaged men could live in peace and security.

Instead of going out to work, the residents were able to learn a trade at the home and start to live a normal life. When they were ready, they were moved to a half-way house where they could learn to look after themselves.

Always ready to meet a challenge, Langley has responded to a variety of situations. At one time there was an urgent need for homes for teenage boys coming out of Borstal. Retirement homes have been established for men over 55 who have nowhere to live. Homes have been opened for the care and rehabilitation of drug addicts.

Langley House Trust now operates 13 homes throughout England. Not every resident is a success story, as Dodd was the first to admit, but many have found Christ at a Langley House and settled down to a new and more purposeful way of living.

### CORPORATE OBJECTIVES OF LANGLEY HOMES

To respond to the love of God in Christ and the needs of offenders by:

* setting up, developing and managing residential communities and other projects consistent with the Object of the Charity.

* recognising the unique qualities and promoting the development of each member, and accepting their contribution to the life and enrichment of others.

* developing working relationships and partnerships with other relevant agencies – local and national, spiritual, cultural and professional.

* acquiring resources and managing them effectively within current legislation.

## MILDMAY MISSION HOSPITAL (1866)
### Rev. William Pennefather (1816-1873)

The foundation of hospitals by the Church aptly illustrates the practical nature of the gospel. Although giving hospitality to travellers in biblical times was widely-practised throughout the Middle East, it was a duty especially incumbent upon every Christian.

Based on the words of Jesus, 'I was a stranger and you invited me in', and following the appeal of Paul, Christians showed hospitality towards all poor travellers, including pagans. This practice was the germ of the idea of the modern hospital.

The word 'hospital' comes from the Latin *hospitium*, which also gives us the words 'hospitality' and 'hotel'. Originally, it meant 'a place (i.e. a room or a house) where you receive a stranger'. But Christianity transformed what began as a private practice into a public duty, and established houses specifically to minister to the needs of pilgrims who became ill on their journey.

Christian hospitality gave rise to two kinds of institutions: hospitals, which cared for invalids, victims of leprosy and those suffering from other sicknesses; and hospices or almshouses, often adjoining monasteries situated along the chief highways or in dangerous mountain passes, and open to travellers in need of accommodation and shelter from wintry conditions.

One of the first hospitals in England was established by Archbishop Lanfranc in Canterbury (1070). The earliest one in London was St Bartholomew's, opened in 1102. During the reign of Queen Elizabeth 1, the Poor Law Act of 1601 required the authorities to become responsible for the care of the sick, both by indoor and outdoor relief. But even though more charitable hospitals were founded, provision for the sick was still woefully inadequate.

In the 18th century, the only hospitals available were the outcome of voluntary effort and subscription. Sir Thomas Guy, for example, began a network of charitable hospitals, and others such as St George's, the Middlesex, the Westminster and the London were also established about this time.

For most people, however, there was nothing but the dreaded workhouse, filled with the chronic sick, disabled and dying. Although medical research was beginning to discover new treatments, outbreaks

### The First Hospitals

One of the earliest references to giving hospitality is that of a wealthy Christian lady, Fabriola from Rome, who in 361 turned her home into a refuge for sick and dying pilgrims returning from Africa.

But the first mention of what appears to be a hospital dates from 370 in the town of Edessa in Syria (now eastern Turkey). When the town was afflicted by a famine, causing the deaths of many poor people, a Christian hermit, Ephraim, persuaded rich people to provide large sums of money for the purchase of 300 beds. These were set up in the porches surrounding the market place, where the suffering received attention.

At Caesarea (Cappadocia, Asia Minor), the bishop opened a hospital in 375 consisting of several separate houses. But Chrysostom, Patriarch of Constantinople, went further by specifying the different classes requiring relief. Between 400 and 403 he built seven hospitals - for travellers, the handicapped, orphans, old people, the destitute and one for the treatment of 'acute complaints'.

From the 5th century Church Councils drew up canons devoted to the relief of the poor and the sick, placing them under the responsibility of the bishop. Initially the sick were left in the care of priests, but orders of hospitallers were founded to take over the work. The best-known were those serving pilgrims en route for the Holy Land.

In the Middle Ages women began to participate in this ministry. Orders of Hospital Sisters were set up, which eventually exceeded in number those of the Brethren.

of disease were still common, especially in slum areas, and life expectancy was short. One of the most frightful diseases was cholera, which was highly infectious and fatal.

## Mildmay Deaconesses

The origins of the Mildmay Hospital date from 1866, when in the July a cholera epidemic swept through the East End of London. It originated in the docks, brought into the country by an Asiatic seaman. The infection spread at an alarming rate; people who were well and strong in the morning were dead by the evening. Pickford's vans called daily at the London Hospital to carry away the bodies for a communal burial.

For three months the epidemic raged, and when it was over it left 3,909 dead; a further 14,000 had been affected less severely. Since the doctors were unable to deal with the huge numbers of people struck down by the disease, medical students – among them the young Tom Barnardo – and the Mildmay deaconesses were called upon to assist.

The deaconesses belonged to the Association of Female Workers, set up by the Pennefathers in 1857, with

WILLIAM PENNEFATHER

Catherine as President. Inspired by the deaconesses of Kaiserwerth, Germany, a Missionary Training Home was opened in 1860, the first of its kind in England, to prepare young women for the mission field. Although their medical knowledge was minimal, they visited the poor and the sick, were trained to lead classes and meetings and generally to make themselves useful. They were not paid a salary, and were even expected to contribute towards their own upkeep.

To be nearer the poor people they wished to serve, the Pennefathers moved from Christ Church, Barnet to St Jude's Church, Mildmay, on the edge of the East End, where they established the Mildmay Institution. This consisted of a widespread network of social services aimed at relieving the needs of the poor people of the East End, who had been largely abandoned by the mainline Churches.

The Pennefathers were a remarkable couple. They co-ordinated much of the evangelical social work of their day, and were associated with leading reformers such as William and Catherine Booth, Barnardo, Annie Macpherson, Grattan Guinness and others.

When the outbreak of cholera occurred, the Pennefathers were asked by the vicar of St Philip's if their deaconesses might come to help. A property was acquired in the heart of the slums of Bethnal Green, and two deaconesses volunteered to begin work. Others were to join them later, and the Mildmay deaconesses – approvingly known as 'angels' – became a familiar sight around the streets of the East End.

After the epidemic had subsided, the deaconesses stayed on in the district; they continued to visit the poor, set up soup kitchens, hold clinics and conduct meetings. Before long, it was safe enough for them to visit the slums unescorted, in places where policemen still only dared go in

pairs. Welcomed wherever they went, the deaconesses not only witnessed poverty and misery, they also saw lives changed by the gospel.

## Mission Hospital

William Pennefather realised that a more permanent work was needed,
and his thoughts turned towards the idea of a mission hospital. In 1869,
he invited Dr William Burns Thompson, founder of the Edinburgh
Medical Mission, to speak at the Mildmay on the subject of medical
missions.

Stirred by what they heard, the Pennefathers visited Edinburgh to see
the work for themselves, and felt the scheme could also work well in the
East End. They recognised that spiritual and physical care went together, and that people appreciated the gospel more when they saw it in
action. But before they could make any plans, William Pennefather died.

A memorial fund opened in his name realised enough money to start
a mission hospital in Bethnal Green. Catherine Pennefather was determined to see the vision realised, and set about making plans.

From Dr Thompson, she received a promise to find a Christian
doctor to supervise the new mission; all she needed now was a suitable
building. So, accompanied by her superintendent deaconess and an
architect, she scoured the passages and alleyways of Bethnal Green for
the right place. And there in the slums was a disused warehouse.

'There's your hospital,' exclaimed the architect. The others were
unenthusiastic, but he insisted it had potential. He turned out to be right.

A small hospital was opened in 1877. It had a ward for men, one for
women, and one for children, plus a doctor, three nurses and five
Mildmay deaconesses to act as probationers. The first time Dr Thompson
visited the hospital, he declared it was the best-equipped medical
mission in Britain, and suggested that it ought to be a training hospital.
No doubt with Florence Nightingale's School of Nursing in mind, he
saw the opportunity for women to be trained as missionary nurses.

## Training School

The scheme for training nurses was launched by Dr William Gauld, an
ex-China missionary who had worked with Thompson in Edinburgh.
Following his appointment in 1880 as medical superintendent, he
secured the voluntary services of lecturers for his nurses, and opened the
training school three years later. Since then hundreds of Mildmay nurses

and doctors have gone on to serve God in mission fields around the world.

As the work grew, it became clear that the hospital was too small, the only fault Dr Thompson could find with it. It was decided that an entirely new purpose-built hospital was needed, and plans were put in hand. Although a site was found on the edge of the district, it appeared too far from the centre.

There were some who suggested that the hospital should be relocated in a quiet, healthy suburb, but that would have denied access to the very people it was intended to serve. As it was, when an order was issued by the local authorities for the slums to be demolished, including the hospital, the new site by Shoreditch parish church seemed just right.

It was in 1892 that the Mildmay Mission Hospital was declared open by Mrs Mathieson, wife of the Mildmay Trust treasurer. Catherine Pennefather was unable to attend the ceremony through ill-health, and the absence of 'the mother of Mildmay' was remarked upon with regret.

It had been intended that she should plant a tree in the courtyard, but when the time came it was planted instead by Miss Coventry, the Lady Superintendent of the Deaconess Home. Fortunately, Mrs Pennefather lived just long enough to see the fruit of her labours; she died two months later.

The new hospital, built in good red brick on three sides of an oblong courtyard, was five storeys high. It had 50 beds, and included doctors' surgeries, a nurses' home and bedrooms for domestic staff.

But the hospital was not the full extent of Mildmay's work. At one point it had 24 branches of outreach – lodging houses, infirmaries, convalescent homes, a home for the aged, the Bible Flower Mission and – for a while – the Mildmay Mission to the Jews.

**Survival**

Over the years Mildmay maintained a high standard of care, and the hospital consequently gained an international reputation. Nevertheless, the hospital had to fight for its survival. It was kept going by the donations and prayers of Christian people, as well as the support of ordinary East-Enders.

Finance was often a problem, as gradually the former wealthy supporters died and legacies dried up. Economies had to be made and funds raised. When repairs or developments came up for consideration, it was usually the case of one or the other: either a new drainage system or an electrically-controlled lift and electric lights in the operating theatre.

During the First World War nearly all the doctors had been called up, and Dr Gauld had to come out of retirement for a couple of days a week. At the beginning of the Second World War the patients had to be evacuated to a hospital on the edge of Epping Forest. But due to customer demand, wards were gradually re-opened and, despite the air-raids, work continued. The hospital was once damaged by a bomb, but it survived to continue caring for the wounded.

The greatest threat to the hospital's future came when plans were being drawn up for the National Health Service. In 1942 the government began to plan the postwar co-ordination of all hospital services. Hospitals not up to standard or those with fewer than 200 beds, and therefore considered to be uneconomic, were likely to be made redundant. Mildmay had 54 beds.

As it happened, voluntary hospitals were allowed to continue in the post-war scheme. But there was one further problem. The threat of coming under state control would probably mean a curtailment to its evangelistic and missionary activities. In 1947 this was compounded by a new regulation, which decreed that hospitals with fewer than 100 beds would no longer be permitted to run a nurses' training school. In both these cases, the very character of the hospital was threatened, indeed if it could exist at all.

**Prayer**

Over these years much prayer went up to God, and his goodness prevailed. A scheme was permitted whereby the nurses' training was to be undertaken in conjunction with the larger London Hospital, in Whitechapel Road. Mildmay accepted the nurses for training, but for specified periods they transferred to the London.

The matter of state control was surmounted by recalling the hospital's trust deeds, dating back to 1892. A clause in the National Health Bill allowed a voluntary hospital 'to preserve its character and association'. On that basis Mildmay was permitted to continue its twofold aim, 'to heal the sick and to diffuse simple gospel truth'.

It was essential for the hospital to retain its distinctive Christian ethos, which meant that staff had to be carefully selected. Although it would have no authority, Mildmay representatives were promised a place on the management committee, and therefore the chance to influence the choice of key appointments. Mildmay was granted a new lease of life.

When the NHS opened in 1948 Mildmay came under the authority of a regional health board. Although state-controlled, there were advantages: finance was provided by government, and through larger NHS hospitals nurses had access to other branches of medicine and surgery not available at Mildmay. Meanwhile, evangelistic work continues.

In 1982 the hospital was forced to close because of NHS rationalization. Shocked by this decision, many Christian and local people petitioned for the hospital to remain open, and two years later the government relented. It re-opened as an independent hospital in 1985.

Since then it has earned the remarkable distinction of becoming Europe's first AIDS hospital. The hospice and continuing care unit has an accent on living, and offers rehabilitation, convalescent, respite and, of course, terminal care for anyone with AIDS – men, women, children and babies.

Mildmay, although now independent, contracts its services to the NHS. However, it has to fund-raise for any new refurbishments or capital projects, and is grateful for any donations and the prayerful support of its friends. It is now becoming increasingly involved internationally and has been invited to build a centre for AIDS palliative care, research and study/training.

While morale in the hospital is boosted by visits from the Princess of Wales and other influential supporters, the magnificent job being done at Mildmay can only be sustained by generous giving.

## MISSION STATEMENT OF MILDMAY

Mildmay is an Independent Christian hospital and health care provider. It provides comprehensive palliative care for men, women and children living with or affected by HIV and AIDS. Care is given with an emphasis on quality, professionalism and respect for the rights and beliefs of each individual.

Mildmay aims to remain at the forefront of research and development in this speciality, by demonstrating innovative models of care and progressive educational programmes, both nationally and internationally.

# NATIONAL SOCIETY for the PREVENTION
# OF CRUELTY to CHILDREN (1884)
### Rev Benjamin Waugh (1839-1908)

Until the late 19th century children were regarded as the property of their parents. Whatever injury they inflicted upon their young, the law was powerless to intervene. When the NSPCC was formed it was able to bring pressure to bear on parliament and an Act was passed in 1889 when, for the first time, child abuse was made illegal. This was more than 60 years after Martin's Act had outlawed cruelty to animals!

The appalling social conditions that existed in Victorian England, particularly in the large industrial centres, and the callous attitude towards children, gave rise to a number of wide-ranging reforms. A number of reformers, especially Lord Shaftesbury, worked tirelessly to alleviate children's suffering by introducing legislation that brought about an improvement in their conditions of employment.

But many children were equally subject to cruelty and neglect from uncaring and drunken parents or guardians, and had no hope of protection or relief. Living in desperate conditions of poverty and overcrowding, children were often forced to work long hours in order to supplement the family income. Others were made to beg in the streets, and failure to bring home more than a few pence resulted in a beating.

A large number of children were actually turned out of the home by their parents who were anxious to lighten the financial burden. Hundreds of children either died on the streets or committed suicide.

## Scandals

There were also two scandals that caused deep public concern. One was the practice of 'baby-farming'. This involved the sale of unwanted or illegitimate children to ruthless masters who starved or worked them to death. The other was that of insuring the lives of young children, and on their death – sometimes by starvation or even murder – claiming on the policy.

A number of people, mainly Christians, responded to these needs. C H Spurgeon (1867), the Rev Bowman Stephenson (1869) and Dr Tom Barnardo (1870) were among those who established residential homes to care for destitute children. But in south east London, the Rev Benjamin Waugh was concerned about another aspect of the problem, that of the ill-treatment of children by their parents.

As the first Director of the National Society for the Prevention of Cruelty to Children, he more than any other brought the problem before the nation and pressured parliament into passing a Bill to outlaw child cruelty.

## Child Cruelty

Benjamin Waugh was a young Congregational minister when in 1866 he became pastor of a church in Greenwich. Appalled by the scenes of child deprivation and cruelty that he witnessed there, he was soon involved in finding ways to help them.

He opened a day institute for the care of homeless boys, called the 'Wastepaper and Blacking Brigade', and was able to find some of them employment in the fishing industry. When some of them were brought before the courts, he acted as bail. Magistrates were quick to see the value of his work and began to hand over first offenders to him rather than send them to prison.

In 1873 he published an influential book, *The Gaol Cradle – Who Rocks It?*, which was a plea for the abolition of juvenile imprisonment.

Around this time a number of other people were beginning to draw public attention to the problem of child cruelty. In 1881 the Rev George Staite, vicar of Ashton-Hayes in Cheshire, asked in a letter to the *Liverpool Mercury* 'whilst we have a society to care for animals, can we not do something to prevent cruelty to children?'

Staite turned to the Earl of Shaftesbury for advice, only to discover that the noble lord felt powerless to help. 'The evils you state are enormous and indisputable,' he replied, 'but they are of so private, internal and domestic a character as to be beyond the reach of legislation, and the subject would not indeed, I think, be entertained in either House of Parliament.'

In that same year, Thomas Agnew, a Liverpool banker, on a business trip to America discovered in New York the existence of a Society for the Prevention of Cruelty to Children. Intrigued, he made enquiries and discovered that the society had been established in 1875. It was formed as the result of efforts to save a young girl from vicious daily beatings from her adopted mother.

As in England, there was no law on the statute books which could be used to protect the girl. In the end, it was due to the efforts of the founder of the New York Society for the Prevention of Cruelty to Animals that protection was secured for her on humane grounds.

## Liverpool

Enthused by his discovery, on his return to England in 1882 Agnew shared his thoughts with Samuel Smith, Liberal MP for Liverpool. The following year they formed the Liverpool Society for the Prevention of Cruelty to Children, the first of its kind in Britain. It remained an independent society until 1953, when it was absorbed into the national society.

The idea spread rapidly and other societies were started around the country. The well-known philanthropist Baroness Angela Burdett-Coutts was responsible for calling a meeting of interested people to set up a London SPCC.

The Mansion House meeting, held on the 8 July 1884, was attended by a number of distinguished people, including the Earl of Shaftesbury (who became the first President), Lord Aberdeen, Dr Barnardo, Rev

BENJAMIN WAUGH WITH HIS FAMILY

Edward de Montjoie Rudolf (one of the founders of the Children's Society), Cardinal Manning and Robert Colam, Secretary to the RSPCA. Benjamin Waugh became the Honorary Secretary, whose contribution to the society was to prove invaluable.

The new society's two main aims were to protect children from cruelty, and to bring about a change in the law which could provide them with legal protection.

Thomas Agnew went on to form other societies, at Hull, Glasgow and Edinburgh, which began to make the public aware of the ill-treatment inflicted on young children.

The work of the new societies was intended to complement that of the recently-established children's homes set up by Stephenson, Barnardo and others. On one occasion, however, Waugh's zealous remarks caused something of an upset. He appeared to attack these children's homes when he declared, 'What is wanted is not the ever-open door of institutions for the unwanted child, but the ever-open door of prisons for those who make children wretched!' The furore eventually died down without causing any damage.

**Energy and Vision**
Much of what the new society accomplished was due to Waugh's energy and vision. Stirred by injustice, he took every opportunity to defend the cause of helpless children. His most urgent priority was to draw public and government attention to the plight of children who had no-one else to speak for them. Such was his vigour and persistence that a joke was put around about him being 'on the Waugh path'.

He spent much time investigating and collating facts about child abuse, especially baby-farming and insuring young children. He also drew attention to what was known as 'over-laying', when children sleeping in the family bed were suffocated as a result of being 'over-laid' by a drunken parent.

The year 1889 proved to be a memorable one for the society. All the country's 31 societies, except Liverpool, agreed to amalgamate, and adopted the title the National Society for the Prevention of Cruelty to Children. Waugh accepted the position of Director, and Queen Victoria became its patron with a pledge of ten guineas.

In the same year, parliament passed the Prevention of Cruelty to Children Act, which became commonly known as the 'Children's

## CHILD ABUSE

In 1994 the NSPCC received a total of 63,736 requests for help, an increase over the previous year of 15,600. It is estimated that three to four children die each week following abuse and neglect.

The Society operates 120 child protection teams, projects and centres providing a variety of services to prevent child abuse, protect children and help them overcome the damage they have suffered. Its National Child Helpline, a free 24 hour service, is a first point of contact for anyone concerned about a child at risk, and offers advice, information and counselling.

The NSPCC also mounts campaigns to draw attention to particular issues, The 1993 'Justice for Children' campaign helped bring about changes in the law which made it easier for children to give evidence in criminal cases. It has also developed support schemes for children from Surrey and Hackney who have appeared as witnesses.

At the end of 1994 a major three year campaign, 'A Cry for Children', was launched that initiated a national debate about the nature of child abuse aimed at encouraging everyone to examine the way we treat our children.

At national level, the Society has begun to lobby for the appointment of a Children's Rights Commissioner, a move supported by the UN Convention on the Rights of the Child. It makes submissions to parliament on matters of law.

The NSPCC is the only voluntary organisation named in statute which can take legal proceedings to protect a child who is being abused or at risk.

Charter'. A jubilant Waugh sent a telegram to his wife, 'Bill at last law of land!'

For five years Waugh had campaigned for legislation to outlaw child cruelty. During this time he became a familiar figure arguing with MPs in the Commons lobby (where he was said to be 'on the Waugh path'!). It was largely as a result of his efforts, and those of Samuel Smith, that parliament passed the new law.

The main benefit of the Act was to give police authority to arrest anyone ill-treating a child, and to obtain a warrant to enter a home if there was reasonable suspicion that a child was in danger. It also laid down guidelines about the employment of children and outlawed begging in the streets.

Under Waugh's leadership the society achieved increasing recognition of the importance of its mission to protect children, and his enthusiasm and zeal inspired his staff. His aim was 'justice for all children', and his rule, 'We know neither clergy nor laity, Protestant nor Catholic, Jew nor Gentile, but only ill-used children.'

During its first year, 29 inspectors were employed to deal with the hundreds of cases brought to the society's attention. The inspectors, known as 'cruelty men', were carefully chosen by Waugh. Married men were preferred, and they had to be of cheerful disposition; most of the men were ex-police officers or retired servicemen. By 1905 there were 198 inspectors working from over 1,000 centres.

**Wealthy Families**

Although much of the society's work was among poorer people, some bad cases of abuse were investigated among wealthy families. When ill-treatment was detected, a formal warning was issued and a number of supervisory visits paid to check on progress. If there was no improvement, a prosecution could follow. After the first few years the number of prosecutions fell dramatically and most cases tended to be ones of neglect.

The inspectors were backed up by voluntary workers, especially Ladies' Committees, which helped with publicity and raised money. A Children's League of Pity was formed to help middle-class children take an interest in the society's work. It continues today as the Young League.

The society's success was recognised in 1895 when it was granted a Royal Charter. This set out its constitution and objectives, the most important of which were 'to prevent the public and private wrongs of children and corrupting their morals' and 'to take action for the enforcement of laws for their protection'.

An Act of Parliament in 1904 further strengthened the hand of the NSPCC. By this act, the NSPCC was authorised to remove children from their home without the police, though the consent of a JP was necessary.

Pressure of work and deteriorating health finally forced Waugh to resign in 1905. He died three years later, the year of the Children's Act, which dealt with the problem of baby-farming and established juvenile courts.

Once asked by a supporter why his speeches were always so impassioned, he replied, 'Madame, I remember only the children and their sufferings.'

Women now play a more prominent role in the society's services, which have been reorganised into a network of 66 Child Protection Teams, designed to draw together the different strands of prevention and protection into a co-ordinated response to child abuse.

Despite the creation of the welfare state, the NSPCC continues to play an essential role in preventing cruelty to the nation's children and as a voluntary organisation still looks to the public to help maintain its

## MISSION STATEMENT OF
## THE NATIONAL SOCIETY FOR THE
## PREVENTION OF CRUELTY TO CHILDREN

NSPCC Vision

All children grow up unharmed, with the opportunity to develop fully with their basic needs being met.

To prevent children suffering from significant harm as a result of ill treatment.

To help protect children who are at risk from such harm.

To help abused children to overcome the effects of such harm.

To work to protect children from further harm.

# PILGRIM HOMES (1807)
## James Bisset (1771-1859)

Until early this century care of the elderly was undertaken solely by charitable organisations. The secular authorities made little attempt to meet their needs. Although some provision was available under the terms of the Poor Law passed by Queen Elizabeth 1 in 1601 (revised in 1834), the arrangements did not favour the old and most of them were forced to live in poverty.

In 1908 the Liberal government of the day introduced a number of measures to ease the burden of the poor, including a pension of five shillings a week for those over 70. This enabled many elderly people to escape the threat of the workhouse and enjoy a degree of independence in their own homes. By 1914 the basis of the Welfare State had been laid and the main responsibility for the well-being of the underprivileged passed from private charity to the state.

In the Middle Ages, hospitals – originally attached to monasteries but later to become independent institutions – provided for both the sick and the old. These places were usually called almshouses, sometimes known as Maisons Dieu (Houses of God).

By the 14th century most boroughs had almshouses for the aged poor. Outside London, the greatest number of these was to be found at York, where the largest almshouse in England, St Leonard's Hospital, provided a home for over 200 'bedesmen'.

An alternative kind of assistance for old people was the charitable bequest. This was given either as a payment or in the form of an annual pension, and by 1485 some 46 such trusts were known to exist.

The upsurge in the population during the Industrial Revolution led to an increase in the foundation of almshouses by both secular and religious bodies. Of the evangelical Christian homes established during the 19th century the earliest, and probably the best-known, was The Aged Pilgrims' Friend Society, now called Pilgrim Homes. It was founded in 1807 by a group of young men and women led by James Bisset from Whitefield's Tabernacle, Moorfields, to provide for the 'aged and infirm Christian poor'.

The society was founded at a time of great economic difficulty, which only served to heighten the poverty already suffered by working class people. The Napoleonic Wars, which raged from 1793 to 1815, pitched the whole of Europe into turmoil. The price of wheat rose dramatically and led to a steep rise in the price of bread. With low wages, rising unemployment due to the onset of the Industrial Revolution, the poor suffered great hardship and were on the verge of starvation.

The idea was formulated early in August 1807, after a Wednesday evening meeting at Whitefield's Tabernacle. John Hyatt, one of the three pastors ministering at the church, preached a challenging sermon to his congregation on Job 29:12-13. He spoke of the need to minister to the Lord's poor, especially those of old age, who had been severely afflicted by the consequences of the war.

A group of about ten young people were very much moved by his appeal. As they moved off towards Peartree Street, off the City Road, to the home of Thomas Green, one of their number, they talked about the implications of the sermon. After a time of prayer in the house, they discussed what practical help they could give. The need was urgent; casual help was not enough.

Their leader, 36-year-old James Bisset, shared his thoughts. 'What I feel,' Bisset told them, 'is that something of a regular form of help is what is needed. Casual help is not enough; permanent assistance and

personal visitation are what is required. Now would it be possible to organise something of this kind?'

The group talked about Bisset's ideas and wondered whether they could expect any support from the Christian public. They adjourned for a week, during which time they gave the matter further thought and prayer. When they met again, they were of one mind that it was the Lord's will they should go ahead with some scheme of relief.

JAMES BISSET

## Household of Faith

The group formed a committee of 13 men and drew up a list of rules. They passed a resolution: 'That a Society be formed for the purpose of granting an Annuity of Five Guineas during life, unto such aged and infirm persons as are of the household of faith, to be called The Aged Pilgrims' Society.' Help was to be offered to men and women over the age of 60 years, irrespective of denomination, who could give 'satisfactory evidence of being members of the mystical body of Christ'.

In time, the committee set out the objects of the society in more detail. It was to be undenominational, for 'poor, aged and infirm Protestant Christians of both sexes and every religious denomination'; it was to be Bible-based, holding to the society's original doctrinal principles; and it was to be for those who were born-again believers.

The society was fortunate in having as its first leaders two officers totally committed to the work. James Bisset was the oldest member of the committee, and his leadership and sound judgment were acknowledged by them all. He was elected as honorary secretary, a position he held for 51 years. The leading spirit in the new venture, he has always been recognised as the 'founding father' of the Society. Then there was Thomas Watkins, treasurer, who died in 1838 while still in office.

On behalf of the society, Bisset published an *Address to the Religious Public* in which he gave a graphic picture of the poverty experienced by working class people in 1807, and set out the aims of the society. He wrote of many of them 'lingering the remainder of their days in distress and wretchedness, deserted by the world' and 'starving with hunger, and destitute of clothing or any bed to rest their infirm limbs'.

Referring to scriptural teaching about caring for the needy, he wrote that it was the duty and privilege of believers to minister to the Lord's poor. He concluded by quoting Matthew 25:40, a text which became the Society's 'Great Charter'.

## Disappointing

Response to the appeal was disappointing and funds were slow to come in. Although their pastor, John Hyatt, supported them, there is nothing to suggest that the people at the Tabernacle backed their efforts. Even a request for the use of the church's vestry for an annual meeting in 1809 was turned down.

There were not sufficient funds to place anyone on their books until

March the following year. Mary Dew, aged 78, was allocated the first pension, and soon afterwards donations reached the sum of £5 2s 9d, barely enough to cover a year's pension. Before the end of the year, however, it was possible to add two more names to the list and a further two in 1809. By 1839 there were over 300 people receiving a pension at an annual expenditure of £1,600.

The first pensioners were from churches and chapels in the vicinity of the City of London. Pensions were delivered monthly by a 'visitor' whose task was to enquire into the pensioner's spiritual as well as physical well-being. By 1821 the work had grown to such an extent that this was impossible. In that year female visitors were appointed for the first time, and they increasingly took over the work of visitation.

The possibility of building a home for the pensioners was first raised in 1819, but was not seriously considered until 1827. It was not until seven years later that a suitable plot of land became available, in Camberwell, south-east London. Rooms for 18 pensioners were dedicated at a ceremony in October 1834, when the blessing was given by James Bisset. Money for the work was slow coming in and it took three years to complete the project. When it was finished, the spacious property finally provided accommodation for 42 pensioners under the care of a resident warden. This home was closed in July 1991 and sold in 1992.

### Extended Care

The opening of this home was the logical outcome of the Society's intention to offer permanent assistance, and marked an important stage in its history. It could now provide extended care that could take pensioners into the eventide of life. In time further homes were opened, at Hornsey Rise, North London (1870), Brighton (1879) and in other areas.

James Bisset, rather late in life, became an ordained minister and held pastorates at three churches in the Hertfordshire area. He continued to carry out his responsibilities towards the society until 1858, when he handed over the reins to his friend, John Box. Bisset died the following April, in his 88th year.

Over the years, the society has attracted the support of a number of prominent Christians, who have used their good offices to encourage an interest in the work. In the early days, the Earl of Shaftesbury and William Wilberforce, needless to say, were both good friends of the society. Others included Lord Gambier, Lady Lucy Smith (granddaughter of Henry Thornton, of the Clapham Sect), Horatius Bonar, C H Spurgeon and F A Bevan, chairman of what is now Barclays Bank.

There was one problem, however, that still deeply exercised the minds of the committee. It was that of providing nursing care for those who were seriously ill.

Normally residents had to be removed to a workhouse infirmary, which took them out of their Christian environment for the last days of their life. In 1924 it was decided to close this gap in their services. A nursing wing was added to the Hornsey Rise home (this home was closed in 1973) and, when funds permitted, at Brighton (1948) and Tunbridge Wells (1951). Since then, other homes have been opened with this facility and the society has become a pioneer in the care of the aged and chronic sick.

The Society currently runs 11 homes throughout the country, four of which are dual registered so that nursing care is provided, as well as residential care. It is hoped that further homes will be similarly registered in the future. The Society would like to open further homes as finance becomes available.

The Earl of Shaftesbury once wrote of the Society: 'Old people are apt to be regarded as burdens, whereas it should be a joy and a privilege to minister to them. For this reason I specially commend the Charity to young people.'

## AIMS OF PILGRIM HOMES

*What we do*
The Society's main work is the running of residential homes for elderly Christians:
* Sheltered Housing (independent bungalows and flatlets under the supervision of a matron or warden)
* Very Sheltered Housing (additional help is available for those who can still live independently)
* Care Homes (full residential care) and
* Full Nursing Care

*Our emphasis is on providing a loving,*
*caring and Christian environment.*

# THE RED CROSS MOVEMENT (1863)
## Henry Dunant (1838-1910)

Of all the relief agencies set up to give help around the world, the name of the Red Cross has probably become the most familiar to ordinary people. Initially intended to supplement army medical services in time of war, it also looks after the victims of disasters and epidemics, refugees, prisoners of war, security detainees, and the sick and disabled.

Now the world's largest voluntary organization, it has societies in 163 countries, with over 125 million members. A secular society, it cuts across barriers of race and religion, providing impartial assistance, based solely on need. Everyone recognises its symbol as a sign of care and protection, and in times of peace and war, wherever great calamities occur, the Red Cross is at hand to alleviate human suffering.

The Movement was founded in 1863, largely through the endeavours of a Swiss Christian, Henry Dunant. Born in the Protestant city of Geneva, Switzerland, Dunant was the son of wealthy parents who held to a strong evangelical faith. His father spent much of his spare time caring for needy people in the city, a concern that Dunant developed as a young Christian.

## Active

Henry Dunant held Bible studies in his home and started the Christian Union of Young People (later, the YMCA). He was also the Secretary of the Geneva Evangelical Alliance and was active in the anti-slavery campaign. But, like his father, he was not only concerned for the spread of the gospel, but was equally anxious for the well-being of the large number of poor people in the Swiss city.

To bring them much-needed relief, he joined with a group of friends who gave up their evenings and weekends to visiting the destitute, carrying with them medicines, food and clothing. On Sunday afternoons they visited the prisons in Geneva, talking to the inmates and reading the Bible to them. When they had no more money, Dunant begged his parents, friends and the churches for funds.

Hearing of the newly-founded Young Men's Christian Association started in London, Dunant pioneered the YMCA in Switzerland. Then he joined forces with George Williams, the British founder, to start similar groups in other parts of Europe. Recognising the need for consultation and mutual encouragement, it was at Dunant's suggestion that the first World Conference of the YMCA was convened. It was held in Paris, in 1855.

When his father eventually insisted that he get a job, Dunant took a position with a bank and was sent to manage one of their branches in the French colony of Algeria. Finding there were many people in North Africa living in poverty, he looked around for ways of bringing them some assistance.

Out of his salary, he bought a small farm and built some corn mills. The idea was to grow corn, grind it in his mills, sell the flour and use the profits to fund his work for the poor. As he needed more land to expand his project, he wrote to the French government for help, but his many requests were turned down. After six years of pleading his cause, the land he wanted was sold to another buyer.

In desperation, Dunant finally decided to seek out the Emperor Napoleon III in person for help. He had written a book about the emperor, praising him for his attempts to improve the lot of his people, and he decided to give him a copy. Perhaps, he mused, if the emperor liked the book he would sell him some land for his Algerian project.

**Battle of Solferino**

It was the summer of 1859. The French and their Italian allies were at war with Austria, fighting to drive them out of Piedmont, northern Italy. As Napoleon had left for Italy, Dunant had to travel to the battle zone to seek an audience. On arrival, he learned that a great battle was to be fought the next day, and he was invited by an officer to watch the conflict.

He did, and witnessed one of the bloodiest battles of his time – the battle of Solferino. Of the 300,000 soldiers engaged in the 14-hour battle, nearly 40,000 were killed, the majority of them Austrians, and hundreds of others were wounded. Such was the carnage that the totally inadequate medical services of the two armies could not cope with the casualties.

Dunant was sickened by the savagery of the fighting – 'a butchery, a conflict between wild animals mad with blood and rage', he wrote later. Some were left to die where they fell; others had their head smashed in by the enemy. Night approached, and the groans of the wounded could be heard as soldiers searched the battlefield for their missing comrades.

It took three days to bury the dead, even with the help of local people, and Dunant feared that some of those injured were buried alive in the mass graves. Recovering the wounded took even longer, and bodies were still being discovered three weeks later.

Without proper stretchers, the wounded had to be strapped to the saddles of pack mules or carried in carts. Most of the 6,000 wounded were taken to the nearest town, Castiglione, where all the buildings were commandeered to provide shelter. They were laid on the floors of churches or private houses, or left under the hot sun in the open street. Though there was plenty of food and water, there were hardly any bandages or medicines. With only two doctors to treat the men or supervise the medical care, someone was needed to take charge of the situation.

**White Suit**
Dressed in a smart white suit, hopefully to meet the Emperor, Dunant took over the arrangements. He organised the women and children of the town into groups to carry out simple first aid, with instructions to care for soldiers of both armies. He was even able to persuade a few English and French tourists to assist.

At first the women only treated the French, and ignored the Austrians. But when Dunant was seen to tend men from both sides, they began to follow his example. He told them always to treat the worst cases first, and not those whose cries were the loudest.

He organised the boys of the town to bring buckets of clean water, and others were despatched to find supplies of straw for bedding. For three days Dunant worked day and night, non-stop; he bathed men's wounds and tried to comfort them as best he could. But without medicines it was impossible, and the death toll continued to rise. The wounded were cared for and then moved out of the town to other centres. Even so, a soldier died every quarter of an hour.

Gradually, the fight to save the wounded was being won and Dunant realised he needed to rest. He withdrew from the battle area and once again attempted to gain an interview with the Emperor. Caked in mud and with his white suit covered in blood, Dunant was again refused an interview, though Napoleon did agree to release captured Austrian doctors to help treat the wounded.

Resolved that what had happened at Solferino should never happen again, he returned to Geneva to write about his experiences. His book, *A Memory of Solferino*, was published in 1862 at his own expense and copies sent to the reigning monarchs of Europe, to politicians, military officers, philanthropists and friends. It received unexpected acceptance, as the majority of people had no idea of the severity of the cruelties of war.

The short book was divided into three parts: in the first part he vividly described the horrors of the battle; next he detailed his efforts to care for the wounded; and he concluded by outlining his ideas for the future.

He proposed forming permanent 'relief societies' which in peace time would train and equip volunteers to act in support of the military medical services in time of war. He also called for an international agreement to provide protection in battle for medical workers and the wounded.

**Committee of Five**

Four of Geneva's leading citizens who read the book were impressed with his ideas: they were General Dufour, Drs Appia and Maunoir, and Gustave Moynier, a lawyer, as well as a practical organiser and administrator. With Dunant they formed the 'Committee of Five', which became the 'International Committee for Relief of the Wounded'. The title was changed in 1875 when it became the International Committee of the Red Cross (ICRC).

The following year (1863), delegates from 12 European governments met in Geneva. The conference adopted ten resolutions that were to make up the founding charter of the Red Cross, defining the functions and working methods of the Committees for the Relief of the Wounded which Dunant had proposed. The resolutions and recommendations of the conference were the foundation of the Red Cross Movement.

After reporting back to their governments, the delegates met again, at a diplomatic conference in August 1864, to adopt a draft treaty prepared by the International Committee. Its acceptance was a milestone in the history of humanity.

Called the 'Geneva Convention for the Amelioration of the Condition of the Wounded in the Armies in the Field', the treaty was based on two main principles: first, that the wounded should be protected and cared for regardless of nationality; and second, that all personnel attending the wounded, together with their installations and equipment – hospitals, ambulances and the like – should be treated as neutral and under the protection of the Red Cross emblem.

## Emblem

At the conference Dr Appia proposed that a badge was needed, partly for recognition, but also to stimulate the movement's own esprit de corps. He suggested a white armband, perhaps because it had long been accepted as the colour of truce, and the conference added that it should bear a red cross.

The symbol of a red cross on a white background is the Swiss flag in reverse. It was not intended as a religious sign, and the Red Cross Movement has no religious affiliations.

The symbol was to be a protective emblem, only to be used on authorised personnel, vehicles, ships, buildings and other installations serving the wounded. The first test of these arrangements came that same year, in a war fought between Denmark and Prussia. Both sides respected the sign and the doctors were able to treat the wounded in safety. Appropriately enough, one of the first people to wear the badge on the battlefield was Dr Appia himself.

Dunant devoted so much of his time to the Red Cross that he had to give up his position at the bank, even neglecting the Algerian farm project. By 1867 he had exhausted his money in forming the new organization and was forced to resign from the Geneva Committee.

He went to France for a time, and during the siege of Paris in the Franco-Prussian war (1870) spent his energies helping the victims of the fighting. Returning to Switzerland, he lived in obscurity in the mountain health resort of Heiden, above Lake Constance.

In 1895 he was found by a newspaper reporter who wrote an article about the start of the Red Cross. News that Dunant was still alive brought him gifts and tributes from all over the world, and in 1901 he was awarded the Nobel Peace Prize. He died in 1910.

The Red Cross Movement, which owed its initial inspiration to him, was awarded the Nobel Peace Prize in 1917, 1944 and again in 1963. It also has its own award, the Henri Dunant medal, which is given to people who have shown exceptional courage while serving the Red Cross, or to mark special devotion to its cause.

## Growth

The Red Cross works at every level, national and international. After the signing of the original Geneva Convention, the International Committee lost no time in encouraging the formation of national relief societies.

## THE ICRC

The ICRC is the founding institution of the International Red Cross and Red Crescent Movement (also known as the International Red Cross), which now has the following components:
1) the International Committee of the Red Cross;
2) the International Federation of Red Cross and Red Crescent Societies (founded 1919); this is the world federation of National Societies, which co-ordinates their work and provides a forum for discussion;
3) the National Red Cross and Red Crescent Societies, duly recognised by the ICRC; in 1995 there were 163 Societies with more than 125 million members.

The three components meet every four years, together with representatives of countries party to the Geneva Conventions, to consider general humanitarian problems, adopt resolutions and assign mandates.

The ICRC is a private, independent institution, composed largely of Swiss nationals, with its headquarters in Geneva. Its supreme body is a Committee whose members are all Swiss citizens, meeting in an assembly to set general policies and guidelines.

The original Geneva Convention has been supplemented and updated by subsequent conventions, and the four Geneva Conventions afford protection to the following:
* wounded and sick members of the armed forces, medical personnel and chaplains;
* the wounded and sick, medical personnel and chaplains at sea, the shipwrecked;
* prisoners of war;
* civilians in enemy or occupied territory.

In 1977 two additional Protocols were formulated, to provide greater legal protection for all victims, especially civilians, in the event of:
* international armed conflict;
* non-international armed conflict.

These treaties confer on the ICRC the right to take certain action to protect and assist the victims of armed conflict. The Movement's Statutes recognise that the ICRC has a right of humanitarian initiative in situations not covered by the Conventions and Protocols.

Within ten years, committees had been established in 22 European states, including Great Britain. Beyond Europe, other societies included Peru (1879), the United States (1881), Japan, (1887) and China (1903).

Each National Red Cross Society is an independent organization (not subordinate to the ICRC), which attends to the needs of its own country, but also has international responsibilities as part of the Red Cross Movement. In times of armed conflict or other emergencies which outstrip the resources of a single country, then National Red Cross Societies are asked to send help. Their efforts in conflict situations are co-ordinated by the ICRC, while their efforts in other emergencies are co-ordinated by the Federation.

With this growth came a strong demand for the Red Cross to use its energies in peace as well as war, and an international conference in Berlin, in 1869, resolved that Red Cross societies should provide help in cases of 'public calamity' requiring immediate and organised assistance.

The origins of the British Red Cross date from 1870 and the time of the Franco-Prussian War, when the National Society for Aid to the Sick and Wounded in War was founded, and adopted the Red Cross emblem. It officially became the British Red Cross in 1905, but it was not until the First World War that it came to play a major part in British life.

Over the years, the Red Cross Movement has enlarged the scope of its activities. Its mandate now covers casualties at sea, prisoners of war, and civilians including refugees. Peacetime services include training medical teams, developing community health programmes and caring for people who are disabled.

Although the Movement originated in Christian Europe, it soon spread throughout the world. Many Muslim countries prefer to use the Red Crescent sign rather than the Red Cross. The second recognised emblem was first used during the Russo-Turkish War of 1876, when the Turkish government was worried about the reaction of its Muslim troops to the Red Cross emblem. The Ottoman Society for Relief of the Wounded decided to change to a Red Crescent (the symbol of Islam) and a number of other countries have since followed this lead.

In more recent times, after the founding of the state of Israel in 1948, the Israelis set up their own Society called the Magen David Adom, using the Star (or Shield) of David as its emblem.

**Peacetime**

A major turning point in the Movement came after the end of the First World War. If this was 'the war to end wars', then the Red Cross needed to give more consideration to its peacetime activities. Under the leadership of the National Societies of the Allied Powers, a new institution was founded.

In 1919 the League of Red Cross Societies was formed for 'the improvement of health, the prevention of disease and the mitigation of suffering'. Ten years later, the League was extended to include Red

Crescent Societies, and is now known as the International Federation of Red Cross and Red Crescent Societies. The Federation encourages the creation and development of National Societies and co-ordinates relief activities in cases of natural disaster, and to refugees outside of conflict zones.

The Red Cross Movement continues to promote humanitarian activities which contribute to the maintenance and advancement of peace in the world.

Its members, cutting across religious, political and other boundaries, are united in seeking to prevent and alleviate human suffering wherever it may be found.

**THE INTERNATIONAL RED CROSS AND RED CRESCENT MOVEMENT IS GUIDED BY THE FOLLOWING FUNDAMENTAL PRINCIPLES:**

> Humanity
> Impartiality
> Neutrality
> Independence
> Voluntary Service
> Unity
> Universality

# ROYAL ASSOCIATION IN AID OF DEAF PEOPLE
## (1841)

Deafness is a hidden disability; people affected in this way are often subject to loneliness and virtually to a life of solitary confinement. Because their condition is invisible, society tends not to notice them. And as communication with them can be difficult, they sometimes 'turn off their voices' because of ridicule or embarrassment. In England, Scotland and Wales there are more than 50,000 people of all ages who have lost or never even enjoyed the faculty of hearing. In addition, there are around three quarters of a million who are hard of hearing.

Since 1841 the Royal Association in aid of Deaf people (RAD) has been working in London and the South-East to meet the spiritual, social and special needs of people of all ages whose hearing has been impaired from birth or childhood. Today it is still a modern dynamic force responding to the needs of individuals.

Deaf children were the first to receive special help. This was partly because their condition was more obvious, though some parents tended to conceal the problem. Since the 1893 Elementary Education Act these children have received special help through the education authorities.

Adults with a hearing difficulty, however, were usually not so ready to admit their need and could often continue with their normal manner of living. They were catered for by voluntary charities, and it was not until 1948 that state provision was finally made for them.

### Children

Deaf children from well-to-do families were usually privately educated. But one of the first schools to educate deaf children of the poor was opened in 1792 by Henry Thornton (of the Clapham Sect) and the Rev John Townsend, a Congregational minister in Bermondsey. They formed a society to educate the 'indigent deaf' in the parish of Bermondsey, and rented a house in which to start a school for six deaf-mutes.

Because of the demand for places it became necessary to build a larger school, and in 1807 it was moved to a more spacious site. The London Asylum for the Deaf and Dumb Children of the Poor was opened in the Old Kent Road, south-east London. It became the leading school for the education of deaf children of the poor.

There were two new features to this school: tuition for poor children was free, and residential accommodation was provided in order to allow for continuous teaching. They were given instruction in both manual and oral methods of communication, and, at the suggestion of William Wilberforce, were taught practical subjects that would afterwards enable them to make a living.

In 1862 the school was moved to Margate, and was the model on which other schools were opened in the large provincial towns.

### After-care

Although similar institutions were set up in other parts of the country, it was left to Christian missions to assume responsibility for the after-care of the deaf. They not only started Sunday services and engaged in evangelism, but also involved themselves in a wide range of welfare activities.

The first societies to make provision for the deaf were founded in Scotland. Elizabeth Burnside started a mission for profoundly deaf adults in Edinburgh (1818) after she discovered a group of deaf men with no place to meet. In Glasgow, John Anderson opened his home to deaf people in 1822 for worship services 'in a way in which they could understand'. Then a congregation was established in Edinburgh (1830) which later became the Edinburgh Deaf and Dumb Benevolent Society, in aid of the deaf and dumb who were poor and elderly.

Mission work on behalf of the deaf in England dates from 1840. This was despite the scepticism of some who suggested at the time that there were hardly enough deaf people in the country to justify the effort.

An 1840s report, however, gives the number of deaf and dumb people in the UK as 14,328. This included 1,018 children who were receiving education in 14 institutions, a figure which is probably underestimated.

Until the Royal Association in aid of Deaf people (RAD) was founded there was no system of care in England for the deaf and dumb, as they were then termed. Many destitute deaf people ended up in the workhouse and others were discovered to have been committed to a mental institution.

### Self-Help

A group of deaf young men who had been worshipping together at the Scottish Hospital in Fetters Lane were increasingly dismayed by their sense of isolation. They felt that neither Church nor State cared about them, and in 1840 decided to set up their own self-help organisation.

They were aided by an Anglican priest and as their secretary had James Simpson, a man who had previously worked with deaf people in his native Scotland. Later that year a number of London businessmen led by George Crouch, father of five profoundly deaf children, began to show an interest in the work.

A new committee was formed under the leadership of the Rev Robert Simpson, who worked tirelessly for some years as honorary chaplain. A series of formal meetings were held, and on 27 August 1841 RAD was legally constituted under the title of The Refuge for the Destitute Deaf and Dumb.

Its chief aim was evangelism, to bring deaf people 'to a sound knowledge of the gospel'. It also aimed to provide welfare services, such as finding employment in the community or in the workshops, or training for a trade. A headquarters was established with a chapel, workshops and living accommodation at 26 Red Lion Square, Bloomsbury.

The only source of income was from charitable donations, and RAD's early years were plagued with financial uncertainty. By 1850 the lack of income made it necessary to discontinue some of the services, and the following year the premises in Red Lion Square were closed down.

In 1854, following a period of reorganisation, welfare services were continued and efforts concentrated mainly on training and finding employment for deaf people in the community. The title was changed to The Association in Aid of the Deaf and Dumb (the prefix 'Royal' was granted by Queen Victoria in 1873), and it was established as a Church of England foundation.

## Chaplains

At the same time, the emphasis on evangelism was stepped up. A small band of dedicated missionaries was recruited in 1855, among whom was Samuel Smith, a teacher from the Doncaster Institution for the Deaf. He later became the first of a succession of dynamic chaplains who were to shape the association's future, and was sponsored by RAD to study for ordination as an Anglican priest.

Smith and his colleagues gave themselves wholeheartedly to their duties and worked many long hours on behalf of the deaf. In their search of London's back streets and workhouses for deaf people who were in extreme need, they discovered many who were unemployed, destitute, physically disabled, even seriously ill or dying. Not only did they bring the comfort of the gospel, they were also able to offer financial help to relieve the circumstances.

Finding schools for children and jobs for adults continued as a major part of the work and it became one of Smith's particular concerns. He built up a network of firms willing to take on deaf workers, and Mr Heal of Tottenham Court Road (founder of the famous store) was one of a number of employers who often provided work for deaf women.

While working as a missionary, Smith studied theology at King's College. He was ordained into the Church of England in 1861 and became the first Anglican priest – and RAD's first full-time chaplain – to minister to the deaf. As a chaplain he was responsible for conducting Sunday services and taking classes for religious instruction, as well as continuing with his usual missionary work.

**A Church**

Unable to participate in ordinary services and unhappy with the secular character of the rooms they were using, RAD wanted its own place of worship. In 1859 a committee of seven deaf men was formed to promote a project for building a church specially for the deaf.

Smith added his weight to the campaign and enough money was raised to erect a building on Oxford Street. St Saviour's, opened in 1873, was also used as a centre for social and educational gatherings. It was closed down in 1924 and a new church built in Acton, west London.

From 1865 to his death in 1883, Smith also acted as RAD's secretary and the work went even further ahead. He travelled the country seeking diocesan support for the establishment of other local societies in aid of deaf people.

A number of Anglican and Nonconformist churches started societies, based on the RAD model, often to supplement the work of local schools for the deaf. A lecture programme was drawn up to encourage the pursuit of more 'intellectual pleasures'. Links were established with the temperance movement to teach about the problems of drink, and a Penny Bank opened to encourage the saving habit.

Smith was very adept at persuading people to contribute to RAD's

work, and people such as Baroness Burdett-Coutts, a leading philanthropist of the day, rallied to his support. He often obtained help in cash
and kind for poor people, and thanks to the generosity of shopkeepers
he was able to organise a system of tickets for providing essentials like
bread and coal.

Under his enthusiastic leadership RAD's work expanded and the
staff increased. In 1870 the Rev William Stainer, formerly a teacher at
the London Asylum in Old Kent Road and an indefatigable worker on
behalf of the deaf, joined RAD as a second chaplain. (It was Stainer who
first suggested that deaf children could be educated in the same schools
as normal children, in separate classes but with special teachers.) The
work in London was reorganised and the capital divided into three
districts, each supervised by a newly-appointed missionary.

From its foundation RAD met a basic need no other group could
satisfy, which was to help deaf people overcome their sense of isolation.
This was achieved by providing them with an opportunity to meet with
other deaf people and communicate with them in their own language.

Some critics argued that the deaf should integrate with hearing
people, and be taught oral speech and lip-reading rather than sign
language. RAD's policy of encouraging sign language gained ground,
however, and became the main method of communication.

RAD is over 150 years old, and it can justly take pride in its history
of dedication to the spiritual and social welfare of profoundly deaf
people.

## MISSION STATEMENT OF RAD

RAD is a charity committed to meeting the individual needs of
people affected by deafness, through its centres situated in south
east England.

RAD provides services which include: advocacy, chaplaincy,
counselling, information, interpreting, leisure facilities and
support groups.

RAD has specialist knowledge and influence which give deaf
people the opportunity to lead confident, effective and independent lives.

# THE ROYAL HOSPITAL FOR NEURO-DISABILITY (1855)
## Rev Andrew Reed DD (1787-1862)

The Royal Hospital and Home, Putney, south-west London, provides medical care and rehabilitation therapy for people with severe physical disabilities resulting from accident or disease. It also offers care for outpatients who can live at home.

Originally a home for 'incurables', it was founded by the Rev Andrew Reed, a Congregational minister and philanthropist. He set up several charitable institutions in the last century, pioneering establishments which served as a model for future developments. His work continues to this day.

Andrew Reed was born of yeoman stock at St Clement Danes in the City of London, in November 1787. His father was a watchmaker and his mother taught at a dame school in Little Britain. Apprenticed to his father's trade on leaving school, he later realised his call to the ministry and cancelled his indentures. At first he considered the idea of becoming a missionary, but dismissed this and began further studies with a view to entering the Congregational ministry.

Reed was a man of tireless ability, and an able and energetic organiser. As a young man of 19 he started a 'Society of Contending Brethren' (in 1806), which was the forerunner of a number of 'mutual improvement societies' for young men, organised by David Nasmith of Glasgow. The purpose was to discuss theological issues, though social and political matters were never far from the surface. Such was his enthusiasm, that a short while later he joined a similar young men's society at the Moorfields Tabernacle, run by the pastor, Matthew Wilks.

In 1811 he was ordained pastor of Wycliffe Chapel, just off the Commercial Road, Whitechapel, where he remained until his resignation in 1861. One of the leading dissenting chapels of the capital, its membership gradually increased under Reed's ministry until it reached just short of 1,000.

During the 1830s Wycliffe enjoyed a series of revivals, though Reed was cautious about the nature of the work. He was against imitating anything American – these were the days of the revivalist, Charles G Finney – and believed that it was God, and not man, who would bring about an awakening. 'If it is the Lord's work,' he remarked, 'it will speak for itself.'

Recognised as one of the outstanding leaders of his denomination, in 1834 Reed was sent as a delegate by the Congregational Union of England and Wales to visit their churches in the United States. He was doubtless already a man of some standing and renown, as Yale University awarded him an honorary Doctor of Divinity degree.

## Homeless Children

Over a period of 50 years in the East End Reed made a tremendous contribution to caring for orphans, as well as for disabled children and adults. His work as a pastor in Whitechapel drew his attention to the hundreds of homeless children who everywhere roamed the streets, begging or somehow scraping a living. He was horrified to discover that many of them had nowhere to sleep and felt he had to do something to help. (This was 30 years before Barnardo discovered the same problem, though Reed's work eventually led him in a different direction.)

Within the space of a few years he had opened two 'asylums' (i.e. orphanages). The first was the London Orphan Asylum at Clapton (Hackney), which was soon recognised as an up-to-date and successful institution. His second venture, in 1841, was an orphanage for younger children, the Infant Orphan Asylum at nearby Wanstead. The foundation stone was laid by the Prince Consort, and Queen Victoria, the Prince and the Queen Dowager were afterwards among his many patrons. The Duke of Wellington was a keen supporter and could always be called upon to preside at charity dinners.

Sadly, the work at Wanstead was marred by dispute, involving the use of the catechism to be used for the infants. Reed objected to the board of governors' decision to use the Church catechism, when there was no alternative asylum for children of Dissenting families. He severed his connexions with Wanstead in March 1843, and did not even attend the opening ceremony by the King of the Belgiums. The following year, on 6 June, he officially ended his association with the Clapton orphanage.

His next move was to open an orphanage on a non-sectarian basis, for which he had the support of several notable London Dissenters, including James Nisbet the publisher and James Shearmam, pastor of Surrey Chapel. The Asylum for Fatherless Children, later known as the Reedham Orphanage at Coulsdon, near Croydon, Surrey, was opened in 1843.

## Mentally Handicapped

Some of the children under Reed's care were mentally handicapped, and in those days were usually classed together with the mentally ill. Termed either 'insane' or 'lunatic', there was no special provision for them and they were usually to be found in workhouses, asylums and even in prisons and lodging houses. The distinction between the two groups was not officially recognised until parliament passed the Idiots Act in 1886, influenced by the results of Reed's endeavours.

When Reed began to appreciate the difficulties faced by mentally handicapped children in his orphanages, he set himself the task of studying the problems. He visited continental Europe to see experimental work being undertaken there, to discover what could be done. This led to his decision to open a separate institution for intellectually disadvantaged children capable of some training. With Queen Victoria and the Prince Consort as patrons, he opened an experimental home in 1848 for 27 'idiot' children at Highgate, north London.

The work proved successful and was later transferred to a more permanent location at Essex Hall, Colchester, the home of a prominent Baptist MP, Sir Morton Peto. With the help of the Commissioners in Lunacy a second establishment was founded in 1855, at Earlswood, near Redhill, Surrey. It was called the Asylum for Idiots, today known as the Royal Earlswood Hospital.

As a result of this lead, other similar institutions opened at Exeter and Lancaster (1864) and Birmingham (1868). Like Earlswood, the aim was 'to take the idiot and the imbecile under its care ... to improve his bodily powers, to prepare him, as far as possible, for the duties and enjoyments of life'. The children were given special care and love, and were also taught such trades as shoe-making, tailoring, carpentry, gardening or printing. Until the Idiots Act of 1886, Andrew Reed's asylums were the only institutions outside London where intellectually disadvantaged children could be educated and trained.

## Incurables

In the course of his work with the mentally handicapped, Reed became aware of the needs of the 'incurable', that is, those suffering from an incurable disease or too disabled to look after themselves. He found that such people were not generally welcomed at hospitals and often ended their days in the workhouse.

It was this realisation that led him to set up what turned out to be the best-remembered of his charitable works. Both the Royal Hospital and Home for Incurables at Putney, and the British Home and Hospital for Incurables at Streatham were founded as a result of his efforts.

As early as 1845 Reed had written that 'it would be a blessed thing if we had provision in this land to give shelter to despairing incurables'. Despite this prognosis, it was some years before he was able to get a scheme started. He lobbied members of the medical profession, who agreed to support him.

In July 1854 he finally inaugurated a scheme for having 'a house and a hospital for the discharged incurables of the great hospitals of the land, where every comfort may be enjoyed to mitigate affliction, (and) where the best medical skill and care may be had'.

That year he convened his first meeting at the London Tavern, in Fenchurch Street, when a provisional committee was formed, followed by a public meeting at the Mansion House.

Six inmates and pensioners were elected to the available places, but only after some difficulty in making the choice. (Election was the usual method by which an entrance was gained to various institutions at that time.) They became the first residents at a small house in Carshalton, Surrey, while several other outpatients were granted a pension. The Home, eventually to become the Royal Hospital and Home for Incurables, opened in the spring of 1855, and the four inmates paid between £50 and £75 per annum towards their maintenance costs.

The number of applicants wanting to enter the Home far exceeded the available places, and Reed resolved to have a larger, permanent building as soon as possible. By the time the first Festival Dinner took place in 1855, with the author Charles Dickens as chairman, the hospital had outgrown its accommodation. From 1857 to 1865 the committee was able to rent Putney House, a spacious mansion on the borders of Putney and Richmond, which allowed him to accommodate the 43 applicants seeking places.

## Opponents

Meanwhile he continued his search for a permanent site which would allow for further expansion of his work, and many properties were considered. But Reed had settled his mind on building a new Home alongside his orphanage at Coulsdon.

However, a few members of the governing body he had established disagreed about the suitability of the Coulsdon site. They held that its position on 'the bleak North Downs' was not ideal for permanent invalids. There was some dissension at the Annual General Meeting in February 1860. While many supporters backed Reed, there were a number of opponents, including the President and Treasurer, who felt strongly enough to resign in order to pursue an alternative plan.

Fortunately the split had a happy outcome and the dissidents' devotion to their cause was undiminished. In July 1861 a second Home was founded, the British Home and Hospital for Incurables. At first housed in the disused premises of the British Orphan Asylum at Clapham Rise, it was moved to Streatham in 1894, when a new building was opened. A chapel was added in 1912 as more funds became available.

Both these institutions were very much alike, it seems, except that the British Home preferred to admit patients who came from a background of comfortable circumstances and steady employment. But the aim, to provide good quality medical and nursing care to the chronically sick and disabled, remained the same.

Reed and his board of governors continued plans to build a new hospital at Coulsdon. They appointed a Building Committee and on 24 February 1862 launched a Building Fund Appeal in the newspapers. However, Reed, whose health had been causing some anxiety, died the following day. He was buried in Newington, north London, which was then a stronghold of Nonconformity.

**Vision**

Although plans to make use of the Coulsdon estate were eventually abandoned, Reed's vision had caught the Board's imagination. In June 1863 they bought Melrose Hall on West Hill, close to Putney Heath, which commanded fine views over Surrey.

The new hospital was set in extensive, picturesque grounds, originally landscaped by Capability Brown, and gave the general effect of 'a substantial English home'. It provided for more residents and had space to allow for future expansion.

Under the new name of the Royal Home and Hospital for Incurables, it opened its doors in 1864, first to women patients. Men were admitted the following summer. There were 81 patients in all, three quarters of whom were women.

As a result of Reed's work other small Homes were founded throughout the British Isles, including the Mildmay Home for Incurable Consumptives at Torquay, the Broomhill Home at Glasgow and the Home for Protestant Incurables at Cork, Southern Ireland.

Patients who were dying were not admitted to the hospital, hence a similar movement began that was to meet this need. The first such hospitals were set up by High Church and Roman Catholic orders, and towards the end of the century hospitals for the dying were opened by some evangelical groups.

When the Royal Hospital first opened, its patients suffered mainly from complaints such as rheumatism, paralysis, and certain spinal and chest diseases. Today some of these illnesses have been conquered, and present-day patients are affected by a wide range of neuro-muscular and musculo-skeletal disorders, all of which are as yet uncurable.

Patients receive the same devoted care as they did over a hundred years ago, but happily much more can be achieved to help them lead lives which are as independent as possible.

The technical section at the hospital invents and constructs special aids to give the patients more mobility and the physiotherapy department works to ensure that crippled limbs are helped to do as much as they can possibly achieve.

While the name of Andrew Reed may be unknown to the majority of Christians today, the Royal Hospital at Putney and the British Home at Streatham stand as a testimony to his abounding energy, tremendous organising ability and untiring devotion on behalf of hundreds of needy men, women and children.

# ROYAL NATIONAL INSTITUTE FOR THE BLIND (1868)
## Dr Thomas Armitage (1824-1890)

An estimated 1,000,000 people in the United Kingdom are known to be visually handicapped. Most of them fall into the over-65 age group, but 13,000 under-16s are blind or partially sighted. However, the problem is more serious still, for fewer than 320,000 visually handicapped people are actually registered, so the needs of very many go unrecognised. To cover them all, the services provided by the government and charitable institutions would need to grow significantly.

One of the earliest attempts to care for blind people arose in the 15th century, with the founding of the first of a number of pension societies to provide for those no longer able to work. The societies usually granted the pensions at around the age of 65, though it was recognised that many blind people needed financial support at an earlier age. It was not until the 19th century that a greater interest was taken in providing voluntary help.

The Christian Blind Relief Society, founded in 1843, gave pensions to any blind people who were badly-off. The amounts were small, but created a precedent eventually followed by the government, which in 1920 began to give a pension to blind people from the age of 50.

Probably the most pressing need, however, was to educate and train young people to become more self-supporting. Several societies had been established towards the end of the 18th century with this purpose in mind, the earliest of which was a work started in Paris by Valentin Hauy. A native of Picardy, Hauy started in 1784 to educate the blind by means of touch, using raised characters. His first pupil was a blind beggar whom he paid to receive instruction, and one year later he founded the first School for the Young Blind.

Other schools followed. The Liverpool School for the Blind was founded in 1791, followed two years later by the Edinburgh Blind Asylum, which became one of the most successful schools of its kind in the world. The Quakers founded the Royal School of Industry for the Blind (1793), in Bristol, and in Yorkshire, the Yorkshire School for the Blind was opened in 1833. One of its superintendents, the Rev William Taylor, was a founder of Worcester College, 'for the blind sons of gentlemen' (1866).

## Problems

By around this time there were some 20 schools, mostly residential, offering an elementary education and training in a suitable trade. There were two problems, however, that needed attention: one was the variety of scripts used for reading, the other was the lack of an after-care system for those leaving to find employment.

In England, the most notable contribution in caring for the blind came from Dr Thomas Rhodes Armitage, founder of the Royal National Institute for the Blind (RNIB). His aim was to find and bring into general use the type best adapted to the needs of the blind and to help blind people discover a more fulfilling and independent lifestyle.

Research resulted in the introduction into England in 1868 of a type invented 40 years before, by the Frenchman Louis Braille. Dr Armitage was largely responsible for popularising the use of Braille writing in this country, which promoted the spread of education, and together with his wife formulated much of the policy followed by other societies in later years.

Born in Sussex in 1824, the young Thomas Armitage moved with his family to live for a short time in France and later in Germany, where he learned to speak the language fluently. He returned to France to study at the Sorbonne University, Paris, and in 1840 became a medical student at King's College, London.

## Concern

By the end of his first year of medical training, his sight was beginning to cause him concern and he was forced to take a long rest from reading. After two years he was able to continue his studies; he qualified as a surgeon, receiving the degree of MD (London) and MRCP.

After a period of service in the Crimean War, he returned to London where he worked both as a GP and consultant. His eyesight began to trouble him again, and in order to retain what vision he had, he was forced to give up his medical practice.

An apparently serious situation became one of God's opportunities. Dr Armitage realised that his experience as a doctor, together with his failing sight, had prepared him for a new direction in his life. Together with his wife he determined to devote his time and energies to the welfare of blind people in England.

He wrote later, 'I cannot conceive of an occupation so congenial to a blind man of education and leisure as the attempt to advance the education and improve the condition of his fellow-sufferers.'

In 1866 he determined to see for himself some of the problems faced by ordinary blind people. He spent time accompanying a missionary with the Indigent Blind Visiting Society, founded in 1834 by Lord Shaftesbury to visit poor blind people in London for the purpose of giving them scriptural teaching.

He soon realised, however, that their basic need was simply the chance to read and write. But as there was no generally accepted system of embossed writing in the country, the task of providing an education seemed quite daunting.

### Braille

Louis Braille (1809-1852) was the inventor of the system of reading and writing for the blind that is known by his name. The system consists of utilising a maximum of six raised dots or points on tough paper. The whole alphabet, numerals and the various punctuation marks etc., are all based on a variation of the six dots. Braille music is available for blind musicians, and a wide range of school textbooks.

At the time, there were various other systems in use, including one by another Frenchman, Valentin Hauy, who used an embossed form of the Roman letter. Other forms of embossed type were also introduced. James Gall of Edinburgh, in 1827, made use of Roman characters, but for ease of recognition changed all the curves to angles. Dr William Moon's type, which became very popular, was a modification of the Roman character, but also used Frere's method, which guided the finger from left to right, and then by an embossed curve to the line below. Books printed in this type were very expensive and bulky.

However, it was soon recognised that Braille had a number of advantages. Letters were more easily recognised; they could be written by blind people in such a way as to be legible for sighted people who know the script; and books printed in this script were smaller in bulk and cheaper to produce.

While at school, twelve-year-old Louis Braille had picked up the idea of using dots from an army captain, who had worked out a system for passing messages to his men in the dark. It took some time before Louis was able to develop the idea, but by the age of 15 years he had devised a system using only six dots with 63 combinations. It was at his teacher's suggestion that it should be called Braille writing.

Dr Armitage believed that blind people themselves were the most fitted to decide on the best system for their needs, saying, 'The relative merits of the various methods of education through the sense of touch should be decided by these, and only these, who have to rely on this sense.'

## Best Possibilities

In 1868 he enlisted the help of three blind men, each of whom had to read by touch and were familiar with at least three of the available systems of embossed writing. They formed a committee and took the name of the British and Foreign Association for Promoting the Education and Employment of the Blind, later to become the RNIB. They set themselves to selecting a system of writing that would prove the best for teaching young blind people.

Over the course of nearly two years, the committee interviewed many people with defective sight who had a working knowledge of more than one system. They discussed the merits of the different systems of embossed writing and finally concluded that Braille offered the best possibilities.

DR THOMAS RHODES ARMITAGE

For the next 20 years Dr Armitage devoted his energies and re-sources to the introduction of Braille. By 1882 he was able to report, 'There is now probably no institution in the civilised world where Braille is not used, except in some of those in North America.'

From 1870 the Association began printing books in Braille, starting with the Bible, 'that the blind by this means might be led from theological darkness into light'. It also produced other kinds of litera-ture, especially school text books, including John Gilpin, the multipli-cation tables and several maps.

## Music

Another significant development at this time was the appearance of embossed music, helping blind people to use a wider range of skills. Dr Armitage persuaded Francis Campbell, Head of Music at the Perkins Institute, Massachusetts, to help him set up what became the Royal Normal College for the Blind, in Upper Norwood, south London. The college attracted many talented blind people who came to learn music.

Most of the pupils were trained as church organists and piano tuners, and in this way they were able to earn a living and support themselves. A report of 1885 stated that of its 1,170 students, most of them were at work with self-supporting jobs.

The college, now the Royal National College for the Blind, is located in Hereford. Students can still follow a piano tuning and repairs course, as well as learning office and computer skills.

After Dr Armitage's death in 1890, the British and Foreign Blind Association took the lead in work on behalf of the blind. It co-ordinated the various developments taking place, set up conferences to discuss methods and share expertise, and gave support to a lending library scheme for the blind. In 1893 school boards had to make provision for blind children, and it was to the association they looked for help. Soon Dr Armitage's methods became the basis on which the education authorities built up their own work.

## Sheltered Workshops

Dr Armitage also set himself the task of tackling the other chief problem facing blind people, the need to find work after their period of training. Initially he tried using agents of the Indigent Blind Visiting Society. The idea was that the agents visited the people in their homes, to oversee their progress and help them find work.

As the scheme was not successful, he tried a method introduced from Germany. Again, the scheme involved agents visiting the homes of blind people, arranging for the sale of the articles they made. However, there were insufficient funds for the scheme and his efforts came to nothing.

### Torch Trust

Since the days of Dr Armitage, other societies have appeared to care for the needs of blind people. One of more recent origin is Torch Trust for the Blind, which began in the 1950s as a club for blind young people. The founders, Ron and Stella Heath, wanted to win young blind people to Christ, but soon discovered there was a lack of suitable Bible-based literature in Braille.

So the Heaths took over from an elderly Christian lady the editorship of a magazine called Torch. Published for blind people, it was built up as a means of contacting blind people all over the world. The Heaths also started a Braille lending service and produced a correspondence course for those wanting to learn Braille.

Now based at Hallaton, near Market Harborough, Leicestershire, Torch Trust produces magazines for blind people of all ages, and publishes Braille Scriptures, Bible study aids, tracts and other kinds of Christian literature in many languages. The library lending service includes large print books, talking books, cassettes and magazines which are sent out worldwide.

Some 150 Torch Fellowship groups established in all parts of the country carry out the ministry of caring for spiritual and physical needs. Sighted people minister to the needs of the visually handicapped of all ages, and there are houseparties through the year.

What began as a meeting for a group of young people in the Heath's Reigate home has now developed into an international 'Torch family' with about 60 staff, some short-term helpers and many sighted workers at the Torch centres.

Later, he opened a series of sheltered workshops where adult blind people worked together under a supervisor, and the goods were sold on their behalf. It was an idea he borrowed from Elizabeth Gilbert, the daughter of the Bishop of Chichester, who had been blind from the age of three. She had devoted her life to caring for the blind poor, and together with William Hanks Levy, a teacher at St John's Wood School for the Blind, had formed the Association for Promoting the General Welfare of the Blind in 1856. They had workshops and a retail shop where their goods were sold.

Today, the RNIB has one of the largest Braille printing houses in the world and runs over 60 services for the visually handicapped. In addition to its education and training programme, it runs four residential homes for people who can't cope independently, designs and sells specially-adapted equipment and games, and produces a wide range of material in Braille and on tape.

## MISSION STATEMENT OF RNIB

RNIB wants a world in which blind and partially sighted people enjoy the same rights, freedoms, responsibilities and quality of life as people who are fully sighted.

Our mission is to challenge blindness. We challenge the disabling effects of blindness by providing services to help people determine their own lives. We challenge society's actions, attitudes and assumptions. Many barriers are put in the path of blind and partially sighted people – our task is to dismantle them. And we challenge the underlying causes of blindness to prevent, cure or alleviate it.

# ROYAL NATIONAL MISSION
# TO DEEP SEA FISHERMEN (1881)
## E J Mather (1849-1927)

The Royal National Mission to Deep Sea Fishermen has been looking after the welfare of British fishermen for over a hundred years. It was founded in 1881 when public attention was first drawn to conditions at sea after the murder of an apprentice boy by the skipper of a North Sea trawling smack. Offering medical, material and financial aid to fishermen and their families, its influence on legislation and social services has improved the lives and working conditions of these 'toilers of the deep'.

Salt fish was a major part of the diet of Europe, not limited to the Catholic tradition of eating fish on Fridays and during the season of Lent. The British, for example, consumed as much fish as they did meat. Since Tudor times, British fishermen have sailed the North Sea, and beyond, as far as Iceland and across the Atlantic to Newfoundland, in search of sea food.

Early in the 19th century it was customary for a single boat to fish for a few days for herrings with a drift net. This gradually gave way to large trawler fleets, fishing the Dogger Bank with the newly-invented beam trawl. There were as many as 200 trawlers or more in a fleet, and each boat carried a crew of at least four men, including a boy apprentice.

Many of these young boys were apprenticed from industrial or reformatory schools. With no relations to be concerned for their well-being, they were badly exploited and often ill-treated; punishments even for minor misdemeanours were severe.

Fishing continued all the year round and, except for Sundays, stopped only when bad weather made trawling impossible. After the catch was lifted, it was transferred to a 'carrier' ship and hurried back to base for transfer to Billingsgate market, London, for the best prices. Originally, this was the busy port of Barking (Essex), but after a railway was built in 1865 it was rushed by train from Yarmouth to London.

## Conditions

To say the least, conditions aboard the trawlers were primitive. Cramped cabins with no facilities for drying wet clothes, poor sanitary arrangements and little cooked food combined to make a very dangerous occupation even more intolerable.

438

Most important, there was no proper medical care. Accidents were regular occurrences, and men had to carry on working with wounds or broken limbs that gradually worsened. Usually the only way to help such men was to send them on the carrier when it returned to market with the fish. By which time the injury could mean an amputation. Each year there were hundreds of casualties on the ships, resulting in as many as 350 deaths, mostly by loss overboard.

As the ships remained at sea for eight to ten weeks at a time, there were periods when the smacks were unable to fish. So when the men had nothing to do, they took to drink - an even worse enemy than the storms. Alcohol was easily available from floating German and Dutch grog-ships - trading ships known as 'copers' (from a Dutch word meaning 'cheap'), which came out to visit the fleet. Ostensibly calling to sell duty-free tobacco and other necessities, the copers tempted many fishermen by offering them cheap drinks. Even men who only wanted tobacco were lured with the offer of a first free drink of gin, spiked to create a thirst, so that many men fell into the trap.

To pay for the drinks fishermen sometimes traded their ship's gear, fish, nets, stores and even sails for liquor; and skippers were known to pawn their ship for another drink. Consequently, smacks were damaged or even lost through the lack of equipment or the recklessness of a drunken skipper. Back on shore there were numerous drinking saloons along the quay-sides of the fishermen's quarters. Wages were usually paid off here, virtually reducing men to penury.

## Challenge

Since 1844 Ebenezer Mather had worked for the Thames Church Mission, caring for the needs of sailors, watermen and bargees and their families along the River Thames. His 'parish' was 76 miles long and had a population of around 3,000 men, women and children. But in 1881 a friend drew his attention to the fishing vessels that sailed beyond the mouth of the Thames, into the storms and hazards of the North Sea.

As the friend painted a picture of life on the deep seas, Mather became concerned and accepted the challenge to find out the truth of the situation. A few days later he joined the steamer Supply of the Short Blue Fleet, at that time the largest fishing fleet in the world, owned by Samuel Hewett. The supply ship carried coal, ice (a recent innovation to keep the fish fresh) and empty fish boxes to the fishing fleets in the

North Sea, returning with the latest catch for market.

On that five day voyage Mather discovered at first hand the conditions under which these deep sea fishermen worked. He learned about the long absence from home and family, the coarseness of thought and language, the threat of a force nine gale, the lack of medical treatment, and the scourge of malnutrition. Cold, wet and hungry he found himself back on shore determined to do something about it.

The new venture became known as the Mission to Deep Sea Fishermen. Although Mather felt that the primary need was to supply medical aid, his Mission had a two-fold purpose: 'To preach the gospel and heal the sick,' an aim that has ever since continued to motivate the mission.

Mather found that he could purchase a second-hand fishing smack for about £1,000, but it would need alterations to fit it out as a mission ship. With no idea where the money would come from, he made it a matter of prayer. After all, the Scriptures said, 'Whatever you shall ask in prayer, you shall receive.'

**Skipper**

His first 'gift' was that of a skipper, Captain Budd, an experienced seafarer who pleaded with Mather for medical help for the fleets. 'We badly need help, especially medical help,' he told him. 'Nobody here at home seems to care.' It was Budd who agreed to skipper the first mission ship; now all that was needed was the ship.

Following a public appeal Mather's first donation was of one guinea, which the donor increased to £1,000 when he learned the full need. With the money Mather was able to purchase a 56 ton yawl-rigged smack from Samuel Hewett of Yarmouth, who also gave him the use of his dry dock for making the necessary alterations.

The Hewetts were well aware of the dangers the fishermen faced from both the weather and from alcohol, and were fully behind Mather in his Mission. Although they were hardheaded businessmen, the company recognised the importance of the work Mather was doing and offered him continued financial support. They also allowed him to use one of the fishing smacks as a first-aid centre and hospital for men injured at sea.

The new ship, named the *Ensign*, had a chapel where men could come aboard for worship, and a cabin for private counselling; known as the 'Bethel' ship, it was recognised at sea by its special flag. It carried medical supplies, fresh food and water, plenty of dry clothes, plus books, Bibles and tracts. Under the motto 'Preach the word, heal the sick', Captain Budd and his crew, after a dedication service, set sail from Gorleston, on the east coast, one Friday in July 1882 to a mixture of jeers and cheers from watching fishermen.

In the early stages the mission ship tried to support itself by trawling. But the task of trying to fulfil two functions soon proved impossible. In any way, as the work became more widely-known, the Mission was able to concentrate solely on fighting the copers.

## Tobacco

The practice of supplying fishermen with tobacco posed a threat to the work at one point. Among the mission's supporters was an anti-smoking lobby, which regarded smoking as much a 'sin' as drinking. Mather demolished the argument, largely on the grounds that if the mission did not supply cut-price tobacco, then the men would visit the copers, exposing themselves to the dangers of alcohol.

Mather asked HM Customs to allow him to buy tobacco from bond and sell it cheaply, but he was refused access to duty-free stores. In which case, they would have had to pay the full price for it and then sell it at a large loss. Instead, he bought tobacco intended for delivery abroad.

E J MATHER

This meant first sending a ship to Ostend to pick up the tobacco before setting sail for the fleets, which placed an extra burden upon the Mission's limited resources.

Turning over the problem in his mind one evening, he committed the whole problem to God. Then he remembered that he had once stayed in the home of someone who knew W H Wills MP, a philanthropist and a member of the tobacco manufacturing family. Next morning, after determining to obtain an introduction to Mr Wills, his clerk unexpectedly announced a visitor – 'Mr W H Wills MP'. Before Wills could speak, to the visitor's surprise Mather informed him that he knew why he had come.

The outcome was that the tobacco company allowed the Mission to purchase tobacco at cost price. They sent it direct to Ostend where the mission could buy it at more advantageous Custom prices. In this way, the Mission ship was able to retain its customers, giving away clothing and portions of Scriptures along with the tobacco.

## Success

The struggle against the copers showed signs of success, and before long many of the fishermen began to prefer the friendliness of the mission ships. It was only the hardened drinkers who patronised the copers. Though still in business, there were now fewer copers afloat, and several European countries started to wage war against them.

Two years later, in 1887, their fate was sealed when an international convention was signed at the Hague, making illegal the sale or barter of spirits in the North Sea. Soon afterwards a letter from HM Commissioner of Customs informed Mather that he would allow mission ships to sell tobacco at duty-free prices. 'What did I tell you?' cried Mather triumphantly. 'The sale of tobacco has turned out for the furtherance of the gospel, and we have won a great battle.'

During its first eight years the Mission was under the leadership of Ebenezer Mather: he was both manager and secretary, backed by a committee of prominent people. He also spent much of his time raising funds, though initially he supplemented the Mission's income from his own pocket. Public meetings were held throughout the country and money came in, so that the Mission was able to extend its work.

More ships were commissioned and their facilities improved, and by 1887 it had seven ships operating in the North Sea. They contained a shop which sold warm clothing and other goods at low prices, a library, a clubroom and recreation room where the men could spend their spare time.

## Medical Care

As well as its evangelistic concern, the Mission tried to provide proper medical care for fishermen taken ill or injured at sea. In the beginning, this was a matter of simple first-aid given by mission skippers. The more serious cases – crushed and broken limbs or acute illnesses – were taken by carrier to the London Hospital, near Billingsgate Market, where they often came under the care of Sir Frederick Treves.

The hospital doctors realised that many lives could be saved and broken bones mended if medical treatment were available on the spot. Dr Treves, elected chairman of the Mission's medical committee in 1886, already had a scheme in mind.

His plan was to equip a number of floating hospitals, each with its own doctor, which would work in the North Sea alongside the fishing fleets. He undertook to find the right doctors for the service, and his first volunteer was one of his young surgeons, Wilfred Grenfell.

When Grenfell learned from his senior, Sir Frederick Treves, that the fishermen's Mission needed a doctor who could also offer the men spiritual help, he readily offered his services. Despite financial difficulties, the Mission approved Dr Treve's plan. A trawler was designated as a hospital ship for a two months trial period – provided it did not interfere with the Mission's evangelistic work.

The trial was a success, and in December 1888 Grenfell joined the Mission staff with a salary of £300 a year. The first mission hospital ship was named Queen Victoria, in gratitude for the queen's generous subscription towards its purchase. It was the first hospital ship to sail the North Sea, and had a fully equipped ward of eight beds and two swing cots.

Shortly afterwards, Mather resigned as mission Superintendent and Grenfell became his successor. Based at Gorleston, Grenfell had several ideas for expanding the work, though he did not always wait for permission from the council. He opened a fishermen's club at Yarmouth, and each spring sent out a dispensary vessel to care for the Scots, Manx, Irish and French fishermen working off south-west Ireland.

While on speaking engagements he did not always follow the Mission's programme, though they often received gifts of money as a

**Dr W T Grenfell (1865-1943)**

Grenfell was converted in 1884 under the ministry of D L Moody, and immediately became an ardent evangelist. A house-surgeon at the London Hospital, he had under his care - though responsible to his senior, Dr Treves - a patient referred to as 'the elephant man' (known today as a result of a film by that title). Grenfell spent his spare time preaching the gospel in the East End. He visited public houses, handing out tracts, taught in a ragged school, launched a total abstinence campaign and held Sunday services in lodging-houses along the Radcliffe Highway. His efforts as a Sunday school teacher, however, were disappointing, and he seemed to be making little progress with his boys.

As there were no YMCAs in the area to give the boys any physical culture, which Grenfell felt to be important, he decided to provide it himself. He gathered a group of boys together and taught them boxing, to encourage them to keep their bodies healthy. An avid sailor since his youth, he took some of his boys with him on his annual sailing holiday on the Anglesey coast, and the following year began a series of seaside camps in Dorset for sailing and swimming. Needless to say, his relationship with the boys grew firmer, and the numbers in his classes increased.

Grenfell never lost sight of the need to present the gospel to the fisherfolk among whom he worked. But he was primarily a doctor, and when he was converted to Christ he determined always 'to do as I thought Christ would do in my place as a doctor.'

result of his efforts. When the council withdrew him from deputation work, he went off to southern Ireland to find out in what other ways the Mission could be of benefit there. Opposed by local priests, he had to restrain his evangelical fervour. But the people liked his ministry, and when he returned later he was warmly received by them.

## Newfoundland

From 1886 the Mission began to receive appeals from Newfoundland for help among the cod fishermen, a request that was at first turned down. However, following the dramatic disclosures of the men's dreadful working conditions and the loss of 40 men in a blizzard at sea, the Mission reconsidered its position.

In 1892 the council decided to send a hospital ship on an exploratory voyage, under the leadership of their young superintendent, Wilfred Grenfell. He was dismayed to discover that the poverty of the Newfoundland fishing communities was worse than he expected, and the need for medical provision was urgent. During the course of that visit he saw over 900 patients. When he reported his findings to the council they agreed to send help immediately.

The following year he returned to Newfoundland and set up the Mission's headquarters at St Anthony, a small settlement on the north of the island. Aware of the urgent need for funds, Grenfell visited Canada and America on a fund-raising tour. News of his exploits, together with his easy-going style of lecturing, attracted many audiences who gave generously to the cause.

Called back to England by the council, unhappy about his spending so much time away from home base, he returned to his responsibility for the North Sea work. Yet the challenge from across the Atlantic continued to draw him back. He resigned his position at the Mission in 1904 and returned to Labrador, though he continued to maintain links with the London office.

In Newfoundland he fitted out a second hospital ship, established five small hospitals, seven nursing homes, two orphanages, a sailors' home and several co-operative stores. He set up a separate organization in 1912, the International Grenfell Association, to take charge of the business affairs pertaining to his work. In 1925 he founded the Grenfell Association of Great Britain to support his interests in Labrador.

The immense value of the services rendered by the Mission and by

Grenfell received public recognition. In 1896 Queen Victoria granted the Mission the title 'royal', and it became the Royal National Mission to Deep Sea Fishermen. For his outstanding work in Labrador, Queen Victoria awarded Grenfell a knighthood.

With modern developments such as refrigeration and the use of steam trawlers, fishermen's working conditions have become less hazardous. Even so, around 40 lives are lost each year in fishing and related industries.

Since 1950 the RNMDSF has withdrawn its ships from service. Instead, it provides shore-based facilities and welfare services for fishermen and their families at its 17 centres scattered around our coasts.

The Mission has earned for itself an enviable record of concern and efficiency, yet still remains true to its motto of 'Preach the gospel and heal the sick'.

## MISSION STATEMENT OF ROYAL NATIONAL MISSION TO DEEP SEA FISHERMEN

The objects for which the Association is established are:

a. To establish and maintain a Mission presence in fishing ports around the coast where fishermen, their families and those connected with the fishing industry can receive spiritual and material help, regardless of race or creed.

b. To support the fishing community in every way through the Christian Mission presence.

c. To promote, through service, example and counsel the message of the Christian Gospel.

## ROYAL SAILORS' RESTS (1876)
### Agnes Weston (1840-1918)

The Evangelical Revival gave rise in the 19th century to a number of missions devoted to the welfare of men and women engaged in a variety of occupations. Among these groups were to be found flower girls, barmaids, cabmen, navvies, costermongers and railwaymen, many of whom faced hardships and temptations as a consequence of their work. Although most of these missions are no longer extant, they were formed to meet an urgent need to convey the gospel to people who would not normally be found in church.

Among these groups were sailors, who spent long months at sea, often leaving behind a wife and family who had to struggle against mounting odds. Several societies were founded to cater for the physical and spiritual well-being of sailors and their dependants, who were for the most part untouched by the revival.

What appears to be the earliest attempt was made by John Thornton of the Clapham Sect, who in his lifetime gave away thousands of Bibles. In 1780 he was largely instrumental in forming one of the earliest of the Bible societies, designed especially to serve soldiers and sailors. It was called simply the Bible Society – later changed to the Naval & Military Bible Society – and during the following 35 years distributed some 100,000 Bibles.

### Influence
But the man who exerted the greatest influence was the Rev George C Smith, who spent two years serving as a chaplain with the British army during the Peninsula War. Smith had spent some time at sea before entering the Baptist ministry, and upon his return from the war determined to see what help he could give to members of the services.

A west country pastor, he concentrated his attentions chiefly upon merchant seamen, and it was as a result of his initiative that most of the subsequent social work for sailors was set up. He was responsible for the formation of several sailors' societies and orphan homes in the 1820s and 30s. Beginning with the Bethel Seamen's Union in 1819, set up to co-ordinate prayer meetings for sailors, several other organisations were established in the Port of London to cater for their spiritual and physical needs.

As a result, chapels were opened for seamen, both on shore and afloat, and 'seamen's friends societies' were started to hold 'bethel' services and provide social care. As well as engaging in evangelism, bethels provided lodgings, refreshments, and rooms for recreation, reading and writing. They also offered a banking service for sailors, to send part of their pay back home to their wives.

Several denominational missions were begun about this time, notably the Wesleyan Seamen's Mission (1843) and the Missions to Seamen (1856), which was an amalgamation of a number of Anglican societies from ports such as Gravesend, Bristol and Liverpool. Other missions provided for foreign seamen, often to be found in British ports, helping them with financial and other problems, and finding them work if they did not wish to rejoin their ship. Strangers' Rests were opened to provide them with suitable accommodation when on shore leave.

## Devonport

So far, however, little attention had been given to ratings – young boys who were in training for the Royal Navy. Ratings were the chaplains' responsibility on board ship, but there was no special provision for them on land. Although allowed to make use of seamen's societies, they were usually otherwise left high and dry.

It was not until the 1870s that Agnes Weston, on a visit to Devonport, observed the needs of these boys and founded her Sailors' Rests.

Agnes Weston, brought up in Bath from the age of five, came from a well-to-do home. Her father was a barrister, and both her parents were earnest Christians. Leaving school at the age of 16, Agnes was faced with the problem of what to do with her life. It was while wrestling with this problem that she was finally converted, and afterwards began to make herself useful in a variety of ways.

Her first form of service was as a Sunday School teacher. Later she commenced visiting patients in a Bath hospital, where she delivered flowers with a text, joined in weekly ward services and was able to speak about the Lord to patients close to death.

Her first contact with the armed services came in 1865, when she helped a family friend set up a coffee bar for soldiers of the 2nd Somerset Regiment stationed in the city. Agnes had already discovered what she considered to be the evils of drink. As a result, she had become strictly teetotal and had taken up the temperance cause. The coffee bar provided soldiers with an alternative to the public house, as well as giving them an opportunity to attend Bible classes.

When the soldiers were posted abroad, she kept in touch with several of them, and found herself corresponding with other Christian soldiers as well. One of the soldiers was aboard *HMS Crocodile*, en route to join a regiment in India. He was befriended by a sickberth attendant, to whom he showed Agnes' letter. Learning of her kindness, the lonely sailor wrote to Agnes and asked if she would also write to him. She did, and it was this contact that started her interest in seamen.

## Letter Writing

The ministry of letter writing was obviously one to which she attached great importance, as did the men with whom she corresponded. It is recorded that at one stage Agnes had been distributing 55,000 letters per month. On one occasion she wrote 36 letters which were put by in monthly batches, made watertight in tin-lined chests and placed on board *HMS Albert* and *HMS Discovery* for regular distribution throughout three years on an Arctic expedition.

One seaman who wrote to her remarked, 'M'am, we think so highly of your letters, we never even use them to light our pipes with.'

With an increasing number of correspondents, in 1868 Agnes found it necessary to start a monthly newspaper, which she called *Ashore and Afloat*, with which she included a personal note to her men. She developed her friendship with the sailors who, anxious to meet the kind lady who faithfully wrote to them, suggested she might like to come down to Devonport.

## Ratings

Agnes Weston paid her first visit to the naval port in January 1873, when she was introduced to Sophia Wintz, a young Swiss lady already concerned for the sailors and their families. Though the two women talked about ways in which they might do something for the 'bluejackets', their attention was at first drawn to the plight of hundreds of ratings who walked aimlessly about the town on a Sunday afternoon with nothing to do. The only place open to them was the public house.

Miss Wintz offered the use of her mother's large kitchen where they could hold a meeting for the boys, with the added attraction of tea afterwards. The idea of being invited into a home appealed to many of them, and the meetings were packed. Boys crammed the kitchen; they sang hymns, read the Bible and talked about it, and ended by eating a huge plate of buns.

The following year, realising the need for a more spacious meeting place for the boys' work, they hired a furniture store for Sunday afternoons. Assisted by dockers and their wives, the two ladies brought boys in from the streets, and there were often as many as three or four hundred each week. Over the course of some 40 years, thousands of ratings heard the gospel and were converted to Christ.

As this work proceeded, Agnes gained permission to visit ships-of-war when in port, to speak to the ratings on board. A firm supporter of the temperance movement and a representative of the Royal Temperance Society, she was given permission to visit ships coming into the port. Always she took the opportunity to speak to the crews on the subject of temperance, and persuaded many of them to sign the pledge.

In 1873 she visited 38 Royal Navy ships, took over 1,600 pledges and formed a great many temperance branches. Ships' captains, many of them Christians, were pleased to offer her an opportunity to speak of the dangers of drink, which caused much damage to sailors and their families.

## Deputation

The next development was to open a Sailors' Rest at Devonport, but the initiative this time came from the men. In 1874 a deputation called on Agnes and Sophia to urge them to open a temperance house, a grog shop without the grog, outside the dockyard gate, and then become responsible for it.

This was not the sort of things well-bred young ladies did in those days, and Agnes realised that it would involve a lifetime of work. Though her first reaction was to say 'No', Sophia promised to support her. After prayer, the two ladies accepted the challenge. They rented an empty grocery store near the dock gates, right among a cluster of grog shops.

Agnes received staunch support from R C Morgan, editor of *The Christian*, who published the story in his paper. Readers responded by sending in enough money to enable her to buy the property outright. The Rest opened in Fore Street, at 5 am one Monday in May 1876, and was immediately filled with dockers and sailors all glad to get a hot drink before starting work.

The facilities included a coffee bar, restaurant, reading and recreational rooms, plus a number of cabins for sleeping accommodation. Rooms were also set aside for the two women who had agreed to live on the premises and manage the new enterprise.

## Success

From the outset, Agnes adopted a business-like approach to the undertaking. The place had to pay its own way and was in no sense to be regarded as a 'charity', even though the helpers gave their services free. Any surplus money was given to the relief of widows and orphans and other needy causes.

She kept two quite separate departments which were kept distinct and yet united. One was the Institute with its coffee bar and other facilities, and the other was the evangelistic work, with Bible classes and meetings for wives and children. There was no membership subscription, and no compulsion to attend Bible meetings. Sailors and soldiers were welcome, sober or drunk, with or without a creed.

The Rest was an immediate success, even though it did not sell alcohol; but men knew that at 'Aggie Weston's' they would be cared for and possibly helped to a better life.

As the Rest became more popular, the nearby pubs and pawn shops were put out of business. She was able to buy the sites and erect a new building that would accommodate 900 guests. Interest in the work spread, and Agnes travelled around the country to draw the Christian public's attention to the needs.

The next centre to be opened was at Portsmouth, another large naval base. It came about as the result of a tragedy, when *HMS Eurydice* sank off Portsmouth with the loss of all but two of the crew. Many of the men who lost their lives were known personally to Agnes, and she went straight away to Portsmouth to comfort the grieving families.

With her attention drawn to the needs at Portsmouth, she made plans to move into the port. She rented a former Music Hall on the Commercial Road, using the small building as a coffee bar and reading room until more permanent premises were available. She organised Saturday night entertainment, with music, songs and recitations, but anything coarse was not allowed. Even though the men enjoyed the concerts, Agnes was criticised by some Christian people for this new departure, just as they disapproved of her taking in drunks.

**Royal Visitors**

From the start, Agnes recognised that larger premises would soon be required, in order to offer servicemen and their families overnight accommodation. A gift of 1,000 guineas set the seal on the project, and in 1881 a new building was opened. But even this proved too small, and seven years later it had to be extended. It was visited by members of the royal family, who themselves had close connections with the sea and who recognised what a good work she was doing. All of them gave generous donations, and some of them also presented a cabin. The cabin donated by the Queen contained her portrait, and proved a popular booking with the sailors.

It was Queen Victoria who also gave the title 'Royal' to the Sailors' Rests, confirming it by Royal Warrant and saying that 'it was a fitting title for a royal work'.

The sad task which befell both Agnes and Sophia Wintz, to bring comfort and relief to sailors' families at times of disaster, was proving to be part of their ministry. A further accident occurred in 1893, when *HMS Victoria* and *HMS Camperdown* collided in the Mediterranean and sank with the loss of several hundred lives.

The ladies again went to the immediate assistance of the families. In many cases they were able to make a small grant or pay off arrears of rent; they also visited many of the bereaved wives and their children. Agnes also set up a Naval Disaster Fund, which supported sailors invalided out of the service, and encouraged members of the Royal Naval Christian Union to visit these men and help them over their initial difficulties.

The name Agnes Weston became renowned throughout the Royal Navy, and the Royal Sailors' Rests were held in the highest esteem. News of her exploits reached foreign shores, and governments enquired of her organisation with the intent of setting up their own Rests. In fact, similar institutions were set up on the continent of Europe, and as far away as America and Japan.

**'Mother' Weston**

Agnes eventually became known as 'Mother' Weston, for many seamen adopted her as their substitute mother. This was because she was genuinely concerned for their welfare, and had a matronly approach to them, treating them with a mixture of indulgence and admonition. She received hundreds of letters of gratitude, both from sailors and their families, and was looked upon with great affection. The parents of one sailor told her, 'We love you because our son loved you, and you taught him to trust and serve his Saviour.'

After many years of loyal service to the men of the Navy, King George V (1910-36) awarded her the GBE. She died just before she was due to receive it. The award was the Grand Cross of the British Empire – the sailors said the initials stood for 'God Bless 'Er'. Later Sophia Wintz was awarded the DBE.

Today there are six Sailors' Rests, providing much the same kind of facility offered in the early days, and complemented by the work of evangelism. Though the emphasis on temperance has changed, the Rests still adopt Agnes' policy of not selling alcohol, and provide an acceptable alternative to the pub for many naval men and women.

Now RSR missionaries work alongside naval chaplains and the social workers in the Navy Personnel and Family Services, and are able to help families which do not want to use the 'official' welfare agencies.

But the RSR motto, 'For the glory of God and good of the Service', stands as a reminder that the gospel of Christ remains the basis of the work.

## MISSION STATEMENT OF ROYAL SAILORS REST

The Mission of the Society is to meet the sailor at his point of need, be it physical, moral or spiritual so that he and his family can feel valued, cared for and supported. To this end the Society is charged under its Governing Instrument to provide in the Rests a setting, free from alcoholic and other pressures, where the Missioners can minister the love of God in a way which commends itself to the Navy and which honours God.

# ROYAL SOCIETY for the
## PREVENTION of CRUELTY to ANIMALS (1824)
### Rev Arthur Broome (1780-1837)
### Richard Martin MP (1754-1834)

The first society in the world for the protection of animals was formed in the early years of the 19th century. This was despite ridicule and opposition from the most respectable quarters. At the time, an increasing number of voices were being raised in protest at the inhumane treatment often meted out to animals, and an emasculated Bill outlawing such cruelty had been passed in parliament. But it was the foundation of an animal welfare society that ultimately brought about a change in the nation's attitudes.

Despite the reverence for all forms of life recognised by world religions, the treatment of animals was often brutal and callous. In the arenas of Ancient Rome, as many as 5,000 beasts are known to have been slaughtered in one day to provide entertainment for the populace. Statesmen and philosophers such as Cicero and Plutarch attacked the barbaric practice, but to no avail.

In the Middle Ages, Francis of Assisi was known for his compassion for animals and did much to encourage Christians to have concern for them. Yet animals were still used for cruel forms of sport, in which they were savagely torn apart or were viciously beaten or otherwise ill-treated by their owners.

## Conscience

Until the beginning of the 19th century animals were not legally protected except as a form of property. Owners could treat them as they liked without any fear of punishment. As a result, animals suffered terrible abuse and few people felt that there was anything amiss in inflicting pain on them.

In England, a number of prominent people began to draw attention to this scandal, and some kind of conscience towards animal treatment began to emerge. It was first noticeable among the Quakers, and John Wesley also joined in condemning the practice of brutal sports. Other famous names who protested included the poets Blake, Cowper and Wordsworth. Hogarth, the engraver and moralist, produced a series of cartoons called 'Four Stages of Cruelty', by which he attacked the ill-treatment of dumb animals.

## Cruelty to Animals

Probably the most brutal form of cruelty to animals was bull-baiting, in which both the bull and the attacking dogs suffered horrible injuries. The bull was tethered to a metal ring and set upon by specially-trained dogs. The idea was to bite the bull's nose, so long as they could avoid being tossed by it. If the animals failed to show enough spirit they were tormented by fire or acid, or pepper was blown up their nose. In Stamford (Lincolnshire), there was an annual festival in which an enraged bull was pursued through the town by dogs, a practice which persisted until the 19th century.

Badger-baiting was also a common sport, in which badgers had their tails nailed down to be savaged to death by dogs. Cock-throwing was another pastime, which consisted of throwing sticks at a bird tied to a post. Although the game ended with the cockerel's death, grease was smeared on the feathers to make it more difficult.

Cockfighting, dating back to at least 1400 BC, was the most traditional of these so-called games. Metal spurs were attached to the cocks' legs, and the birds fought it out until one, or sometimes both of them, died either of wounds or of exhaustion.

Domestic animals were sometimes treated with equal severity. Horses were beaten or worked to death, especially cab horses. Sheep intended for slaughter had their faces slashed and tendons cut; calves were strung up, their mouths taped to still their cries, and were slowly bled to death. Fights were arranged between dogs and cats, until the stronger of the two tore the other one apart.

As the voice of protest began to swell, there was the first hint of the idea that cruelty should be banned by law. It was suggested by Jeremy Bentham, an English philosopher and reformer, in a book published in 1780. Twenty years later Sir William Pulteney MP initiated the first attempt to secure legislation to protect animals from cruelty. It was a Bill to prevent bull-baiting, which he said 'depraved the onlooker'. The Bill was narrowly defeated, by two votes.

It was another eight years before a further attempt was made. The new champion of animal rights was Lord Erskine, a lawyer. Erskine was said to have once reprimanded a carter on Hampstead Heath for beating his horse. 'Can't I do what I like with my own ?' the man asked. 'Yes,' came the reply, 'and so can I – this stick is my own.' And with that he proceeded to give the carter a thrashing.

Erskine's Bill, introduced in the House of Lords, was designed to prevent the 'wanton cruelty to animals', which included horses, sheep and dogs. Anyone found guilty would be liable for up to one month's imprisonment. Although it was defeated in the Commons, much to the disgust of the Gentlemen's

Magazine – which spoke out against 'the unnecessary cruelty of man to animals' – by now the climate of opinion was beginning to change.

William Wilberforce MP added his weight to the cause, and joined the campaign through the agency of his Society for the Suppression of Vice (formerly called the Proclamation Society).

## Leading Champion

But the leading champion in the House of Commons was Richard Martin. Already Martin had helped to abolish capital punishment for forgery, and had pioneered moves to provide free legal aid for those who could not afford it. Though it was some time before his moment of triumph was to be, it was he who introduced the first successful Bill to limit cruelty to animals.

Richard Martin was the son of a well-to-do Irish landowner. Born in Dublin, he had a passion for duelling, and at one time was nicknamed 'hairtrigger Dick'. Educated at Harrow school and Trinity College, Cambridge, Martin afterwards qualified as a barrister at the King's Inns, but gave up the idea of practising law to enter politics.

From 1776 he was a member of the Irish Parliament, and after the Act of Union in 1800 he represented Galway at Westminster. Although born into a Roman Catholic family, he was brought up as a Protestant, which made it possible for him to enter parliament.

Despite his reputation as a duellist, he was widely known for his kindness and generosity. Heir to a 200,000 acre estate, he provided work and shelter for homeless children, and even built a model prison so the local offenders need not be sent away from home.

In the House of Commons he joined a group of reformers who fought for the poor and underprivileged. Since 1800, when he had supported Pulteney's Bill, he constantly campaigned for the cause of animal welfare. This concern for animals stemmed from his school days at Harrow. As a nine-year-old-boy he came under the influence of a remarkable master, Samuel Parr, who taught his pupils to be kind to animals and condemned those who inflicted them with 'wanton barbarity'.

Campaigning for animal welfare, Martin made it his business to visit slaughterhouses and bear-baiting pits to learn at first hand of the cruelties inflicted upon them. On his travels he would inspect the horses drawing a stagecoach, and if one of them was suffering he would order the coachman to see the animal was attended to.

## Humanity Dick

It was not until 12 years after Erskine's attempt, in June 1821, that Martin presented a Bill to the Commons, aimed at preventing 'the cruel and improper treatment of cattle', amended to include mares, geldings, mules and asses. The Bill wisely excluded dogs and cats; if they had been included, it would have had less likelihood of being passed. And it was aimed at anyone in charge of animals rather than their owners, providing for such persons to be brought before a justice of the peace or other magistrate.

By this skilful presentation, the Bill was passed by 48 votes to 16. Although it was defeated in the Lords, it was passed by both houses the following year and received royal assent in July 1822.

It became the first national law anywhere in the world, passed by a democratically elected legislature, which dealt specifically and entirely with cruelty to animals. It soon became known as 'Martin's Act'. As a result of his humanitarian ideals and campaign for animal rights, Martin was nicknamed 'Humanity Dick', probably by his friend, King George IV.

The first hurdle had at last been cleared. But the question remained, would the new law be effective, and would magistrates risk unpopularity by sentencing offenders ?

Martin and Erskine often reprimanded people they saw beating their horses, and were said to have instilled fear into the hearts of London's cabmen and carters. Not surprising, it was Richard Martin who brought the first prosecution under the law when he charged a costermonger called Bill Burns with cruelty to his donkey.

At the trial it seemed the magistrate was about to dismiss the charge, so Martin rushed outside and brought in the donkey for all to see its wounds. There was no option but to find the man guilty. The case was widely talked of and even gave rise to a popular song:

> If I had a donkey wot wouldn't go,
> D'ye think I'd wollop him? No, no, no!
> By gentle means I'd try, d'ye see,
> Because I hate all cruelty.
> If all had been like me, in fact
> there'd ha' been no occasion for Martin's Act.

On another occasion he prosecuted a cabman for flogging his horse in Cheapside. But when Martin discovered the man had just got his job after being out of work for some months, he unsuccessfully tried to get the case withdrawn. The magistrate fixed the penalty at the minimum of ten shillings, which Martin paid himself. This was a gesture he frequently made, as he preferred to educate the poor rather than punish them.

Between 1822 and 1826 Martin presented a series of Bills in the Commons intended to extend the terms of his original Act. His main targets were bull-baiting, slaughterhouse conditions and the protection of cats and dogs, which were not previously included. But without the skilled support of Lord Erskine, who died in 1823, and with opposition in the Commons from Sir Robert Peel, his efforts were defeated.

Furthermore, Martin lost his seat in the Commons in 1826 when his opponents protested about what appeared to have been a more than usually disorderly Irish election. (It was said that some of Martin's supporters had voted twice.) Martin was a flamboyant, witty figure, quick-tempered yet kind. Weighed down by debts, inherited with his estates, he fled to Boulogne where he died as a refugee in 1834.

**Arthur Broome**

Outside parliament other moves were afoot to support the new law and bring pressure to bear on all sections of society. An attempt had been made in Liverpool as early as 1809 to form a society for the prevention of cruelty to animals, but it was short-lived.

The idea was resurrected in 1822 by the Rev Arthur Broome, of St. Mary's Church, Bromley-by-Bow, East London. Broome, an ordained Church of England clergyman, was a graduate of Balliol College, Oxford, and became vicar of St Mary's in 1820. He urged the formation of a society that would uphold the terms of Martin's Act and work for the rights of animals. He first floated the idea in an advertisement in the John Bull magazine (1822). Though nothing came of this move, Broome persisted with his efforts. He employed a man, Charles Wheeler, to watch for cases of cruelty which could be prosecuted under the Act, paying him out of his own pocket.

The following year he published a tract by Henry Primatt, *A Dissertation on the Duty of Mercy and Sin of Cruelty to Brute Animals*. A footnote was added to the effect that profits arising from sales would be given to the Society for Cruelty to Animals, even though this was not yet in existence.

Broome's second attempt to form a society was successful. Several distinguished gentlemen met at Old Slaughter's Coffee House in St. Martin's Lane, Westminster, in June 1824. They included Sir Thomas Foxwell Buxton MP, a well-known Quaker and a member of the Clapham Sect, as chairman, three clergymen, five MPs (including Wilberforce, also of the Clapham Sect, and Martin) and a Jewish man called Lewis Gompertz.

The minutes of the meeting do not specifically name the society, but describe it as 'instituted for the purpose for preventing cruelty to animals'. The prime aim should be, Martin stressed, 'to alter the moral feelings of the country'; he felt it should not become known as a prosecuting society.

Broome, the moving spirit behind the meeting, was appointed Secretary and in 1824 gave up his living in order to devote himself full-time to the work. Two committees were set up, one to 'superintend the publication of tracts, sermons and similar modes of influencing public opinions', and the other 'to adopt measures for inspecting the markets and streets of the Metropolis, the slaughterhouses, the conduct of coachmen etc.'.

Within four days of that first meeting, Broome gathered the publications committee together to make a start. A tract on *Cruelty to Brutes* (about bull-baiting) was written by a Mrs Hall and published later that year, and there is a record of a £50 donation which presumably covered the tracts put out by the society.

**Debts**
Initially, the society was funded by donations and by Broome himself (although he was not wealthy). By January 1826, however, the society had debts amounting to £300 – it may be that Broome was financially inept – and the idea of closing the work was discussed. Despite receiving a £100 legacy, Broome was thrown into prison for the society's remaining debts. He was later rescued by Martin (himself in debt) and Gompertz.

When Broome resigned in 1828 he was succeeded by Gompertz. A committee minute indicates that Broome had not been attending meetings nor looking to the duties of his office, possibly despondent because of the society's financial problems. Nevertheless, the committee respected the man and appeared sorry to see him go.

Under Broome, the society had proved a success. A number of tracts were published and Charles Wheeler continued as an inspector to gather evidence. An assistant inspector was appointed, and the two of them appear to have been effective – in the first six months of 1824 they brought 63 offenders to court, and gained nearly 150 prosecutions before the end of the year.

In 1832, however, there was a disagreement between some committee members and secretary Gompertz, probably because they believed his ideas to be rather extreme. The committee finally resolved that 'the proceedings of this society are entirely based on the Christian faith and on Christian principles', which led Gompertz – a practising Jew – to resign. He continued to fight for animal causes; he founded the Animals' Friend Society, and in 1852 published a tract attacking cruelties to horses and cattle, hunting, vivisection and the 'barbarity of whale fishing'.

By this time, the character of the society had changed. Martin, Wilberforce and Buxton were no longer involved, and aristocratic patrons of the SPCA were exercising more influence. Although Martin was no longer an MP he continued to use his influence for the good of the cause. Broome continued to take an interest in the Society until his death in 1837, though he does not appear to have attended any more meetings.

Others in parliament took up the cause of animal welfare as the climate of opinion gradually turned in favour of further legislation. The first successful Bill since Martin's Act was passed in 1835, which increased protection by including bulls and domestic animals in its terms. It also improved the conditions in slaughter houses and, in theory, put an end to bull-baiting and cockfighting.

During these years the Society was able to encourage the spread of the animal welfare movement overseas. In 1834 a member of the committee influenced the starting of a French society, and a German work was begun in Stuttgart in 1837. Both the Dutch and Belgium governments passed similar laws as a result of an approach from the SPCA. Henry Bergh, who founded the New York SPCA in 1866, did so after being enthused by a meeting with the RSPCA's Chief Secretary in London.

The Society's public image was tremendously helped when it received royal support, by way of the patronage of the Duchess of Kent and the Princess Victoria. In 1840, after her accession to the throne, Queen Victoria granted the prefix 'Royal' to the Society – now the Royal Society for the Prevention of Cruelty to Animals – thereby marking the final arrival of animal welfare as an entirely respectable concern.

One further creditable development is worthy of mention. As a consequence of the founding of the SPCA in New York, a Society for the Prevention of Cruelty to Children was also formed in that city. A similar organization was started in England, under the influence of the society's chief secretary and the RSPCA committee. The London Society for the Prevention of Cruelty to Children was founded in 1884, proposed by Lord Shaftesbury. Since then, there has been a long and happy co-operation between the RCPCA and the NSPCC.

The credit for founding the RSPCA appears to be shared between the two men who persisted in their efforts when everything seemed stacked against them. Both Broome and Martin, in their different ways, greatly contributed to establishing the world's first animal welfare society, the one complementing the work of the other.

But there is a committee record that refers to Broome as 'the benevolent Founder of the Society', so it seems he should be given the credit.

### AIMS OF THE RSPCA

The objects of this Charity are to promote kindness and to prevent or suppress cruelty to animals and to do such lawful acts as the Society may consider to be conducive or incidental to the attainment of those objects. The twin policies of humane education and enforcement of animal protection law are the same today as when the Society was first established in 1824.

## ST CHRISTOPHER'S HOSPICE (1967)
### Dr Cicely Saunders (born 1918)

St Christopher's Hospice in south-east London is probably the best-known of all hospices in England. It is acknowledged to be in the vanguard of the modern hospice movement. Founded by Dr Cicely Saunders, it provides skilled and compassionate medical care for patients dying from advanced incurable diseases and motor neurone disease. Dr Saunders has redefined what hospice care can mean. Her work has proved to be the starting point of a totally new approach to the terminally ill, and many other hospices have taken up her ideas.

The term 'hospice' comes from the Latin *hospes*, which means guest or host, and was linked to the idea of giving hospitality. It eventually came to refer to the building where hospitality was given to pilgrims and travellers.

The first hospices can be traced back as far as the 4th century and the beginnings of Eastern monasticism. It was the monks who created a special form of Christian hospitality – the almshouse or hospice, attached to monasteries along the chief pilgrim routes.

### Hostel of God

The modern hospice movement, however, did not begin to blossom until the 19th century. One of the first homes in Britain to make provision especially for the dying was the National Free Home for the Dying, or the Hostel of God, on Clapham Common, south London. It was launched on Christmas Eve 1891, following a letter to *The Times* written by banker William Hoare on behalf of St James' Servants of the Poor.

From 1895 the hostel was staffed by Anglican nuns from the Order of St Margaret, East Grinstead. In 1977 a new management team brought in state-trained nurses and changed the name to Trinity Hospice. Today the patients are cared for by some 100 staff, supported by a home care team and social workers.

In the East End of London, Roman Catholic Sisters of Charity from Dublin started another work in the 1890s. Visiting the poor and the sick in their homes, they realised the need for a hostel in which to care for the dying. They started to pray for a suitable house in Hackney. Their faith was rewarded when a generous Jewish lady, who wished to remain anonymous, bought a villa for them, the very house for which they had prayed.

## Hospice Movement

By the 7th-8th centuries there were hospices in Rome, erected for pilgrims visiting the tomb of St Peter. They offered rest and shelter, but no medical assistance; whilst no care was given to the sick, minor cuts and sores were treated. As time went on, however, it was inevitable that proper treatment should be offered to those who were taken ill on their journey.

In Britain, the hospice movement flourished in medieval times, between 925-1170. A hospice was built in York in 925 and two others were established by Saxon bishops, until there were some 750 of these charitable institutions, including monasteries and friaries.

The early hospice movement reached its zenith in Europe at the time of the Crusades, when thousands of pilgrims were on the move across the Continent. Launched by Pope Urban in 1095, the aim of the Crusades was to recover the Holy Land from the 'infidels'. The first hospital for sick and dying pilgrims was opened in Jerusalem around 1100 by the Knights of St John, and others were set up at Acre, Tyre and on the island of Cyprus.

From the 15th century the hospice went into decline; pilgrimages became less fashionable and pilgrims were usually labelled as 'vagrants'. The hospice in England was replaced by the workhouse and the charity ward, though some religious groups such as the Benedictines and Augustinians maintained care for the dying.

St Joseph's Home was opened in 1905 when two patients dying of tuberculosis were received into care. Supported by four local doctors, the work quickly expanded and within two years offered 29 beds and two cots for children. The modern hospice of St Joseph's is still in Mare Street, and cares for the dying of any creed or race.

Although these hospices were providing high quality care, no in-depth research had been carried out into the needs of terminally ill people. Doctors thought only in terms of curing the sick and not about treating the dying, who were often left alone and in constant pain. Dr Cicely Saunders was struck by this failing in hospital care, and came to believe that care of the dying must consider the whole person and not simply aim to relieve pain.

## Determined to Serve

Cicely Saunders was born into a well-to-do but unhappy home, and eventually her parents separated. At her boarding school she became a shy and sensitive pupil, but sang in the chapel choir and was chosen as head of house. Perhaps it was her childhood experiences that gave her a sympathy for people in need; she had wanted to become a nurse, but was discouraged by her parents. Despite this opposition, she was subsequently able to take up her first love, though her medical career started somewhat later in life.

After leaving Roedean School, Cicely entered Oxford University but left after one term to do something more practical and useful. The war against Germany had broken out when she moved to London in 1940 in order to train as a nurse at St Thomas' Hospital. Her time at St Thomas' was a success; she was a popular student and showed she had the makings of an excellent nurse. Qualifying with high honours, she gained a Silver Medal Honours Certificate and the future seemed to hold bright prospects for her.

However, dogged by back trouble – she had a congenital curvature of the spine – she was forced to leave the profession, and so returned to Oxford to qualify as an almoner (now known as medical social workers). Despite time off for an operation, she completed her degree and also gained a Diploma in Public and Social Administration.

As a teenager Cicely had described herself as an atheist, but at Oxford she returned to the religion of her childhood and began attending church. Challenged by the writings of Archbishop William Temple and C S Lewis, and befriended by a group of Christians, she began to yearn for what she called a 'real conversion'.

Her search ended in the summer of 1945 while on holiday in Cornwall. It was, she said, 'as if a switch had been flipped'. She realised that God had forgiven her sins and that she had been reconciled to him. From that moment she was determined to serve God in whatever way he would lead her.

## Cancer Patients

After graduating in 1947 she returned to St Thomas' Hospital, this time as an assistant almoner with the Northcote Trust, which specialised in caring for cancer patients. Still unsure about her real call, she continued praying and waiting for two years. It was her friendship with one of her first patients that provided the answer.

David Tasma was a Polish Jew and an agnostic. He had escaped from the Warsaw ghetto and found his way to England. When Cicely met him, he was dying of an inoperable cancer, in great pain and desperately lonely. She took a special interest in him, and a warm friendship developed during the remaining few months he had to live.

They frequently discussed what could be done for other people suffering as David did, and Cicely shared with him her thoughts about the need for a home where such people could be cared for. Ready to share her faith with him, she offered to read the Bible to him. 'No thank you, I only want what is in your mind and in your heart.' Just before he died, David made his peace with God.

In his will David made provision for Cicely to receive £500, all he possessed, with which to start her home for the dying, suggesting to her, 'I'll be a window in your home.'

Cicely's friendship with David Tasma underlined the need for a radical change in caring for the terminally ill. Relieving constant pain was not enough; dying people had spiritual, emotional and social needs as well. The money from David meant that the idea of a hospice could take a more definite form.

### Vocation to the Dying

For further experience Cicely volunteered to help at St Luke's Hospice, a home for the dying in Bayswater, London. She worked in her spare time as a Sister, and this gave her valuable insights into treatment of the incurably ill. Previously, she had been used to seeing patients dosed with drugs to reduce their pain, but here the drugs were given at regular

intervals before a patient's pain became intense. This was a new idea to her, and she later adopted this method herself.

Now certain that her vocation was to the dying, Cicely followed a surgeon's advice and began to study to become a doctor. She was 33 years old. When she qualified in 1957, she followed this by taking up a research fellowship at St Mary's Hospital, Paddington, working on pain in the terminally ill.

Part of her time was spent at St Joseph's Hospice in the East End, where she could care for patients and evaluate drug use.

DAME CICELEY SAUNDERS

She also had full clinical care of 45 beds, and was able to use the pain control technique she had learned at St Luke's. Nuns and doctors alike were impressed with her results. The patients' pain could now be eased without making them comatose, leaving them alert, serene and happy.

Her research reinforced her conviction that there was a better way to care for the dying. In the right setting, with the right care, she believed she could offer her patients a 'good death'.

As the project, she believed, was of God, then money would be no problem. So she wrote in her Bible, 'Apart from him I can do nothing. All the fruit that I ever bear comes wholly from his life within me.'

For a while Cicely could not make up her mind about her aims : were they medical or spiritual? As a Christian, she wanted patients to come to the Lord; but she was also deeply aware of the need to provide the right kind of medical treatment. She finally resolved the tension with a decision to provide medical care, but in a Christian context.

Although nourished during her early Christian life in the evangelical tradition, when she opened her hospice the spiritual ethos was more broadly-based: it was to be an undenominational community.

### A Place for Travellers
Cicely circulated her ideas among a number of influential Church and medical people, who rallied to her support. She began fund-raising in earnest, and by 1961 about a third of the necessary amount of money had been received. A site was discovered in Sydenham, south-east London, and the building work started in 1965. It was completed in two years, and was opened on 24 July 1967 by Princess Alexandra.

The name, St Christopher's, came as a result of a chat with a patient who became a personal friend. 'A place for travellers?' she had remarked. 'Then it will have to be St Christopher's, won't it?'

Cicely became the first person to introduce priorities in nursing the dying. Her first aim is to relieve the distress sometimes experienced by patients dying of cancer or other incurable diseases. At the same time, she intends to provide all-round care, allowing them to live out their last days in their own way.

She also makes the hospice as much like a home as possible, so that patients can feel at ease. They are encouraged to bring some of their own personal belongings with them, and visitors are allowed to drop in almost at any time. Families, in fact, are involved at all stages, and counselling services are available following a bereavement.

The Christian ethos of the hospice is maintained not in an overt manner, but by the loving care and attention invested by the staff. Consideration is given to small details that help make the patients' stay at St Christopher's more relaxing – fresh flowers, favourite food, time to stop for a chat.

Central to life at the hospice is the chapel. There are daily prayers in the chapel and Communion twice a week, as well as a Roman Catholic mass.

For Cicely, the spiritual needs of the dying are summed up in Christ's words in the Garden of Gethsemane: 'Stay here and keep watch with me.' At St Christopher's no one dies alone; 'watching' means above all just being there.

When Cicely built St Christopher's she did not realise she was starting a new movement. But now others have followed her ideas, and today she is recognised as the founder of the modern hospice movement. She has been awarded many honours, and in 1980 the Queen made her a Dame of the British Empire.

Perhaps the extent of Cicely's success can be appreciated from the words of an elderly Christian lady who, just prior to her death, said of St Christopher's, 'The nurses are so kind here – it's just like heaven.'

---

## AIMS OF ST CHRISTOPHER'S HOSPICE

St Christopher's exists to provide skilled and compassionate palliative care of the highest quality.

*Beliefs*

* To affirm life; not to hasten death but to regard death as a normal process.

* To offer relief from pain and other distressing symptoms.

* To help patients with strong and unfamiliar emotions. To assist them to explore meaning, purpose and belief in their lives. To help them to reconcile and heal relationships and complete important personal tasks.

* To offer a support system for family and friends during the patient's illness and in bereavement.

# SANDES SOLDIERS' AND AIRMEN'S CENTRES (1869)
## Elise Sandes (1851-1934)

During the second half of the 19th century, Christians began to take an increasing interest in the condition of British servicemen. In the 1850s, accounts of the Crimean War and the Indian Mutiny brought home to the British public not only the dangers of battle, but also the terrible conditions under which these men lived.

The situation was further highlighted by the publication of a biography by Catherine Marsh, *The Memorials of Hedley Vicars*, a Christian officer killed in the Crimea. More than anything else, it brought home the difficulties and temptations endured by servicemen away from home, and led to the feeling that something should be done for them.

One of the main problems facing soldiers was the lack of suitable recreational facilities. Some of the larger camps could boast a library and games rooms, but many others provided only a 'wet canteen' where drinking alcohol was the only means of relaxation. Young recruits were especially tempted by the ready availability of drink. Often, unscrupulous landlords opened up public houses of the worst description close to the camps, with a highly demoralising effect upon the men.

A number of private individuals began to show a concern for soldiers, and a start was made on opening soldiers' institutes outside army barracks. Prominent among them were several Christian ladies who came from well-to-do families. With time on their hands, they could afford to become involved in charitable works, though convention would often have dictated otherwise. They became 'mother' to many tough, foul-mouthed, often drunken men whose only soft spot was the thought of a mother back home who wept and prayed for them.

The first alternative leisure-time facilities for soldiers in England were institutes opened in 1858, at Shorncliffe (Essex) and Portsmouth. In 1862, at the suggestion of the Rev William Pennefather of Mildmay, Mrs Louisa Daniell, the widow of an army officer, opened an institute at Aldershot, where a new base for 15,000 men had recently been established. It provided a dining room, recreation and classrooms, and accommodation for men on leave. When she died in 1871 the work was carried on by her daughter, who opened other branches throughout the country.

A Home was opened by Alice Todd near the Gallowgate Barracks,

Glasgow, to provide soldiers with an alternative to the public house. After her marriage she continued her efforts, and as Mrs Todd Osbourne of the Mission to Mediterranean Garrisons (afterwards the Mission to Military Garrisons), founded in 1883, she went on to open a total of 60 homes for servicemen.

The situation facing soldiers became known to the War Office when a report to the Secretary of War was published in 1862. It warned of the increasing number of public houses and music halls of ill-repute being set up near army camps. The army authorities responded by opening special institutes outside the barracks at Aldershot and Portsmouth.

## Ireland

At this time there were many British troops stationed in Ireland which, under the Act of Union (1800) had been made part of the United Kingdom. (The division into Northern Ireland and Eire did not take place until 1922.) To the soldiers, Ireland was a 'foreign' country where many of the people seemed unfriendly – certainly in the years after the great potato famine – and the language sounded strange. Many of the men felt isolated and far away from home.

In the town of Tralee, on the south-west coast of Ireland, a young woman of aristocratic background rented a small terraced house in 1869 and opened what was to be the first of more than 60 Sandes Homes. Elise Sandes took a personal interest in her soldiers, and corresponded with them when they were posted away. She adapted ordinary houses to suit local needs, and tried to make them a 'home from home'. Not only were soldiers given a chance to escape the temptations of alcohol in the local bar, but they were also enabled to hear the claims of the gospel.

Elizabeth Sandes – it was her French teacher who gave her the name Elise, which she kept – was born into a well-to-do landowning family. She lived with her parents, brothers and sisters in an imposing house called Oak Villa on the outskirts of Tralee (Kerry). Small and slight for her years, Elise was often ill and needed nursing, a weakness that remained with her throughout her adult life.

As a girl, Elise had a yearning to know peace with God and she came to faith in the wake of the 1859 Ulster Revival. It happened at a special children's meeting at her local Presbyterian Church.

Her father, who also became a believer about the same time, confided to her, 'My prayer for you is that you may lead other young girls to the Saviour.' Elise, though timid and shy, felt she must talk to others about Jesus, but found difficulty in what to say. 'Don't be thinking about yourself or about the words you use', her father taught her. 'God has promised that his Holy Spirit will give you the right words, and that he will bless them.'

At the age of thirteen she was sent to a private school at Bray, south of Dublin. She realised that in the close confines of a school, if she were to help others then she must at least live up to the same standard. As she prayed for opportunities to witness, she asked God to give her the right words to speak. In this way she managed to talk to her school friends about Jesus and several of them became Christians.

## The Future

News of her father's sudden death was brought to her at school by sixteen-year-old Marie Fry, who lived nearby in Bray. Despite her great sense of loss, Elise found comfort in her new friendship with Marie. They used to meet on the rocks of Dublin Bay and read their Bibles, pray and discuss what God might have them to do in the future. Perhaps, they thought, God might give them a work together, and considered the possibility of evangelism among shop girls.

Quietly, however, a work among soldiers began to unfold itself. Marie had begun to take a prayerful interest in the garrisons stationed in Dublin, and the recently-formed Royal Irish Constabulary. Though convention did not allow any personal contact, Marie was able to invite some of the men to gospel meetings. Afterwards, she followed them up by letters and prayer.

She did, however, manage to invite some of the young drummer boys – each regiment contained a small number of them – to her home. She taught them hymns, and they talked about the Bible and its message. Elise at first frowned upon the idea, but she was soon won round.

When one of the drummer boys visited Tralee, Elise was able to contact him and invite him to a gospel meeting. The boy brought another drummer boy with him, the only Christian soldier in Tralee barracks. Elise's mother invited them back to Oak Villas, which proved to be the first of many visits paid by soldiers from the Tralee barracks to the Sandes' home.

When Elise discovered that some of the drummer boys from the barracks could neither read nor write, she agreed to give them lessons at her home. One of her text books was the Bible, and as a result two of the boys learned to read and to love the Lord too.

## Life Work

As the small group met regularly for Bible study and prayer, the numbers attending the meetings grew, as did their faith and enthusiasm for the Lord. Elise realised that although she was only a girl of 19, she was actually leading and speaking at meetings for men, and that this was the life work which God had given her.

When the 89th Regiment left Tralee, Elise kept in contact with her soldier friends by writing them long letters, a practice she maintained all her life. They were replaced by the 65th Regiment, which allowed further opportunities for gospel outreach. She and her mother visited the barracks and invited men to their home. Though diffident at first, the ice was eventually broken. Before long, it was necessary to rent premises in the town of Tralee to allow space for bigger meetings.

Having gathered these men together in spite of dif-

### Mission to Military Garrisons

The MMG exists to serve British Armed Forces personnel and their families by providing tea rooms and, in some cases, shops in locations which tend to be isolated. By offering this service, the Mission is able to minister to the moral, physical and spiritual needs of its patrons, and to assist the Service Chaplains in their role.

The Mission was founded in 1883 by Mrs Alice Todd Osbourne as the Mission to Mediterranean Garrisons. Alice was born into an army family, and her father and two of her uncles were officers in the Scots Greys. Knowing the rigours of army life and the scourge of alcohol, she was especially aware that there were no attractive places for soldiers to go when off duty.

To introduce men to the Lord, she started Bible classes in the barracks at Gallowgate, Glasgow, and rented a small house nearby where they could find a haven from 'the bar'. When the Regiment moved to new barracks in Maryhill, she started the first Soldiers' Home with the help of a Mrs Allen, whose husband was a shipping magnate.

In due course the Regiment moved to Gibraltar, where at the request of the men she opened a tea room. Similarly, when they moved to Cyprus and then Egypt, the men asked her to open more rooms. Over the years, more than 50 homes have been opened overseas and ten in the UK. During World War II there were 19 Homes in operation, mostly in the Middle East.

Now with reductions in the Armed Forces, there are not so many openings, but there are Centres (as they are now called) in Ascension, Benbecula, Cyprus, the Falkland Islands and London (Mill Hill).

ficulties, she grew discouraged because she could not see any results for her efforts. Perhaps for a girl of nineteen the task was too much, she thought. Driven to her knees, she admitted to God her own limitations and inexperience, and asked should she give up the work. If she did, many of the men would return to their old ways, she felt.

Finally Elise asked God for a token – would he save one soldier, quickly, if she was to go on with the work? Within a short time not one, but three men came out for Christ. Never again, she vowed, would she doubt that this was the work God had for her.

It was perhaps the death of her friend Marie, at Bray, that triggered off her thoughts. She realised that there were at least 25,000 soldiers in Ireland, most of them stationed in lonely places, and not one Soldiers' Home. Few people were interested in trying to help, and even fewer had approved of Marie's efforts. But it could be that already there was the germ of an idea in Elise's mind.

## Soldiers' Home

Some of the Christian men from the 89th Regiment had been posted to Cork, on the south coast, and Elise visited them to help get a prayer meeting started. Although they found a room for prayer, there was nowhere for the men to go in the evenings.

As she remembered how her own home had been used to attract men away from the wet canteens and public houses, the idea of a home for soldiers began to take shape. In Cork, she shared with the men her vision for setting up a Soldiers' Home, and they began to pray that God would give them a place. An unexpected gift of £16 – a substantial sum of money in those days – proved to be the first instalment of thousands of pounds God was going to send her.

It was not until two years later, in 1877, that the money for a home was forthcoming. A retired naval officer, visiting Oak Villas, bought the lease on a house in King Street for her use. Enough money came in to furnish the Home, which had a coffee room, a reading room and a meeting room, plus a sitting room and bedrooms. There was also accommodation for Elise and a helper, a Miss Wilkinson, who was to supervise the work.

Many of the men had longed for a Home, and now their wish was fulfilled. The two young ladies had a rough crowd to deal with, but were determined to make the house a proper home. They determined not to post strict notices around the building, but expected the men to treat it as their home. The only rule they had was to make the men welcome.

It was Miss Wilkinson who pointed out the need of a mother for the Home, and suggested Mrs Sandes. 'I'll be the mother,' replied Elise mischievously. 'But you're only 26 – not much older than most of the men. How can you be their mother ?' came back the reply. 'You'll see,' retorted Elise. 'I've prayed about it and am sure this is the way to reach them.'

So it was that Elise became 'mother'. The men soon adopted her as their 'mother' and they frequently looked to her for counsel and advice. And when they wrote to her, many of them addressed her by her new title.

Elise, who had never enjoyed good health at the best of times, found the work in Cork very demanding. After a few months she was taken ill; as she recovered, her companion's health also broke and she had to give up the work. Other helpers came to her aid; one of them, Mary Stokes, was stricken with scarlet fever and died shortly afterwards.

## Funds

Despite setbacks, the work grew and plans were made to build a larger Home to accommodate the many men she often had to turn away. Money from Ireland for the project seemed in short supply, and on the advice of a friend Elise went to London to try and raise further funds.

ELISE SANDES

She had letters of introduction to a number of wealthy men, and after six weeks, and with several other visits, she was able to raise all the money needed for the Home.

The year 1886 was a crisis year for Elise. She had a serious attack of rheumatic fever, and was advised by the doctor to give up her work. But there was much to be done, and she prayed that God would restore her to health, as she believed he would. In the New Year her strength gradually began to return, and despite an attack of scarlet fever she came through.

Following several pressing invitations, Elise travelled to Belfast, to explore the possibility of setting up another Home. She felt rather strange moving to a city in the North, but received a warm reception and was able to gain public support for the project. Money and workers came in, and a Home was opened in 1891 opposite the entrance to the Victoria Barracks.

With responsibility for three centres, Elise had less and less time for her soldiers. She became more of an administrator, rather than personally serving the soldiers. Anxious to continue her letter writing, she took up a friend's suggestion that she produce a printed letter with all the news on it, and simply added a personal note on the end. The newsletter idea developed and in 1887 it began to appear monthly as *Our Soldiers' Magazine*, today called *Forward*.

Over the next few years the work expanded. Further Homes were opened along the south coast of Ireland and in other parts of the country. For the first time a Home opened in the port of Queenstown (now called Cobh) was also used by sailors. The building was formerly a public house, opposite the landing stage where ships from abroad tied up.

Each Home was an answer to prayer and the outcome of hard work, and in some cases was a response to an appeal from soldiers themselves. In each instance, the necessary money came in. Although Elise never felt comfortable dealing with matters of finance, she trusted God for each project and found that believers gave what was needed.

At Dublin, Elise took over the Parkgates Home and soon became a familiar figure on the streets and quays. Her search was for drunks – for whom she had a great heart of compassion – to bring them into the Home.

## India

In 1895 a cheque for £600 from an unknown supporter in India drew Elise's attention to the needs of soldiers on the sub-continent. The soldiers' barracks were without proper recreational facilities, and the men had nowhere to go to escape the oppressive heat when on leave. There were numerous prayer rooms set up for Christians at several military camps, provided under the support of W. B. Harington, a Christian construction engineer. But something more was needed for the ordinary soldier.

Elise sent one of her workers to India to set up a Home at Rawalpindi

(Pakistan), as well as a 'furlough' house at Murree in the cool hill country. Further Homes were established, including one at Quetta in Baluchistan, destroyed in an earthquake in 1934.

During the Boer War (1899-1902) the Soldiers' Christian Association (SCA) set up a number of temporary Homes in tents, which did stalwart work among the soldiers. The success of the SCA canvas homes in South Africa gave Elise the idea of setting up similar tent Homes in Ireland for the weeks when the troops were on their summer exercises. Large marquees were hired to provide the customary needs, and although the venture was bigger than she had visualised, she overcame the difficulties involved.

The onset of the First World War placed even greater demands upon the Homes, which had to be reorganised and enlarged. Elise now had more correspondence to deal with, for she also wrote to the families of men killed in the fighting.

After the War, Ireland was torn by political troubles which led to the north-south division. As British troops were pulled out of the South, Elise was forced to close down 13 of her Homes.

Over the years Sandes has learned to adapt to changing circumstances. This has involved closing down Homes and opening up new ones in garrison towns and camps as far afield as Jamaica, Iceland and Borneo.

### Letter to Elise

A letter written to Elise Sandes a few days before the Relief of Ladysmith (1900), during the Boer War, by one of her soldier boys who lost his life in the fighting, shows how much her Homes meant to him:

*Dear Mother,*
*I know full well that your great heart of love will rejoice to hear how God is leading your once prodigal boy. His love to me is more than tongue can tell. He is with me, and Jesus with me is the secret of all joy – of everything. He makes the darkest valley light.*

*God is answering our prayers, for we have glorious times here in Natal. Sinners and backsliders are returning to God. So amidst all the horrors of war, there is joy in heaven over souls saved. Imagine my delight when a few days ago I met two old folk who reminded me of the dear old Cork Home, which to me is the dearest, sweetest place on earth.*

*I expect to be fighting in a few days. God bless you! I would like to see you again, Mother, but if I see the King in his beauty first, I shall be watching for you at the gate.*

In 1922 Elise herself was forced to move, and made her home at
Ballykinlar (Co Down), Northern Ireland, where she continued her
work. It was a blow from which she never fully recovered. A serious
illness forced her more and more to hand over the work to another, and
she often longed to 'go home'. When she died in August 1934, the Last
Post was sounded at the barracks, and she was buried with full military
honours.

Since her death the work has continued to develop, always keeping
abreast of the times. In 1938 the first Sandes Home for airmen was
opened at Aldergrove, near Belfast. The Indian Homes were closed
down in 1947 when the nation gained its independence and the army left
for Britain.

Over the years other Homes have come and gone, and seven centres
(as they are now called) remain. The Ballykinlar centre stands as a
testimony to the dedication of the staff, for in 1974 it was completely
destroyed by an IRA bomb which killed two soldiers and injured 31
others.

A new centre has arisen from the ashes, built within the garrison
compound. It is this sort of determination that signifies the intention of
Sandes to maintain their long-standing tradition of selfless service in the
cause of the gospel.

## MISSION STATEMENT OF SANDES

### Soldiers' and Airmen's Centres

To lead service men and women and their families to trust in
Christ for salvation;
to build up believers to Christian maturity;
to offer warm friendship in the warmth of a Christian home.

## THE SHAFTESBURY SOCIETY (1844)
### Thomas Cranfield (c1760-1835?), John Pounds (1776-1839)

Education was a privilege enjoyed almost exclusively by the rich until the charity school movement began towards the close of the 17th century. Although primarily set up to teach the Protestant religion, this aim was possible only after children had first learned to read. It was therefore essential to provide an elementary secular education as well as religious instruction. As a result, charity schools were the first to provide working class children with a system of education.

Charity schools were started by Dr Thomas Bray under the umbrella of the Society for the Promotion of Christian Knowledge, founded in 1698. The purpose was to promote the spread of Christian knowledge through the distribution of Bibles and tracts, and by founding schools where the poor could be taught to read. The movement spread to Scotland and was taken up by the General Assembly of the Presbyterian Church.

During the 18th century child labour was in great demand. Many children were forced to work a six-day-week, and often parents could not afford to release their children to attend school. As charity schools declined towards the end of the century, Sunday Schools provided an education for these children on their one day off work. Schools of industry were also started for children not in employment, to give them a basic education and teach them a trade.

Efforts were made in parliament in 1807 to introduce elementary education on the rates, but Samuel Whitbread's Parochial Schools Bill was rejected by the House of Lords. The churches, however, were more successful, and two societies were established to provide day schools in urban areas for the poorer classes. The British and Foreign Schools Society (1808) gave interdenominational teaching in schools attached to Nonconformist churches. Not to be left behind, in 1811 the National Society was established to promote the principles of the Established Church in Anglican schools.

Despite the growth of the voluntary schools, many children remained outside the system. The church schools did not cater for the large number of destitute children – usually dirty, verminous and ill-clothed – who roamed the streets of our large cities and industrial towns.

Often thrown out of their homes by callous parents, these children slept in the open, and survived by selling matches, begging or stealing.

It was for street urchins such as these that ragged schools were started. Staffed mainly by evangelical Christians, they offered not only an elementary education but also provided urgently needed welfare services.

### Ragged Children

Although John Pounds is usually acknowledged as the founder of the ragged school movement, a major contribution was also made by Thomas Cranfield of Camberwell, London. It was the work of both these men that subsequently led in 1844 to the foundation of the Ragged School Union, later to become known as the Shaftesbury Society.

Cranfield was brought up in Camberwell, and as a boy was apprenticed to a tailor. But he was rather wild and rebellious, and ran away from home to join the army. After service in Gibraltar, he came back and was reconciled to his father who had regularly prayed for his safe return. To show his gratitude, the young man joined his father in going to church on his first Sunday home, and was soundly converted.

He opened a tailor's shop in Goswell Street in the City. Every day a group of friends gathered together in his living room for prayer and Bible study. In 1791 he moved to Kingsland Road in the East End. Concerned about children too destitute and ragged to attend church, he opened a Sunday School in his home 'to facilitate the spread of the gospel among the poor'.

The numbers at his Sunday School quickly grew to 60 and he was forced to find larger premises. With the work firmly established, he entrusted the school to a group of friends and started another one in Stoke Newington. As the process was repeated, he eventually started 19 Sunday Schools in north London.

Cranfield next turned his thoughts to Southwark, south of the Thames, where the slums were among the worst in the capital. Working among children who were said to be 'unsuitable' for the Sunday Schools, he wrote of the area: 'Men, women, children, asses, pigs and dogs were living together in the same room. Children were in a deplorable condition, half clad in rags and so dirty and unkempt it seemed possible that they had never been washed or combed since birth.'

He opened a voluntary school for boys and girls where he provided them with a basic education. To encourage the children to attend regularly, he offered the gift of a cap for boys and a bonnet for girls. Well aware that the children needed to be clothed and fed, he started a valuable social work that supported both pupils and families. He set up soup kitchens, and distributed bread, rice and coal to needy families. At the age of 70 he began a class for very young children, left in his care while their mothers went to work.

Without being aware of it, Cranfield had pioneered one of the 19th century's most powerful agencies for good, some ten years before John Pounds started his first ragged school.

## Ragged Schools

The credit for founding the ragged school movement, however, is usually given to John Pounds. This is possibly because the methods he evolved were later adopted by others.

John Pounds was born in Portsmouth and was apprenticed at the age of 12 to a shipwright in the royal dockyard. A tall lad, and stronger than his workmates even while still a youth, at the age of 15 he fell into a dry dock and was left permanently crippled. His body was bent and distorted, so that he was only able to do light work. Placed under instruction to a shoemaker in the High Street, a job where he sat down at a bench, when work permitted he often spent time in reading his Bible.

Eventually – in 1803 – he was able to start up his own business as a cobbler in St Mary's Street. It was some years before events unfolded that were to shape his life and lead to the formation of a nationwide movement.

His brother had a large family, including a disabled five-year-old son, born deformed in the ankles and feet. The child had crossed feet, and his scissor gait deformity meant that he could not walk. In 1818 Pounds asked permission to take his nephew into his home, in order to see what he could do for him.

Having learned to face his own disability, he put his cobbling expertise to good use by making the child a pair of wedged shoes. Although at first they caused the boy some pain, Pounds persevered with daily exercises until his nephew was able to walk.

News of this remarkable achievement became known throughout the city. Attracted by the prospect of finding help, a number of parents from the slums of Portsmouth brought their handicapped children to Pounds. Unable to offer much hope, he took them in simply as company for his nephew, and told them stories from his only book, the Bible.

When he realised there were many other needy children in the slums, he started to take them in as well. As his concern for them grew, he went out and around the streets and harbour area in search of homeless children, in order to befriend them, giving out hot baked potatoes to the 'drifters' who slept out on the quayside.

Gathering together a group of about 40 children, including 12 girls, and with an apparent gift for teaching, he started daily classes for them in a room above his shop. In addition to telling Bible stories, he gave them reading lessons using handbills and old school text books, that they might learn to read the Bible for themselves. He taught them simple arithmetic, instructed them in how to cook their own food, mend shoes and make toys. Sometimes he took them out into the countryside around Portsmouth for elementary nature study lessons.

People dubbed his classes as a 'ragged school', which aptly described what he was doing. Ragged schools differed from Sunday Schools in that they did not expect the children to attend washed and clean (Robert Raikes taught his pupils to come with clean hands and faces). For Pounds, however, they were accepted as they were, and so he attracted the neediest group of pupils.

The idea spread to London, where barns, stables and sheds were taken over by voluntary teachers who followed Pounds' example. Some of the first ragged schools were started by missionaries of the London City Mission, who were themselves from the working class. From around 1840 they began to open schools in the East End and other areas of the capital.

### Lord Ashley

About this time, Lord Ashley (who became the Earl of Shaftesbury in 1851) read an advertisement in *The Times* headed 'Ragged Schools'. It was a plea from the teachers of the Field Lane ragged school in Holborn, inviting 'any lady or gentleman willing to assist as teachers' on Sunday and Thursday evenings. Already concerned for the welfare of destitute children, Lord Ashley contacted the teachers and visited the school.

This was one of many visits Ashley paid to some of the worst parts of the capital. Accompanied by a district missionary of the London City Mission, he toured the slums to find out the dreadful facts for himself, even though the stench of the places turned his stomach. Throughout his early visits his identity went unknown; and he never received an insult as he listened to the grievances recounted by the East Enders.

**Earl of Shaftesbury (1801-1885)**

Born Anthony Ashley Cooper, he succeeded to the title in 1851 on the death of his father, the sixth Earl. As a boy he was deprived of parental affection and was brought up by Maria Millis, a much-loved housekeeper who encouraged the youngster in a love for God.

About the age of 14 he one day witnessed a pauper funeral on Harrow Hill, and was deeply shocked by the drunkenness and profanity of the coffin bearers. It is said that this incident led to his decision to devote his life to serving the poor and oppressed.

As Lord Ashley he entered parliament in 1826 as member for Woodstock, and then for Dorchester in 1830. His first social concern was the treatment of lunatics (1828), followed by efforts to reform the law relating to the employment of workers in mills and factories. In the 1840s he fought to improve the lot of 'climbing boys', to establish lodging houses for poor workers and to improve public health.

A member of the evangelical party of the Church of England, he supported a wide variety of Christian societies, and was either patron or (vice) president of some 50 missions. The cause dearest to his heart was the ragged school movement, but he was closely involved in the London City Mission, Bible Society, the Cabman's Shelter Fund, the temperance movement, homes for destitute or disabled children, rescue societies, and many others. Frequently he was requested by various Christian bodies to chair their annual meeting, or to allow them to use his good offices as a parliamentarian.

From the autumn of 1884 his health began to fail, and he died 1 October the following year. The poor people of England had lost their staunchest supporter.

Impressed by the fine work being done by the ragged schools, he gave himself to supporting their efforts – by seeking funds from well-to-do benefactors, encouraging the teachers and speaking to the children at their school anniversaries. On one occasion he even stood at the entrance to the House of Commons with a collecting box, for donations for the work.

Soon the movement spread to Scotland, and in 1841 Dr Guthrie (of Edinburgh) and Sheriff Watson (Aberdeen) opened a work north of the border. They provided their pupils with meals as well as giving them an education and industrial training. This was not generally the case in England, though the London City Missionaries made attempts to provide for their starving children.

In 1844, teachers from seven ragged schools banded together to found The Ragged School Union. Its aim was 'to give permanence, regularity and vigour to the existing ragged schools, and to promote the founding of new ones.' Lord Ashley became their first President, and the work of the ragged schools remained his dearest cause until his death in 1885, a commitment noted even by Queen Victoria. Ashley once remarked, 'I would rather be President of the Ragged Schools Union than have the command of armies or wield the destiny of empires.'

**Rapid Growth**

The movement grew rapidly. By 1861 there were some 26,000 children under its care, and similar unions were started in other cities. The union's work was extended in the early 1850s when Lord Ashley persuaded the government to give him two ships, used for teaching destitute boys a trade and for training them for service at sea. He also started a farm for the benefit of poor boys who wished to work on the land.

Despite the good work being done by the ragged schools, it was thwarted by the children's lack of a home. After classes were over, the majority of them had nowhere to sleep, and bedded down under the arches of bridges, in barrels in the markets or under whatever kind of shelter they could find. During the daytime they returned to their usual activities, many of them stealing or living by their wits.

Although the idea of opening children's homes was still in its infancy – George Müller had opened his first home in Bristol in 1836 – Ashley's response was to set up an emigration programme. From 1848, an opportunity was given for destitute children and adults who had fallen into crime to start a new life in Australia, New Zealand and Canada. The scheme was a success, and many letters of gratitude written to Ashley assured him that his assistance had been appreciated.

When the 1870 Education Act was passed providing elementary education for all, there was no further place for ragged schools. They ceased to function and many of them became interdenominational missions providing welfare services.

At the jubilee of The Ragged School Union in 1894, the title was changed to 'The Ragged School Union and Shaftesbury Society', in honour of their former President. In 1944 it became simply 'The Shaftesbury Society'.

The tradition of caring for children is continued through the society's residential schools and holiday centres for the physically handicapped; its housing association provides care homes for the handicapped and sheltered housing for the elderly, and its mission centres in London maintain an outreach into their locality.

In the name of Jesus Christ, the society continues to provide the same high standard of personal care, love and attention that has characterised its work for over 150 years.

---

**STRATEGIC OBJECTIVES OF THE SHAFTESBURY SOCIETY**

To achieve The Society's Strategic Vision, the following key Strategic Objectives have been identified:

Deploy the right number, variety and scope of operational centres.
Provide well-defined models of good practice (the service products).
Secure growing and fruitful links with the Christian community.
Enhance the level of voluntary income.
Achieve the necessary financial reserves.
Achieve consistent standards of quality and practice throughout The Society.
Achieve a high level of staff training and development.
Achieve partnerships where they enable The Society to be more effective.
Secure the right public image.
Secure effective prayer support.

# THOMAS COOK TRAVEL (1841)
## Thomas Cook (1808-1892)

One of the most remarkable social developments to take place over the past 200 years has been that of the annual holiday. A number of factors have given rise to this phenomenon, especially the increase in leisure time and wealth, and improvements in the means of communication. For many people it now stands as the highlight of their year and the focal point of their life.

More than any other, it was Thomas Cook, a Baptist preacher from Melbourne in Derbyshire, who laid the foundation for the modern package holiday business. He pioneered cheap excursions for ordinary people, and by the middle of the 19th century had founded a tourist agency that served as a model for its rivals.

The idea of a holiday, a break from everyday work, was originally linked in the Roman empire to religious festivals. They were 'holy days' – holidays or rest days, when the Romans stopped work to celebrate the heathen deities. For Christians, the most important celebration was the first day of the week. By the beginning of the second century it was widely recognised as the day of worship, when it was known as 'the Lord's Day'.

Towards the end of the century, the writer Tertullian suggested that, like a Roman festival, the first day was almost a holiday. Yet the practice was not established until 321, when the Christian emperor, Constantine, regularised it by law. The name in the Roman empire of the first day of the week was 'the day of the sun', which some Christians began to call 'Sunday'. It was this day that was now officially set aside as a rest day.

The commemoration of the Lord's birth, celebrated on 25 December, is first mentioned in a calendar dated 336, which suggests that it was already the practice of the Roman Church. Good Friday was eventually declared a holy day and, in some sections of the Church, saints' days and the anniversaries of martyrs were later added to the list.

Over the centuries, holy days were not always strictly observed; it often depended upon the prevailing religious climate. By the 18th century, for many working class people – especially those in the new towns thrown up by the onset of the industrial revolution – holy days were like any other day; only the middle and upper classes could afford to take time off.

## Holidays

As social life became increasingly secularised, the idea of holidays became disassociated from religion, a process which has continued to this day. Gradually, they were accepted as a necessity and from the early 1800s some benign employers began to concede the occasional break to their workers. In the second half of the century, the acceptance of a weekly half day holiday, though not in shops and agriculture, marked a further step forward.

The idea of a break from work gathered momentum, and was further strengthened in 1871 by the statutory award of four 'Bank Holidays'; though, with one exception, these were already acknowledged on the days of the great Christian festivals. However, these holidays were no longer regarded as 'religious', but as secular days of leisure. By the end of the century the practice of an annual holiday, in some cases with pay, was beginning to take hold.

Around the same time, a number of villages and towns were beginning to be recognised as places of entertainment. The spa towns, which had so far served as 'holiday resorts' for the well-to-do, were challenged by the new fashion for sea-bathing, a pastime popularised by the Prince of Wales' visits to the small fishing village of Brighthelmstone (Brighton).

While upper and middle class people enjoyed the privilege of trips to spas and seaside resorts, it was the coming of the railways that provided the working classes with their opportunity for travel. The first passenger line, from Liverpool to Manchester, was opened in 1830. By the 1840s most of the main line railways had either been laid or planned, and the idea of reduced fares for special occasions accepted.

Thomas Cook recognised the potential of the railways and began to organise excursions on a commercial basis. His enthusiasm and business acumen stood him in good stead, and he has ever since been recognised as the pioneer of cheap travel.

## Evangelist

Cook was born into a working class family with a Christian background; his grandfather was an evangelical and probably attended the local Baptist Church. After Cook's father died and his mother remarried, the young Thomas was apprenticed at the age of ten to a market gardener. Even at this early stage, he displayed signs of initiative and drive.

His master was unfortunately given to bouts of drunkenness and frequently neglected his business. Thomas, however, took upon himself the responsibility for selling the garden produce in the market and around the streets of Melbourne. Needless to say, he eventually looked around for a new job. At the age of 14 he was further apprenticed, this time to his uncle, John Pegg, a wood-turner. Once again he was faced with the problem of a drunken employer, yet stayed in his position for five years.

These years, nevertheless, proved to be the most formative ones of his life, as he came under the influence of the local Baptist minister, J F Winks. It was probably about this time that Cook became a Christian, and at the age of twenty responded to a call to become an evangelist. As a teenager his chief pastime had been fishing, and sometimes he used to rise at 4 am in order to finish work early and get down to the river. As an evangelist, he became a 'fisher of men'.

Cook appears to have travelled considerable distances on his preaching tours, and in one year (1829) covered 2,692 miles, mostly on foot. When the Baptist Church could no longer afford to pay his salary, he decided to return to his wood-turning and set himself up in his own workshop. In 1832 he moved to Market Harborough where he married 23-year-old Marianne Mason whom he had met while working as an evangelist. They had one son, John Mason, and a daughter, Annie.

**Temperance**
At Market Harborough Cook met the Rev Francis Beardsall who was the local agent for the British and Foreign Temperance Society. Although, like many others of his day, Cook was in the habit of drinking beer, he was persuaded by Beardsall to 'sign the pledge'. (This involved abstaining from the use of spirits, and taking other alcoholic drinks only in moderation.) A year later his wife followed his example, but became a total abstainer; after listening to a teetotal advocate known as 'the Birmingham Blacksmith', Cook took the same step.

With the same zeal he had brought to his evangelism, Cook fought for the temperance cause and became fully involved in the movement. He was appointed secretary of the South Midland Temperance Association and took over the publication side of its work. Opposed by brewers and publicans who sent thugs to break up their meetings, Cook was once felled by the leg bone of a horse, but managed to arrest his attacker and bring him to justice.

In 1840 the newly opened Midland Railway experimented with a half-price excursion from Leicester to Nottingham. Its success persuaded Cook to organise a similar trip the following year in connection with a temperance demonstration. On 5th July 1841 he hired a special train at his own risk, and took 570 passengers from Loughborough to Leicester at a return fare of one shilling each.

Further excursions were arranged and by 1845 he had started to run them as a business proposition. Although other 'pleasure trips' were being arranged up and down the country – nearly 15,000 passengers travelled from London to Brighton over three Easter holidays – it was Cook who became known as 'the pioneer of convenient travel'.

## Great Exhibition

The turning point in his career came when he organised travel to two international exhibitions. The first was the Great Exhibition of 1851, held in Hyde Park, London, when he brought 165,000 excursionists

THOMAS COOK

from Yorkshire alone. Cook and his 17-year-old son, John, worked night and day to ensure its success, and both of them accompanied parties to the capital.

He charged five shillings for a ticket, and set up clubs to help workers save up the fare. Many started off on Saturday night and spent Sunday and Monday in London. They stayed in dormitories provided with clean sheets, towel and soap, and were given a hearty breakfast. They returned home in time to start work on the Tuesday morning.

In 1854 Cook gave up his work as a wood-turner, and made plans for his first continental journey – a trip to the Paris Exhibition of 1855. This proved to be the most important step of his whole life, as it launched him on a completely new course of foreign travel. He did for the tourists what they were not able to do for themselves: he provided them with a courier who was able to deal with language problems, money exchange, passport and all their other difficulties.

The French tours proved most popular, and he took his clients to Paris and to Chamonix, where elegant ladies in crinolines scrambled over the glacier. He escorted parties to Switzerland and Italy, where his son bought the Vesuvius funicular railway (which his company ran until 1948).

## London Office

By 1865 Cook felt confident enough to open a London office, at Ludgate Circus, which led to further expansion of his business. Already over one million passengers had passed through his hands and his agency was developing into an international organisation.

From here on, the possibilities for travel were limitless, and Cook took his clients to the four corners of the earth. In 1866 his first tour to America took place. When the Suez Canal opened in 1869, he set up an office in Cairo and arranged tours to Turkey and the Holy Land, and organised cruises up the Nile. And when General Gordon was besieged in Khartoum in 1884, John Mason Cook was called in to organise transport for 20,000 relief troops.

In 1874 Thomas Cook introduced a system of travellers' cheques (the only universal currency at the time was gold) and used coupons for paying hoteliers. In 1878 he founded a banking service. Meanwhile he himself was leading a party of 12 travellers on one of his round-the-world tours, which took 220 days and cost 200 guineas.

Cook's travel agency proved to be the prototype for all other operators, including a number run by Christians. There was John Frame, a temperance man, who popularised the Highlands of Scotland; his first tour was in connection with a temperance demonstration in 1881.

Sir Henry Lunn, formerly a medical missionary, started with tours to Grindelwald, Switzerland, for Free Church and Anglican clergy and their families; he later formed the Hellenic Travellers' Club, famous for its lecture cruises to Greece.

And the Rev T A Leonard, a Congregational minister from Colne, founded the Co-operative Holidays Association to encourage 'the healthful ways of an out-of-door life among the hills'.

Although now a successful business man, Cook's enterprise was not entirely motivated by finance; it served to support his concern for Baptist missions in India and an evangelical witness in Rome. He also regarded his work as a moral crusade : he felt that the working classes would be better-educated and better-off if they could spend their money on travel rather than drink.

Sadly, Cook's involvement in the business was brought to a premature end, and he retired in 1880 following a disagreement with his son. By this time his agency had become internationally-known, and more than any other had contributed to the growth of popular travel, both home and abroad.

# PHOTOGRAPH ACKNOWLEDGEMENTS

Page 22 - Action Partners; Page 29 - Africa Inland Mission; Pages 35 and 38 - Arab World Ministries; Page 46 - European Christian Mission; Page 56 -Full Gospel Business Men's Fellowship International; Page 88 - The Messianic Testimony; Page 105 - OMF International; Page 116 - OMS International; Page 125 - Operation Mobilisation; Page 138 - Qua Iboe Fellowship; Page 152 - South American Mission Society; Page 164 - Transworld Radio; Page 170 - Youth With A Mission; Page 187 - Christian Herald; Page 195 - Christian Literature Crusade; Page 200 - The Gideons International; Page 209 - Scripture Gift Mission; Page 212 - Scripture Union; Page 222 - Wycliffe Bible Translators; Page 235 - Evangelical Alliance; Page 241 - Keston Institute; Pages 247 and 251 - League of Prayer; Page 254 - Missionary Aviation Fellowship; Page 262 - The Navigators; Page 269 - Evangelical Library; Page 279 - Boys' Brigade; Page 303 - N.C.H. Action for Children; Page 309 - Teen Challenge; Page 317 - YMCA; Page 338 - Church Army; Page 346 - Home Evangelism; Page 350 - London City Mission; Page 358 - Earnest Walton-Lewsey; Page 366 - SASRA; Page 381 - John Groom's Association for the Disabled; Page 389 - Langley House Trust; Page 395 - Evangelical Library; Page 402 - NSPCC; Page 408 - Pilgrim Homes; Page 434 - Royal National Institute for the Blind; Pages 441 and 444 - Royal National Mission to Deep Sea Fishermen; Page 465 - St Christopher's Hospice; Page 473 - Sandes' Soldiers and Airmen's Centres; Page 481 - Evangelical Library; Page 487 - Thomas Cook Travel.

# ADDRESSES

Action Partners, Bawtry Hall, Bawtry, Doncaster, South Yorkshire DN10 6JH.

The AD 2000 & Beyond Movement, 2860 S. Circle Drive, Suite 2112, Colorado Springs, CO 80906, USA.

Africa Inland Mission International, 2 Vorley Road, Archway, London N19 5HE.

Arab World Ministries, PO Box 51, Loughborough, Leics LE11 0ZQ.

Bethnal Green Medical Mission, 305 Cambridge Heath Road, London E2 9LG

The Bible Society, Stonehill Green, Westlea, Swindon, Wilts SN5 7 DG.

Book Aid, 271 Church Road, Upper Norwood, London SE19 2QQ.

The Boys Brigade, Kings Terrace, 1 Galena Road, London W6 OLT.

The British Red Cross Society, 9 Grosvenor Crescent, London SW1X 7EJ.

The Christian Herald, Herald House Ltd, 96 Dominion Road, Worthing, West Sussex BN14 8JP.

Christian Home for the Physically Handicapped, 58 Purbeck Road, Hornchurch, Essex RM11 1NA.

Church Army, Independents Road, Blackheath, London SE3 9LG

Christian Literature Crusade, 51, The Dean, Alresford, Hants, SO 24 9BJ

DEF Centre, 211 Wick Road, Brislington, Bristol BS4 4HP.

European Christian Mission, 50 Billing Road, Northampton NN1 5DH

Eurovision, 75 Moorlands Road, Dewsbury, West Yorkshire WF13 2LF.

Evangelical Alliance UK, Whitefield House, 186 Kennington Road, London SE11 4BT.

FEBA Radio, Ivy Arch Road, Worthing, West Sussex BN14 8BX.

FGBMFI, PO Box 11, Knutsford, Cheshire WA16 6QP.

The Gideons International, Western House, George Street, Lutterworth, Leics LE17 4EE.

The Girls' Brigade (National Council for England & Wales), Girls' Brigade House, Foxhall Road, Didcot, Oxon OX11 7BQ.

Girls' Friendly Society, Townsend House, 126 Queens Gate, London SW7 5LQ

Home Evangelism, Tyndale House, 3 Grange Road, Egham, Surrey TW20 9QW.

Hope UK, 25 (F) Copperfield Street, London, SE1 0EN.

International Nepal Fellowship, 69 Wentworth Road, Harborne, Birmingham, B17 9SS.

Interserve, 325 Kennington Road, London, SE11 4QH.

Japan Evangelistic Band, 275 London Road, Portsmouth, Hants PO2 9HE.

John Grooms Association for Disabled People, 10 Gloucester Drive, Finsbury Park, London N4 2LP.

Keston Institute, 4 Park Town, Oxford OX2 6SH.

Langley House Trust, 46 Market Square, Witney, Oxon OX8 6AL.

League of Prayer, 69 Fitzwalter Road, Sheffield, S2 2SJ.

London City Mission, 175 Tower Bridge Road, London SE1 2AH.

The Lord's Day Observance Society, 6 Sherman Road, Bromley, Kent BR1 3JH.

The Messianic Testimony, 93 Axe Street, Barking, Essex 1E11 7LZ.

Mildmay Mission Hospital, Hackney Road, London E2 7NA.

Mission Aviation Fellowship, Ingles Manor, Castle Hill Avenue, Folkstone, Kent CT20 2TN.

Mission Care, 5 Oaklands Road, Bromley, Kent BR1 3SJ

Mission to Military Garrisons, 23 Royal Exchange Square, Glasgow G1 3AJ.

National Christian Education Council, 1020 Bristol Road, Selly Oak, Birmingham, B29 6LB

NCH Action for Children, 85 Highbury Park, London N5 1UD.

National Bible Society of Scotland, 7 Hampton Terrace, Edinburgh, EH12 5XU

NSPCC, 42 Curtain Road, London, EC2A 3NH.

The Navigators, Adyar House, 32 Carlton Crescent, Southampton SO15 7EW

OAC Ministries International, 102 Dukes Avenue, Muswell Hill, London N10 2QA.

OMF International, Belmont, The Vine, Sevenoaks, Kent TN13 3TZ

OMS International, 1 Sandileigh Avenue, Manchester M20 3LN.

Operation Mobilisation, The Quinta, Weston Ryn, Oswestry,Shropshire SY10 7LT.

Qua Iboe Fellowship, 14 Glencregagh Court, Belfast BT6 0PA

Pilgrim Homes, 175 Tower Bridge Road, London SE1 2AL.

The Royal Association in Aid of Deaf People, 27 Old Oak Road, London W3 7HN.

Royal National Institure for the Blind, 224 Great Portland Street, London W1N 6AA.

Royal National Mission to Deep Sea Fishermen, 43 Nottingham Place, London W1M 4BX.

The Royal Hospital for Neuro-Disability, West Hill, Putney, London SW15 3SW

Royal Sailors' Rests, 5 St George's Business Centre, St George's Square, Portsmouth, Hants PO1 3EY.

RSPCA, Causeway, Horsham, West Sussex, RH12 1HG

Sandes Soldiers' & Airmen's Centres, 3A Belmont Road, Belfast BT4 2AA

St Christopher's Hospice, 51/59 Lawrie Park Road, Sydenham, London SE26 6DZ.

SASRA, Havelock House, Barrack Road, Aldershot, Hants GU11 3NP

Scripture Gift Mission, Radstock House, 3 Eccleston Street, London SW1W 9LZ.

Scripture Union, 130 City Road, London EC1V 2NJ.

The Shaftesbury Society, 18-20 Kingston Road, London SW19 1JZ.

SIM International (UK), Joint Mission Centre, Ullswater Crescent, Coulsdon, Surrey CR5 2HR.

South American Mission Society, Allen Gardiner House, Pembury Road, Tunbridge Wells, Kent TN2 3QU.

Thomas Cook, 45 Berkeley Street, London W1A 1EB

Torch Trust for the Blind, Torch House, Hallaton, Market Harborough, Leics. LE16 8UJ.

Trans World Radio, 45 London Road, Biggleswade, Bedfordshire SG18 8ED.

Wycliffe Bible Translators, Horsleys Green, High Wycombe, Bucks HP14 3XL.

Teen Challenge Centre, 50 Penygroes Road, Gorslas, Llanelli, Dyfed SA14 7LA.

YWAM, 13 Highfield Oval, Ambrose Lane, Harpenden, Herts AL5 4BX.

YWCA, Clarendon House, 52 Cornmarket Street, Oxford OX1 3EJ.

YMCA, 640 Forest Road, London, E17 3DZ.

# SELECTED INDEX